A History of Ethiopia

Updated Edition

A History of Ethiopia

Updated Edition

Harold G. Marcus

UNIVERSITY OF CALIFORNIA PRESS

Berkeley / Los Angeles / London

University of California Press
Berkeley and Los Angeles, California

University of California Press, Ltd.
London, England

© 1994 by the Regents of the University of California
Updated Edition © 2002 by the Regents of the University of California

Library of Congress Cataloging-in-Publication Data

Marcus, Harold G.
   A History of Ethiopia Updated Edition/ Harold G. Marcus.
     p. cm.
   Includes bibliographical references and index.
   ISBN 978-0-520-22479-7 (alk. paper)
   1. Ethiopia—History. I. Title.
DT381.M33 2002
963—dc21   93-17987
                                               CIP

Manufactured in the United States of America

23 22 21 20
10 9 8 7

The paper used in this publication meets the minimum requirements of
ANSI/NISO Z39.48-1992 (R 1997) (*Permanence of Paper*). ∞

For Emma, still a creation better than any book

The publisher gratefully acknowledges the contribution provided by the General Endowment Fund of the Associates of the University of California Press.

Contents

LIST OF PHOTOGRAPHS   ix

PREFACE   xi

PREFACE TO THE 1994 EDITION   xv

1
Beginnings, to 1270   1

2
The Golden Age of the Solomonic Dynasty, to 1500   17

3
The Decline of the Solomonic Dynasty, to 1796   30

4
Political and Economic Transformations, to 1855   48

5
Imperial Resurrection, to 1877   63

6
Imperial Consolidation, to 1889   77

7
The Defeat of European Imperialism, to 1897   91

8
Menilek's State, to 1916   104

9
Ras Tafari, to 1930   116

10
Haile Sellassie, to 1936   130

11
Haile Sellassie, to 1955   147

12
Haile Sellassie, to 1973   164

13
The Revolution, to 1977   181

14
The Failure of the Revolution, to 1991   202

15
The New Rulers, to 1995   221

16
Peace and War, to 2000   246

EPILOGUE   265

MAPS   269

GLOSSARY   279

SELECT BIBLIOGRAPHY   285

INDEX   299

Photographs

1. Plowing   4

2. Obelisk at Axum   6

3. Church of Medhane Alem   13

4. The Blue Nile during the dry season   14

5. Northwest Shewa at Harvest time   15

6. Hamlet in Gurage   20

7. Sidama house   21

8. Crowns held at Church of Mary, Axum   25

9. Small mosque, Harer   27

10. Abba Gada of the Boren Oromo   33

11. Tomb of an Oromo Muslim saint in Arsi   35

12. Oromo funerary stela, Arsi   36

13. Ceiling of the Church of Debre Birhan, Gonder   41

14. Detail of a crumbling castle, Gonder   42

15. Rock houses, northern Shewa   50

16. Woman spinning thread, Gojam   51

17. Emperor Menilek II   88

18. Keren Hotel, Asmera   100

19. Just across the Eritrean frontier, facing into Ethiopia   101

20. Haile Sellassie opening parliament in 1934   135

21. Haile Sellassie reviewing troops in 1935   141

22. Oromo patriot and family   149

23. The Italian fort at Maji   152

24. Abandoned Italian tractor in 1961   153

25. Addis Abeba in 1970   165

26. Imperial Bodyguards in ceremonial uniforms, 1962   168

27. Haile Sellassie presiding over university
     graduation, 1966   177

28. Military review for the Declaration of Socialism   191

29. Students in the uniform of the Development through
     Cooperation Campaign   192

30. Eradicating the past in Addis Abeba   197

31. Slogan from 1977–1978   198

32. Feeding camp at Bati, July 1985   207

33. Survivors, Bati, July 1985   208

34. Bomb damage, Mitsiwa, December 1991   215

35. The imperial palace in Mitsiwa, bombed by
     government planes   216

36. Triumphal arch in Asmera   217

37. Eradicating the past in Asmera   218

38. Money to die for   251

39. Center of Zalembessa when recovered
     on 26 May 2000   261

40. Commemorating the tenth anniversary of
     independence, Asmera 2001   266

Preface

I realized that *A History of Ethiopia* needed a second edition to explain the genesis of Ethiopia's present ruling party and its unusual ideological approach to federalism based on ethnic units defined largely by language. In recent history, Ethiopia was governed first by the decentralized, though unitary, state of Haile Sellassie I (r. 1916–1974) and then by the highly centralized administration of Mengistu Haile Mariam (r. 1974–1991). According to Meles Zenawi, Ethiopia's current prime minister, these two approaches to the unitary state led to elitism, despotism, authoritarianism, and the sacrifice of ethnicity on the altar of transcendent nationalism. At the core of Meles's ruling coalition, the Tigrayan Peoples Liberation Front (TPLF) fought as much for the integrity of Tigrayan culture as for provincial autonomy. The TPLF has applied a provincial and particular solution to Ethiopia as a whole, and ethnicity has replaced national culture in shaping the country's destiny. Chapter 15 interprets the ethnic factor in terms of the Tigrayan Peoples Liberation Front, the ruling Ethiopian Peoples Revolutionary Democratic Front (EPRDF), and the Federal Democratic Republic of Ethiopia (FDRE).

I also thought that it would be instructive to compare and contrast Ethiopia's contemporary constitutional, administrative, and political developments with those of neighboring Eritrea. Although the two countries share historical, cultural, religious, and linguistic characteristics, Ethiopia has sought stability in reorganizing politics according to ethnicity, whereas Eritrea has opted for a highly centralized unitary state in which ethnic status is not an official political factor. In their different approaches, one may find some of the divergences that led to the Ethio-Eritrean war of May 1998 to June 2000.

I have not attempted to integrate the history of various Ethiopian nationalities into this new edition. The available literature is insufficient for such an ambitious undertaking. Historians cannot be so creative as some of our more demanding critics would like. Researchers have to go into the field, accomplish difficult and time-consuming work, and publish their findings. Only in this way will the history of Ethiopia's many nationalities become known and subsequently integrated into the public record of the larger political unit. Those of us who write general accounts will welcome the new scholarship, since having ethno-national histories to refer to will permit us to reassess, redefine, and revise our writings.

I was in Addis Abeba during the Ethiopian blitzkrieg of May through June 2000, and I was able to differentiate the situation on the ground from the situation in the heads of the spin-doctors and the propagandists. There remains much ignorance about the Ethio-Eritrean war, especially among those who claimed special insight and knowledge. They were afflicted by wishful thinking conditioned by the history of warfare between the two adversaries, or by what they had hoped would happen. Their notions of field tactics and war objectives were contradicted by the reality of the strife and its conclusion, to which I have devoted chapter 16.

I have been able to make use of the developing methodology of contemporary history by reading the available political literature and journalism and assessing them in conventional scholarly terms. In this effort, my forty years of experience as an Ethiopia watcher have given me a perspective that only a few others enjoy. I continue to travel widely and visit areas well off the beaten track. During my 1999–2000 sabbatical leave from Michigan State University, I chose to live in Gonder, a city of 160,000 with a total foreign population of four, where it is impossible not to experience Ethiopia, its myriad problems, and its culture of poverty; and where one must conform to the local culture or be isolated from the community. I grow weary of foreigners and Ethiopians who see everything from the vantage of Addis Abeba. The countryside *is* Ethiopia, more so than a primate city and certainly more so than the fictitious country in which expatriate Ethiopians imagine they once dwelled.

I want to thank those who reviewed the first edition of this book. Their comments were kind and well intentioned, none mortal in nature. Given the economics of publishing, I have not been permitted to integrate their valid suggestions into the updated edition, which leaves the original text intact, but adds two chapters, a new preface, and an epilogue. In chapter 15, there is some repetition of materials covered in chapter 14, but the data are presented from a specific perspective and with a wholly different goal in mind.

I promise to act on the helpful advice of my reviewers in an all-new third edition, which will be written before 2010. Meanwhile, let me respond to one reviewer who was irate that I had sullied the reputation of some British and Commonwealth officers and men who served in Ethiopia in 1941–1942. He was correct in his charges, and I apologize for my overly purple prose. I hope he will be pleased with my better-informed treatment of his military compatriots to appear in chapter 11 of my forthcoming full-length biography, *A Man Out of His Time: A Political Biography of Haile Sellassie I.*

Finally, I owe much gratitude to those who made my 1999–2000 sabbatical in Ethiopia so worthwhile. First, I want to acknowledge the Fulbright program, which can still support worthy research even if it lacks the funding fully to carry out its excellent programs. Second, I want to credit the American embassy under Ambassador Tibor Nagy and its Public Diplomacy Unit under Alice LeMaistre for treating Fulbrighters as responsible human beings and not as swamp critters. We enjoyed semiofficial status and were respected for our academic talents. May this approach overwhelm the rest of the Foreign Service. Third, I am, as always, grateful to Solomon at the library of Addis Ababa University's Institute of Ethiopian Studies. He is a welcoming librarian who works closely with his researchers to get them what they need, regardless of where the material is located. He is responsible for more good scholarship than he realizes. Fourth, I want to correct an oversight and offer my belated thanks to the American Philosophical Society for its support, in 1991–1992, of some of the research necessary to complete the first edition of this book. Fifth, I want to recognize Cressida for helping me to see Ethiopia anew and afresh, and for suffering with me some of the worst roads in the world. Sixth, I rededicate this book to Emma, still a better creation than any book.

Harold Marcus
Asmera, July 2001

Preface to the 1994 Edition

I began writing this book in January 1986, and I fully anticipated its completion within six months. Although I knew much of the story, I discovered that I needed to learn more. Many new books and articles had to be perused, and not a few old works had to be reread. Moreover, ongoing civil conflict raised the question of what Ethiopia was. Several of the "liberation movements" argued against Ethiopia as a nation, defining it as an obsolete empire-state, a prison house of peoples. Though I was predisposed toward the Ethiopia I had studied since the late 1950s, I appreciated that within its frontiers were a variety of peoples.

The Tigray and the Amhara of highlands Eritrea, Tigray, Welo, Gonder, Shewa, and Gojam are the inheritors and avatars of Orthodox Christianity and its political traditions. They use plows to cultivate grains, and they also herd cattle, sheep, and goats. Their primary affiliation is to the Orthodox church, and they are loosely organized into parishes. Priests and itinerant holy men keep the banner of Christianity high and drill their auditors to believe in their moral and religious superiority. The clerics have kept alive the myth of a Christian empire whose origins go back to Axum and even to King Solomon's Israel.

Within Ethiopia there are also large populations of Muslims: the Cushitic-speaking Afar, Saho, and Somali in the desert lowlands in the eastern parts of Eritrea, Tigray, Welo, and Harerge; and the Semitic-speaking Adari of Harer. Islam is also well represented in the large mercantile communities of Gonder, Addis Abeba, and other centers. Since the overthrow of Haile Sellassie in 1974, Islam has spread throughout Ethiopia, as evidenced by a large number of newly built mosques.

In the Gibe region, Harerge, and Arsi are millions of Cushitic-speaking Oromo Muslims; in Borena, hundreds of thousands of Oromo traditionalists; and in Welega, Welo, and southern Shewa, millions of Christian Oromo, many of whom speak Amharic as their mother tongue. As the country's majority and most widely dispersed people, the Oromo are present in at least twelve clusters in ten provinces. Over the last three centuries, most Oromo have transformed themselves into farmers, although they continue to revere animal keeping.

In Ethiopia's southern lacustrine regions live a variety of peoples, of whom the most important are the Semitic-speaking Gurage and the Cushitic-speaking Konso and Sidama. They are hoe agriculturists who cultivate ensete. The Gurage are mostly Muslim, but they number some Christians among them. The Sidama include Muslims, Christians, and traditionalists, whereas the Konso mostly follow a traditional African monotheism.

Besides the small Omotic-speaking family inhabiting a region adjacent to the Omo, an important population of Sudanic peoples dwell along Ethiopia's western border. Among them are the Koman, Kunama, Berta, and Annuak, who speak Nilo-Saharan tongues and live in largely segmented societies. Although these and other groups were essentially peripheral to the main strands of the history of the highlands Ethiopian state, recently scholars have studied their social history, to include them in the record. Not surprisingly, they were found to harbor grievances against the northern state builders, whose government they considered elitist and exploitative.

The government of Mengistu Haile Mariam (1974–1991) was also interested in Ethiopia's national composition, for reasons dictated by Marxist-Leninist theory and politics. It posed as its peoples' savior and envisioned their prosperity and happiness within the Socialist motherland that it was building for the so-called broad masses. As Mengistu's government grew increasingly authoritarian and intrusive, spokesmen for this or that nationality rose to the challenge and waged propaganda wars against the regime's politics. The assertions made by Ethiopians at home and abroad often were distorted by hyperbole, disaffecting a whole generation of Ethiopianists from the object of their scholarship. They left Ethiopian studies or became politicized for or against the warring factions.

As I watched the intellectual mayhem and continued my research, I came to realize that Ethiopia's history contained an analytical truth validating my decision to consider Ethiopia's wider geographic limits as my canvas: from time to time, the nation had disintegrated into component parts, but it had never disappeared as an idea and always reappeared in fact. The Axumite Empire may have faded after the seventh century, but the Zagwes followed in the eleventh century; and, of course, the succeeding Solomonic dynasty created a state that incorporated at least two-thirds of the country's present area. In the sixteenth century, that empire lost its will to rule after being ravaged by Muslim armies waging holy war, and it sharply contracted in the seventeenth century as the Oromo successfully invaded the devastated and depopulated highlands.

Even as the Solomonic monarchy weakened in the eighteenth century, the imperial tradition remained validated in Ethiopia's monasteries and parish churches. The northern peasantry was continually reminded of Ethiopia's earlier greatness and exhorted to work toward its renaissance. From 1896 to 1907, Menilek II (1889–1913) directed Ethiopia's return into southern and western regions abandoned in the seventeenth century. Modern firearms gave the emperor's soldiers a strategic advantage, but their morale was inspired by expectations of booty and the belief that they were regaining lands once part of the Christian state. By the end of the expansion in 1906, Ethiopia (without Eritrea) had reached its present size, comprising the highlands, the key river systems, and the state's central core, surrounded by a borderland buffer zone in low-lying, arid, or tropical zones.

From the Axumite period, public history in Ethiopia has moved from north to south, and the twentieth-century state developed along this well-trodden path. Menilek and his governors ruled Ethiopia's heterogeneous population indirectly, largely through accommodation and co-option. Haile Sellassie centralized the state and expanded Ethiopia's civil society as a counterweight to ethnic forces. He fostered unity through the development of a national army, a pan-Ethiopian economy, modern communications, and an official culture whose main feature was the use of the Amharic language in government and education.

As Ethiopia's economy moved toward capitalism in the 1960s, considerable social unrest among the intelligentsia and in the provinces undermined the national consensus. Indeed, the Eritreans rebelled, claiming that they were a separate people largely because of their experiences under Italian and British colonial rule. Throughout the 1960s and 1970s, the authorities resorted to police or military repression to keep Ethiopia intact or enlisted clients to bolster its administration, as in the case of the Ogaden.

Haile Sellassie's government was overthrown in 1974 and replaced by an ideologically driven inclusivist state determined to extirpate any competing civil society or ethnic activity. Ruthless suppression of ideological adversaries fostered the growth of nationality movements and ongoing civil wars. The military government's tightly centralized authority imposed land tenure and supposedly "progressive" social policies that undermined the peasants' historic connection to the state and the land. Resettlement, villagization, mass political organizations, and the command economy conspired to alienate the people from their natural allegiances. The state's inability to compromise politically further encouraged the breakup of the larger nation.

Yet, if history is to be our guide, such a development will give way inevitably to renewed national unity as the logic of geography, economics, tradition, and political culture once again come to dominate politics. Some people may disagree with this hypothesis or other aspects of my book. I make no apologies but rather submit my synthesis as a challenge: prove me wrong, clarify my points, reveal where my work is insubstantial, and show where other and better analyses might have been offered. If this book stimulates scholarship and amplifies our knowledge of Ethiopian history, then it will have proved its worth beyond merely being a guide through a complex and difficult story. This achievement is my great hope.

This volume is the culmination of many years' work, and its faults are all mine. Blameless are those of my friends, colleagues, and students whose criticisms helped bring the book to completion: John Hinnant, Donald Crummey, James McCann, Guluma Gemeda, Daniel Kendie, Patrick Gilkes, Ezekiel Gebissa, Charles McClellan, Yakob Fisseha, William Hixon, David Robinson, Richard Greenfield, and Jay Spaulding. Once again, I offer a special appreciation to Susan Drabik, who survived life with me during the book's long gestation. To the National Humanities Center—truly the "southern part of heaven"—where the first part of the book was written and the final draft edited, I present my deep and enduring gratitude. I am a fan for life. To the Social Science Research Council, the American Philosophical Society, and to Michigan State University, I say keep up the good work of supporting research, reflection, and scholarship. Thank you very much for your confidence in me.

Harold Marcus
National Humanities Center, July 1992

ONE

Beginnings, to 1270

Four million years ago, near Hadar in the most easterly part of Ethiopia's Welo Province, there was a lake in a verdant setting. Its subsequent desiccation safeguarded a treasure for future paleoanthropologists: in 1974, an old shore or marsh yielded up the fossilized remains of "Lucy *Australopithecus afarensis*," a relatively young hominid woman.[1] Her almost complete skeleton reveals an ape-faced species that had just begun its evolution toward intelligence. Her small brain, one-third the size of that of a modern human, directed a compact and rugged body, little more than a meter tall and weighing about thirty kilos, set on pelvic and leg bones dense enough to support erect and sustained walking, if not speedy locomotion. She and her larger male counterpart scavenged meat from carnivores, caught smaller animals, and collected fruit, vegetables, roots, and tubers. Though they used sticks and stones, they did not hunt; they spent most of their lives gathering and collecting near water and sheltering trees. Even with its obvious limitations, *Australopithecus afarensis* survived for at least two million years before giving way to its closely related cousin *Australopithecus africanus*, present about three million years ago in Ethiopia's Omo region.

Africanus was followed by the large-brained *Homo habilis*, who lived in groups clustered at campsites offering water and protection from

1. The Ethiopians call her *Dinkenesh*, or "she is wonderful."

predators. *Homo habilis* flaked stone into knives, hand axes, choppers, and other pointed tools for domestic use and for hunting. While the women and the juveniles foraged nearby and collected 75 percent of the group's food, the males usually ranged away from the campsite in the quest for game. Stalking depended on communal effort and a skillful strategy to compensate for the hunters' relative weakness and slowness. Success hinged likewise on the quality of the weapons carried by each male, and campsite groups supported experts in stone work and specialists who invoked the assistance of the supernatural for a successful hunt. The group came together in the evenings to eat a communal meal and to defend itself against predators, whose approach would be met by salvos of rocks. *Homo habilis* prospered and spread into most parts of savanna Africa.

In fact, *habilis* was so successful that, about 1.5 million years ago, it evolved into *Homo erectus*, the brawnier and brainier species associated with much of the later stone ages. Its much larger skull contained about 1,000 cubic centimeters of gray matter, and it had a fine, erect carriage and a body over twice the size of *afarensis*. In Ethiopia, *Homo erectus* ranged from the coast east to around Harer and the Awash valley and southwest into the Omo valley and to Lake Turkana. Though *erectus* spread widely throughout Africa, which it came to dominate, its growing numbers pushed some groups farther afield, and about 1 million years ago they traversed then existing land bridges into Asia and Europe.

Thus, *Homo erectus* is known in many variants, of whom Peking man and his cousin in Java are the most prominent. In eastern Africa, including Ethiopia, their artifacts reveal members of *Homo erectus* as intrepid hunters, able to track and kill large animals. They butchered the meat with increasingly more efficient, miniaturized, and well-made knives, choppers, scrapers, and cleavers; and, starting about 70,000 years ago, they used fire to prepare the steaks, chops, and roasts that constituted their main source of protein. The flames also provided warmth, protected people from predators, and extended the waking day to permit leisure and reflection, perhaps even illumination, about the meaning of life.

The heat of the campfire also nurtured the slow evolution of *Homo erectus* into *Homo sapiens*. In Ethiopia, individuals of the latter species first show up in the Dire Dawa region about 60,000 years ago and shortly thereafter at Melka Kontoure in the Awash valley. With a 1,300 cubic centimeter brain cage, their high intelligence was manifested almost immediately in their superior manufacture of hafted and chiseled tools and weapons. The improved technology permitted the establishment of several seasonal campgrounds linked to more or less distant bases, from which hunting parties could rove far afield. The net result was population growth and greater vitality and health. From the surrounding savanna lowlands, *Homo sapiens* spread into the foothills of Ethiopia's central highlands, especially in the west and northwest, to interact with peoples and cultures of the Nile valley. Yet, historical distance and scholarly bewilderment combine to obscure a full understanding of the emergence of Ethiopia's peoples and their material cultures.

Evidence is strong that the Afro-Asiatic (Hamitic-Semitic) group of languages developed and fissured in the Sudan-Ethiopian borderlands. There Proto-Cushitic and Proto-Semitic began their evolution. In Ethiopia, the Semitic branch grew into a northern group, today echoed in Tigrinya, and a southern group, best heard in Amharic. It simultaneously spread to the Middle East, whence, millennia later, it returned in a written form to enrich its cousins several times removed.

Much of the linguistic development came after the eighth millennium B.C., as population grew consequent to the domestication and herding of cattle, goats, sheep, and donkeys and the intensive collection of wild grains. This development was followed, perhaps as early as the third millennium B.C., by the cultivation of thirty-six crops, for which Ethiopia was either the primary or the secondary point of dispersion. Most important were teff (*ragrostis tef*), a small-kerneled grass, whose flour was baked into large, round, flat breads, the staple still preferred by many Ethiopians, and ensete (*ensete edulis*, the "false" banana), the pulp of whose pseudostem can, after a complex process, be made into a flour for the bread or porridge still eaten in large parts of southern and southwestern Ethiopia.

The greater versatility of these cultivated foods enabled proto-Ethiopians to advance into the temperate plateaus and to clear the land, which they cultivated with the plow, a feature of the highlands as old there as agriculture itself. As Middle Eastern grains, especially barley and wheat, and pottery from the Sudan spread during the second millenium B.C., the Semitic-speaking northerners came to dominate the plateaus. Coming into contact with Sabaean traders, whose language was uncannily similar to their own, the pre-Axumites fashioned a South Arabian-like state, the Kingdom of Da'amat, which dominated the highlands of western Tigray from Yeha, its capital. It exchanged ivory, tortoiseshell, rhinoceros horn, gold, silver, and slaves for such finished goods as cloth, tools, metals, and

1. Plowing

jewelry. When, between 300 and 100 B.C., rivals diverted trade and merchants to such new towns as Malazo, Kaskase, and Matara on the central and eastern Tigrayan and Eritrean plateaus, where access to the Red Sea was easy, Da'amat collapsed.

The successor mini-states were places where Ethiopians continued to be exposed to South Arabian customs and religion. The towns featured adjacent, irrigated, intensive agriculture fed by the same type of reservoirs found in South Arabia. Farther away, traditional dryland agriculture was practiced, best exemplified archaeologically in the region around Axum. The use of both farming techniques created a vital synergy, one also evidenced in the high culture that developed.

The earliest inscriptional fragments appear to be in Sabaean, but a closer perusal suggests an amalgam, with features that can derive only from Ge'ez, a local Semitic language. The domination of the indigenous culture became more marked after the fourth century B.C. That fact is clearly apparent in surviving monuments, especially in the architecture and sculptures found at Yeha, Haoulti, Malazo, and elsewhere. The stiff forms of the heavily stylized seated figures, the characteristic placement of the hands on the knees, and the drape of the long chemiselike garment may be based on South Arabian prototypes but are typically Axumite in realization. The few examples of bas-relief portray men who are characteristically Ethiopian but rendered in poses that can be seen at sites from Egypt to Iran. Altars and figurines were decorated with South Arabian religious symbols—the crescent of Almouqah, the circle of Shams, for example—not representations of the traditional snake god and other Ethiopian deities. In an ideological sense, therefore, Ethiopia early joined the Middle East and participated in the region's rich religious history. Similarly, it also shared in the evolving mercantile life of the eastern Mediterranean–Red Sea regional economy.

Trade brought the wealth that permitted the rise of elites who assumed honors and titles. Ambition and greed made for wars of aggrandizement; luck and talent brought consolidation; and success led to greater wealth, more followers, and additional pretensions. The five hundred years before the Christian era witnessed warfare that increased in scale as the stakes became greater. The winner was the inland state of Axum, comprising Akele Guzay and Agame, and dominating food-rich areas to the southwest largely inhabited by Agew-speaking farmers. The rise and then the hegemony of Axum over the coast inland into Tigray and even its subsequent expansion within and without Ethiopia appears linked to the stimulus given to regional trade by Ptolemaic Egypt (330–320 B.C.) and then by the Roman world economy.

When the state of Axum emerges into the wider light of history at the end of the first century A.D., it is a full-blown, if not well-integrated, trading state. The anonymous author of the *Periplus [Geography] of the Erythraean Sea* mentions Ethiopia's main port at Adulis, twenty miles inside the Gulf of Zula, where visiting foreign ships anchored in the channel to protect themselves against attack at night by unruly local peoples. Nevertheless, Adulis offered profit enough to receive a continuous stream of merchants who, in return for ivory, offered cloth of many types, glassware, tools, gold and silver jewelry, copper, and Indian iron and steel used to manufacture high-quality weapons. Befitting its centrality in Ethiopia's economy, Adulis was an impressive place with stone-built houses and temples, a dam, and irrigated agriculture.

Five days to the west-south-west lay the city of Axum, which dominated the ivory trade west into Sudan. The state's leaders not only monopolized the commerce but also sought to dominate trade routes and sources of supply. During the fifth century A.D., for example, Ethiopian armies campaigned northward to establish control over the

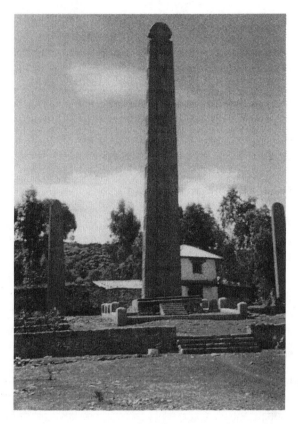

2. Obelisk at Axum

commerce that flowed toward Suakin and to pacify the Beja of the Sahil, through which caravans passed en route to Adulis; south of the Tekeze to subdue the Agew-speaking agriculturists of productive but mountainous Simen; southeastward into the Afar desert to command the incense trade; and even across the Red Sea to force Hejaz (a province of modern Saudi Arabia) to pay tribute and to guarantee the seaborne trade.

Our information comes from an inscription copied at Adulis in 525 by the seafaring Cosmas Indicopleustes and subsequently published in his *Christian Topography* (ca. 547). The book reveals that cut pieces of brass and coins were imported in the first century A.D. to use as money in Ethiopia's markets, suggesting a commerce requiring easier exchange. Ultimately, Axum responded by issuing its own coins late in the third century. Significantly, the first mintings were rendered in Greek and were fractions of the Roman solidus, clearly indicating that the specie was used primarily in international trade. The mere existence of Axumite money signaled Ethiopia's major role in the Middle East, where only Persia, Kushanas in India, and Rome circulated specie. The Ge'ez-speaking masses, however, continued to use traditional salt and iron bars as money and remained aloof from events that brought not only commerce but also Christianity to Axum's shores. They avoided both the coin and the cross—not so the ruling elites, whose interests came to include both.

From the third century, or even before, Axum's Hellenized elites had learned about the new faith from Christian traders. At court, the ideology was discussed philosophically but also, as befitted a place of power, in economic and political terms. Context was paramount: by the early fourth century, Christianity had become the established religion of the eastern Roman Empire. Since Roman trade dominated the Red Sea, it was inevitable that Christianity would penetrate Axum. Conversion was slow and occurred first in the towns and along the major trade routes. The shift was heralded, during the first third of the fourth century, by coins suddenly embossed with a cross and then by monuments carrying imperial inscriptions prefaced by Christian incantations.

According to Ethiopian church tradition, two Syrian boys, Aedisius and Frumentius, brought Christianity to Ethiopia. Shipwreck victims, they were brought to court as slaves and put to work by Emperor Ella Amida (r. ca. end of the third century A.D.). Over the years, their piety, reliability, and especially Frumentius's sagacity and wisdom as royal secretary and treasurer earned the monarch's gratitude, and his will manumitted them. His widow, as regent, asked them to remain in the palace and advise her until her infant son, Ezanas, was ready for the throne. While so engaged, Frumentius sought out Christian merchants, urged them to establish churches, and cooperated fully with them to spread the gospel.

When the young king came to power (ca. 303), Frumentius traveled to Alexandria to urge the patriarch to assign a bishop to Ethiopia to speed its conversion. He must not have been surprised—since his life had normally been astonishing—to hear the prelate nominate him. And back Frumentius went to Axum sometime around 305 (?) to begin a lifetime's work of evangelism, in so doing wresting Ezanas from his traditional beliefs. As linked to trade, Christianity proved a boon to the monarch.

Around 350, Emperor Ezanas followed his commercial star westward into the Nile valley to secure Axum's trade in ivory and other commodities. He acted because the Sudanese state of Meroë, in its decline, was unable to protect the caravan routes from raiding by the nomadic Beja. The Axumite army encountered little resistance as it made its way into Sudan (Kush), and, at the confluence of the Atbara and Nile, Ezanas raised a stela on which he described the ease of his conquests and thanked the Christian God for His protection. For the next few centuries, no state is known to have challenged Axum's trading monopoly on the African side of the Red Sea.

The trade not only brought prosperity but stimulated important cultural changes. Greek remained the courtly language, but Ge'ez was increasingly the language of the people, and often royal inscriptions used the vernacular. There were Ge'ez versions of the Old and New Testaments, which tradition claims were translated from the Antioch version of the Gospels during the period of the "Nine Saints," who came from greater Syria toward the end of the fifth century. Recent philological scholarship is skeptical about the role of Syriac influences in Axumite Ethiopia and finds no evidence of such a provenance.

Yet the folklore claims that the monks were good Monophysites who believed that Christ had one nature, the human subsumed in the divine, the theological view of the savior's persona championed by the see of Alexandria[2] and transmitted to Ethiopia by Bishop Frumentius 150 years earlier. The monks had been forced into exile after the Council of Chalcedon (451) defined Christ "as perfect God and man, consubstantial with the Father and consubstantial with Man, one sole being in two natures, without division or separation and without confusion or change." As the story goes, they found safe haven in Ethiopia, where they were warmly welcomed and then directed east of Axum into the countryside to preach the Word.

Proselytizing among people hostile to the new faith, the monks demonstrated the falseness of the old gods by establishing religious centers where they found temples and other shrines, among them the still active and rightly famous establishment at Debre Damo. They fashioned their monastic rule around communalism, hard work, discipline, and obedience, while introducing an asceticism and mysticism that attracted

2. The connection also yielded the Pseudo-Canon of Nicea (325), which robbed the Orthodox church of authority to name its own prelate and to ordain its own bishops, a power retained by Alexandria for sixteen hundred years.

young idealists. After education and training, the newly ordained went into the countryside, establishing the tradition that monks would be the main purveyors of the Gospels in Ethiopia.

With the new faith came traders responding to overseas demand manifested in Adulis, the region's most important commercial center. It was the destination of choice for Byzantine and other traders who sought to transship goods to Arabia, India, and regions even farther eastward. They came to Adulis by July, to transact their business before the Ethiopian fleet, composed of sturdy vessels made from tightly roped, fitted boards, left for Asia with the summer monsoon winds. At their destinations by September, Axum's traders would sell their cargoes and purchase export goods, and when the prevailing winds changed in October, sail back to Adulis, where the awaiting foreign merchants would buy items in demand in the eastern Mediterranean and themselves return home. Commercial prosperity therefore depended on the safety of the trading lanes and access to foreign markets. Whenever these were threatened, the Axumite Empire intervened to restore security, as was the case in South Arabia in the early sixth century.

There Judaism was resurgent, and Christians were being persecuted, among them the Axumites involved in commerce. The victims appealed across the Red Sea for help, and Axum responded in 517 by sending forces that garrisoned strategic points in Yemen. The Jews retreated into inaccessible country, attracted converts who abhorred foreign rule, raided towns, and interrupted the import-export trade. In 523–524, Emperor Caleb (ca. 500–534; otherwise known as Ella Asbeha) requested and obtained supplies and support from the patriarch of Alexandria and from the Byzantine government—which also had a strong interest in safeguarding commerce—for a major campaign against the Jewish leader, Dhu Nuwas. Caleb immediately ordered the building of a large fleet at Adulis, rented other vessels, recruited a substantial army, and himself led the expedition to Yemen.

After hard fighting, Dhu Nuwas and his forces withdrew, as did Caleb after he had established an interim administration. With the status quo more or less restored, the Jews quickly returned to raiding government outposts and garrison towns from sanctuaries in the mountains and desert. Piecemeal pacification failed, and in 525 Caleb returned with another army that caught the rebel forces in a destructive pincer near the sea. Loath to witness the disaster, Dhu Nuwas spurred his stallion into the sea, and nothing more was seen of horse or rider. The emperor named

Abreha, one of his generals, as viceroy, left him with an army of five thousand men, and returned home in triumph.

Axum was then at the apogee of its power: Christianity had developed apace with the empire's expansion, was firmly established to the south of Tigray in Wag and Lasta, and was growing in adjacent Agew areas (northern Welo), from which Axum continued to obtain export commodities. Trade from Sudan also moved through Agew, especially gold from Sasaw, today identified with the Fazughli region on the Blue Nile. Overseas, however, Axum's effort to build an empire was failing.

In 543, General Abreha rebelled and established himself as the independent ruler of South Arabia. Caleb and his successors fought back, but their limited efforts only helped consolidate and augment Abreha's authority, and he came to dominate the routes to northern Arabia and the east. His success actually advantaged many Axumites, who expanded their commercial activities internationally and locally, especially in San'a, Abreha's capital.

The self-proclaimed monarch kept his options and trading connections open by paying an annual tribute to both the Axumite and Persian emperors. While Abreha ruled, South Arabia was prosperous and well governed; he improved public works and built monuments and churches, since he sought to convert his subjects. He overextended himself, however, in campaigns against Mecca, activities that disrupted the intricate web of desert trading patterns, thus helping to cause a commercial crisis. The Persians became anxious as they saw the lucrative caravan trade dissipate.

They decided to intervene when Abreha's successors proved weak and vacillating, unable to retain the support of either the people or the army. The Sassanids reasoned that South Arabia's current rulers were Ethiopians, who paid tribute to Axum—conveniently forgetting that the same people paid them, too—and that the African power was allied to Byzantium, their bitter political and trade rival. A success in Yemen, therefore, would weaken their enemy and probably would not provoke a counterattack. In around 570, perhaps even on the day Muhammad was born, a ragtag Persian expedition of eight ships and eight hundred soldiers arrived on the South Arabian coast and proceeded systematically to destroy Ethiopian authority, helped by the people, who massacred Axumites throughout the land.

The mother country stood by, apparently impotent to intervene, thus signaling the end of Axum's political authority in Arabia. Commercial life in Adulis continued, however, and the links to South Arabia were maintained, especially with Mecca, where resident Ethiopians were important as traders and soldiers. Ships from Adulis regularly sailed to and from the Bay of Soaiba, Mecca's debouchment. The connection was destroyed, however, in the mid-seventh century as Islam triumphed in Arabia.

As Muslim power and influence grew in the eighth century, Ethiopian shipping was swept from the Red Sea–Indian Ocean, changing the nature of the Axumite state. It became isolated from the eastern Mediterranean ecumene that for centuries had influenced its culture and sustained its economy. The coastal region lost its economic vitality as trade decreased, and Adulis and other commercial centers slowly withered. The state consequently suffered a sharp reduction in revenues and no longer could afford to maintain a large army, a complex administration, and urban amenities. The culture associated with the outside world quickly became a memory, and Ethiopia turned inward.

Axum's weakened forces lost control over the trade routes into the interior and its monopoly over ivory and gold. In order to support itself, the Christian state moved southward, to the rich grain-growing areas of Agew country. By the early ninth century, the kingdom was well established as far south as the Beshlo River (then the Angot region; currently Wadla Delanta in west-central Welo). The drive southward was characterized by the implantation of military colonies, whose members established a feudal-like social order based on the productivity of the Agew cultivator. Soldiers, of course, took local wives and otherwise helped to assimilate the Agew, but priests and monks acted as the instruments of pacification and acculturation.

During 900–1000, the kingdom was overextended and its soldiers thin on the ground, permitting the majority Agew speakers to fight back. From the fragments of information contained in later chronicles, we learn that there were continual warfare and skirmishing against the isolated government fortresses.[3] Inevitably Axum lost its periphery: churches were destroyed, thousands of Christians died, and the Begemdir region and the area south of the Jema River were lost to state control. A rump

3. One persistent tradition tells of the Agew Queen Gudit, who persecuted Christians and fought their kingdom. In light of subsequent events, the tale suggests that an inland Agew people led by a woman destroyed or turned out the Axumite ruling class. Most active at the end of the tenth century, Gudit was nonetheless so long-lived that she must be a composite of individuals.

central government survived only through enlisting Agew officers and men to throw off their more unruly brethren. The more successful the Agew leaders were, the more they became assimilated into the Semitic culture and integrated into the ruling elites. From their ranks came the progenitor of a new line, the Zagwes, who, however, retained the Axumite social and political order.

The new rulers came from the mountains of Lasta, long a part of the Christian kingdom. Its Agew speakers had quickly absorbed the new religion, and the local nobility had joined the Axumite government. The province was strategically sited astride major north-south communication links, and it is not surprising that its princes originated the Zagwe dynasty. The Agew period witnessed the continuing Ethiopianization of the state, although the Zagwes have been derided in Solomonic chronicles and their achievements obscured. Even at the height of their rule, churchmen considered them usurpers, and the Zagwes created myths that they descended from Moses. In order physically to demonstrate the primacy of the new order over the Axumite line, Emperor Lalibela (r. ca. 1185–1225) directed the building of eleven rock-hewn churches at his capital at Roha (now Lalibela).

The monarch intended a stupendous monument to faith, and certainly the idea of hewing churches from the Lastan mountains was inspired. Although there are other monolithic structures in Ethiopia, the edifices at Roha are amazing, especially the chiseled-out access, courtyards, and interiors and the rich, mostly geometric and linear decorations. The churches' conception and style are very much Ethiopian, and possibly each one is an example of a particular kind of Axumite church, or even of some of Tigray's rock-hewn edifices, altogether forming a museum of sacred architecture. As a technically difficult achievement, it is in many ways unrivaled, and Lalibela denuded the countryside of its tools and masons and recruited craftsmen from as far away as Egypt and the Holy Land.

The largest of the eleven structures, Medhane Alem (savior of the world), is 33.5 meters long, 23.5 meters wide, and 11 meters high. It displays an external colonnade on all four sides supporting a gabled roof, the sides of which show carved arches cleverly arranged as if atop each column. The sanctuary itself, comprising a nave and aisles, is a square carved out of the stone, broken by four rows of seven rectangular pillars. The walls are flat and massive, reminiscent of Axumite prototypes, and the few windows are mostly at the top, making for a dim interior, perhaps

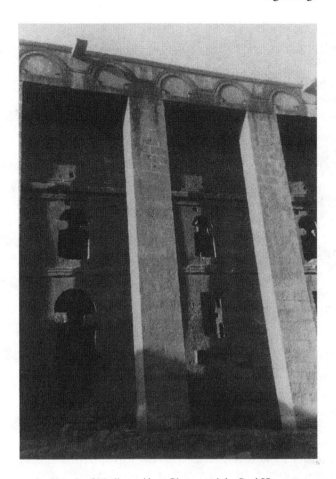

3. Church of Medhane Alem. Photograph by Paul Henze.

explaining why Medhane Alem's walls are not so elaborately decorated as some of the other, better lit, churches. The obscurity within Medhane Alem matches our knowledge of the entire Zagwe period.

Ethiopia then enjoyed commercial relations with Egypt and Aden, but Muslims at the coast and Arab shipping took most of the profits. There was a large slave trade, especially to Egypt, where Ethiopians were used as soldiers. In return, Cairene and Alexandrian merchants shipped textiles and finished goods to the port of Mitsiwa, by then Ethiopia's most important emporium. Relations with Egypt were cordial, although both

4. The Blue Nile during the dry season, downstream from Tissisat Falls

its Muslim civil and Christian (Coptic) religious authorities were resolved, if for different reasons, to refuse the Ethiopian church the right to appoint its own metropolitan and suffragan bishops. The lack of provincial prelates impeded the development of clergy and the spread of Christianity, and the Egyptian primate selected to head the Ethiopian church rarely understood the country, its politics, language, or culture. The Zagwes sought to evade Egypt's jurisdiction by turning to the Monophysite patriarch of Antioch, a useless ploy but one that brought Ethiopia to the attention of the crusaders and, in a distorted and romantic way, to the Western world.

In twelfth-century Europe, legends began to circulate about a remote and fabulously wealthy country in the east ruled by a priest-king who had vanquished the infidel Persians. Prester John, as he came to be known, was reportedly a devout Christian who claimed suzerainty over Christendom and ruled a kingdom strategically placed to outflank Islam. Full of exotic people and bizarre animals, his realm was peaceful, crimeless, and united. This vision became a conception of Ethiopia that long dominated Europe's imagination and stimulated its greediness for Ethiopia's resources.

5. Northwest Shewa at harvest time

During the reign of Lalibela, certainly the Zagwe dynasty's high point, Ethiopia comprised an assortment of fiefdoms under the emperor's suzerainty. The monarch made an annual progress to inform himself about local conditions, to act as Ethiopia's supreme judge, to feed himself and his court, and to settle political squabbles. The entire political economy depended on the farmer, who used plow and oxen to turn the high plateau's rich, volcanic soils during May and June in time for sowing when the long rains began. After the harvest in October–November, the cultivator paid taxes in grain and other foodstuffs to the local lord, who, except for a somewhat larger house and a retinue, lived very much like his subjects, mostly making do with locally made tools, cloth, and furnishings. Both noble and commoner suffered from the imperial visit, which resembled an infestation of locusts, so thoroughly did the movable court have a movable feast.

The Zagwes were unable to forge national unity; even in their home province, they could not stop squabbling over the throne, diverting men, energy, and money that could have been used better elsewhere to affirm the dynasty's authority. In the late thirteenth century, for example, the Zagwes were unable to control a small Christian kingdom in northern

Shewa, which had grown rich from diverting trade away from traditional routes through Lasta. The Shewans were ruled by Yekuno Amlak (d. 1285), who was supported strongly by local clerics, since he promised to make the church a semi-independent institution. When the Shewans rebelled, the church therefore remained neutral, though Yitbarek, the last of the Zagwes, had been anointed monarch and deserved fidelity.

In a series of battles from Lasta to Begemdir, the emperor was consistently defeated, finally falling in 1270 in the parish church in Gayint, murdered in front of the altar by Yekuno Amlak, who thereupon proclaimed himself emperor. As a usurper, the new monarch encountered considerable resistance, and, in order to win over Tigray with its many Axumite traditions, he and his supporters began to circulate a fable about his descent from King Solomon and Makeda, Queen of Saba, a genealogy that, of course, gave him traditional legitimacy and provided the continuity so honored in Ethiopia's subsequent national history.

TWO

The Golden Age of the Solomonic Dynasty, to 1500

Article 2 of the revised Ethiopian constitution of 1955 claimed that the ruling line descended from Menilek I, the son of Makeda, queen of Ethiopia, and King Solomon. Tourists visiting Addis Abeba often purchase the comic-strip painting that recalls the mythic birth of the progenitor of the Solomonic dynasty. Its forty-four scenes are drawn from the *Kebre Negast* (The glory of the kings), a pastiche of legends conflated early in the fourteenth century by six Tigrayan scribes. Yishak, the chief compiler, claimed that he and his colleagues were merely translating an Arabic version of a Coptic work into Ge'ez. In fact, his team blended local and regional oral traditions and style and substance derived from the Old and New Testaments, various apocryphal texts, Jewish and Islamic commentaries, and Patristic writings. The *Kebre Negast*'s primary goal was to legitimize the ascendancy of Emperor Yekuno Amlak and the "restored" Solomonic line. Most of the book is devoted therefore to the parentage of Emperor Menilek I.

According to the story, his mother, Queen Makeda, had little experience in government when suddenly called to the throne in the tenth century B.C. Feeling inadequate to the task, she decided to journey to Jerusalem to observe and learn from the wise and beneficent rule of King Solomon. Arriving in the Jewish capital, she was received with pomp by Solomon, who agreed to cooperate as long as she paid her way and took

17

nothing without his permission. The rich but inexperienced Makeda readily agreed and commenced to learn Middle Eastern statecraft, which Solomon taught disarmingly well. The young woman was not only impressed but also enthusiastically converted to Judaism and gave her mentor gifts of gold, gems, and spices. He, however, wanted something more precious.

With celebration as the pretext, Solomon invited his precocious student to dinner. He directed his cook to serve the best wines and to prepare the spiciest dishes, both of which happily suited Makeda. After having eaten and drunk her fill, the queen fell into a stupor, during which Solomon had jugs of water, labeled as his property, placed strategically around her sofa. When Makeda reawakened, she immediately gulped down some water, an act that permitted King Solomon to satisfy his lust. The cartoon-paintings show a large lump under a coverlet and two heads jowl by cheek, a surprised and resigned woman's face squeezed under a smiling male countenance. That night, Solomon's sleep was interrupted by a dream revealing that God would transfer responsibility to a new order, represented by the baby growing in Makeda's womb. The king therefore sent her home to await delivery, directing her to send a male child to Jerusalem for training in Jewish lore and law.

The queen bore a son, Menilek I, who traveled to Jerusalem when he came of age.[1] A pleased Solomon housed the lad at court and affectionately offered to make him crown prince. Menilek, however, was determined to return home, and Solomon graciously anointed his son king of Ethiopia, assigning a number of young Israeli nobles as courtiers. Menilek's retinue could not contemplate life without the Ark of the Covenant, which they stole. The larceny was apparently approved by God, who levitated the youths and their holy cargo across the Red Sea before discovery and chase by Solomon's forces. The *Kebre Negast*'s messages are clear: Menilek had bested his father, in a way avenging Makeda's humiliation, and God had consigned his covenant with man to Ethiopia, making it Israel's successor.

Ethiopians became the chosen people, an honor reinforced by their acceptance of Christianity. The *Kebre Negast* is thus a national epic that glorifies a particular monarchical line and tradition and also indelibly associates Ethiopia with the Judeo-Christian tradition. The epic sought

---

1. According to Jewish tradition, he would have been thirteen.

to arouse patriotic feelings of uniqueness, to glorify Ethiopia, and to provide a proud identity.

The myths surrounding the "restored" Solomonic dynasty provided the basis necessary for a renaissance in church and state. Under the new dynasty's banner, Ethiopia expanded southward, confirming Amharic and Christianity as integral parts of the imperial tradition dominating the government until late in the twentieth century. Crown and church were thus inextricably linked, a relationship clearly revealed in the reign of the great Emperor Amda Siyon (r. 1314–1344), who consolidated the new dynasty's authority.

A rough and tough military man, he quickly moved against his enemies in Tigray and fractious ethnic groups in Hadiya, Damot, and Gojam, who sought to transform feudal autonomy into sovereign independence. Upon victory, he reorganized rebellious provinces into more easily ruled smaller jurisdictions controlled through strategically placed imperial garrisons. He used the same methods in newly conquered southern regions, where his armies spread the gospel as well as the *Pax Ethiopica*.

As imperial control grew, so did the economy, which delivered gold, ivory, and slaves from south and central Ethiopia to the coast for export to the Middle East. Ethiopia's commodities flowed to the coast along three routes: from Sudan to Mitsiwa north of Lake Tana via Lasta; from the central provinces through southern Shewa to Mitsiwa or Zeila; and from the southern provinces connecting up with the route through Shewa to Zeila. Amda Siyon shrewdly invited the Muslim communities that dominated commerce and the trade routes into a symbiotic relationship. To continue their activities, they had to recognize his suzerainty, pay him taxes on trade, and otherwise conform to his administration.

Amda Siyon shaped a pragmatic form of administration that derived from the natural economy and from Zagwean, perhaps even Axumite, precedents. As the theoretical owner of all land, the emperor assigned *gults*, or fiefs, to worthy followers. They administered their localities, supplied soldiers and animals during wartime, demanded service from their subjects, and collected taxes in kind. The dues and corvée varied widely from region to region, depending on fertility, security, recency of conquest, religion, social cohesion, and whatever the emperor demanded for tribute.

The gult lords enjoyed almost untrammeled local power, which they exercised in the monarch's name under the watchful eyes of the local imperial garrison. Given Ethiopia's terrain and difficulty of communications, the early Solomonic monarchs could not construct a bureaucratic

6. Hamlet in Gurage

empire. Although the court periodically moved around the country to demonstrate the emperor's might, administrative flexibility and continuity could be provided only through the gult lords. As long as they kept their jurisdictions tranquil and tribute was delivered regularly, the fiefs could be passed from father to son, until the personalized authority became hereditary right.

In newly conquered territories, the emperor named gult holders from among outstanding soldiers. At first, they were little more than warlords, controlling their holdings from strategically placed military posts, which, as time passed, became trade and administrative centers. By the end of Amda Siyon's reign in 1344, his empire had come to control all of Shewa—Damot had been reduced to vassalage—and the surrounding and widely dispersed Muslim states of Yifat, Hadiya, and Dawaro.

Since Zagwean times, Muslim leaders had sought to unite their jurisdictions into one large and powerful state to struggle for souls, terrain, and trade. Upon accession in 1270, Yekuno Amlak had quickly subdued Yifat, the Muslim center adjacent to Shewa. Authorities in Cairo sought to defend their confreres by refusing to send a new bishop to Ethiopia, thus crippling the Orthodox church and the unanointed

7. Sidama house

emperor. In the quest for legitimacy, the king's immediate successors resorted to appeasement, seen as a sign of weakness by Yifat, which renewed raiding along the frontier.

Amda Siyon soon became frustrated with Yifat's razzias and Cairo's refusals. He concluded that he could force the sultan's hand only by taking control of Ethiopia's Muslim population, which would, of course, permit him to administer and tax the country's growing trade. In 1316, the king attacked Yifat, easily took and plundered its capital and looted smaller Muslim principalities to the south and the east. His suzerainty was accepted, and his new subjects agreed to pay an annual tribute in return for autonomy.

Yifat used the peace to build up its army while Amda Siyon was preoccupied by rebellions in Tigray, Damot, Dawaro, and Hadiya. By the late 1320s, exploiting a decade of royal neglect, Sabradin of Yifat confidently organized a united Muslim front composed of peoples dissatisfied with Christian domination and tired of paying heavy taxes. In 1332, Sabradin declared a holy war against the Solomonic state, invaded its territory, destroyed churches, and forced conversions to Islam.

Calling up troops from all over his empire, Amda Siyon led a bloody campaign against Yifat and its allies. He even took the battle to the lowlands, where imperial armies rarely went, and he lost many soldiers to desertion, disease, and thirst. Still, the king went on, determined once and for all to end the Muslim threat and to replace local governments with imperial officials. He led his forces brilliantly, feinting here, probing there, attacking the weakest units in the Muslim federation, and never permitting his enemy to counter in a mass attack. Pushing his army to the limits of its strength, he even outmaneuvered an enemy that contained units of highly mobile, if fractious, nomads. It was a magisterial effort by a charismatic and resourceful man who also had mastered and united an empire around him. His great victory carried the frontier of Christian power into the Awash valley and beyond.

After their defeat, the Muslims of Yifat called to Cairo for help, and, not surprisingly, in 1337, Abuna Yakob found his way to Ethiopia, proof indeed of Amda Siyon's great success. The new metropolitan immediately set about ordaining desperately needed clergy and consecrating churches often built years before. A fervent evangelical, Abuna Yakob deployed a corps of monks in the newly conquered empire. The obvious objectives were central and southern Shewa, Damot (Gojam), and the Beta Israel (Falasha)–inhabited areas of Begemdir, which the bishop subdivided and assigned to particular monks.

They had their task cut out for them, since they worked among devout people, whose priests and shamans fought hard to retain their allegiance. Many monks were killed or injured by those they sought to convert, especially as the interlopers chose to build churches on traditional sacred sites. The evangelists ultimately won, however, in much the same ways that Christian missionaries have always succeeded, through hard work, faith, and persistence; by convincing the local elites that conversion guaranteed continuation in office; and by ignoring for a time such folk practices as witchcraft, magic, or devotion to household spirits. Over the longer term, the people became more conventional Christians, and the conquest zones were absorbed to a greater or lesser extent into the Solomonic heartland.

The quality of Christianity greatly concerned the more fervent monks, who sought to uphold the ethical tone of the church and its dogma. In the mid-fourteenth century, Abba Ewostatewos (c. 1273–1352), an abbot in Seraye, shaped a new monastic ideology which stressed that spiritual independence necessitated isolation from corrupting state influences. He accused the secular clergy of loose morality and the aristocracy of venality by participating in the lucrative slave trade to Arabia, Sudan, and Egypt. The people and the church, the abbot thundered, must return to the great teachings of the Bible, including observance of the Sabbath to honor the Old Testament. Meanwhile, his followers would neither accept money from the gult lords nor pay tribute and other traditional dues.

Church and state establishments quickly united to protect their interests and attacked Ewostatewos's stubbornly held notions, but his righteousness armored him against slander and his intellect against conventional dogma. Outdone in the theological war, his opponents declared him a deviant according to the Alexandrian church's thirteenth-century anathematization of Old Testament customs. Ewostatewos and his followers were actively persecuted, and the unyielding leader was forced into exile, first in the Holy Land and later in Armenia, where he died in 1352.

In Ethiopia, Sabbatarians were refused ordination, hounded from monasteries and churches, driven from the court, demoted or fired from official positions, and even forced out of towns and settled areas. The zealots retreated into remote areas of northeastern Ethiopia, where they formed isolated communities. A few settlements in Begemdir might have "purified" their Christianity to the point of returning to a form of Judaism. No other explanation accounts for the unique pre-Talmudic faith of the Beta Israel, in which Ethiopian Christian borrowings abound.

For the most part, however, priests and powerful lay abbots ensured the continuity of Ewostathian practices. The Sabbatarians were filled with a religious zeal that overflowed in missionary activities among adjacent non-Christian communities. Within a few generations, the Ewostathians were flourishing as never before, and their monasteries and communities, dominated by Debre Bizen, dotted the Eritrean highlands. That they managed to attain prosperity while being pariahs alarmed the official establishment, and in 1400, Emperor Dawit I (r. 1380–1412) acted to control the outlaws.

He invited the Sabbatarians to court for a debate, ostensibly to seek compromise, when, in fact, he and Abuna Bartolomewos (1399–1436) wanted only conformity. The Sabbatarian leaders, led by Abba Filipos of Debre Bizen, oblivious to any possibility of perfidy, argued their case with the courage of Ewostatewos a century earlier. Time after time, they refused to repudiate the Sabbath, until in frustration the *abun* ordered Abba Filipos and the others fettered and thrown into prison. Many conforming abbots believed that the now leaderless movement would dissipate, but its local nature ensured survival among the masses. The cleavage in the church developed into a social chasm, pitting rulers against a mass movement.

Jailing Abba Filipos proved a blunder, which Dawit recognized in 1403, when he ordered his release, ostensibly to celebrate a military victory over Muslims. By then, feelings of Christian nationalism were running high, and it was easy and politic for the emperor to seek compromise with the homegrown ideology. He decreed that the Ewostathians be permitted to observe the Sabbath and to return to their normal activities, including proselytization. He paradoxically decided, however, to maintain at court the Alexandrian view of Sunday as the sole Sabbath.

Dawit's successor, Emperor Zara Yakob (r. 1434–1468) finally was able to meld a fractious church and state into unity. His excellent education at a leading Eritrean monastery school had sensitized him to the issues involved in the Sabbatarian controversy. Having witnessed the impressive growth of the Ewostathians after Dawit's decree of toleration, Zara Yakob recognized that their energetic conviction ought to be exploited to renovate the church as a vehicle of national unity.

During the previous two centuries, Ethiopian Christianity had attracted whole countries of converts of varied languages and cultures. They were served by the many new monasteries and parishes that dotted the landscape from north to south, disseminating often different messages. Even at court, clergy presented opposite views: the abun, the hierarchy, and the secular clergy stood with the Alexandrian church, but royal chaplains and monks taught the holiness of the Sabbath. Although the Ewostathians' stubbornness had won them recognition and legality, their monks continued to refuse the church's discipline.

The moment for compromise came when Abuna Bartolomewos died in 1436. Zara Yakob asked for two bishops to help reform the church, and the see of Saint Mark agreeably sent co-abuns Mikail (1438–1458?) and Gabriel (1438–1458?). They and the emperor forthrightly discussed the church's problems and the overriding need for theological uniformity. Zara Yakob advised the cobishops that Alexandria's acceptance of the Ethiopian view of the Sabbath would restore religious unity. He reasoned that once the church conceded the point, the Ewostathians would have to accept Holy Orders and episcopal discipline.

Meanwhile, Zara Yakob traveled to Axum in 1436 for his coronation and remained in the north for the next three years. His symbolic goal was to identify himself and his state with the First Ethiopian Empire, but his

8. Crowns held at Church of Mary, Axum

real intention was to begin reconciling with the Ewostathians. Their payment of feudal dues to the emperor signaled the end of the schism between renegades and ruling elites, although it was not until 1450, at the Council of Mitmaq, that Bishops Mikail and Gabriel conceded the observance of the Sabbath and the Sabbatarians agreed to Holy Orders. With Zara Yakob presiding, the event formalized the crown's importance in fostering national reconciliation and reform.

Since the Islamic challenge was sometimes a reality and always a threat, Zara Yakob continued to mold Christianity into Ethiopia's main line of internal defense. Together clergy and king created an ideology for a united state, an idea spread by the many deacons and priests newly ordained by Zara Yakob's two bishops. In the more remote areas, the emperor liberally endowed monasteries and churches, making land grants with property confiscated from defeated rulers. Even the most radical clergy and monastics were integrated into the political economy, further uniting church and state. Zara Yakob was a great leader of Ethiopia. He was remarkably consistent in working for Ethiopia's unity from Eritrea south through Shewa into Sidama country. The choices he made—Christianity and feudalism—were rational, indeed inevitable, in terms of terrain and communications, and led to a largely peaceful and prosperous reign.

The emperor was secure enough to establish a permanent capital in northern Shewa at Debre Birhan (mountain of light), on an austere, cold, and windswept plateau, reflecting the emperor's celebrated asceticism. During a fourteen-year residency there, he established a large palace and endowed churches, and the *makwanent* (high nobility) and abbots built villas, whose needs attracted craftsmen, workers, farmers, and merchants. As Ethiopia's first major town in centuries, it attracted teachers and savants from throughout the empire; even Zara Yakob participated in its rich cultural life by lending his name to several religious pamphlets. The new capital even drew the interest of the outside world, a consequence that pleased the emperor.

He had an active, if vague, awareness of when Ethiopia had been known in the outside world and was interested in restoring his country's international relations, especially with Christian powers. Ethiopians had ventured to Jerusalem often during the previous century, to open contacts with their coreligionists. The West was, of course, bemused by its attractive, if distorted, vision of the empire of Prester John, but access into the Horn of Africa was blocked by the determination of Egypt's rulers not to let Europeans travel to Ethiopia, lest they sell modern firearms to the emperors. Throughout the 1440s, Zara Yakob therefore tried to break the Muslim hold over access into Ethiopia.

In the east, the Muslims were led by Adal, Yifat's militant successor. Located around Harer, it was able to dominate the trade routes to the coast at Zeila from Ethiopia's largely Muslim provinces of Yifat, Fatagar, Dawaro, and Bale. From time to time, usually when Ethio-Egyptian relations were strained, Adal's highly mobile Somali and Afar cavalry entered Solomonic territory and, with the cooperation of their fellow Muslims, waged guerrilla war against Christian garrisons. The Adal became particularly worrisome in the late 1430s under Ahmad Badlay, an ambitious and ardent leader who exemplified the increasingly militant nature of Ethiopian Islam. Between 1443 and 1445, he directed harsh, if intermittent, campaigns in Ethiopia's largely Muslim-inhabited provinces before falling in battle in Dawaro, thereby breaking his army's morale.

In return for peace, Adal was made to pay a heavy tribute but was permitted to continue under its own rulers. The region was too vast for the imperial government to garrison, and highlanders hated living among Muslims in the hot, dry country. Since Zara Yakob sought full access to the sea, he looked northward to the Red Sea coast near the Christian-inhabited central highlands of Tigray. In 1448–1449, he settled military

9. Small mosque, Harer

colonies in what is today Eritrea, reorganized the highlands into one administration under a "ruler of the seas" (*bahr negash*), and then attacked the Muslim principalities at Mitsiwa and on the Dahlak Islands. He refurbished the old port at Girar, opposite Mitsiwa, and diverted all highlands trade there.

Reports of Zara Yakob's success made their way to Europe, burnishing the spurious luster of Prester John. Some Westerners exaggerated the importance of Ethiopia, which they hoped would destroy Muslim power in Egypt, Arabia, and even Syria. Europe's leaders therefore welcomed a mission sent by Zara Yakob in 1450, its arrival another signal that the Solomonic empire wished to break the Muslim encirclement and its isolation. The Ethiopians sought technical assistance, which the West was willing to provide if travel was made safe. Some artisans apparently reached Debre Birhan, but the Egyptians managed to keep most of them away. One European who made an indelible mark on Ethiopia was the painter, Niccolo Brancaleone, whose fluid renaissance style influenced traditional Ethiopian artists to graft a more natural modeling of faces and bodies onto their previously stylized religious scenes. Meanwhile, the art of government and politics had stultified, with dangerous prospects for the future.

The fault lay mostly with the nature of the monarchy and its supporting institutions. Succession had always been a problem, since there was no concept of primogeniture, and kings could choose from among their male children, causing intrigue, squabbling, and civil war. To ensure tranquility, emperors stored their potential rivals on Amba Gishan, a steep-sided, flat-topped mountain fortress with only one closely guarded access. On a monarch's death, an ad hoc committee of high churchmen and officials met and selected a successor from the princely filing cabinet. Obviously, the process was not so simple, and family, political, economic, and military considerations informed it. For example, Zara Yakob became emperor because the army concluded that he would make a good commander in chief. The selection process probably worked in a rough way to establish the best candidate for the job but invariably created factions, took too long, and left the new emperor with a difficult task of consolidation and pacification.

The periodic disunity at the center was matched by centrifugal forces on the periphery of Solomonic political power. By the sixteenth century, Ethiopia was a feudal, conglomerate state centered in the northern-central highlands among people who shared cultural, economic, linguistic, and religious affinities. The core area was ringed by more or less recently conquered provinces, whose inhabitants were at least superficially Christian and whose administration resembled government in the traditional provinces. At the outer periphery were tributary states whose traditional rulers presided over people culturally, religiously, and economically different from those of the heartland and its environs. Whenever there was a crisis, or, indeed, royal instability, death, or succession, the state began to contract. Even in the heartland, political squabbling often eroded the fragile unities of religion, language, tradition, economics, and mythology. Most of Ethiopia's peoples continued to think locally, and, for them, the state was at best a shadowy entity that manifested itself only in its demand for taxes. Unity was thus the consequence of strong rule, and Zara Yakob's successors were weak. Dynastic instability led to short reigns, youthful and inexperienced monarchs, and ambitious royal councillors, among them the Dowager Queen Elleni. She was an exceptionally intelligent person, whose political talents took her from Zara Yakob's harem to an influential position at court during the reign of Baeda Mariam (1468–1478). Originally from Hadiya, her instincts were attuned to Ethiopia's periphery, where, she believed, the best imperial government was the least imperial government.

In line with such thinking, Baeda Mariam ignored the mechanisms of central government established during Zara Yakob's reign. In the provinces, he replaced his father's carefully chosen partisans with scions of locally important families, clans, and dynasties; and at court, he transferred authority over the government's daily business to the *bitwodeds* (literally, the "beloved" ones). Debre Birhan was permitted to run down, while Baeda Mariam took to the road in search of sustenance, instead of insisting that tribute and taxes be delivered to a central location. Whereas fifteenth-century Western Europe was reinventing the town and the related market mechanisms that would overwhelm feudalism, Ethiopia was slowing the forces of change and strengthening the process of division.

The weakening of the central state reduced the flow of revenues, more of which could be retained by local authorities as imperial garrisons withdrew or decayed. The decline of the Solomonic monarchy led, in the central highlands, to Christian heterodoxy, social strife, and friction between clergy and crown, a weakening therefore of the central axis of the state. Conversely, the decline of the Solomonic state advantaged the long-suffering Muslim states, who increasingly avoided paying tribute and a percentage of trading profits to the hated Christians. Adal grew increasingly stronger, until it was able to defeat Christian armies. Emperor Naod (r. 1494–1508), for example, was killed trying to push Adal invaders out of Yifat, where the enemy had been welcomed. The Christian state had failed to satisfy the aspirations of its Muslim subjects, who remained susceptible to external mobilization. For a time, however, the potential storm was hidden by the successful reign of Emperor Lebna Dengel (r. 1508–1540).

THREE

The Decline of the Solomonic Dynasty, to 1769

As a child, Lebna Dengel was lucky. He was enthroned when he was only eleven, but his imperial scepter was handled wisely enough by the elderly Elleni to ensure his survival. Moreover, thanks to internal squabbles in Adal, the Christian state was able to contain incursions, even to advance into Muslim territory and win some major battles. Beneath the surface, however, pressures were building up that would erupt into disaster for the Solomonic empire. Lebna Dengel's fate as a young man was to preside over tragedy.

The Muslim explosion into the Christian kingdom had been long in the making. Strife between the cross and the crescent provided the ideological justification, and Ethiopia's maladministered and exploited periphery furnished the battlegrounds. For several centuries, Ethiopia's mostly non-Christian nomads had sought to quit their lowlands and deserts for the adjacent salubrious high plateaus. The demand for more territory stemmed from the herders' need for more and better pasture for their flocks and progeny. Over the years, some pastoralists, especially among the southern Oromo, had mounted the highlands, mostly to be savaged and thrown back by Christian armies or frontier garrisons. Between the thirteenth and sixteenth centuries, overpopulation and overgrazing grew among the Somali and Afar of eastern Ethiopia. The pressure led at first to raiding at water holes and to animal rustling, then to clan warfare, and finally to population movement. Yet, people in the Awsa-Awash plains and in the Chercher-Harer uplands could not have understood that their existence was being upset because of population pressures felt by obscure people living far to the east and close to the coast. They merely observed an unusual amount of political turmoil.

There had always been political dispute in Ethiopia's Muslim mini- and microstates between pragmatists and zealots. The former chose to work with the Christian monarchy, whereas the latter preferred to spread the Prophet's word. In the early sixteenth century, differences between the two groups led to humiliating defeats by Lebna Dengel's armies and consequent civil strife in Adal. The religious fervor of the Muslim state eroded, and Harer, so tradition claims, became a center of debauchery and anarchy. When trade declined, the people called out for new leadership.

Adal's savior was to be Ahmad ibn Ibrihim al-Ghazi (1506–1543), known to the Ethiopians as Ahmad "Gran" (the "left-handed"). He soldiered for Sultan Jared Abun of Adal (r. ca. 1522–1525), who during his few years of power sought to impose Islamic puritanism on his fractious people. The righteous road appealed to the pious Ahmad, who was raised by his devout kin in Jeldesa, one of the major oases along the trading route to Zeila. Although his Islam was the most rigorous and doctrinaire, deeply influenced by the discipline of the desert, it was tempered by an understanding of commerce.

When Jared Abun was assassinated, Ahmad found the rule of secular Muslims repulsive. He retired to the countryside (or Zeila, as local tradition claims) and exhorted his brethren to join him in returning the state to pristine Islamic practices. As imam, his fiery message and its charismatic delivery electrified his audience, and he shortly recruited an enthusiastic, if unruly, force of tribesmen to lead against the backsliding enemy. Adal quickly fell to Ahmad's army, but the levies, flush with treasure and tales, rapidly fell away from him to return to their flocks and families. Ahmad determined to win them back by proclaiming holy war against the Christian state.

And return they did, though probably more for the possibility of plunder than for proselytization. When Ahmad thought them ready for confrontation, he ostentatiously refused to pay Adal's tribute, triggering a Solomonic invasion in 1527 that was decisively thrown back. Once again, the victorious warriors took their booty and made for the desert, demonstrating to their commander that the army's allegiance to God and to him remained opportunistic and episodic. Ahmad sought to counter their fickleness by whipping up a religious frenzy over the competition between Islam and Christianity. He declared a jihad, rigorously disciplined his enlistees, and trained them in the use of the new tactics and firearms the Ottomans recently had introduced into the Red Sea region.

In 1527, once on the highlands and distant from their desert sanctuaries, the imam's men fought magnificently. They first subdued the periphery, revealing the fragility of its attachment to the center. The erstwhile Ethiopians abandoned their clergy, northern settlers, soldiers, and officials to Ahmad's men, and, to survive, people accepted the demolition of their churches, holy books, and relics. Bale, Sidamo, and Hadiya, and Kembata were gone quickly, placing the heartland at risk.

Emperor Lebna Dengel mobilized a vast force from Tigray, Amhara, the Agew territories, Begemdir, Gojam, and Shewa and encamped about fifty kilometers east of what is now Addis Abeba. The huge army suffered from poor logistics and a leadership more concerned about authority and precedence than with adopting a common strategy to defeat the enemy. Imam Ahmad's army, by contrast, was united in its command structure, and its smaller size permitted mobility and flexible tactics. Moreover, the Adal soldiers enjoyed superior weapons and were led by a brilliant leader. His great success had filled each soldier with enthusiasm for the battlefield. It is not surprising therefore that, in 1528, the Christians were defeated at the decisive battle of Shimbra Kure, allowing the Muslims to occupy Dawaro, Shewa, Amhara, and Lasta.

They pushed inexorably northward, traversing the rich Amhara plateau north of the Awash, destroying settled life and razing churches and other cultural centers, among them the monasteries that stored Solomonic lore. As he moved, Ahmad built a civil administration composed of his own men and collaborators, often the remnants of the pre-Solomonic ruling classes. By 1535, he headed a vast and ephemeral Islamic empire stretching from Zeila to Mitsiwa on the coast and including the Ethiopian interior.

Yet Lebna Dengel remained at large in the Christian highlands, where he was welcomed and protected by a fiercely proud people for whom the Solomonic state reflected not only their inheritance but also their destiny. Chronicles about the time display not so much hatred against the Muslims as embarrassment that Christians permitted infidels to enter and devastate their country and holy places. In the empire's embattled heartland, the ethos of Ethiopia was present in fable and tale, the stuff

10. Abba Gada of the Boren Oromo

from which a new state later would be conjured. When Lebna Dengel died in 1540, the Solomonic mythology was not interred with him. In fact, he well may have ensured the survival of Christian Ethiopia by having sent an SOS to Europe.

In 1535, the emperor's cry for help reached the Portuguese, who had long sought contact with Prester John. In January 1541, after Ethiopia had agonized through six terrible and wearying years of war, four hundred musketeers disembarked at Mitsiwa. When they arrived in the highlands, the governor of Tigray raised an army to be reorganized and retrained in European tactics. The Imam Ahmad immediately recognized the danger, but when he finally caught up with the Ethio-Portuguese army in April 1541, he was defeated by the well-directed firepower of four hundred muskets. The great leader was pained only by a slight wound, but his movement was mortified by the Christian affront.

The imam quickly turned to Turkey, the leading Muslim state, then a superpower. Istanbul was competing with the Portuguese for hegemony in the Indian Ocean and naturally saw Lisbon's activities as threatening its interests in the Horn of Africa. After regional Ottoman authorities provided nine hundred Muslim, mostly mercenary, musketeers and ten cannon, Ahmad's army was ready for the Christians. It won a significant victory in late August 1542, taking weapons and ammunition and killing hundreds of the Christian enemy, including two hundred Portuguese and their commander, Christopher da Gama, who was captured and beheaded. A happy and now confident imam thanked his Turkish allies for services rendered, rewarded them with goods doubtless looted from the church, sent them home, and ordered his army back to their camp.

Meanwhile, the Christian survivors prepared for a final confrontation under the leadership of Emperor Galawedos (r. 1540–1559). Given limited resources, the monarch decided to abandon positional war and to take the initiative. His hit-and-run strategy was so successful that the imam's forces were thrown off balance and often caught off guard. Ahmad never knew where his adversary would strike and had to station his forces in defensive positions, where they lost all mobility, originally his army's greatest quality. He and his personal troops acted as a strategic reserve and shifted from post to post in an apparently random way. He was in the open, encamped near Lake Tana, when, on 25 February 1543, Galawedos and a flying column attacked. After hard fighting, Ahmad ibn Ibrihim was killed, and his soldiers broke and ran, leaving the field and Ethiopia to the Christians.

The country had lost hundreds of thousands of lives, a measure of confidence in itself and its religion, and much of its capital. Ethiopia would not be able to follow Europe into commercial and then industrial capitalism. By the early 1550s, Galawedos had fashioned a reasonable facsimile of the Solomonic empire as it had existed at the beginning of his father's reign, but without its deep strength. Muslims, especially in the border provinces of Yifat, Dawaro, and Bale, remained disaffected, and in the extreme south the Oromo awaited their chance to occupy large areas of the fertile highlands.

The original homeland of the Oromo, a Cushitic-speaking pastoralist people, has been located in northwest Borena. First their Afar-Saho and then their Somali brothers hived off northeastward to the African littorals

11. Tomb of an Oromo Muslim saint in Arsi

of the Indian Ocean, Gulf of Aden, and the Red Sea. Some Oromo may have attained the high plateaus as early as the late thirteenth century, only to be contained by the garrisons that the Solomonic state established along the empire's periphery. When the defenses were destroyed during the Muslim war, the Oromo resumed infiltrating, even as Lebna Dengel restored a semblance of Solomonic government in the empire's periphery.

The Oromo, among other East African peoples, had developed a generational-grade form of government, the *gada* system, which defined male activities in eight-year segments. The pastoral nature of Oromo life dictated a loose, egalitarian society led by officials elected by the gada responsible for government. In the sixteenth century, the Oromo probably were divided into exogamous moieties, the Borena and the Barettuma. They identified themselves as members of moieties, gada classes, clans, and lineages. The elders, the *jarsa biyya*, dealt with day-to-day moral and legal issues, ceremonies, and religious life.

The *qallu*, Oromo leaders who represented the forces of nature, had a powerful, if vague, authority over religious and political matters great and small. They validated the leadership of the gada council from a list

12. Oromo funerary stela, Arsi

supplied by a committee of the ruling gada cohort. The qallu grade, the sixth and perhaps most important level of the gada cycle, ideally extended from the forty-seventh to the fifty-fifth year of male life. By then, men theoretically had been exposed to the major aspects of Oromo life, especially marriage and military service. Success in the latter led to the former, so that every eight years, when a new warrior (*luba*) class was inaugurated, there was a cycle of violence often outside of Oromo-inhabited lands.

The Oromo need to raid and restore herds reflected the poverty of their semiarid environments in Bale and Borena, and they fought adjacent pastoralist people for grazing, water, and animals. Such activities became deeply ingrained, even happily anticipated by self-conscious youths en route to manhood. Should environmental imperatives demand—however obscurely they impinged upon individual consciousness—long-distance expeditions could and were easily substituted for local razzias.

The Oromo made for the high plateaus. Helped by their adversaries' war weariness, demoralization, and depopulation, the Oromo won territory after territory in the seventeenth century. The Ethiopian monk and historian Bahrey rationalized Oromo success as being largely due to the failure of Solomonic society effectively to mobilize its resources. Feudalism, according to Bahrey, had created too many privileged classes and not enough soldiers to fight the socially homogeneous Oromo warriors. He explained that the latter moved in natural response to their inhospitable homeland, pushing northwestward into Arsi, Shewa, Welega, and Gojam; and northeastward into Harerge and Welo (traditional Amhara), stopping only where they were blocked by forest and population or by the effective mobilization of Christian or Muslim forces. By the end of the century, the Oromo came to dominate areas with different ecologies, environments, climates, and cultures, factors tending toward social differentiation.

Some Oromo remained pastoralists, others became agriculturists, and a large number practiced a mixed mode of production. Tens of thousands of people came to identify with the host society, while others remained apart or selectively borrowed new methods of production, social organization, and thought. Some Oromo became Muslim, others Christian, and many retained the faith of their fathers, even if they incorporated Allah, Muhammad, Jesus, and the Virgin Mary into their rituals. The Oromo thus came to live within varied social formations and to speak dialects of the mother tongue. They had little to hinder their development, since Emperor Sarsa Dengel (r. 1563–1597) had decided, for defensive reasons, to reduce Ethiopia's size.

First he reorganized the military and showed surprising political talent as he won the support of northern magnates. By 1578, Christian Ethiopia was united enough to move against the Turks, whose efforts to transform the Red Sea into a Muslim lake had taken them from a landing at Mitsiwa onto the highlands and deep into Tigray. Once Sarsa Dengel moved, the intruders quickly retreated to the coast, but they did not abandon their territorial ambitions until 1589, when Istanbul agreed to a formal peace. By then, the emperor's social policies and campaigns had reshaped Ethiopia, which at the time comprised most of modern Eritrea, Tigray, and Begemdir and parts of Gojam, Shewa, and Welo, later termed Abyssinia.

But a mere rump of the earlier state, it was an easily defensible, socially cohesive unit that included mostly Christian, Semitic-speaking peoples, although there were important populations of Agew, Oromo, and Beta Israel. With few exceptions, the people were sedentary agriculturists, who lived within the political economy characteristic of the Solomonic state. The Christians never forgot that their rulers once held sway over a much larger state, and *Ethiopia irredenta* was a political idea dunned into the heads of prince and peasant alike, merely adding to the *Kebre Negast*'s legitimation of the activities of the Solomonic dynasty.

Shewa, where the indigenous Amhara had been driven from the middle highlands into the highest and coldest parts of Menz and Mahrabete or into the relatively unhealthy adjacent lowlands, became a center of anti-Oromo sentiment. Elsewhere, parish clergy railed against the infidels and exhorted congregants to work for the liberation of their coreligionists. Overall, the Orthodox church on the local level was the most important purveyor of the Solomonic lore and the related nationalism that united the rump state and kept alive the idea of the extended empire.

A revived and reformed military had an obviously important role in the new Ethiopia. Sarsa Dengel recruited more soldiers and established more units under the crown's direct command. First, he strengthened the imperial guard and other palace units and made them responsible for internal security. Then he withdrew obviously ineffectual provincial garrisons, now islands awash with Oromo, and repositioned them in the north, transforming some of them into a quick-deployment force while resettling others, as watch dogs, in provinces controlled by the more important nobles. His military policy confirmed that the old empire was gone, at least for a time, and that the very survival of Abyssinia and its monarchy was paramount.

The twin Oromo-Muslim crises had raised questions about the effectiveness of the Orthodox church. The church's ideology appeared flawed, since Christians had abandoned clergy, property, and territory to Muslims and continued to give way to the Oromo. The ruling classes could neither appreciate the social fissures of feudalism that weakened peasant resolve to fight nor comprehend the pressures behind the Oromo expansion. With impeccable logic, since they considered themselves blameless, court officials reasoned that, just as the Ethiopian army had required new men, new tactics, and redeployment, the Orthodox church needed renewal. Since military revival had come from Western Christendom, why not religious revival? Indeed, the emperors may have regarded a dalliance with Roman Catholicism as a tactic to secure sufficient modern weaponry and training to win back the Solomonic empire.

With the Portuguese had come priests, who were welcomed at court, where their ideas had a stimulating effect. Emperor Galawedos (r. 1540–1559) responded by writing his famous *Confession of Faith*, an affirmation of confidence in Orthodox church teachings, which he clarified for his Portuguese friends. Fifty years and many provinces of Oromo expansion later, Emperor Za Dengel (r. 1603–1604) was unable to share his predecessor's trust in the church's teaching and despairingly and secretly converted to Roman Catholicism. Found out, he was quickly deposed by horrified provincial lords and replaced by Susneyos (r. 1607–1632), one of Lebna Dengel's grandsons. The new emperor had an interesting and creative mind, and his policy of integrating Oromo into the Solomonic state's political life was a daring gambit.

On taking the crown, Susneyos's situation was precarious: he had no real counter against the provincial lords, whose members not only refused to remit their tribute but also sheltered various pretenders. Meanwhile, the military threat to the state had grown: the Fung of Sennar attacked along the northern frontier into Begemdir, and the Oromo continued infiltrating into Shewa and Gojam.

His previous experience with the Oromo—he had lived among them and had married a daughter of a ranking gada official—convinced him that the newcomers might have a role to play in Ethiopia's politics. As Rome's Emperor Aurelian had done in the late third century, the Ethiopian sovereign chose to settle his interlopers in the marches and to integrate their units into the forces of the central government, thus transforming one enemy into a weapon useful to subdue the others. So far, so good, but the emperor's fundamental aim was to return Ethiopia to its previous greatness.

To do so, Susneyos imagined, required an alliance with Western Christendom, now personified in the dignified and diplomatic Pedro Paez, a Spanish Jesuit. The priest worked behind the scenes as adviser, educator, and diplomat to bring the Ethiopian sheep into the Roman flock. In 1612, Susneyos himself converted, refraining, however, on Paez's advice, from a public declaration until 1622. By then, the auspices were not good, since in 1617–1618 several anti-Catholic risings had occurred. For the Ethiopian church and its faithful, conversion required fundamental changes in liturgy, theology, and religious practices, not merely a shift in the chain of apostolic authority.

Such a transformation became moot after 1625, when Paez's intolerant successor, Afonso Mendez, another Spanish Jesuit, became Ethiopia's Catholic bishop. He decided that Holy Mother Church could not wait one more day to save the souls of the heretical Ethiopians. He ordered the suspension of male circumcision and the observance of the Sabbath as outmoded Jewish customs; and he directed that churches be reconsecrated, altars rebuilt, priests removed or reordained, people rebaptized, fasts and festivals rescheduled, and the liturgy refashioned. Resistance led to a series of rebellions and repressions, until it appeared that the country was coming apart. The emperor's most loyal followers, including his son and successor, Fasilidas (r. 1632–1667), grew alarmed at the destruction of the social fabric, especially as the Oromo exploited the anarchy and pleaded with the emperor to reconsider his religious policy.

When Susneyos concluded that his personal commitment to Catholicism had led to imminent disaster, he abdicated in favor of Fasilidas, who ordered the Jesuits from court and then from Ethiopia. The rejection of Roman Catholicism was ipso facto an admission that for the time being the Solomonic state would limit its activities and imagination to Abyssinia, a focus that the new emperor tried to ensure by signing agreements with Mitsiwa and Suakin seeking to prohibit the entry of Europeans into the Christian highlands.

For the next two centuries, Ethiopia's extent was essentially limited to Abyssinia, but not its reach. The highlands exploited the hinterland's primary products, connecting Ethiopia's economy to the commerce of the Red Sea and Nile valley. A complex caravan network linked Mitsiwa and the interior, and Gonder became a regional center, doing business with Sennar and Fazughli for slaves and gold bought and paid for with coffee obtained from Enerea. The market for Ethiopian beans grew considerably during the last quarter of the seventeenth century, as Yemen, a major trading partner, sought increasing amounts of coffee for transshipment to Europe to satisfy burgeoning Western demand.

Gonder was at the height of its prosperity at the turn of the eighteenth

13. Ceiling of the Church of Debre Birhan, Gonder

century, when it may have had a population of seventy thousand.
Emperor Fasilidas, who founded the new capital around 1635, obviously
hoped to create a strong center around which the remnants of the
Christian north could rally. He picked a beautiful site, a flat volcanic ridge
at seven thousand feet surrounded by mountains on three sides, but with
easy access to Lake Tana in the south. Gonder's climate is warm during
the day, cool at night; its two streams afforded plentiful water supplies and
its hinterland abundant wood and produce.

14. Detail of a crumbling castle, Gonder

Enough of an urban economy arose to sustain architecture, music, poetry, literature, painting, calligraphy, and educational, religious, and social institutions. The emperors appeared in considerable state, surrounded by courtiers, clergy, and soldiers. Iyasu I ("the Great"; r. 1682–1706) sat on throne-divans made of gold- and silver-threaded fabric, and he wore gold-embroidered clothing and jewels. On ceremonial occasions, he walked under a splendid purple canopy, preceded by bandsmen playing trumpets, flutes, oboes, and drums, and followed by gorgeously arrayed nobles in the middle of whom walked the bearer of the imperial crown.

The aristocracy and the monarchy supported the artists and artisans who put up buildings, illuminated manuscripts, decorated the interior of churches and palaces, and worked stone, wood, or pottery. The town's castles and other monuments were built of hewn brown basalt blocks and contained features that derived from Axumite and Zagwe times as well as Portuguese models. They were concentrated in the center of the town and provided a sharp contrast with the traditional round, thatched, mud and wattle homes of the people.

Living in a special quarter were the Beta Israel, whose ancestral farms had been confiscated by Christian conquerors. Over the previous two centuries, they had survived by moving into such marginal occupations as weaving and smithing, the crafts that Christians avoided as the gift of the devil. The growth of Gonder and its need for workers allowed the Beta Israel to augment their skills. The men became masons, stonecutters, carpenters, and plasterers; and the women specialized in paint making and interior decoration. Since the Beta Israel were far outside of the power structure, they were often recruited into the imperial guard and used in particularly delicate or confidential situations. Both as technicians and soldiers, they came to be an important component of Gonderine society.

Muslims handled domestic trade, in which high-born Gonderi, among them the royal family, shared. The ruling classes also held interests in the import-export trade dominated by resident Indians, Armenians, and Greeks, whom the emperors occasionally used to run diplomatic errands. A large Oromo population comprised farmers, day laborers, and soldiers. The Oromo represented Ethiopia's past problem and also its future hope. The monarchy tied its fate to the social and political integration of the Oromo. The idea was surely wise, even if the feudal political order deceived the emperors by ultimately transforming them into the puppets of the Oromo political leaders whom they legitimized.

This subversion of the Solomonic monarchy stemmed from Susneyos's decision to incorporate Oromo leaders into Ethiopia's nobility and to use their forces against his feudal enemies. His new allies were adept students of politics, just as the Oromo masses rapidly learned efficient methods of highlands agriculture from the farmers they had conquered. Oromo not only assumed the material culture of the Christian farmer but also their language, religion, and, inevitably, Abyssinia's feudal political economy. Above all, the Gonderine period was marked by the political assimilation of the Oromo into the Solomonic state, although the imperial goal of political unity remained elusive.

Fasilidas, for example, spent most of his long reign enmeshed in a long-term controversy about the nature of Christ, an issue the Jesuits had raised in questioning Monophysite theology. The church hierarchy and the more traditional monastic orders followed the Alexandrian position that Christ's human nature had become perfect through its union, or *tewahdo*, with the divine, from which it had become inseparable. The more fundamental Ewostathians, especially those in Gojam, believed that the unction, or *k'ibat*, of the Holy Ghost, had acted to combine the two natures of Christ, thereby making him the Son of God and part of the Trinity. The unionists were scandalized that the unctionist position could not explain the scriptural references to Jesus' humanity and therefore the need for salvation through Christ's redemption.

The controversy faced Fasilidas with a serious political decision. The Ewostathian clergy and monasteries were influential in the countryside, especially in more remote regions, where they were bringing Christianity to the Oromo. The ecclesiastical hierarchy, the abbots of the more conservative monasteries, and many of the parish clergy—the spine of the church—were unionist but closer to home and consequently easier to control. In 1654, at a church council convened in Gonder, the emperor, as the head of the church, therefore came down on the side of the unctionists and quickly put down the ensuing unionist insurrections. Theological controversy then translated itself into political terms as provincial nobility, spurred on by clerical partisans, took sides.

The emperor's decision for the unctionists alienated most of the Amhara nobility because the monks at Debre Libanos, the leading monastery in Shewa, were traditional unionists, following the lead of their abbot, who was then also the *etchege*, the church's highest Ethiopian official. They tended therefore to isolate themselves from the Solomonic state, which increasingly had to rely on the strength of the newly assimilated Oromo aristocracy. The latter were called on to protect the frontiers of Christendom, but, ironically, even they failed to stem the Oromo movement into southern Tigray and southeastern Begemdir. Fasilidas and his successor, Yohannes I (r. 1667–1682), therefore concentrated on consolidating their authority in areas adjacent to Gonder, west of the Tekeze River, with the rest surviving as best it could. Thus, by the turn of the eighteenth century, Abyssinia was really a trifurcated rump comprising Gonder and its dependencies: Dembea, Wegera, Begemdir, and Simen; the traditionally Christian parts of Tigray and the north; and portions of southern Gojam, northern Shewa, and southern Welo.

Transition and decline best sum up the entire Gonderine period. The Oromo roamed virtually at will, the religious controversies sapped the ideological underpinnings of the Solomonic state, the feudal lords grew strong enough to challenge the power of the monarchy, and the emperors slowly became the captives of their generals. In 1690, Iyasu I decreed that the imperial *ras* (equivalent to duke; literally, "head"), or commanding general, had primacy over all court officials. The ras was invariably the most powerful provincial lord, a counterpoint to imperial weakness.

The contrast was hidden for a time behind the smoke screen of Iyasu's fruitless activities to shore up the state, to augment revenues, and to regain lost territories. His efforts were only temporarily successful because his armies had neither the strength nor the resilience to retain the periphery. In the Gibe basin, the Oromo were undertaking a process of agricultural development that would lead to state formation in the nineteenth century; the Gonga states were growing in the Kefa highlands; and in northern Shewa, a line that claimed descent from Emperor Lebna Dengel was busily resurrecting Christian power there. These phenomena evolved outside of imperial control, because after Iyasu's death, the reality of the Solomonic empire slowly devolved into an insubstantial, if persistent, concept.

The monarchy became increasingly captive, first within the limits of Gonder itself and then within the royal compound. Abyssinia as an organized entity slipped into rapid decline as the provinces went their individual ways. The regression was, in fact, the delayed but inevitable result of almost two centuries of crisis. The emperors at Gonder became little more than local magnates, who occasionally sallied forth to punish nearby malefactors, but mostly they stayed in their deteriorating palaces. Their guards, increasingly keepers, became the servants of a crown council composed of the magnates who really ran the country.

Soldiers helped to assassinate Emperor Tekle Haimanot I (r. 1706–1708) and, after the death of his successor, Tewoflos, in 1711, later cooperated with the members of the nobility to place Yostos (r. 1711–1716) on the throne. Strictly speaking, he was a usurper, since he illegally claimed Solomonic blood only through his mother, but his position as ras made his candidacy acceptable to the crown council. The church, however, railed against such lèse-majesté, a theme repeated in the parishes, and Yostos spent his time fighting intrigue and explaining himself until the imperial guards saw to his poisoning and the proclamation of one of Iyasu's grandsons, Dawit III (r. 1716–1721). The latter also had an unhappy reign, fell victim to his praetorians' fatal brew, and was followed by their nominee, this time one of Iyasu's sons, Bekaffa (r. 1721–1730), who proved to be the bane of his guards and the crown council. Indeed, for a time it appeared as if he might restore the monarchy to some semblance of authority.

Gonder's power brokers mistakenly considered him malleable and weak, whereas he was strong, capable, and opinionated. He loathed the court nobility, believing them responsible for the decline of the monarchy and the state. He took every opportunity to purge them and closely supervised his male relatives, making them unavailable for conspiracies. Last but not least, he recruited new Oromo, especially from among the Mecha of Damot, and armed them with muskets to use against the corrupt imperial guard and household units. He also turned his new forces against rebellious provinces, especially those east of the Tekeze, returning Wag and Lasta to the Solomonic fold in 1724, and cowing the nobility of Tigray and Bahir Meder into submission. By the end of his reign, Bekaffa ruled a relatively stable polity stretching from Tigray in the east to Damot in the west, which he left to his young son and successor Iyasu II (r. 1730–1755).

As his regent and later coruler, the new emperor had his shrewd and capable mother, Dowager Empress Mentewab (consort, 1722–1730; queen mother and grandmother, 1730–1769), an Oromo from Kwara (Chilga) and a sign of the times. Bekaffa had married her for political reasons, to satisfy the aspirations of the newly acculturated peoples upon whose support the Solomonic crown rested. The young queen saw that her kinsmen were given important palace positions and named her brother Wolde Lul as ras. After an attempted coup by the traditional nobility in 1735–1736, Mentewab placed Kwarans in the high command and in the army. To obtain further Oromo support, she married Iyasu to the daughter of an important Welo chief, who came to the capital with so many followers that Oromo was more often heard in the court than Amharic.

When the newcomers threatened Gonder's ethnic balance, Mentewab appointed Mikail Sehul of Tigray ras of the provinces east of the Angereb River. By making Mikail the dominant force in the north, the dowager empress thought to hold Abyssinia together. Yet, when her grandson Iyoas (1755–1769) came to the throne, the Solomonic realm was small and weak. Never one to miss an opportunity, Mikail Sehul worked behind the scenes to undermine the house that Yekuno Amlak had first built in 1270.

He monopolized the trade that passed through his province en route to Mitsiwa and withheld duties and fees from Gonder, diverting them to recruit an army, eight thousand of whom he equipped with muskets. A ruthless politician, he exploited the natural anxieties of Abyssinian conservatives, who saw their capital full of Oromo soldiers, administrators, and courtiers. As traditionalists, they believed that the Solomonic state was sliding down a rapidly inclining slope toward Islam, a conclusion amplified when Iyoas removed a popular figure from the governorship of Christian Amhara, the only remaining bulwark against Muslim Welo expansion westward. Finally, the mostly Ewostathian clergy became alienated when it appeared that Iyoas, in seeking Shewan support, had endorsed a radical anti-unctionist interpretation of Christ's nature.

Derived largely from unionist notions, the new theory, as reified by the monks at Debre Libanos, posited that Christ had been born three times (*sost lidot*): first in eternity, then in Mary's womb through the anointment of the Holy Spirit, and finally physically, but free of original sin (thanks to his first birth). The Ewostathians objected to any notion that Christ had several natures or was not inherently divine. The controversy had important national implications, since Christian Ethiopia, thanks to Mikail, now divided into two camps along provincial lines, Amhara-Shewa (three births) versus Tigray-Gojam (Ewostathian).

In 1766, civil war broke out between assimilated (Kwaran) and nonassimilated Oromo (Welo). For Ras Mikail Sehul, it was the moment of opportunity, and when Iyoas and Mentewab called on him to save the Solomonic state, he rushed to the rescue. After being named imperial ras, he proceeded to destroy the power of the Kwarans and then of the Welo. Iyoas immediately became wary about the future, formed a coalition of anti-Tigray forces, and ordered Mikail back to his province. The ras disobeyed, and in January 1769, with the support of the unctionists, marched against his master, whom he defeated and assassinated, ushering in a century of feudal anarchy and mayhem, the Zamana Masafent, the "age of the princes," which lasted until 1855.

FOUR

Political and Economic Transformations, to 1855

Between 1769 and 1855, before Tewodros II (r. 1855–1868) took power and reinvigorated the crown, a series of all but powerless emperors reigned in Gonder. Although they were involved in apparently empty pomp and ritual in increasingly dismal and crumbling palaces, their existence, along with the mythology of the Solomonic dynasty, symbolized the historic traditions of highlands Ethiopia. The real actors were the mayors of the palace, often Oromo, who took their place in the Abyssinian power structure, vying with more or less pristine descendants of the old order for control over the sovereignty represented in the person of the emperor. The complex facts of the age of the princes mask the point that it witnessed the culmination of historical factors set in motion by the Muslim wars and the Oromo population movements.

Significantly, the Oromo-inhabited Gibe region (Gera, Jima, Goma, and Limu-Enerea) had entered into a phase of state building sustained by the development of agriculture and commerce, especially in slaves. Ambition led to a struggle for more territory and to the emergence of a war-born aristocracy as the main political actors and accumulators of wealth. The Gibe Oromo took much of their new political structure and symbolism from nearby and highly successful Omotic (Gonga) monarchies, especially Seka and Kefa. When the Oromo appeared, Kefa established a feudal system of leadership based on northern models[1] and expanded their armies, which they concentrated at the frontiers. To feed the soldiers, the hoe gave way to the more efficient northern plow, and peasants were placed under the authority of overlords, who controlled access to land and taxed the harvest. The political economy of north and south thus coalesced, as did the panoply and much of the terminology of state, mostly borrowed from northern governmental organization. Ironically, the Gibe region prospered while the north suffered political decline and decreasing trade revenues.

Red Sea commerce had eroded, owing to the onset of the political illness that was to make Turkey the sick man of Europe. The Ottoman Empire, as an economic system, was deteriorating along its periphery, especially in the Red Sea–Indian Ocean. As the region's trading networks were disrupted, demand for Ethiopia's products slackened. Intra-Ethiopian trade continued, with regional products, such as wool blankets from Menz, salt from Eritrea, and coffee from Kefa, being marketed everywhere. The Gibe rulers were deeply influenced by the Muslim traders who had brought them prosperity, and they were naturally attracted to Islam. The faith permitted the Oromo fully to share the trading network to greater Ethiopia and the world; and it differentiated them from the Christian north.

In Abyssinia, meanwhile, Oromo parvenus joined the ruling aristocracy in Gonder, Begemdir, Lasta, and Yeju. In Shewa, Ethiopia's center, a Menzi dynasty alternately cooperated or fought with Oromo, the northernmost of whom were assimilated politically. Yet, in the Christian heartland as a whole, the old elites struggled and managed to survive either as provincial leaders—although here there were upstarts galore—or as farmers. In Gonder especially, the nobility resorted to such traditionally unsavory occupations as smithing, weaving, and trading, and they developed the *alakenat*. This new device endowed one individual with a major portion of a family's property and power, more or less in trust for the next generation. Certain families also ensured their futures by tying church endowments to the transgenerational support of specified lineages. While the continuities helped some to survive and prosper, the political changes made peasant life less secure.

In the countryside, most individuals could claim but not own land, and one's holdings depended on personal position, age, influence, soil fertility, competing claims, and the political situation. If the gult (fief) holder could contrive a genealogy adequate to acquire land on the basis

---

1. Or since the area had once been a part of the pre-Gran Ethiopian state, it reverted to earlier traditions.

15. Rock houses, northern Shewa

of descent, then some might lose part of their best plots. Moreover, fief holders themselves had no security of office in face of the ever-changing politics of province and palace. Neither peasant nor patrician was willing, therefore, to invest in or otherwise improve the land. Indeed, during the age of the princes, Ethiopian feudal lords were unlikely therefore to spark innovation, commission art and architecture, or build with an eye to posterity.

For most Ethiopians, therefore, life in the eighteenth century was difficult, full of toil and devoid of reward. There was little concept of change, growth, and development. Everyone had a niche in society, few moved from class to class, and practically nobody questioned the social order. Although there were occasional peasant insurrections, differentiation between the classes had little to do with quality but with quantity. The ruler enjoyed a spacious compound, which had large buildings and storage facilities. He had more locally made clothes, household items, and food, the latter probably the most important single difference in standard of living. He might sport a chemise made of imported fabric, but mostly he and his dependents dressed in the same stuff, ate the same kinds of foods, slept in the same type of beds, sat on the same stools, and used

16. Woman spinning thread, Gojam

the same tools. The rural economy was self-sufficient; people knew and cared little about the outside world, which rarely impinged upon their way of life; and they probably understood the chronic political crisis in Gonder in terms of local strife.

Mikail Sehul did no less than Pandora when he assassinated Iyoas. From the open box, every possible misery afflicted Ethiopia, often in a confused and bewildering sequence, although ambition was the taproot of the troubles. A coalition of envious Amhara and Oromo lords resented the Tigrayan ras and, with unionist clergy, railed against the regicide and his unctionist notions about Christ's birth. In 1770, Mikail responded with a reign of terror in Gonder, even executing high churchmen. He failed, however, to pacify the countryside, where Fasil of Damot, Goshu of Amhara, and Wond Bewossen of Begemdir allied to fight him. In January 1771, after a hard-fought battle, Mikail was captured and exiled to Shewa. Goshu became leading ras (ras-bitwoded) to Emperor Tekle

Haimanot II (r. 1769–1777), whom Mikail had installed to replace the aged and uncooperative Emperor Yohannes II (r. 1769). Before long, Goshu gave way to Fasil, who, in his turn, was killed by a coalition of Amhara nobles in 1775.

Emperor Tekle Haimanot was helped out of office by his brother Salomon III (1777–1779). He subsequently gave way to Tekle Giorgis I, whose erratic record of office—1779–1784, 1788–1789, 1794–1795, 1795–1796, 1797–1799, 1800—captures the reality of the age. When he was sometimes able to exercise personal power, Tekle Giorgis I used Muslim troops under Ali I of Yeju (d. 1788), who, subsequent to his conversion to Christianity, was made ras-bitwoded by a grateful emperor. The latter was, understandably, a chronic paranoid who soon came to distrust Ali, insisting that he abandon his position and title. Ali responded by toppling the emperor in 1784.

Thereafter, power became the prerogative of provincial leaders. The emperor's keeper was only first among equals, even if he was ras-bitwoded. Continuation of power and retention of the title depended largely upon his ability to organize the support of provincial lords. Though some agility was required, the bitwoded was usually successful, since his colleagues were involved in ruling and exploiting their provinces, controlling their ambitious subordinates, or in fending off their covetous neighbors. The peasantry suffered greatly as armies, large and small, traversed Abyssinia, ruining the countryside and the economy. Many a farmer was forced off his land onto the field of battle, a shift that led to the impoverishment of the rural sector and the repeated looting and torching of Gonder.

Meanwhile, the clergy disdained Ras Ali's adherence to Christianity, and the nobility scorned his Yeju origins. Ras Ali, his compatriots, and their allies from Ambasel, Lasta, and Wag were strong enough to suppress repeated rebellions, though the Yeju lost control over the area west of the Tekeze. Ali's enemies were therefore pleased when he died in 1788. In the ensuing power struggle, the Yeju savaged each other, ravaged Gonder and Begemdir, massacred innocent peasant bystanders, and enslaved others. When Ras Gugsa of Yeju (r. 1803–1825) finally triumphed in 1803, he determined to be ever vigilant and to exercise close personal control over every aspect of government, treating everyone, including the nominal sovereign, harshly.

Above all, he had to control Wolde Sellassie (d. 1817), who had wrested Tigray from Wolde Gabriel (d. 1820), Ras Mikail's heir, and was trying to restore confidence in the province's traditional leadership. Wolde Sellassie, a conservative Christian who valued Ethiopia's monarchical traditions, hated the Yeju parvenus. He hit out at them by conquering the Azebo and Raya Oromo and by taking control over all the important passes in Lasta leading to Tigray. He then turned his attention to the coast, slowly but surely imposing his suzerainty over the Muslim authorities there until he finally could control and tax their trade inland. He used the revenues, as had Ras Mikail, to reform and reequip his army. When the nineteenth century opened, Wolde Sellassie was probably Abyssinia's leading figure and certainly the main champion of the Solomonic tradition.

He inevitably thought about removing the eastern Oromo leadership, reuniting Christian Ethiopia, and restoring the monarchy. Among the Amhara and the Tigray leadership, considerable bitterness remained over the two-centuries-long record of helplessness before the Oromo advance. The hard feelings had been exacerbated first by the rise of Amharicized Oromo elites, whom the hard-pressed emperors had invited to share power, and then by the ascendancy of the Yeju rases and their manipulation of the enfeebled emperors. Wolde Sellassie harnessed the general anti-Oromo prejudice to move against the Yeju.

In around 1809, he approached Gebru the *dejazmach*[2] of Simen and the self-denominated Ras Wossen Seged of Shewa (r. ca. 1808–1813), the major Christian actors. The Amhara-Shewans generally were unctionists, and the Tigrayans were more conventional unionists. In 1811–1812, Ras Gugsa manipulated his control over the emperor and the abun to exacerbate the religious differences among his foes and to destroy their unity. Shewa quickly retreated from the national scene to concentrate on internal issues and politics as a new ruler, Sahle Sellassie (r. 1813–1847) began consolidating his government. Meanwhile, Wolde Sellassie grew old in his single-minded opposition to the Yeju, and by the time of his death in 1817, Gugsa had broken the anti-Oromo front by arranging a matrimonial alliance with Dej. Haile Mariam, the new ruler of Simen. The Yeju ras and his people remained the masters of the Gonderine monarchy.

If the political disunity of traditional worship helped the eastern Oromo to retain power, the commercial strength of Islam would undo them. In 1811, the capable and imaginative Muhammad Ali of Egypt (r.

2. "Commander of the gate," equivalent to a count.

1801–1848) embarked upon a slow but successful conquest of Arabia and the Red Sea coast. The reappearance of Cairo's influences in the region restored trade in the Red Sea to its previous importance. Demand grew for southern Ethiopia's slaves, coffee, hides, skins, musk, and ivory, immediately affecting the north, since trading centers in Shewa, Begemdir, and Tigray were involved in moving the commodities to the sea.

Indeed, Ethiopia's basic currency, the rectangular, half-kilo salt bar called *amoleh*, came from the north. The money's value stemmed from the biological need for salt and the consensus that the bar was a measure of value better than unfamiliar coins. All amoleh came from the Taltal flats in the Afar depression, one hundred miles south and east of Mitsiwa, whose inhabitants made a living either through bringing salt to the highlands or by facilitating the work of the annual salt caravans from Inderta and Agame. The visitors, mostly young men, stayed only a short time, working hard in terrible heat to pry loose enough large salt blocks to take back to their cool highland homes, where the bars would be shaped with chisel and adz.

At their source, eighty to one hundred amoleh could be purchased for a Maria Theresa (MT) dollar,[3] and their value inflated as they were carried inland, making them a profitable trade item. For the rulers of Tigray, taxes on the commerce in amoleh augmented the revenues they garnered from the transit trade to and from Mitsiwa. With their relatively high incomes and easy access to the sea, they were able to purchase enough weapons to outgun their rivals elsewhere in Ethiopia. They would retain this advantage until rulers elsewhere were able to divert or control the growing trade from southern Ethiopia.

The Gibe states exported commodities to Gojam and thence through Begemdir and Welo to the Afar coast and Mitsiwa for export to the Red Sea or to Metema for trade with Sudan. Gonder was the most important transit center in the Abyssinian highlands, although Harer retained significance, even if its route from southern Ethiopia to Zeila and Berbera was losing carriage. At the turn of the nineteenth century, Shewa did not benefit directly from Ethiopia's growing commerce, but, later, its self-

3. Maria Theresa (1717–1780) was variously archduchess of Austria, queen of Hungary, queen of Bohemia, and the wife of Francis I of the Holy Roman Empire. The dollar bearing her effigy was first issued in 1751, and the one that continues to be minted carries the date of 1780. The coin, reliably 28.0668 grams of 0.8331 fine silver, was immediately and continuously popular in the unstable Red Sea region and in Ethiopia, where no specie had been struck since the tenth century.

proclaimed King Sahle Sellassie (r. 1813–1847) determined to gain his fair share. His province was located closer to producing and shipping areas, and he and his successors generally worked to expand southward, combining Solomonic irredentism with economic aggrandizement.

Middle Easterners long had bought Ethiopian slaves for their armies, their fields, their homes, and their beds. The *habasha* slaves, as they were generically classified, were not usually from Abyssinia but from southern and western Ethiopia, whose societies could not protect themselves against the raiders' firearms. Religious law did not permit Christians to participate in the trade, but they could buy, own, and use slaves; and rulers such as Sahle Sellassie could tax transactions as the slaves were marketed or as the traffic passed through Shewa and its dependencies. Since Christians could not be involved, Muslims dominated the slave trade, often going farther and farther afield to find supplies.

Slaves were often provided by Oromo and Sidamo rulers who raided their neighbors or who enslaved their own people for even minor crimes. The merchant villages adjacent to the major markets of southwestern Ethiopia were invariably full of slaves, which the upper classes exchanged for the imported goods they coveted. The slaves were walked to the large distribution markets, such as Basso in Gojam, where they were sold on site. In some cases, Christian rulers established an isolated slave market some distance away from a larger, general commercial center. For example, when Sahle Sellassie made Ankober his capital, Aliyu Amba, situated in the adjacent lowlands at the intersection of several caravan routes, became Shewa's major depot for the south's "legitimate" commerce. The less seemly trade in slaves was carried on a few kilometers to the south, at Abdul Resul, where three thousand to four thousand slaves were annually sold to merchants from Harer, Tadjoura, Awsa, Rahita, Welo, and northern Ethiopia. Abdul Resul was more conveniently placed than was Basso for export to Arabia, where a growing economy created increasing demand for slaves.

Every year in January (after the main harvest and just before the short rains in March–April), June (after the harvest following the short rains), and after October (when the long rains ended and the fields had been planted), Sahle Sellassie led expeditions southward. By 1840, the king controlled most of Shewa to the Awash River and enjoyed suzerainty over regions as far south as Gurage. He redirected trade through Aliyu Amba and Abdul Resul, thereby augmenting their importance and popularizing the route through Shewa to the sea and increasing his revenues from transaction taxes, transit charges, and duties. The monarch and his high officials directly profited from investments they made in the caravans of the larger merchants and also received gifts from merchants who sought favors or advantageous legal judgments.

Thus, during Sahle Sellassie's reign, Shewa was obviously becoming the center of Ethiopia's economy, even if that development was obscured by the continuing importance of Basso, Gonder, Axum, Mitsiwa, and Harer. Together, however, the quintet did not account for the number of slaves nor the amount of coffee which Shewan centers expedited and shipped onward. Nevertheless, there would be a time lag before the province's leaders would be able to translate the economic truth into political hegemony. Meanwhile, Shewan rulers continued to expand their power and authority toward the rich southwest.

In the Gibe River basin, the old Oromo democratic form of government had given way to such monarchical states as Goma, Guma, Limu-Enerea, Gera, and Jima. The last had strayed far from its egalitarian traditions. By 1830, it was a highly centralized, well-organized, and strong monarchy under Abba Jifar I (d. 1855), whose dynasty emerged supreme after long and bloody warfare against eight other *abba dula*, or war leaders. Once Abba Jifar had won his country, he set about subordinating the peasantry, who lost control over their lands to a patrilocal extended family headed by the equivalent of a feudal lord. The latter appropriated surplus from the members of his lineage, now analogous to tenant farmers. The produce was sold to the hundreds of caravans of coffee and slave buyers that passed through the excellently sited country. From all the commercial activity, Abba Jifar and the ruling classes grew wealthy and strong enough to dominate the surrounding states, including Enerea, hitherto the region's leader. Yet, Jima's fate was tied to the north, where the complications of the Zamana Masafent were coming to a climax.

After the death of Ras Wolde Sellassie in 1817, his descendants and those of Mikail Sehul battled over Tigray. In northern and western Begemdir, Dej. Haile Mariam, who had succeeded his father Dej. Gebru, struggled with Dej. Maru of a competing house, although both men acknowledged the suzerainty of their mutual father-in-law, Ras Gugsa. Dej. Alula, Gugsa's son, administered Gojam; and in Yeju the descendants of Dej. Aligaz (Ras Ali's brother), who had lost out to Gugsa on the national front, quietly ruled, as did Welo's Dej. Ahmade, who was building a feudal state based, as in the Gibe region, on Islam.

Ras Gugsa's death in June 1825 ushered in another period of frenetic political warfare in Begemdir and Gojam. Naturally enough, the then reigning Emperor Sahle Dengel had no role, since his major preoccupation was eking out an existence on the MT$300 annually paid to him by Gonder's Muslim (!) merchants. Sahle Sellassie also remained aloof, as his energies were devoted to expanding Shewa's domains and in consolidating his authority. Interestingly, Dej. Sebagadis, from 1822 the new ruler of Tigray, stayed outside of the fray building his administration, and remained indifferent until 1828, when the political possibilities became too seductive.

By then, Dej. Maru had fallen in battle, and Ras Yimam, Ras Gugsa's son and heir, had died of natural causes, to be succeeded by his brother Ras Marye. Seeing the Yeju dynasty weakened, Sebagadis turned to Dej. Wolde Sellassie's old goal of building a coalition to restore the Amhara-Tigray to their rightful place in Gonder. Unity, however, was not easy to achieve in a country accustomed to fraction, and it was not until 1830 that the Tigrayans formed a loose alliance. The delay permitted Ras Marye to make good his succession and to organize a countercoalition composed of Begemdir, Yeju, and Welo. He first campaigned against, punished, and gained the submission of Sebagadis's erstwhile allies, Wube of Simen (Dej. Haile Mariam's successor), Goshu Zewde of Gojam, and Kinfu (Dej. Maru's nephew) of the Sudan borderlands (from Agew Midir in the south to Metema in the north). They joined up with the ras's army in 1831, when he marched north from Gonder to Debre Abay on the Tekeze, where his superbly led Oromo cavalry defeated Sebagadis's army. Marye, however, died in combat, and Sebagadis was executed.

Marye's brother Dori took over and led his mostly Welo troops into Tigray on a looting expedition, cut short when the new ras became ill and died. Wube remained behind as the province's new ruler and cleverly named some of the traditional aristocracy, including Sebagadis's sons, as subgovernors. By so doing, he united all of northern Ethiopia from Tigray to Wegera, a fact of potential importance in the struggle against the Oromo. Meanwhile, Dori had been succeeded by his nephew Ras Ali II (r. 1831–1853), a minor whose regent was his politically brilliant mother, Menen,[4] a Welo, who had accepted Christianity to marry into Ras Gugsa's family.

---

4. After 1840, she was called *itegue*, or empress, in recognition of her marriage to the powerless Yohannes III (r. 1840–1855), the last of the Zamana Masafent emperors, whose last official act of obedience was to vacate the crown in favor of Tewodros II (r. 1855–1858).

Her origins were suspicious to good Christians, and she sought to gain legitimacy through marriage to the nugatory Emperor Yohannes III (r. 1840–55). She also rallied the Christian-Oromo nobility and her Muslim kin and followers to support her son. Oblivious to political niceties, he surrounded himself with Muslim and Oromo sycophants and showed considerable indifference to the Christological debates that long had characterized Abyssinia's politics. The tocsin of apostasy quickly sounded; in Tigray, Dej. Wube was immediately concerned, and he involved the newly arrived Abuna Salama in the emerging anti-Ali coalition.

The metropolitan had been a long time getting to Ethiopia—Kerelos had died in 1829—since the Gonderine establishment had been content to permit the church to be run by the etchege, the Ethiopian administrative officer. The leadership knew that a new bishop would seek to bring the Orthodox church into conformity with the conventional Alexandrian view. Any movement in that direction would strengthen the unionist wing of the Orthodox church, benefiting Tigray. By now, Gonder was rife with supporters of the new three-birth heresy, and when church authorities there delayed requesting a new abun, Wube, as ruler of Tigray, successfully petitioned Cairo to send a primate.

Wube quickly drew Salama's attention to Ras Ali's apparent apostasy: did he not have many important and influential Muslims at court; did he not honor his Muslim Yeju relatives; did he not affect Muslim attire from time to time; did he not sleep with Muslim concubines?[5] Such concerns were enough to convince Salama to excommunicate Ali, since he wanted to start his episcopacy in Gonder without having to propitiate any powerful adherents of the triple-birth heresy.

The abun's cooperation helped Wube to recruit soldiers and to attract the assistance of Gojam's Biru Goshu. When the battle came on 7 January 1842, outside of Debre Tabor, Ras Ali and his Oromo allies made a poor showing against the firearms arrayed against them but won anyway thanks to a series of botched events and missed opportunities by his adversaries. The ras was so aware that serendipity had been his secret weapon that, after remission of excommunication, he accepted Salama's submission and his recommendation that Christianity would best be served by pardoning Wube.

By 1845, the knotty doctrinal issues heated up, again convulsing

5. The same charges were made against the uncrowned Emperor Iyasu in 1916, when he was deposed in favor of Empress Zawditu and the heir apparent Tafari Makonnen (later Haile Sellassie I). See below, chapter 6.

Abyssinia. Armies ostensibly sponsoring one, then the other, brand of Christianity roamed the countryside, when, in fact, the real squabble was about political power in Ethiopia. Abuna Salama excommunicated all followers of *sost lidot*, including King Sahle Sellassie, Ras Ali, Itegue Menen, the etchege, and ordinary adherents by the tens of thousands. In March 1847, in the midst of the chaos, the Egyptians occupied Mitsiwa and environs from the sea. Alarmist rumors circulated that Muhammad Ali's soldiers were preparing to move inland, a threat that brought Wube to the northwest frontier and Ali to a truce with him and Abuna Salama.

Perhaps Ali responded to the threat of foreign invasion. It is more likely, however, that he temporized to deal with the more direct menace of his own son-in-law, Kassa Hailu, later Tewodros II (r. 1855–1868). He was from Kwara, the borderlands region due west of Lake Tana, in whose lowlands people survived mostly by looking the other way and by paying respect to whatever strongman happened by. In this no-man's-land lived many smugglers who carried contraband to and from Abyssinia and the Sudan, and *shifta* (thieves or bounders) who were running away from authority or demonstrating their displeasure with the government. For a nobleman whose path to success was otherwise blocked, banditry was a major vehicle of social mobility. Kwara's difficult terrain made it Ethiopia's Sherwood Forest, but there is as much validity in regarding Kassa Hailu as a social reformer as there is in the case of Robin Hood. The future emperor neither came from the people nor did he work for the masses, whether as a bandit or as a governor.

Born in 1818, Kassa's parents were Dej. Hailu Wolde Giorgis, who governed Kwara, and Woizero Attetegab, both of whom later received invented Solomonic genealogies. There was no binding church marriage, and around 1820, the dejazmach chose a new consort, and Attetegab took her son to Gonder, where she eked out a living by selling *koso*, a powerful purgative. Unable to provide adequately for her son, she sent him back to Kwara when Dej. Kinfu (d. 1838?) took over. He took the boy into his court, where he was taught the basic lessons of Ethiopian government, administration, and warfare. On the academic side, Kassa became an avid reader, being especially interested in ancient and modern European history. His education came to an end in 1839, when, on Kinfu's death, he and other young officers were forced to leave Kwara and forge their own careers.

After several years of frustration working for Goshu in Gojam, Kassa returned to Kwara, the only place he felt truly at home. His presence was not welcome to Menen, whose officers so harried him that he fled as a shifta to the anarchic safety of the lowlands. Starting with only twelve followers, he prospered as a highwayman and slave raider and soon attracted three hundred men. His raiding upset the region and reduced the tax revenues the empress expected. She sought to gain Kassa's cooperation by offering her granddaughter Tewabetch (d. 1858) in marriage. A love match from the beginning, it nourished Kassa's confidence to have such a beautiful and well-connected wife by his side. She was, as a true daughter of the Zamana Masafent, ambitious and devoted to power.

She understood the practical importance of marriage, and, with her husband, she wanted to perform on a stage larger than Kwara. She stood with Kassa, therefore, in October 1846, when he invaded and looted Dembea, immediately to the south of Gonder, and applauded when he twice defeated her grandmother's troops and then audaciously took the city in January 1847, when Ali and Menen were in Wegera trying to fight Wube. Already annoyed, they became irate when Kassa collected the taxes due Menen, appointed officers to run the capital, ransacked the royal warehouses, and allowed his men to denude the adjacent countryside of food and forage. The empress marched back to confront her disrespectful grandchild and her unruly husband.

Having made his point, Kassa withdrew from Gonder, but Menen pursued him, and on 18 June, north of Lake Tana, she was defeated and captured with her husband, Emperor Yohannes III. When Ras Ali considered his response, he realized that war against Kassa was senseless; why alienate a leader who might then ally with Wube, Goshu, and Biru Goshu to take over in Gonder? Wisdom dictated that the ras enlist and use Kassa's strength in fending off his enemies, just as the latter realized that it was easier to deal with his relatives than with other ambitious feudal leaders. When Ali offered, Kassa agreed to become governor of the borderlands, with the title of dejazmach, promised his fealty, and, of course, released Menen and Yohannes. For the next few years, Kassa was true to his word.

During this period, the dejazmach had his first experience with modern weaponry. The episode that led up to it is interesting and significant: he had failed to come to Gonder's assistance when Dej. Goshu and Biru Goshu, in Ali's absence in Lasta, had entered and sacked the city and carried off the etchege, the main exponent of sost lidot. He reasoned that their activities only weakened Ali and Menen, working ultimately to his advantage. The same was not the case in early 1848, when he responded to Egyptian cross-border raiding by marching to Metema, defeating its small garrison, and looting its rich market. The victory was so easy that he directed his sixteen thousand men toward Sennar, hoping to regain some Ethiopian territories Muhammad Ali's men had occupied. Taking no chances, the Egyptians rushed reinforcements to the border, and in March 1848, at Dabarki, between the Rahad and Dinder rivers, the confident and contemptuous Kassa launched a frontal attack against a fortified camp defended by eight hundred regulars and two cannon. He was astounded when his army was cut to ribbons by the well-placed artillery fire and the disciplined Egyptian musketry. On the long retreat to the highlands, he reflected on his defeat and determined to train his men in modern tactics and to acquire the latest weapons.

Meanwhile, he had an army short of weapons and morale, facts carefully considered by Ras Ali, who thought only of Kassa's general insubordination, the humiliation done to Menen, and his failure to defend Gonder. He summoned the dejazmach to appear at Debre Tabor to explain his actions, a request that Kassa parried until June, when he wrote that the trip from Dembea would have to await the end of the rainy season's impassable streams and mud. When the ground had hardened enough, Ali's messengers came to remind Kassa of his rendezvous. By then, the dejazmach had rebuilt his forces, commanded six thousand to seven thousand well-armed soldiers, and was not about to satisfy Ali.

The latter refused negotiations and in January 1849 marched on Dembea with an army so large that Kassa withdrew before it and finally agreed to submit. That Ali accepted reflected his assessment that Wube and Goshu could be controlled if Kassa cooperated with him. Until 1852, the dejazmach kept his side of the equation, although he was working diligently to upset the balance of power by building up an army that could challenge and defeat all the princelings of the Zamana Masafent.

During the triennium, collective Abyssinia heaved a sigh of relief, took a deep breath, and relaxed—the calm before Kassa stormed the established order. He tired of keeping the balance of power for his father-in-law and of having his finely tuned army act in another's interest. In 1852, he refused an order to join up with Ali's army for his perennial expedition to Gojam, a disobedience that immediately brought an attack by Ali's new helper, Goshu, whose support had been bought by giving him Kwara. The ras's strategy was excellent: let the new-old allies fight it out and exhaust each other. However, at the Battle of Gur Amba on 27 November

1852, Goshu was killed, and Kassa's newfangled army easily destroyed the Gojami force. Astonished at the unforeseen turn of events, and with his flank unprotected, Ras Ali hastily evacuated Gonder and with his army and the government made for Debre Tabor.

From there he called up units from Welo, Yeju, Tigray, and Gojam. In March, under the command of Dej. Biru Aligaz of Yeju, the forces of Ethiopia's disunity marched on Gonder, which Kassa had occupied. He and his soldiers immediately quit the town for the maneuverability of the countryside. On 12 April at Takusa, Kassa, one man, directed a battle against the Zamana Masafent and resoundingly won a united future for Ethiopia. Shortly thereafter, Kassa marched on Debre Tabor, which he put to the torch before continuing his pursuit of Ras Ali to the plains of Ayshal. There, on 29 June 1853, Kassa's riflemen defeated the Oromo cavalry in one of the bloodiest battles of the period. Ras Ali fled the field to Yeju; he died there in bed in 1856. The Zamana Masafent was virtually over: one man again dominated Ethiopia.

FIVE

Imperial Resurrection, to 1877

Around Abyssinia, the old politicians were assessing the new situation. In Tigray, Dej. Wube put aside personal ambition for the sake of the general good, sending emissaries to Kassa, not in submission but with gifts of conciliation. The new ras accepted, to secure his rear against Biru Goshu, who had escaped the rout at Takusa and now prepared a vengeful attack into Dembea. Moreover, Kassa wanted Abuna Salama returned from Tigray to Gonder, where the two could work together to reconstruct the nation. At the beginning of 1854, as the patriarch made his way westward, Kassa and his army moved southward to confront the Gojami dissident.

In March, in the vicinity of Amba Jebeli, whose protection a confident Biru Goshu had left, Kassa's highly maneuverable army won a magnificent victory over a much larger but poorly organized force. A fugitive Biru Goshu remained at large, but when Kassa consolidated his authority, Biru surrendered in May and was sent into a fourteen-year captivity. Kassa triumphantly returned to Gonder, where he was met by a delighted Abuna Salama.

The two agreed about the necessity of unity in the Orthodox church, a key ingredient in any national reconciliation, and both strongly supported the Alexandrian view of Christ's persona and his birth. In July 1854, Kassa presided over the Council of Amba Chara, which condemned triple birth notions and supported the view that Christ's human nature had been perfected through its union with the divine, which in turn made both inseparable—the old tewahdo line. The call to Orthodoxy was buttressed by proclamations and threats of excommunication and anathematization by Salama, now named the formal head of the clergy. He replaced the Ethiopian-born etchege, who was subordinated to the bishop and made to denounce *sost lidot*. Abuna Salama thus reclaimed authority over the priesthood and, as the functional head of the church, control of the church's property.

By putting through these important reforms, Kassa won an important ally in Salama, who could be expected to work for the greater unity of Ethiopia. Although no formal deal was made, the Abun understood that henceforth the civil head of government would not interfere in churchly matters, just as he would refrain from involvement in the secular realm. Kassa thus obtained the cooperation of the one man in Ethiopia needed in the ceremony of imperial coronation. We do not know when he decided to become *negus negast* (king of kings, or emperor), but he must have had the goal in mind when Salama anointed him Negus (king) Kassa in late 1854, just before he embarked on a campaign to confirm his rule.

In Tigray, Wube still had not formally recognized the new order, though Kassa had offered the title of ras in exchange for submission. Wube by now had several thousand muskets and some artillery, and he was negotiating for more firearms through various European agents. After the church failed at mediation, Negus Kassa marched his excellent little army north into Simen, where, before Wube's capital at Deresge, on 9 February 1855, the last important dejazmach of the Zamana Masafent was defeated. On 11 February, in Wube's own church, Deresge Mariam, Abuna Salama crowned Kassa as Tewodros II, king of kings of Ethiopia.

By taking this regnal name, the new emperor laid claim to the national myth about the hallowed reign of Tewodros I (r. 1412–1413), who reputedly redistributed land to the peasants and who came to be regarded as a "hidden Mahdi" who would return to bring justice to the people. Significantly, the millenarian notions had circulated widely in the 1830s, when demoralized and war-weary peasants sought relief in faith and fable. Possibly Tewodros II was convinced that he was the promised ruler. Shaped by monastic education and mysticism, he was a profoundly religious man, who deeply believed in the personal morality and social responsibility of the Gospels. In fact, the first years of his reign were characterized by compassion, a sense of social justice, and a commitment to improve the life of the poor. He swept aside all political and social opposition and was even able to reintegrate Shewa into the evolving imperial matrix.

During the reign of King Sahle Sellassie (r. 1813–1847), Shewa had quietly continued its growth remote from the destructive insecurities of northern Abyssinia, its star tied to the economic wealth and importance of central and southern Ethiopia. The province's expansionary drive was assisted by the irredentist views of its Christian subjects, who believed that Shewa's frontiers should be extended southward to the storied limits of the old Solomonic empire. Sahle Sellassie directed these ambitions toward immediately productive ends, conveniently combining ideology with capturing territory, booty, and trade. By 1840, the king's army, built around a few hundred matchlockmen, had brought Shewa's frontiers to the Awash, beyond which Sahle Sellassie received tribute from several Oromo jurisdictions and parts of Gurage. He conquered the Finfinni region, presently Addis Abeba, and prophesied that his grandson would build a city there. It is said that he ordered his tents erected where later Menilek II (r. 1889–1913) established his palace, the government complex that is still Ethiopia's political center.

The strength of the Shewan effort derived partly from the political weaknesses of the Oromo, unable to unite even against a mutual enemy. Moreover, once the king had established his hegemony, he was able to recruit Oromo elites as allies. Throughout the eighteenth and nineteenth centuries, the Oromo near Shewa had become peasant farmers living in a political economy resembling that of their Amhara neighbors. Since Sahle Sellassie was mostly willing to allow the ruling classes to remain in place in return for tribute, he recruited allies whose interests he clearly served. They in turn were willing to provide supplies or soldiers, especially cavalry, for the king's seasonal campaigns, making them Oromo participants in the Shewan process of expansion.

Yet, the Shewan empire had so little structure and continuity that any crisis brought immediate Oromo efforts to break away. The monarch's longevity and experience were the biggest factors working to keep center and periphery united. During the first years of his reign, Sahle Sellassie fought often to retain his patrimony. Thereafter, his durability and record of success gave him the charisma necessary to expand his dominions and to surmount threats to his rule. In 1847, however, the king sickened and named his son Haile Malakot (r. 1847–1855) as heir. He obtained the agreement of his Oromo and Amhara vassals to the succession, and just before he died on 22 October 1847, Sahle Sellassie went to Debre Birhan to proclaim his son king.

Haile Malakot was a strong, bluff, and good-natured fellow. That he was a womanizer showed up early, when he impregnated a palace servant named Egigayahu. Sahle Sellassie was delighted by such sexual precocity, and when the young woman bore a son, the king called for legitimation through a civil marriage. He ordered the boy baptized as Menilek, and Haile Malakot is remembered more as his father than for any other achievement because, after only an eight-year reign, he died shortly after Tewodros invaded Shewa.

He probably could have made some arrangement with the new emperor, but he did not appreciate the revolutionary nature of Tewodros's challenge, which he regarded merely as Gonderine politics. Shewa hitherto had remained immune from Abyssinia's chronic civil war because it was remote from northern battlefields and was willing to support the status quo in return for feudal autonomy. Sahle Sellassie had felt secure enough to take the title of king (negus) and to sign a treaty of friendship and commerce with Great Britain on 16 November 1841 and a specious military agreement with France on 7 June 1843. The king had hoped thereby to entice foreign craftsmen to Shewa and to obtain a better supply of arms and munitions. Haile Malakot followed his father's lead and took an independent line when he came to Shewa's throne.

He favored the three-birth dogma and therefore enjoyed a certain cordiality with Ras Ali, whom he inevitably came to support in the struggle for power in Gonder. Kassa naturally came to regard Haile Malakot as an enemy, more so when he heard reports after Ayshal that the negus had facilitated Ali's flight to Yeju and that he was in close contact with Welo. The new emperor had much to fear from a Shewan-Welo alliance in which Ras Ali would have a role. He decided therefore to transform both autonomous areas into provinces under his new crown, and, after his coronation, he ordered his victorious army eastward into Welo.

Although the seven normally fractious Welo clans united against Tewodros, they were defeated after a relatively short campaign in which firepower and mobility dominated. They even lost their major stronghold, Mekdela, whose strategic importance the emperor recognized by making it his most important fortress in central Ethiopia. He established there a prison for political hostages, whose first inmates were the vanquished Welo leaders. His rear secure, Tewodros turned to Shewa, the jewel in the Ethiopian crown.

Contrasting sharply with the rest of war-ravaged and impoverished Abyssinia, Shewa was well governed and prosperous. Its fields were well tended and planted in cereals and cotton, interspersed with pastures on which cattle, sheep, goats, horses, mules, and oxen grazed, watched over by ubiquitous little boys. In the innumerable and comfortable villages spread widely over the countryside, the Shewan dynasts had a good reputation for charity, justice, and generosity, especially during times of famine. Sahle Sellassie was applauded for the bridges and churches he built, and he was a patron of the arts and handicrafts. Thanks to him, Shewa had remained peaceful and prosperous. To Tewodros, who was accustomed to northern harshness, Haile Malakot's province flowed with milk and honey.

In Shewa, meanwhile, a crown council had revealed a serious split about strategy: the governor of Efrata, which bordered on Welo, argued for submission, and, in truth, many Shewans wanted an imperial renaissance. Haile Malakot appeared willing to become the first formally recognized and anointed monarch of Shewa under the charismatic new emperor. However, his brother, Seifu Sellassie, who administered Merhabete, ridiculed any thought of accommodation and retired to his province, determined to fight to the end. An embarrassed Haile Malakot changed his mind and fortified Debre Birhan, hoping the rainy season would weaken the imperial army, forcing retreat. Instead, the Shewan army suffered desertions; the king fell sick, probably from malaria; the emperor marched into the province; and Efrata opted for the empire.

The general crisis sparked a series of debilitating insurrections among the least assimilated Oromo and inspired Haile Malakot to attack the emperor before the situation worsened. In mid-October, at Balla Warka in Gishe, the small and poorly equipped Shewan army lost to a much larger and better-armed imperial force. Haile Malakot, Menilek, and a small troop of survivors returned to Debre Birhan to brood, but when the governors of Menz and Gedem joined Tewodros, the ailing king and a small entourage marched southeastward, to recruit an army among still-loyal subjects. On 9 November, however, Haile Malakot died, leaving his brother Ato Darge in charge of the heir apparent.

Darge was impressed that Tewodros had visited Haile Malakot's grave at Debre Beg, that he had shown clemency toward Shewan soldiers and officials who submitted, and that he had announced publicly that he would treat Menilek as a son. With his small entourage already harried by imperial troops, Darge, against Menilek's expressed wishes, decided to surrender. The emperor treated them kindly but decided nonetheless to name his own Shewan administration and took Menilek and Darge into comfortable exile at court.

By early 1856, Tewodros ruled all of Abyssinia, becoming the last prince of the Zamana Masafent and the first emperor of a new age. He began transforming the traditions of provincial politics into national themes, since he fully believed that he was destined to revive the empire. He combined his ambition with energy, purpose, and creativity to endow the Tewodros legend with substance. He coveted the peoples' support, affection, and affirmation. He wanted to ensure their security and well-being through the provision of justice and economic development.

Regrettably, although his goals were progressive, his methods of achieving them alienated the people. He lost massive popular support when he tried to institute a nationwide system of garrisons to be supplied by already heavily taxed peasants. When he decided to confiscate church lands, arguing that parishes were overstaffed, he lost the local clergy, who railed against the emperor as an illegitimate upstart. When the people and the church turned against him, surviving members of the traditional aristocracy took heart and returned to the comforts of conspiracy.

Tewodros had returned the governorship of Lasta to Wagshum Gebre Medhin, its hereditary ruler, seeking to transform him into a faithful follower, as if such a gesture would eradicate the political conditioning of the Zamana Masafent. True to form, in 1858, the wagshum threw in with Neguse Welde Mikail, Wube's nephew and political heir, who operated with relative impunity in parts of Tigray and Begemdir. Agew Neguse, as he was known because of his mother's origins, was involved in a series of negotiations with French officials and Catholic missionaries for support and had shown himself a resourceful leader merely by evading Tewodros for such a long time. In light of his alliance with the wagshum, his dealings with the Europeans threatened Tewodros, and he hurried to Lasta, where he fought and won a pitched battle. Although Gebre Medhin and eight of his lieutenants were captured and executed, Agew Neguse escaped into Tigray, where he remained at large.

Tewodros himself could not follow through, since he had to go immediately to eastern Welo to put down insurrections. During one year's hard fighting, the imperial army accomplished little before Tewodros had to return to Shewa, where a rebellion by Seifu Sahle Sellassie had grown beyond the ability of his half-brother Meridazmach Haile, now the emperor's man, to control. Quelling Seifu's uprising did not take long, and by late 1859, Seifu had been driven from Ankober and his army dispersed. Meanwhile, Agew Neguse and his brother Tesemma were bedeviling central Tigray. The emperor quick-marched his men to Adwa, forcing Neguse to flee westward to sanctuary. Instead of following, Tewodros had to return to Welo to deal with another mutiny; thence to Kwara, where he brutally put down an insurgency led by his own nephew; and to Tigray in January 1861, finally to catch up with Neguse and Tesemma near Axum, where the imperial army devastated the rebel force and then hung its two leaders.

Clearly, Tewodros's state was not working. Unable to secure the allegiance of people and princes, he held Ethiopia together only through warfare, precisely what he sought to spare his subjects. He had intended to construct a government based on respect for law and order, but violence founded the order of his law, and he was never able to rule on any other basis. Tewodros found himself the emperor of only that part of Ethiopia through which he and his large army marched, and no amount of pillaging and looting and terrorism seemed to make much of a difference. In 1861, finally understanding his conundrum, he decided to win over his people through the application of a bold foreign policy conceived to gain Western technological assistance and to transform Ethiopia into a modern state.

He sought technical assistance from Protestant missionaries, mostly because they were not associated with the Catholic church. Tewodros and also Abuna Salama made clear that Ethiopia did not need religious instruction, already plentiful, but wanted craftsmen, technicians, and secular teachers. The chosen instruments, from the Saint Chrischona Institute of Basel, were skilled worker-missionaries, whose method combined quiet instruction in spiritual matters with education in the trades.

To demonstrate the value of national unity, Tewodros had hoped to thwart and turn back Islam. As a man of the Western frontier, he had long been concerned with Cairo's encroachments, and at Dabarki in 1848 he had suffered the one unforgettable defeat of his rise to power. He was also keenly aware of the Turks, infiltrating slowly inland from Mitsiwa obviously en route to the highlands. That both threats to sovereignty came from Muslim powers fed the anti-Islamic prejudices that he had absorbed growing up. He regarded the record of Islam in Ethiopia as one of mayhem and subversion and concluded that his state was once again threatened by Muslim encirclement. He decided that alliance with the West was state salvation. With naive optimism, Tewodros sent a letter to

Queen Victoria seeking an Anglo-Ethiopian alliance against the Turks. Meanwhile, the internal crisis deepened.

Many of the emperor's problems stemmed from social and political protest in Tigray and Begemdir brought on by drought and famine. In Tigray, Tewodros intensified the natural disaster when he destroyed homesteads and crops in rebellious areas. Unable to control local insurgents in Begemdir and Gojam, the emperor again hit out against the population, even sacking and burning Gonder! After the escape of Menilek of Shewa from Mekdela in July 1865, Tewodros ordered twenty-nine Welo dignitaries massacred and a dozen Amhara notables beaten to death with bamboo rods. As he lost control of the country, his frustration was characterized by burning, looting, killing, and more mass executions. In mid-1867, when the imperial garrison in Gojam defected, Tewodros mindlessly ordered eight hundred innocent Welo soldiers slaughtered because he felt, with no evidence, that they were about to desert.

He clung to the idea of an anti-Muslim entente, especially with Great Britain, as a life raft. He and Queen Victoria would reign over the destruction of Islam, in the process reuniting Ethiopia and defeating his nation's reactionary internal enemies. Since his demarche had been ignored by London, he decided to get Whitehall's attention by imprisoning some minor diplomatic personnel and a few missionaries, thereby stepping on the lion's tail. The Foreign Office was conciliatory enough to draft an innocuous letter for Queen Victoria's signature, which was delivered to the emperor in January 1866, by Hormuzd Rassam, an official of the Aden civil service not empowered to undertake serious negotiations. A frustrated Tewodros detained the envoy and sent one of the missionaries to London with requests for armament experts and equipment.

London was surprisingly willing to meet the demands in return for delivery of the hostages to Mitsiwa; otherwise, it threatened to send an army to Ethiopia to retrieve Her Majesty's subjects. The emperor received this warning in January 1867, when he no longer controlled the route to the coast. By then, he was deeply embittered by the realization that he could save neither himself nor his empire. As if inviting a British invasion to end his reign, he sent no reply to the Foreign Office ultimatum that he received on 16 April 1867.

The British government geared up for a military expedition to free the captives. Under the command of Sir Robert Napier (later Lord Napier of Magdala; d. 1890), a combined Anglo-Indian army of thirty-two thousand landed near Mitsiwa in January 1868 and began marching inland. To ease the way, Napier arranged a liaison of convenience with Dej. Kassa of Tigray (later Yohannes IV, r. 1872–1889), who in return for money and weapons pledged to secure British supply lines from Mekdela to the coast and to deliver specified amounts of wheat and barley. Since 1865–1866, the pious and self-proclaimed dejazmach had been in rebellion against the crown, scandalized by Tewodros's efforts to appropriate church lands and funds. He had acted when the emperor, frustrated in his efforts to tame the clergy, had flung Abuna Salama into Mekdela's dungeon.

Kassa was also convinced that the country required a new leader, and Britain was a convenient hatchet man. Kassa, of course, shared the dream of his kinsmen, Ras Wolde Sellassie and Dej. Sebagadis, of a united and Christian Ethiopia ruled from Tigray. He also believed that the British would leave after they had achieved their goals, since Napier had proclaimed Tewodros his sole enemy, not the Ethiopian people, and London had denied any territorial ambitions. The disclaimer fueled Kassa's ambitions, which were made obvious in late 1867, when, in correspondence with the British, he described himself as Ethiopia's leader.

Meanwhile, in October, the emperor had evacuated and burned Debre Tabor, his capital, and then slowly made his way to Mekdela, where he arrived only two weeks before Napier and his strike force of five thousand appeared. Tewodros's once large and effective army was down to several thousand demoralized men, no match for the disciplined troops they confronted on Good Friday, 10 April 1868, on a small plain just below the amba. As some four thousand Ethiopians came within range, British fire mowed them down. From above, the emperor directed his grab bag of homemade artillery that either misfired or missed their mark, a fitting comment, indeed, on Tewodros's reign.

The next day, he released the hostages and sent a delegation to Napier seeking an honorable peace, but the Englishman refused quarter without the emperor's personal surrender. Tewodros responded, not in his imperial guise, which he now shed, but as Kassa the Christian, explaining that he had been conquered not by the foreigners but by the undisciplined Ethiopian people. On Easter Sunday, the missionaries and some longtime political prisoners were freed, and the next day Tewodros sent his army away and awaited the attack, which came at 4:00 P.M. after an intense bombardment. The British successfully stormed up the slopes and quickly entered the amba, where they discovered that, moments before, Tewodros had committed suicide. The next day, the emperor was buried in the local churchyard, and Napier ordered bastion Mekdela razed. The British evacuated the area on 17–18 April, thus completing an affair of honor that had cost London £9 million.

Helped on its way by Dej. Kassa, the expeditionary force quickly reached the coast. A satisfied Napier granted his Ethiopian ally military aid worth approximately £500,000, including artillery, muskets, rifles, and munitions, important additions to Kassa's already formidable military capability. He made no immediate claim to the vacant imperial throne, preferring instead to strengthen his army through European-style training and to consolidate his hold over Tigray, where, in 1868, he still had rivals. By 1870, however, the province was firmly under his authority; he had obtained a new bishop, Abuna Atnatyos, to replace Salama, who had died in captivity on 25 October 1867, and he claimed to lead Ethiopia's nobles. Meanwhile, he refused to accept Wagshum Gobeze, his brother-in-law since 1866, as Emperor Tekle Giorgis II.

The self-proclaimed emperor had been anointed in mid-August 1868 by the etchege, himself the wagshum's appointee. The pretender ruled impoverished Begemdir, and he could not purchase weapons for his large army since Kassa had siphoned off all trade revenues. Moreover, the very irregularity of his coronation in a land devoted to form and legitimacy weakened Gobeze's case further. An angry Menilek in Shewa refused to recognize him and instead took to calling himself Emperor Menilek II, but Kassa was the more immediate problem. After he refused to be named ras in the new regime and to pay sorely needed tribute, Gobeze marched into Tigray in June 1871. His sixty thousand troops encountered little resistance until Kassa's twelve thousand well-equipped and trained men confronted them outside Adwa on 11 July. During the two-hour battle, the pretender was wounded, many men killed and wounded, and all of his generals and thousands of soldiers captured. In an act of Christian charity, Kassa refused to execute his rival and instead imprisoned him on an amba, where he died a few years later.

Kassa immediately took the title of emperor, and, on 21 January 1872, he was crowned Yohannes IV by Abuna Atnatyos. The ceremony was held in Axum's Church of Mary, following ancient rituals last used for Fasilidas in 1632. The latter had gone to the ancient capital to reclaim Ethiopia's heritage of unity and to demonstrate his devotion to tradition and faith. The new emperor's intent was identical, and throughout his reign he worked faithfully to reintegrate Ethiopia.

He stood for religious uniformity, since he understood the need for a commonly understood ideology around which Ethiopia's population could rally. At the same time, he did not seek to centralize authority, instead opting for a form of federalism in which rulers enjoyed autonomy as long as they pledged fealty and paid periodic homage and tribute. The emperor's flexibility did not immediately win over eastern Welo, Begemdir, and adjacent areas of Tigray, where he campaigned during 1871–1873, and it did not convince King Menilek of Shewa to submit.

With Yohannes preoccupied in the north, Menilek had strengthened his power locally and regionally, especially in southern Welo, where the Imam Muhammad Ali (later Ras and then Negus Mikail; d. 1918), repulsed by the imperial distaste for Islam, became the king's ally and friend. In Yeju, Menilek enjoyed good relations with Dej. Wole Betul, the scion of the old Gonderine rulers, with whom he had been imprisoned in Mekdela and whose sister, Taitou (ca. 1850–1918), he would later marry. Yohannes was fully aware that during Gobeze's interregnum Menilek had claimed the emperorship, but he virtually forgot about these ambitions when confronted by a renewed threat from Egypt.

By about 1870, no buffer zone remained between the khedive's administration in Sudan and an Ethiopian government that had strengthened its hold over the borderlands. Yohannes was of course sensitive to the fact that Tigray, which then included Eritrea, had a long frontier with Sudan. Mitsiwa, Tigray's historic debouchment, was under Egyptian rule. Cairo commanded a relatively modern and powerful state with a European-style army equipped with current weaponry. In mid-1872, the khedive's army took Bogos in the Eritrean highlands, and Werner Munzinger, Cairo's governor in Mitsiwa, banned the export of arms and munitions into Ethiopia. He fully expected that Yohannes would attack the enlarged Egyptian colony.

The emperor, however, had learned from Tewodros's experience and immediately called for arbitration, believing that right was completely on Ethiopia's side. His pleas for fairness and equity—his country's territory had been violated and its commerce unfairly impeded—were ignored by most European chanceries, who were unconcerned about remote Ethiopia, and deprecated in London by racist officials who regarded the Ethiopians as barbarians. Yohannes quickly moved to unite the country around him, should he need to fight the Egyptians.

In 1873, he went to Gonder, to receive Begemdir's homage and the city's recognition of his status of emperor. The next year, he finally maneuvered Gojam under Ras Adal (ca. 1847–1901; after 1881, Negus

Tekle Haimanot) into submission, he forced Wole of Yeju to accept his overlordship, and he was actively pacifying Welo. A worried Menilek, his shield removed, agreed informally not to subvert the empire in return for autonomy. He did very little to help the emperor, since but when Yohannes returned to Tigray in 1875, he had a reasonably united country behind him.

In the meantime, however, the Egyptians had occupied Gallabat and all the ports south of Mitsiwa. Munzinger had been promoted to pasha and made governor-general of eastern Sudan and the Red Sea Coast. His successor at Mitsiwa was Arakil Bey Nubar, who grandly advised that further conquest of Ethiopia would require only some good maps, a few competent officers, and three or four thousand well-armed soldiers. By early September 1875, he had them, and shortly thereafter, Khedive Ismail (b. 1830; r. 1863–1879) ordered four expeditions to take control over the Horn of Africa. Two were successful, and Cairo won the important inland trading center of Harer and consolidated its hold over the Somali coast. Munzinger's expedition, ordered to cross the hinterland of Tadjoura and contact Shewa, failed disastrously on 14 November 1875, when he and one-third of his men lost their lives in a trap sprung by the Afar of Awsa, who fought to retain mastery over key trading routes.

Meanwhile, a much larger force under Arakil and Soren Arendrup Pasha had advanced into Seraye and Hamasen, with local forces retreating before them. After forming up recently mobilized troops in Adwa, the emperor crossed the Mareb on the night of 15–16 November, and, with perhaps as many as seventy thousand men, immediately attacked the Egyptians at Gundet, on the high ground immediately adjacent to the right bank of the Mareb. The twenty-five hundred Egyptians had the better equipment—modern Remingtons, artillery, and rockets—but the more numerous Ethiopians enjoyed high morale, the righteousness of patriotism, and good leadership. Even so, the ineptitude of the Egyptians transformed the battle into a disastrous rout: most of them were killed, including Arakil and Arendrup, and the emperor confiscated the excellent weapons found on the field or in the baggage train. These would shortly be turned on another army sent by the khedive to avenge the defeat at Gundet.

Ismail was convinced that the debacle had resulted solely from the size of the Ethiopian army, and in February 1876, a force of twenty thousand men appeared in Akele Guzay at Gura, where two forts were constructed. Yohannes once again mobilized, this time presenting the issue as a struggle between Christianity and Islam. A reported one hundred thousand men answered, with soldiers coming from as far away as Gojam, although once again Menilek in Shewa remained an observer. By early March, the Egyptian soldiers once again were considerably outmanned, and their leadership this time was worse, with general officers disagreeing about the chain of command. During a three-day battle, 7–9 March, inept officers and unreliable soldiers allowed the Ethiopians to break through defensive lines, catch about six thousand men in the open, and either kill, wound, or capture all but five hundred. When the Egyptian commander found his fort under siege and some of his own artillery being fired in his direction, he asked for a truce. Yohannes, concerned that his supplies would not allow time for a long siege, agreed, if the Egyptians quit the highlands.

The enemy evacuated everything except Bogos, the original bone of contention, which Yohannes believed would be won back in the negotiations that Cairo now requested. Besides, the emperor had successfully rallied most of the nation behind him in a way no sovereign had in centuries. His increased political strength was matched by the infusion of another 12,000–13,000 Remington rifles, sixteen cannon, munitions, and other supplies taken as war booty. Thus, after the war with Egypt, Yohannes was well and truly emperor, that is, everywhere but in Shewa. Menilek remained brooding and sullen, still refusing to recognize the emperor as such, though in June 1876, well after the fighting was over, he had written to Ismail denouncing Cairo's activities in Ethiopia. He was especially concerned about the occupation of Harer and its effect on Shewa's trade and access to modern weapons.

Even before Yohannes had become overwhelmingly strong, Menilek had appreciated that his army needed current weapons. He had tried to obtain them through a variety of European intermediaries and in 1872 had sent an Ethiopian priest to France and Italy to start a traffic in arms. In a sense he succeeded, since his speech before the Italian Geographic Society of Rome sparked an expedition to Shewa in 1876[1] and the subsequent opening up of a route inland from Zeila, which avoided imperial- or Egyptian-controlled territory. Yet, neither the new road nor the new weapons came in time to save Menilek from submission.

1. In 1870, during the year of Italian unification, the new Romans signaled their intentions toward the Horn of Africa. An expedition supposedly under the auspices of the Geographic Society laid claim to Aseb and environs in the name of the Rubattino Company, a steamship line that wanted a coaling station on the Suez route.

The king had concentrated for so long on remaining independent, paying scant attention to Shewa's domestic situation, that he began to lose control of his government. First, in 1875–1876, he had led a campaign into Gurage, which ended in an embarrassing defeat. When the king subsequently decided to war against Yohannes, many Shewans were reluctant to fight an emperor who had defeated the hated Muslims. They certainly did not want to confront their well-equipped northern brothers nor to travel great distances through unfriendly territory. In short, they felt an allegiance to the emperor and, ipso facto, considered themselves his subjects.

In 1876, when Menilek was campaigning in Gojam against Ras Adel, who was allied to Yohannes, an insurrection broke out in Shewa, which also inspired Welo renegades to raid into Menz. Menilek returned quickly and suppressed the uprising and the razzias, but Yohannes knew his rival was considerably weakened and kept advancing toward Shewa from the east, assisted by Menilek's erstwhile ally Muhammad Ali. Bowing to reality, Menilek sent clergymen to negotiate submission with honor. Unwilling to plunge Ethiopia into civil war, the emperor agreed to talks and refrained from further action in return for supplies for his hungry army.

After hard negotiations, Shewa's domains were defined in the north by the Beshlo River, in the west by the Abay, and to the east and south by the Awash. In return, Menilek renounced the title of king of kings and undertook to pay periodic tribute, render homage, provide military assistance, and make his church conform to unionist theology. On the morning of 20 March, Menilek formally submitted. The next day, he took a formal oath of submission prior to being officially invested as king. Following the ceremony, the emperor delivered a gracious speech welcoming Menilek into the imperial fold and swore to respect Shewa's sovereignty as long as the province remained faithful. Some months later, Menilek came north to present Yohannes a magnificent tribute, making him the first emperor in centuries to wield authority from Tigray south to Gurage. Yohannes had accomplished this feat mostly through patience, conciliation, and compromise.

SIX

Imperial Consolidation, to 1889

As long as Menilek did nothing to compromise the balance of power in the north, Yohannes merely kept a wary eye on Shewa. He observed the king's preoccupation with expanding his province's power southward, in part to garner the riches necessary to pay the heavy imperial tribute but also, he believed, to Christianize the heathen and to redeem Ethiopia irredenta. Not so obvious to the emperor was Menilek's realization that he needed new sources of wealth to purchase weapons that one day he might use to acquire the Solomonic throne.

Yohannes's decision to permit Menilek relative freedom in the south made Shewa the center of Ethiopian expansionism. The emperor did not understand that the impinging world economy was changing the subsistence-based Ethiopian feudalism into a complex absolutist system sustained by a more rigorous exploitation of the natural economy and international trade. By Yohannes's reign, the Western world's growing appetite for commodities helped stimulate Menilek's successful thrust into the south. The king, in sharp contrast to the emperor, was willing to exploit Europe's needs in a diplomacy of commerce that ultimately helped keep imperialism at bay. Menilek also made better use than did the emperor of the Westerners attracted to Ethiopia through opportunism or recruitment.

In 1879, Menilek hired Alfred Ilg (1854–1916), a young Swiss engineer who would remain in the king's employ until 1908, serving as architect, builder, plumber, medical adviser, concessionaire, and, finally, foreign affairs adviser. Many other Westerners came to assist Menilek in establishing a rule qualitatively different from governments found elsewhere in Ethiopia and in sub-Sahara Africa. And there were Asians, Arabs, and Europeans who helped open access into Shewa from the Gulf of Tadjoura, where the French were establishing a coaling station along the route to Indochina. Menilek, eager to have an outlet to the sea across territory not controlled by Yohannes, began to send large caravans there and, in return, obtained an ever-increasing flow of finished goods and arms.

He was also receiving weapons via an Aseb-Shewa route, thanks to a transit agreement with the sultan of Awsa and Menilek's cooperation with the Italian Geographic Society mission, in Shewa since 1876. Its leader was Count Pietro Antonelli (1853–1901), well connected in Rome and eager to negotiate a treaty of amity and commerce with Menilek. In 1879, when he presented a draft of the agreement, the king was reluctant— given his recent submission to Yohannes and his military weakness—to undertake such a commitment, but he agreed to open a trade link between Aseb and Shewa. Antonelli demonstrated the connection's potential by delivering two thousand Remingtons on 29 April 1883, inducement enough for Menilek to sign a treaty of amity and commerce on 21 May 1883, worded as if it was an agreement between two sovereign powers.

By this time, the king was reconsidering his political ambitions. He had been steadily expanding Shewa's frontiers southward in order to amass the resources needed to pay Yohannes his biannual tribute. In December 1880, Menilek delivered six hundred mules and horses with gold- and silver-trimmed tack, $80,000 worth of cotton goods, and $50,000 in cash, and in May 1881, $50,000 worth of grain and flour, cattle, and butter and $10,000. Shewa, a land without industry, could not have provided such wealth without impoverishing its inhabitants, and Menilek was forced to looked southward, where people mustered only traditional weapons. For example, in 1880–1881, he sent a large expedition into animal-rich Arsi, which returned to Shewa reportedly with one hundred thousand head of cattle. Occasionally, the king's armies returned empty-handed or even defeated, but usually their firearms ensured booty and victory.

Ethiopia's weather permitted two major expeditions (*zamacha*) annually, in October–November and March–April, following the long and short rains and after the heavy farming tasks had been completed. Each campaign lasted from two to four months, although shorter, punitive raids were often undertaken as necessary; and some zamacha were organized during times of famine or drought in order to settle refugees in relatively underpopulated territories. Menilek could easily mobilize tens of thousands of men, of whom only the royal guard of perhaps five thousand were armed with modern rifles, although at least half of the rest mustered firearms. On march, the army appeared a mob, but in camp, each officer and man took his place according to his rank and importance. The king's tents occupied the central position, surrounded by those of his major lieutenants.

Once in enemy territory, scout units spread out to find the enemy army and to establish where property and animals were hidden. After the critical intelligence had been obtained, the Shewans attacked, taking booty and prisoners until the enemy formally surrendered and submitted. Depending on the severity of the fighting, Menilek or his surrogate would either confirm the old rulers as agents of the crown or assign a nobleman and his retainers to reorganize and administer the ravaged land as a royal province. Only when the main force returned home was the booty divided, with the king receiving one-half to two-thirds of the total.

The road south was thus paved with dreams of wealth and success for many of Menilek's subjects, among them Shewan Oromo. Over the years, they had been acculturated and assimilated into the provincial political and military structure, ipso facto cooperating in the integration of more and more Oromo as Shewa grew. Sahle Sellassie's most successful general was the Oromo Matako, who grew so powerful as the governor of Gedem that he rebelled and ultimately was killed. Menilek, however, enjoyed the services of the ever faithful Gobana (ca. 1821–1889; dejazmach and ras), a high-born Oromo, who submitted to the king when he returned to Shewa in 1865. By 1876, he was devoted to conquering his fellow Oromo with his formidable cavalry and infantry. By the time of Menilek's submission to Yohannes, the general had pushed Shewan sovereignty southwest of the Awash, and he had commenced the conquest of the prosperous Oromo Gibe kingdoms.

The effort brought Menilek into conflict with Ras Adal of Gojam, who taxed southern commodities as they moved through his province en route to Gonder and Mitsiwa. Menilek, just as Sahle Sellassie before him, was redirecting commerce through Shewa. Yohannes tried to balance the situation by using Ras Adal's vital interests to stop Shewa's expansion. On 20 January 1881, the emperor crowned Adal Negus Tekle Haimanot of Gojam and Kefa, the latter designation an order to conquer, and gave him eight thousand rifles, the wherewithal. Menilek politely issued congratulations but also ordered Ras Gobana southwest to Jima and Kefa, the same destinations given to Ras Dereso, Tekle Haimanot's general. When the Gojami army encountered Gobana's much bigger and better equipped force, Dereso blinked, handing over the tribute already collected from Jima, thus acknowledging Shewa's authority there.

A humiliated Tekle Haimanot responded by sending his son Ras Bezabeh (ca. 1865–1905) south with reinforcements, but Shewan units forced the youth to turn back. An infuriated Tekle Haimanot challenged Menilek to select a place for battle. Calling up his guard and some Welo auxiliaries, the Shewan marched westward into Welega, to join up with Ras Gobana's army. Adding to the challenge, Menilek chose to await his adversary in Gudru, on the plains at Embabo near the Abay and the frontier with Gojam. Tekle Haimanot soon arrived, and at 10:00 A.M. on 6 June 1882, his small cannon opened the battle. Both sides fought fiercely, but late in the afternoon, after taking many casualties, the Gojami center collapsed, and King Tekle Haimanot was captured.

The emperor was not amused, especially because his man had lost. The imperial army immediately marched toward the Shewan frontier, a move that brought Menilek and his captive to Yohannes's camp at Were Ilu. Neither the Shewan nor the Tigrayan desired a fight: the emperor wanted unity above all, and Menilek wished to retain his gains in the south. In return for a renewed pledge of fealty, the emperor recognized Shewa's authority in the southwest, shifting to Menilek the sobriquet of King of Kefa. The Shewan ruler had to transfer his holdings in Welo to Yohannes's son, Ras Araya Sellassie (1870?–1888), as dowry for his daughter Zawditu (b. 1876; later empress, r. 1916–1930). Her tender age was not important to the emperor, who was eager to have Menilek recognize Araya Sellassie as heir to the throne, one of the conditions of the marriage.

The emperor consented to another liaison, a wedding on 23 April 1883, between Menilek and Taitou Betul (ca. 1850–1918). There probably was an element of political chess in Menilek's choice, since Taitou came from Yeju, the strategically important northern province whose governor was her brother Wole, Menilek's friend from Mekdela days. More to the point, however, were Taitou's undoubted qualities: she was well educated, tough, self-assured, politically experienced, and deeply nationalistic. Where the king was inclined to be impulsive or adventurous, she was thoughtful and cautious. When involved in serious negotiations with foreigners, she acquitted herself with shrewd confidence, although she could throw a political tantrum when necessary. Of sound judgment and stable temperament, this proud woman was the perfect wife for her husband. She was his sounding board, and they worked well together in their years of marriage.

Private and political lives in order, Menilek intensified his exploitation of the south. The slave trade provided the biggest profits, though the king did not participate directly, always leaving the seamy side of the business to his Muslim agents at Abdul Resul. The supply came through warfare or from Jima, which in 1884 submitted to Menilek in return for autonomy.

Abba Jifar II's (r. 1878–1932) wealth and the well-being of his state were intimately tied up with the slave trade from the southwest and slavery as a mode of production. He facilitated the trade through Jima as a source of transit revenues and as a way to obtain ivory from the south; and he and other officials used slaves on the large farms they had formed from land appropriated from the traditional users. Abba Jifar's exploitation of slaves supported his court and government and paid Menilek his tribute. Similar situations in Leka, Guma, and Gera benefited Menilek, who also taxed sales of slaves in Shewa or their transit through the province or both. Meanwhile, Yohannes was busily safeguarding Ethiopia's independence.

He had won the war with Egypt, but consolidating the peace took seven hard and complex years. Yohannes had to pry the enemy out of its Eritrean holdings, especially from the Christian-inhabited Bogos, and ordered almost continuous raiding into the lowlands around Mitsiwa. The emperor argued that Egypt was the aggressor, that Ethiopia was the aggrieved party, that occupied territory should be restored to him, and that the country's access to the sea should be guaranteed. Since the khedive refused even to discuss these matters, Yohannes declined to see Col. (later general) Charles George Gordon (1833–1885), the governor-general of Sudan, who came to Ethiopia in March 1877 to negotiate peace. Gordon returned in 1879 but again failed, since the emperor then could rely on Menilek and was much stronger in his assertion of Ethiopia's sovereignty.

Yohannes and his general, Ras Alula (ca. 1847–1897), applied unremitting pressure on Egyptian holdings, isolating Mitsiwa from its hinterland, thereby impeding trade and reducing government revenues. Meanwhile, the Egyptian empire was breaking apart internally, as the khedive's schemes of economic development failed. Thus, the situation for the Egyptians was already compromised when the rise of the Mahdi (Muhammad ibn al-Sayid Abdullah, 1844–1885) in Sudan destroyed Cairo's hold over northeast Africa. Since the khedive could no longer retain his imperial real estate, British advisers recommended that Egypt's isolated Sudanese garrisons be evacuated through Ethiopia.

In compensation, the khedive was willing to give back Bogos, but he tried hard to retain Mitsiwa. Yohannes stubbornly held out for unconditional and total evacuation of all Egyptian holdings, supported in London by Lord Napier who favored an Ethiopian-controlled port to open the country to commerce and modernization. Yet, when Admiral Sir William Hewett (1834–1888) came to Adwa in late May 1884 on behalf of Britain and Egypt, his instructions did not permit Mitsiwa's cession, although he was able to concede the Ethiopian reoccupation of Bogos and free transit of all goods to and from Mitsiwa, including arms and ammunition. The Treaty of Adwa, signed on 3 June 1884 by Ethiopia, Great Britain, and Egypt, featured these stipulations in return for Yohannes's pledge to facilitate the evacuation of Egyptian troops through Ethiopia.

For the emperor, the treaty was a considerable success: patience and pressure had been rewarded with the return of territories wrongfully taken and with free access to the sea at Mitsiwa. He may have assumed that the port would shortly become Ethiopian, but nothing in the diplomatic record supports such a conclusion. Besides, even if the treaty had been so written, it would have been broken. Though Ethiopia scrupulously fulfilled its obligations under the treaty, Britain's behavior was perfidious.

London was sensitive to the impending power vacuum in the Red Sea, fearing that the French in Tadjoura might obtain a strategic advantage. In its search for a counterweight, the Foreign Office refused to take Ethiopia seriously as a regional power. Indeed, Hewett recommended that Rome be ceded Zula, which he knew would incite Yohannes to fight. The Englishman believed that five thousand European troops would suffice to punish the Ethiopians for believing themselves equal to white men. Such overweening prejudice, indeed ignorance, especially from one facing the Mahdist armies, pushed London toward a European ally. In October 1884, the Foreign Office encouraged Italy to take Mitsiwa, to act as Britain's gate keeper along the Ethiopian Red Sea coast, thereby preventing French entry into the Nile basin from the east.

Rome was easily seduced, since it was a latecomer to the world of modern European imperialism, and the Ethiopian region was one of the few African areas not dominated by either France or Britain. Italy, a relatively weak if ambitious power, had helped Britain in 1882 to put down the Egyptian nationalists who had sought to eject the Europeans from the country. From London, Rome appeared a convenient and reliable surrogate in the southern Red Sea region. The Italians, of course, had been interested in the Horn of Africa since the early 1870s and believed they knew something about the territory and its personalities. They were delighted to cooperate with Britain in safeguarding northeast Africa, particularly since their scientific experience in Ethiopia had whetted their ambitions for empire.

On 5 February 1885, the Italians landed at Mitsiwa, an event that Menilek realized might lead to war between Ethiopia and Italy. At the outset, the emperor viewed the matter indifferently, awaiting events, although he expressed his exasperation with the British. He was in fact preoccupied with an uprising in Welo against his son and would have been content to see the Italians fulfill the mandate of the Hewett agreement. Within a short time, however, the Europeans were attracted by the alluringly cool and salubrious Bogos highlands only about forty-five miles from Mitsiwa. When the Italians began blocking arms shipments, Yohannes discovered that Ethiopia remained landlocked and that, in the Italians, he had a new enemy.

Menilek, after his fashion, remained faithful to his suzerain, giving the emperor the security he needed to counter the imperialistic threat. He nonetheless remained on cordial terms with the Italians, whose presence at Aseb and in Shewa had helped him obtain thousands of rifles. With them, he was building an empire, which ironically Yohannes was seeking in part to defend. The contrast in activities was clearly apparent in 1887: on 25 January, at Dogali, Ras Alula annihilated a column of 550 Italian troops sent to break the siege of a small post in territory the Hewett treaty had specified as Ethiopian. Meanwhile, Menilek was taking Harer, which he had coveted since its evacuation by the Egyptians in May 1885.

The city and the adjacent region had been taken over by Emir Abdullahi of the old ruling clan. He had a few hundred riflemen, some cannon, and munitions, hardly a force sufficient to garrison Harer, let alone police the trade routes. The emir was also a Muslim fundamentalist, who soon began persecuting European and Ethiopian Christians, forcing many to leave for Shewa and the coast. In January 1886, the emir introduced a new monetary system impoverishing the local Oromo, who immediately rebelled. An already nervous Menilek grew anxious when Abdullahi stopped the transshipment of weapons and munitions through his territories. In April 1886, the massacre in Ogaden of Italian explorers, allegedly on the emir's orders, gave Menilek an excuse to intervene.

The Shewan army was strong: Menilek's men brandished thousands of new Remingtons, were battle hardened and enjoyed high morale, thanks to an almost unbroken string of victories. Menilek nevertheless sought to avoid war, and in early January from his camp at Chelenko, about thirty-eight miles west of Harer, he offered Abdullahi the same type of autonomy that Abba Jifar maintained under Shewan suzerainty. The proposal was, of course, refused, and Abdullahi decided to attack on Ethiopian Christmas, 6 January 1887, when he thought the Shewans would be off guard, glutted with food and drink. Menilek, however, worried about a surprise attack, had put his men on alert.

When the emir's men started shooting about 11:00 A.M., the Shewans immediately counterattacked and, with a minimum of casualties, quickly routed the enemy. Abdullahi and other survivors fled to Harer, followed by Menilek and his troops, who appeared before the city's barred, if fragile, gates on 8 January. Once again Abdullahi refused an offer of benign submission and fled into the Somali desert, permitting his uncle, the local qadi, to arrange the surrender. Menilek named his cousin Dej. Makonnen (1852–1906; later ras; the father of Haile Sellassie I) as Harer's governor.

Under Makonnen's guidance, the city became the center of Shewa's arms trade, making the French-controlled Gulf of Tadjoura and its port of Obok dependent on the Ethiopian connection. French traders came to Harer and provided the Shewan government better weapons at lower prices. With so much competition, Makonnen was able to raise taxes and duties and arrange favorable payment schedules. By September 1887, the arms traffic in Harer overshadowed all other commerce. The business was so lucrative that the French colony at the coast was able to live off its proceeds, making it axiomatic in Paris that this source of revenue should be safeguarded.

In sharp contrast, Mitsiwa suffered through Yohannes's boycott, and the Italians sought to regain lost "prestige." In Italy, the parliament voted funds for an expeditionary corps strong enough to reoccupy positions from which Ras Alula had chased the colonizers in January–February 1887, but not powerful enough to move onto the highlands. In late

November 1887, Gen. Alessandro Asinari di San Marzano, commander of the special corps, began to fortify the small Italian colony: he built roads and bridges to ensure mobility and communications and constructed a railway from Mitsiwa to Sahati, the outpost that Yohannes had argued was within Ethiopia according to the Hewett agreement. San Marzano fortified Sahati, Mitsiwa, Hargigo, and Hitmulo, hoping that the emperor would attack and destroy his army against the colony's new defenses.

Meanwhile, at Entoto (Addis Abeba's precursor), Antonelli was seeking to transform Menilek into an active ally against Yohannes, or, failing that, to obtain his neutrality. The Italian offered to trade Rome's assistance in winning the imperial crown for unspecified territorial, economic, and political concessions, which, judging from subsequent events, mostly related to Eritrea. Menilek was nonetheless noncommittal, since the emperor was popular at court, the imperial army remained a threat, and the Shewan had sworn fealty to Yohannes. Wisdom and irresolution led him to offer to mediate between Yohannes and Italy, not only to safeguard Shewa's gains but also to avoid embarrassing and dangerous circumstances.

His effort failed, since the Italians were being unreasonable about resolving the conflict. They argued that Ras Alula was the aggressor, that Ethiopia should apologize for Dogali, and that they should retain control over Sahati and other disputed territories. Rome conveniently forgot that the places were Ethiopian under the terms of the Hewett agreement and that its forces might therefore have provoked Ras Alula's action.[1] By contrast, Yohannes showed himself seriously interested in peace with honor, seeking arbitration of the dispute by Great Britain, the other signatory to the Hewett treaty. In response, London sent Gerald Herbert Portal (1858–1894; later sir), second secretary at the residency in Cairo, to talk to the emperor. En route in Asmera, he got a foretaste of the imperial position from Ras Alula, who adamantly refused to allow the Italians any role on the highlands. The emperor's stance was even harder: he would cede no land, Mitsiwa was Ethiopian by right, and he would negotiate only a confirmation of the treaty of 1884. Italian policy and Ethiopian national interests were so stubbornly irreconcilable that Portal's mission aborted.

1. Italy made a similar series of arguments about Welwel in 1935–1936. See chapter 10, p. 146.

When the emperor's patience eroded, he and a large force appeared before Sahati at the end of March 1888. In face of the Ethiopian attack, General di San Marzano sensibly did not leave his fortifications. Whatever the emperor hoped to accomplish, his army was too big for a siege. His supplies quickly ran out, and he was forced to order a retreat in early April, by which time his hungry men were ill with dysentery and his draft animals were dying from rinderpest caught from mules the Italians had imported from India. He had weakened his army and lost considerable face, apparently for nothing, and while he was preoccupied at Sahati, the Mahdists had invaded Gojam and Begemdir.

Tekle Haimanot immediately sent messengers to the emperor asking for assistance and then marched off, only to be disastrously defeated by the Sudanese on 18 January. Since the king lost most of his soldiers and all of their weapons, he could not raise a new force, leaving northwestern Ethiopia open to the enemy. The Mahdists followed up their victory by entering, sacking, and burning Gonder, including most of the city's churches. Thousands of Christians were captured, enslaved, and marched off to Metema. Ethiopia was aghast at the news, and the emperor, still licking his wounds in Tigray, ordered Menilek and the Shewan army to the rescue. Sensing a shift in power, Tekle Haimanot negotiated a defensive alliance with Menilek, who thereby broke the agreement of 1878 and directly challenged his sovereign.

After Menilek's army had secured Gojam and Begemdir, the emperor ordered the Shewan to return home via Welo, where the two men would meet. When the king temporized, the emperor was unable to respond forcibly. He was further shaken by the death of his son Ras Araya Sellassie and by the onset of the rinderpest epidemic. Yohannes actually considered abdication during the long rains of 1888, but when he received reports that the Mahdists were raiding into western Gojam, he was quickly on the march hoping for a military success to help regain his luster and authority.

When Tekle Haimanot refused to cooperate in late September 1888, the emperor reacted by turning his army against the people, a decision more characteristic of Tewodros. The emperor blamed the terrorism on Menilek for misleading the Gojami king into a traitorous alliance. The Shewan denied everything, prepared his kingdom's defenses, and in November 1888 declared war against the emperor, warning his people that they must fight or, citing Gojam's experience, lose all their property through looting. At first, Menilek's proclamation was received enthusiastically, but Shewans became anxious when they learned that Tekle Haimanot had submitted to Yohannes and that Ras Mikail of Welo had joined the imperial camp. Menilek was unconcerned, however, since he believed that he had arranged an Italian move in Eritrea necessitating Yohannes's quick retreat north.

During a conversation on 2 July 1888, Menilek had told Count Antonelli that he was breaking with the emperor, that he sought Rome's cooperation, and that he wanted ten thousand Remingtons with adequate ammunition. The Italian reasoned that the time was right for the king to make a move and that the impeding civil war could be used as cover to advance from Mitsiwa onto the highlands. Antonelli therefore advised his government to send Menilek what he wanted and to schedule the occupation of Asmera and Bogos for the outbreak of civil war. He then pushed the king to agree that the additional territories would provide a better frontier with Ethiopia and a temperate environment for European soldiers. Menilek saw through the sophism, but needed the Italian diversion more than he required Bogos. Antonelli advised the king that Italian troops would occupy the region as soon as he attacked Yohannes.

Menilek interpreted Shewa's mobilization as an assault on the emperor and awaited the riposte from Mitsiwa. When the promised rifles and munitions did not appear, courtly tongues wagged about Rome's perfidy and its abandonment of Shewa after seduction into treason. By November, the king grew uneasy and played for time, entering into a correspondence with the emperor to defuse the crisis. Yohannes remained skeptical about the king's loyalty, and the negotiations deteriorated into name calling and accusations. In late December, when Antonelli arrived in Shewa from the coast with the ten thousand rifles and ammunition, civil war appeared inevitable. The crisis was averted, however, when the Mahdists once again attacked Begemdir, and Yohannes marched off to defend his beloved Christian empire against the infidels.

Victory would have repaired most of the damage done to the emperor's military reputation, and he arrived in Metema in late February with a large army and great optimism. He warned the commander of the garrison that he had come to take revenge, and on 9 March when the battle opened, it appeared as if God favored the Ethiopians. The emperor and his command breached the center of the Mahdist lines and surged forward toward victory until Yohannes was shot, first in the right hand, and then, as he again advanced, by a bullet that lodged mortally in his chest. The

17. Emperor Menilek II. Reprinted from Eric Virgin, *The Abyssinia I Knew* (London: Macmillan, 1936).

Christians wavered and then broke, giving an undeserved triumph to the Muslims. With his dying breaths, Yohannes declared his natural son, Dej. Mengesha, heir, creating a minor succession problem. On 25 March 1889, when Menilek learned about the tragedy at Metema, he immediately proclaimed himself negus negast, king of kings.

He did not really have much competition: the imperial army had disintegrated as it marched mournfully home, with only Rases Alula and Mikail retaining small forces intact. Menilek nonetheless quickly toured the north in force, receiving the submission of local officials in Lasta, Yeju, Gojam, Welo, and Begemdir. The new emperor concluded nevertheless that Mengesha's pretensions needed to be blunted, first by the Italian occupation of Bogos, which would render Ras Alula impotent, and then by Rome's formal recognition of his new status. He decided therefore to initiate talks for an agreement Antonelli had proposed before Yohannes's death.

During the negotiations of April 1889, held in the Welo town of Wichale, each phrase of the treaty was explained to Menilek. He insisted on various changes, which Antonelli wrote into the Italian version and which were put into Amharic by Geraz. Yosef Neguse, who knew no Italian. Although the intermediary was Antonelli, who used both languages, the emperor foresaw no possible dangers in the text as negotiated and, on 2 May 1889, signed and sealed a treaty of amity and commerce, the so-called Treaty of Wichale.

The Italian text of the infamous Article 17 bound the emperor to use the Rome government as an intermediary for Ethiopia's foreign relations. The Amharic version, however, contained no obligation but permitted the possibility of requesting Italian assistance. Menilek read no constraint in Article 17, which he approved because it made the Italian diplomatic network available for Ethiopia's use and because, as Antonelli insisted, it demonstrated Rome's goodwill and regard for the Addis Abeba government. The great difference in intent between the Italian and Amharic versions had much to do with Antonelli's imperialistic ambitions for Italy. He obviously hoped that when the textual discrepancy was discovered, Rome would be in such a commanding position in the Horn of Africa that Menilek would accept the fait accompli. Meanwhile, Italy reaped the benefits of the treaty.

The Mitsiwa command peacefully occupied Keren on 2 June 1889, and Asmera on 10 August. In October, Italian diplomatic missions were instructed to notify their host governments that, on the basis of Article

17, Rome claimed a protectorate over Ethiopia in conformity with Article 34 of the General Act of the Congress of Berlin of 26 February 1885. The Russian and French governments objected, since there had been neither effective occupation nor a formal proclamation of protection, nor was the geographic extent of the claim clarified. Of course, Menilek knew nothing about this small contretemps in Europe but went ahead with consolidating his power.

On 3 November 1889, before a glittering crowd of dignitaries and clergy, at the Church of Mary on Mount Entoto, Abuna Mattewos (b. 1857; bishop of Shewa, 1881–1889; metropolitan of Ethiopia, 1889–1927) crowned Menilek emperor of Ethiopia. Before and after this event, the Shewan sent out letters to the various European powers on a range of matters. The responses they drew were fundamentally distressing to Menilek and revealed that he had the makings of a major crisis on his hands.

SEVEN

The Defeat of European Imperialism, to 1897

In December 1889, the Eritrean command unilaterally decided to move troops into Tigray, ostensibly to fight Menilek's enemies. The Italian occupation of Adwa on 26 January 1890 neverthe-less brought into question Rome's long-term intentions, especially since the emperor became the object of Tigrayan charges that he had sold out to the Italians. From Addis Abeba, the new capital now sited in the valley below Entoto, Antonelli agreed with Dej. Makonnen's complaints that the Treaty of Wichale had been violated, especially the supplementary agreement the two men had signed on in Rome on 1 October 1889, which stipulated a frontier along the Mareb River on the basis of effective occupation. When the Italians withdrew from Tigray proper by 25 February 1890, thanks to the emperor's ratification of the Antonelli-Makonnen arrangements, the Eritrean border now included all of Hamasen.

We do not know why Menilek made this historic cession of territory—the first for an Ethiopian ruler. The decision may have stemmed from Menilek's political anxiety about the north and the empire's continuing economic crisis. Since he believed his army's shortage of supplies and draft animals precluded an expedition to Tigray, he might have concluded that he had to rely on the Italians to control Rases Mengesha and Alula. The Europeans were, of course, content to be Ethiopia's policeman, a role relished by Gen. Baldassare Orero, Eritrea's governor (1889–1890). Orero regarded the colony as a military base for the conquest of Ethiopia, revealing the extreme position that a northeast African empire was Rome's destiny.

A leading proponent of this view was Francesco Crispi (1819–1901), the deeply nationalistic and paranoid prime minister, who believed that Italy's newly won national unity required the grandeur of a second Roman Empire. By 1889–1890, however, so much of Africa had already been spoken for that only independent Ethiopia offered opportunity. Crispi attempted to obscure his intentions by playing Ethiopia's good friend, even advising Menilek to circulate, through Italy's diplomatic missions, a document defining Ethiopia's frontiers. The emperor's enthusiasm—he claimed most of Kenya and much of northern Sudan—matched Crispi's fondly considered imperial plans. The basis of such a convenient marriage was quickly eroded after July 1890, when Menilek received replies to the letters he had sent to Europe announcing his accession.

Their contents were unimportant except for the revelation of Italy's declaration, in mid-October 1889, of a protectorate over Ethiopia on the basis of Article 17. Queen Victoria expressed her happiness at learning of Menilek's accession but advised him to send all subsequent messages to London through the king of Italy. Kaiser Wilhelm's reply was insulting, referring to the emperor in nonroyal terms. A great furor resulted at court, and the Italian Resident, Count Augusto Salimbeni, was called in and shown the Amharic version of the treaty and the obvious mistranslation of Article 17 in the Italian copy. The count's hopes for a comfortable sinecure in Addis Abeba, engaged in a profitable business to restore his family's fortunes, were doomed.

He concluded, in fact, that peace between Addis Abeba and Rome had been threatened the moment Italy had left Mitsiwa for the highlands. Since then, Menilek had been assailed by domestic critics for having "sold" the country and harangued by the deeply patriotic Empress Taitou, who came close to accusing her husband of treason. Salimbeni regarded her spirit an accurate reflection of Ethiopia's determination to remain free, and he foresaw the costly failure of Crispi's imperialism. He was, however, powerless to correct the situation, since he had no real authority to negotiate.

In late August 1890, the emperor appealed directly to King Umberto I (r. 1878–1900) to rectify the treaty error. Salimbeni hoped for a change of heart in Rome, since otherwise he foresaw war. On 5 October, he cabled Crispi that the Wichale problem impeded all other business and that Menilek the emperor was a vastly more powerful and confident person than Menilek the king. Indeed, the monarch was busy subverting Italy's declared protectorate by writing letters to the powers explaining Ethiopia's position. Crispi, a racist, thought he could fob off his black adversary by returning Antonelli to Addis Abeba with kind words.

The count and the emperor exchanged several amiable conversations in December, but Menilek insisted that Italy would have to renounce its declared protectorate over his country. When, later, Antonelli cited the humiliation Rome would suffer thereby and tried to assign the blame for Article 17 to Geraz. Yosef, who knew French, but not Italian, the emperor became irate. An indignant Taitou pronounced that the mortification was all Ethiopia's and unbearable for a sovereign state. The most husband and wife would concede was recognition of Article 17 in its Amharic version. Antonelli and Salimbeni advised Rome to accept and to await circumstances more favorable to Italy's plans. Crispi, however, remained obdurate that Article 17 and Italian honor remain intact, and on 12 February 1891 the two diplomats left Addis Abeba with the issue unresolved. Menilek began to prepare for a war his country was then in no condition to sustain.

During the previous few years, the great pandemics and famines afflicting East Africa had devastated Ethiopian society and life. The trouble had begun with the rinderpest that had killed most horned animals, especially the oxen so crucial in the agriculture of the highlands. A healthy population might have been able to mobilize themselves to undertake some plowing, but Ethiopians were struck with a particularly virulent cholera that killed many people and sapped the strength of survivors. Never one to accept fate, Menilek urged his subjects to work harder and produce more, ordered his personal troops to return to farming, and sent tools and implements to the provinces. As much as possible, the imperial couple and the aristocracy opened their granaries to relieve the suffering, and the clergy prayed for divine intervention.

The calamity, however, merely continued along its course. Many people took to the forests to live on grubs, roots, and berries; and others reportedly turned to cannibalism. The social fabric unraveled: relatives refused to aid each other, children were left to starve, and old people were driven from their children's households. People took to the roads, seeking survival by following the armies southward into newly conquered territory. Many governors and leaders resorted to raiding areas in the lowlands and in semi-arid zones that the rinderpest had bypassed. Dej. Makonnen, governor of Harerge, increased forays into the Ogaden, where he took camels, goats, and sheep from its largely Somali, pastoral population.

The clans were historically in competition for the Ogaden's limited resources, and some Somalis sensibly joined and assisted Ras Makonnen's men to subdue common enemies. After the conquest, they ruled under orders from their Ethiopian patrons, who tended to garrison fortified forts and hamlets sited mostly at water holes. Thus, the constant campaigns established a pattern of indirect rule through clientage, used long thereafter to administer the Ogaden. Similar arrangements were worked out in southern Ethiopia as raiding and conquest increased the extent of Menilek's empire.

The expansionism of 1891–1893 helped to end the immediate crisis but also confirmed the shift in economic power in Ethiopia from the north to the south. Begemdir, Gojam, and Tigray, long fought over and often devastated, would never recover their earlier power, except in combination with Shewa. At Ethiopia's center, the province was the geopolitical gate through which the south's economic resources were transferred to bolster the north's sagging economy and to ensure the continuation of Amhara-Tigrayan political and cultural hegemony. More important was Menilek's use of the region's gold, ivory, musk, coffee, hides, and slaves to purchase modern weapons to defeat Italian imperialism. At Obok, France's coastal station, the emperor found profit-seeking gunrunners and budget-conscious administrators eager to assist him. In February 1893, the emperor advised Rome that he would denounce the Treaty of Wichale as of 1 May 1894 and also informed Paris of his intentions.

France was Italy's greatest impediment to isolating Ethiopia diplomatically and commercially. Rome tried hard to convince the French of the legality of Article 17, but the Quai d'Orsay repeated its refusal to recognize the Treaty of Wichale. In Obok, the ambitious, pro-Ethiopian Governor Léonce Lagarde (1860–1936; later, duke of Entoto) labored to sustain the arms trade to Ethiopia that flowed through his microcolony. He invariably exceeded his instructions when it came to his good friend Dej. Makonnen of Harer. In 1893, as the Italo-Ethiopian crisis worsened, his extraordinary diversion of funds from the colony's coffers and weapons from its armories was especially welcomed as a sign of Paris's conviction that Ethiopia should remain free.

In fact, the French government as such did little to provide Menilek with the large numbers of rifles, bayonets, and good cartridges his army needed. Ironically, Italy did more to assist its enemy, donating thousands of rifles and millions of bullets to Ethiopia as goodwill gifts intended to soften Menilek's stance against Article 17. Instead, they would be turned against Rome's army, along with several hundred tons of weapons and munitions the emperor and Dejo Makonnen were able to obtain through the many arms dealers resident in Harer. Had Lagarde not been governor in Obok, had Paris not been at least morally supportive of Ethiopia, it would have been impossible for Menilek to have acquired the modern weaponry necessary to confront Italian imperialism.

France did of course have serious geopolitical interests in Ethiopia, since it was striving for power in the Nile valley. On 5 May 1894, however, an Anglo-Italian protocol was issued, which placed Harer within an Italian sphere of influence, right in the middle of what Paris considered the hinterland of its Obok colony. The Quai d'Orsay complained to the Foreign Office that the protocol contradicted an Anglo-French exchange of notes on 2 February 1888 that had denied the town to both powers but pledged them to oppose colonization by other European states. The British replied that the Treaty of Wichale had made Harer, an Ethiopian dependency, part of an Italian protectorate and that the recent protocol merely recognized that fact. Paris quickly understood that the British were trying to close off French access to the Nile valley from the east. For the Quai d'Orsay, the survival of Ethiopian independence thus became an important consideration.

Isolated in Tigray, Ras Mengesha also concluded that a sovereign Ethiopia was better than a colonial state. He was frustrated by Asmera's professions of support while Rome continued to arm the emperor. Swallowing his pride, Mengesha decided to make his peace with Menilek and arrived in Addis Abeba on 2 June 1894, ready to submit. Within the Grand Palace's newly constructed reception hall, the emperor awaited, seated on his throne, a large crown on his head. Mengesha and his three major lieutenants, including Ras Alula, approached, each man carrying a rock of submission on his shoulder, then prostrated themselves, and asked for forgiveness. Menilek simply declared them pardoned, thus bringing Tigray back into the empire.

Highlands Eritrea also tried to rejoin the motherland because traditional leaders were alienated by an Italian settlement policy that expropriated prime agricultural land on behalf of European settlers. The church was especially upset, since it owned some of the best acreage, which it ordinarily gave as usufruct to priests or rented to sharecroppers. The local aristocracy, as the second big loser, campaigned vigorously against the European interlopers and, claiming to act for Ras Mengesha, led their followers into rebellion in mid-December 1894. The Italians quickly suppressed the insurrection, but misunderstanding its local nature, warned Ras Mengesha to remove his troops from areas near the frontier.

On his refusal, the Italian command sent an army across the Mareb to destroy the alleged military threat. When Mengesha rushed to counter, the Italians withdrew, enticing him into Eritrea, where after a series of battles his army was routed near Senafe on 15 January 1895. The feat had been accomplished by sixty-six European officers, with an army of thirty-nine hundred men (96 percent of whom were Eritrean), and, best of all, at a cost of only £19,000. The ease of this small victory misled the Italians into believing that they could just as easily defeat the imperial army and its rapidly growing arsenal of modern weapons. They failed to appreciate that they had encountered not the imperial army but only the soldiers of a provincial governor.

Ethiopia's situation then was generally satisfactory: the emperor had just conquered prosperous Walamo and taken rich booty; the harvests during the previous three years had been good; there were no annoying dissidents; and the new 10 percent agricultural tax (*asrat*) was yielding increasing revenues. The treasury in Addis Abeba was overflowing; the regional granaries were brimming; and the imperial armories were filling. The news from Tigray, however, was annoying, but the emperor appreciated that Mengesha, whom he had promoted to ras-bitwoded, served a useful purpose there as a cat's-paw. He sent him weapons and munitions to stiffen his morale but also advised nearby commanders to hold themselves in readiness should the Italians try to exploit their local victory by moving southward.

Menilek proclaimed national mobilization on 17 September 1895, warning his people that the Italians wanted to take over their farms and their churches. Besides directing his soldiers to prepare for war, he asked noncombatants for their assistance and prayers. An equally determined Crispi ordered his governor in Eritrea, Gen. Oreste Baratieri (1841–1901; military commander, 1891–1896, and civil governor, 1893–1896), to ready for attack.

The general planned to occupy the high ground in Tigray, to counter Ras Mengesha's rearmed forces, which, in early 1895, were raiding into Eritrea. Whenever the Italians pursued them, they took sanctuary across the Mareb frontier, convincing Baratieri that Eritrea's best defensive positions were in the mountains in Tigray. By entering Ethiopia, the general, however, gave up the moral high ground to Menilek, who whipped up his people's patriotism by charging that Italy had violated Ethiopia's sacred territory. When the emperor proclaimed mobilization in September, he knew that he would be marching north to eject the enemy from positions within Ethiopia.

Baratieri had a relatively small army of 35,000 men, mostly Eritreans. He and his masters in Rome believed that the force could contain Menilek's massive military. Blinded by racism and cultural arrogance, the Italians had little respect for its enemy's modern weaponry. They also ridiculed the notion of Ethiopian nationalism, disbelieving that the Solomonic empire's masses could be united and mustered for any confrontation with European imperialism. With great internal logic but with complete ignorance of the facts, Crispi and Baratieri regarded Menilek as the barbarian leader of primitive African peoples. In their immense miscalculation, they concluded that even a small force of well-trained modern and motivated soldiers would destroy Menilek's minions.

The empire's peoples proved them wrong by rallying around their leaders and marching off to assist their monarch. The Italians had no inkling that Menilek was gathering a force of well over 100,000 troops and garrisoned forward positions with relatively few men. In one case, Ambalage in Tigray, thirty-six miles in advance of Baratieri's most southern defensive position, 2,150 Italian soldiers were isolated in an area where as many as 50,000 imperial troops were concentrated. On 7 November, the Ethiopians attacked and overran the enemy's lines, killing 1,300 colonial troops and twenty Italian officers. This success was an omen that even the optimistic Baratieri could not misread.

Ethiopia was moving from strength to strength. Almost all of the important provincial figures supported the emperor, and weapons and munitions kept arriving from Djibouti. In late December 1895, Ethiopia's combined armies were in the north, looking to destroy the Italians. In Rome, meanwhile, Crispi believed that soon Baratieri would impose the following conditions on a vanquished enemy: Tigray to be ceded to Eritrea; Harer to become an Italian protectorate; Rome to handle Ethiopia's foreign relations; and an Italian resident to direct the Addis Abeba government. Menilek would be permitted to remain on the throne, although Italian policy was purposely vague on that point. Rome's officials, especially the prime minister, lived in racist self-delusion.

The more realistic Menilek was meanwhile seeking to lure Baratieri into open combat against his numerically superior force. He marched into northwestern Tigray and camped at Adwa virtually under the eyes of Baratieri's forces. The general and his army of 8,463 Italians and 10,749 Eritreans held the high ground between Adigrat and Idaga Hamus. Baratieri was prepared to outwait his enemy, whose limited supplies would have forced retirement southward, permitting Baratieri to claim victory and also advance deeper into Tigray. The same strategy could have been repeated annually until the Ethiopian empire succumbed either to exhaustion or to internal division.

Baratieri's reasoning was sound: by late January, the imperial army was experiencing severe supply shortages and was having to forage over a wider and wider range from Adwa. The Italian position was better, although guerrilla bands were attacking Baratieri's supply lines to Eritrea, and his men were on half-rations. The general should have stayed where he was, watching his enemy weaken and finally retreat. Instead, his hand was forced by Crispi's insulting fulminations. Telegram after telegram urged attack for the sake of Italian grandeur, the honor of the army, and the prestige of the monarchy, implicitly questioning Baratieri's strategy and, by implication, his courage.

The general's brigade commanders felt their careers would best be served on the battlefield. Baratieri's resolve to remain in place eroded when he heard rumors that he was to be replaced by a more aggressive commander and evaporated completely when he was misinformed, possibly by a double agent, that much of the Ethiopian army was either too ill to fight or was away from camp foraging for food and fodder. Suddenly abandoning his caution, Baratieri ordered battle preparations, jeopardizing Rome's chance for an empire in Ethiopia.

At 9:00 P.M. on 28 February, the Italians began a forced march to the three hills that dominated the Ethiopian camp, to surprise and challenge Menilek's army. To secure his left, Baratieri sent his reserve brigade to an unnamed, nearby fourth hill, but the Ethiopian guide, either through misdirection or sabotage, led the Italians astray. Not only was the left flank uncovered but also a quarter of the Italian force was rendered useless and vulnerable. So, even if Baratieri's army had occupied the high points and deployed in strong defensive positions on the frontal slopes, it was foredoomed to defeat. Indeed, the timing of the Italian attack, as a surprise on early Sunday morning, was all wrong.

At 4:00 A.M., on 1 March, Menilek, Taitou, and the rases were at mass, which the Orthodox church celebrates early. It was a sad time, since the food situation had forced the emperor to order camp to be struck on 2 March. His relief must have been great when a number of couriers and runners rushed in to report that the enemy was approaching in force. The emperor ordered men to arms, and, as the soldiers lined up, priests passed before them hearing confession, granting absolution, and offering blessings. The green, orange, and red flags of Ethiopia were unfurled when the emperor appeared, and the soldiers cheered and cheered. At 5:30 A.M., Menilek's 100,000-man army moved forward, to confront an Italian force of 14,500 soldiers.

By 9:00 A.M., the outcome was obvious. The Italian center had crumbled, and other units were in danger of being flanked by Ethiopians who had found the gap in Baratieri's defenses. By noon, when retreat sounded, the Italians had paid dearly. Four thousand Europeans and 2,000 Eritreans had died, 1,428 of Baratieri's soldiers had been wounded, and 1,800 prisoners were held by the Ethiopians. All told, the Italian lost 70 percent of its forces, an incredible disaster for a modern army.

In sharp contrast, Menilek's forces army suffered an estimated 4,000–7000 killed and perhaps as many as 10,000 wounded, which made for an acceptably low loss ratio. The Italian enemy had been destroyed, whereas the Ethiopian army remained in being, strengthened by the weapons and matériel abandoned on the field. The victory was unequivocally Ethiopian. A wise Menilek decided not to defy the fates and retired southward into Ethiopia, leaving Eritrea to Rome.

The Eritrean command had expected otherwise, fearing that its remnant army would have to face the full onslaught of Menilek's victorious forces. They misunderstood that the Ethiopian army was ill and hungry, conditions that could not be rectified en route to Eritrea, in poor country already ravaged by Baratieri's men. Finally, Menilek reasoned that the Italians might not acknowledge their defeat and renew the fighting the next year. He therefore had to rest his men and also raise money, supplies, and reinforcements for the next campaign.

As it turned out, a demoralized and chastened Rome lacked the political will to continue, though its defeat in Ethiopia constituted a rankling embarrassment later exploited by the Fascists. For now, however, the Italians offered peace, conceding the abrogation of the Treaty of Wichale and recognition of Ethiopia's sovereign independence. Both conditions were incorporated in a peace treaty signed in Addis Abeba on 26 October 1896, which also accepted Eritrea's Mareb frontier. The

18. Keren Hotel, Asmera

agreement did far more than guarantee Ethiopia another generation and one-half of virtually unchallenged independence; it gave the country a status similar to that of Afghanistan, Persia, Japan, and Thailand as accepted anomalies in the imperialist world order.

The West explained Ethiopia's victory through sophistry. Since racism did not permit Westerners to acknowledge that black men could vanquish whites, Europeans suddenly discovered that Ethiopians were Caucasians darkened by exposure to the equatorial sun. Whereas previously Ethiopians shared sloth, ignorance, and degradation with their African brothers, they suddenly became energetic, enlightened, and progressive. The Orthodox church, often reviled by visiting white clerics as debased and corrupt, now was seen as a proper vehicle of the Holy Spirit and the true keeper of Ethiopia's national spirit.

19. Just across the Eritrean frontier, facing into Ethiopia

Menilek, earlier regarded as a barbarian princeling, became the epitome of monarchical virtues, full of wisdom and sagacity. His noblemen, depicted before the war as decadent and grasping, were transformed into an order of chivalry, whose only goal was selflessly to serve their sovereign and his subjects. The Ethiopian army, hitherto composed of a cowardly rabble, was suddenly pictured as a magnificent force of heroic marksmen. The abruptly revived Ethiopian state attracted a flood of journalists and adventurers.

Menilek was pleased by the attention, since his first interest was to obtain recognition of the country's independent status, especially from Britain. The Italian defeat in Ethiopia stimulated London to act more quickly against the Sudanese. The British had believed that Rome would make good its Ethiopian empire, thus removing the country from the arena of imperialism. More specifically, London wanted to ensure that the French would not use Ethiopia as an entry into Sudan. Paris remained uneasy about Britain's occupation of the Suez Canal, its dominance over Egypt, and, consequently, its leading position in the eastern Mediterranean. French strategists came to believe that the strong British stance might erode if Paris could obtain control over the Nile in Sudan. They dreamed of an unassailable French redoubt on the White Nile near Fashoda, from which they might also threaten British East Africa. The French strategists may have been good chess players, but they were poor geographers.

Their chosen site was difficult to access from any direction. And, once there, the sandy terrain offered no materials with which to build a barrage to threaten the Nile's flow. Indeed, the engineering required was probably well beyond the skills normally offered by military engineers and possibly beyond even the then most advanced technicians and scientific personnel. The Fashoda area was also indefensible, with no hills or other obvious sites to fortify and no place to hide or to which to retreat. In other words, the French efforts were doomed from the start, a fact realized neither by the British nor the Ethiopians.

Menilek was in a delicate situation. The French had offered moral and military support during the recent war and would be seeking repayment in the form of assistance for their mission into Sudan. It was conceivable that Paris might succeed in its venture. The emperor's dilemma was simple: how to provide assistance to France without alienating Britain or, for that matter, the Mahdists, who might survive in power. Ethiopia's national interest stemmed from the need to protect and extend its frontiers, and, given the diplomatic complexity and the consequent dangers, the emperor's best tactic was to dissimulate, to cooperate with all but to side with none.

The Italian crisis already had moved Ethiopia to establish peaceful relations with the Sudanese on the basis of their common interest in containing modern European imperialism. After Adwa, the emperor and the Khalifa Abdullahi (d. 1898) exchanged information, declared good intentions, and facilitated regional trade. Menilek carefully refrained from formal commitments to his Muslim neighbors, and cynically negotiated with the French about the future of Sudan.

Paris was pressing for an alliance and in November 1896 sent Lagarde, the governor of Obok-Djibouti, to Addis Abeba to win Menilek's agreement. Negotiations led first to the convention of 29 January 1897, which conceded duty-free transit of weapons through Djibouti, recognized by Menilek as his country's official outlet, and which reduced France's paper claims over its colony's hinterland, now effectively occupied by Ras Makonnen's men. In return, on 30 January the emperor signed a secret agreement pledging support for France's aspirations in the upper Nile region and promising to contain the British with French-armed Ethiopian soldiers.

Menilek never had any intentions of fulfilling his obligations, which would have damaged his detente with Sudan and made an enemy out of Britain. Subtle evasion was his guide to a secure future: he would therefore cooperate on one level, while ensuring sub rosa that Paris's efforts failed. Whenever the French complained about ignorant guides, soldiers who failed to appear, uncooperative officials, and undelivered supplies, the emperor shrugged his shoulders and apologized profusely for the "imbeciles" who disobeyed his orders. He then commanded new letters of authorization, which, however, never reached their destination or were too late to affect events. Though Menilek proved useless in helping to attain Paris's goal in the upper Nile, he showed enough goodwill that he would have been able to capitalize on any French success. The emperor's smiles toward Lagarde and others were sufficient, however, to cause anxiety in London.

Aware of the contacts between Addis Abeba and Omdurman, the Foreign Office feared that Ethiopia might direct its surplus, obsolete weapons into Sudan, appreciated the need to negotiate colonial frontiers with Menilek, and wanted good relations immediately. The emperor quickly realized that London's policy was defensive and reactive and welcomed a British mission led by Rennel Rodd to Addis Abeba in April 1897. Menilek cooperated by agreeing, secretly of course, not to ship weapons to Sudan, in return for which he obtained duty-free transit of all Ethiopian government goods passing through Zeila. Later, thanks to Ras Makonnen's determined bargaining on the basis of effective occupation, the emperor gained virtually all of the Ogaden, whose Somali inhabitants now had to cross an international frontier—largely ignored until after World War II—to reach their December–March pasturage.

The Anglo-Ethiopian settlement of 14 May 1897 marked the end of Europe's threat to Menilek's empire. The major powers now recognized Ethiopia's sovereignty and independence, even if racism and feelings of cultural superiority would continue to color diplomatic relations. The victory at Adwa was a great achievement for Ethiopia, since its emperor had been able successfully to mobilize men and resources throughout his vast domains to overcome a powerful enemy. The subsequent diplomacy revealed Menilek as an astute and wily statesman: his carefully designed, noncommittal foreign policy consolidated his battlefield success, safeguarded Ethiopia's position on all sides, and won territorial and economic concessions from his powerful neighbors. Ethiopia's improved international standing and recognition permitted Menilek to embark on a period of nation building.

EIGHT

Menilek's State, to 1916

From 1896 to 1907, Menilek directed Ethiopia's return into southern and western regions abandoned in the seventeenth century and into areas never before under its rule. Many of the newly incorporated peoples lived in nonhierarchical societies, practiced animal husbandry or nonplow agriculture, followed traditional religions or Islam, and spoke non-Semitic languages. The superior weapons of the northerners and their hierarchical social organization gave them significant advantages, but they also were inspired by the notion of regaining Ethiopia irredenta. Menilek certainly believed that his was a holy crusade, and his soldiers presumed, with considerable justification, that they would help their sovereign to restore Ethiopia to its historic grandeur and size.

And they did so, with a vengeance. First, in March 1897, Ras Wolde Giorgis (1851–1918), one of Menilek's cousins and a leading general, invaded Kefa. Although he deployed twenty thousand modern rifles against their three hundred muskets, the Kefa defended their country fiercely, causing many northern casualties before they surrendered in September. Thereafter, the ras ordered his armies southward into Gamo Gofa to Lake Turkana (formerly Lake Rudolf), where he had learned a British expedition had camped. The thinly populated region offered little opposition, and the ras's army raised the Ethiopian tricolor at the lake before returning to Kefa.

The European threat to the Ethiopian periphery worried Menilek enough to order Ras Makonnen westward into Beni (or Bela) Shangul country. The imminence of British rule in Sudan gave urgency to the acquisition of the gold-producing area. And it was sufficient, finally, to permit some very frustrated Frenchmen to accompany Dej. Tesemma Nadaw (later ras-regent; d. 1911) as he proceeded through Ilubabor toward the White Nile, firming up imperial rule as he traveled. Understandably enough, Tesemma's men never reached Fashoda, although an Ethiopian flag was planted on the right bank of the White Nile, which is all that really mattered to the emperor.

Meanwhile, Menilek had ordered forces to move into what were to become the empire's extreme peripheries, especially Borena, directly in the path of British expansion northward from Kenya. Ethiopia's policy was slowly but determinedly to infiltrate such remote areas with irregulars and, then, to build an effective occupation. The adjacent powers were regularly surprised by the extent of Ethiopian administration in regions they considered their own either through treaties, to which Addis Abeba was not signatory, or through asserted rights over colonial hinterlands. Between 1896 and 1906, Ethiopia expanded to its present size, comprising the highlands, the key river systems, and a borderland buffer zone in low-lying, arid, or tropical zones to protect the state's central core.

During the decade, the Ethiopian periphery was legalized through a series of frontier agreements that Menilek negotiated with the adjacent colonial powers. It was consolidated on the ground from fortified villages, or *ketema*, generally situated atop the highest points, dominating the regions below. They were in communication with each other through runners, so that during crises, men and arms could be concentrated quickly. Since the ketema were largely inhabited by northern administrators and soldiers and their families, they were diffusion points for Christian culture; and as market centers, they helped to stimulate regional economies and thereby to shape a new national economy.

Northern soldier-settlers, or *neftennya*, also helped to spread the new order. Situated throughout the countryside to discourage disorder and to assist local administration, they were assigned farmers, or *gabbar*, who provided them food and services. The gabbar were administered by the *ballabat* (headmen) and their assistants, the *korro*, officials often chosen from among the traditional elites and ruling families. The two local administrators mediated between the subjects and their overlords, and, as landowners with rights over gabbar, they were class allies of the neftennya. They and their families often intermarried with the settlers, and, given the attractive power of acculturation, became little different than their northern colleagues.

Some traditional political leaders also benefited from the structure of the imperial state. Moroda of Nekemte (r. 1868–1889), once a gada official, decided that his holdings in Welega deserved political ties with the powerful northerners. His son, Kumsa Moroda (r. 1889–1932) agreed, even converting to Christianity in order to satisfy his larger ambitions. As Dej. Gebre Egziabeher (literally, "servant of God"), he had an important role in national politics, managed an autonomous state, and retained some semblance of an Oromo political order.

Gebre Egziabeher annually delivered a rich tribute in gold and ivory to Addis Abeba. He also had to make exceptional payments during times of crisis or for extraordinary expenses. Gebre Egziabeher was always writing to Addis Abeba bemoaning the heavy imperial taxes his people bore. He was quick also to counter any government effort to assume his administrative responsibilities. He was able to retain his country's autonomy until his death in 1932, bequeathing to his people a better economy, more educational facilities, and a better communications infrastructure than were available in most of Ethiopia's provinces.

Menilek also managed to make Ethiopia a better place to live. He was highly intelligent and quick-witted, curious about everything, especially machinery and technology. Although the monarch was a progressive man, his political education made him unlikely to alter his country's social order. As a triumphant general who had safeguarded Ethiopia's sovereignty, he saw no need to change an effective social and economic formula. He therefore chose to import manufactured goods into Ethiopia but not Europe's mode of production nor its social structure. Unlike the Japanese state, the Solomonic empire would not undergo the social revolution required to attain security thorough industrial modernization.

The Ethiopian people were not so well disciplined as the Japanese; the empire was newly established and its administration still rudimentary. The Solomonic state was vast, its communications primitive, and its population heterogeneous: there was no insular cultural homogeneity to exploit and reshape. Capital resources and trade revenues were limited by Ethiopia's narrow markets, its limited range of exports, and its practically nonexistent banking and credit facilities. There were relatively few skilled and educated Ethiopians who had significant roles in political and economic life. Indeed, the traditional elites were fully engaged in an empire that had the capacity to absorb their interests and ambitions and that presented no structural danger from an impoverished warrior class. In short, there were no compelling reasons to change Ethiopia.

The emperor did, however, bring some of the modern age to Addis Abeba: stone buildings were constructed, bridges were built, a few streets were paved; and piped water, plumbing, and electricity were introduced in the imperial palace. The government post office offered mail services adequate enough to gain Ethiopia entry into the International Postal Union in 1908; and it also offered telephonic and telegraphic services. After 1905, the capital's inhabitants were linked to the world's financial marts through the chartered Bank of Abyssinia, an affiliate of the National Bank of Egypt. Advances in education and health were made with the opening of several schools and hospitals and the establishment of a government press.

For most of Ethiopia's population, however, the limited trappings of the modern age were novelties that left their lives unaffected. For them, Menilek's only real innovation was the construction, under concession to a French company, of an Addis Abeba–Djibouti railway. It not only physically linked Ethiopia to the outside world but it also spurred the articulation of capitalism and the exploitation of the country's bulk produce as cash crops. Easy access into Ethiopia and its peripheries attracted the attention of capital-rich Indian merchants, who were already working to integrate East Africa into the world economy. In Ethiopia, they stimulated capitalist practices in cooperation with the ruling elites. They exploited the railway link and the credit facilities of the Bank of Abyssinia to join Ethiopia to the world system, a basic change that would affect the lives of its inhabitants.

During its building, the railway was the object of much controversy. The French concessionaire was always short of funds, and when British capital sought a takeover, Paris intervened as if the line was national property, forgetting that it ran mostly through Ethiopian territory. An irate Menilek ordered that goods addressed to his government be shipped by camel caravan from Djibouti, robbing the railway company of revenues sufficient to cover expenses and to pay interest on its bonds. When, in 1902, he refused to sanction construction of the line beyond Dire Dawa, the first main terminus in Ethiopia, the company was in deep trouble. It muddled through, however, until 1908, when, in a new agreement, France agreed that Addis Abeba held sovereignty over the Ethiopian portion of the line.

There was an irony here, since on 4 July 1906, France, Britain, and Italy had initialed a tripartite agreement that defined their interests in Ethiopia as if the country was a transitory phenomenon or less than sovereign. Paris won a French-administered railway and an economic zone of influence stretching from Djibouti to Addis Abeba; the British gained recognition of its overriding interests in the Nile basin; and the Italians obtained a vague acknowledgement that it might exploit western Ethiopia, through which some link connecting Eritrea and Italian Somaliland might be built.

The treaty's preamble claimed nonetheless that the signatories wished to maintain Ethiopia's integrity, and one of its eleven articles pledged the trio's neutrality and nonintervention in the country's internal affairs. Ethiopia in fact gained considerable stability from the treaty, which marked the end of active British and French imperialism in the region and eliminated, for a time, the likelihood of Italian expansion. While the treaty did not respect Ethiopia's full sovereignty in international affairs, the Tripartite powers promoted Ethiopia's national integrity at a time when the empire's internal stability was shaken by Menilek's illness and a troubled succession.

The old emperor had been the rock of determination on which modern Ethiopia was built. In 1902, he held a military review in Addis Abeba to commemorate the memory of those who had fallen at Adwa. Over three hundred thousand soldiers from the provinces participated, but the day was capped by a review of the imperial army. Close to one hundred thousand men under Fit. Habte Giorgis (later minister of war; d. 1926) marched past, and elite units demonstrated the efficient use of machine-gun and cannon fire, followed by disciplined rifle salvos. No provincial ruler could withstand such fire power, rendering the emperor's internal position unassailable.

After the victory at Adwa, he had contained all internal dissent, including a rebellion in Tigray led in 1899 by the nettlesome Ras Mengesha. Subsequently, the emperor redistributed the province's subgovernments to competing politicians, all, to be sure, relatives of Yohannes IV. In 1901, when Negus Tekle Haimanot of Gojam died, Menilek similarly consigned the province to three carefully chosen individuals, each well balanced against each other.

Yet, the emperor was also increasingly isolated at the center of government. Early in the twentieth century, several of his trusted advisers and confidants died, among them Ras Makonnen in 1906. That year, the emperor also lost the services of Alfred Ilg, his longtime adviser and foreign affairs consultant. The emperor, moreover, was aging, unable to travel periodically to the provinces to show his grandeur and to supervise provincial officials. He now governed by telephone, and while the line to the provinces held daily terrors for officials, his workday nonetheless revealed how much he had slowed down.

The emperor rose early in the morning and immediately went to one of the palace's three churches for prayer. He returned to his living quarters to breakfast with the empress and some of his cronies and discuss the day's business. At 9:00 A.M., he went to the throne room to deal with diplomats or high officials. Immediately thereafter until 1:00 P.M., the emperor served as Ethiopia's supreme court, hearing final pleas from litigants empirewide. When the morning's work was done, the emperor returned to his apartment for lunch with Taitou and invited officials and then took a short nap before returning to the throne room for further business.

Around 4:00 P.M., Menilek would often order his mule or his coach to tour the extensive palace grounds or to venture into his rapidly growing capital. Surrounded by selected young protégés and guardsmen, he inspected public works and showed himself to his subjects. He often stopped to talk to petitioners and to passersby, in order to gauge public opinion and to learn firsthand the peoples' anxieties and problems. He returned to the palace before dusk, to sit on the veranda of his apartment, gossiping and sipping honey wine with his cronies until the sun went down. Dinner would be taken with friends, distinguished visitors, foreign advisers, or diplomats. After 10:00 P.M., the empress and emperor, like most Addis Abebans, retired for the day.

In the early 1900s, the heavily forested capital, with a population of perhaps sixty-five thousand, was a strange, spread-out town, dominated on the hills by either the imperial palace or the large, traditional manors of the very high nobility. On knolls adjacent to each establishment were satellite communities such that the city resembled a conglomeration of villages. An occasional church or European-style building was interspersed among the predominating traditional, wattle-and-thatch dwellings, although square houses with tin roofs had begun to appear. Only in front of Menilek's palace, in the market area, was there the dense population characteristic of the later city. Here lived merchants, artisans, day laborers, shopkeepers and bar owners, prostitutes, and palace workers and servants.

Most had come to Addis Abeba after the victorious war against Italy and the subsequent territorial expansion, some, indeed, as captives or slaves. The townspeople crossed religious, caste, and ethnic lines in their quests of career and fortune. And, ultimately, they were employed in a very real, if inchoate, national economy, working for money, clothes, food, and housing. The prestige of their employers was not so important as their level of wages and security. A well-paid worker could hope to make a monthly salary of $12 (£1) and be allotted clothes twice a year. Palace personnel could hope for bonuses, pensions, and land grants, and they were fed daily as part of their wages.

Providing such largess was normal for Ethiopian rulers, who used institutionalized feeding for charitable, representational, and redistributive purposes. The imperial palace daily served about three thousand people, and on Sundays as many as four thousand took their meal with Menilek. Perhaps forty-five thousand were served during the three-day celebrations of important holidays. These were enormous events that required the almost total mobilization of the palace's staff and resources. Arrangements had to commence well in advance of the holiday, and all women workers dropped their usual tasks to assist in the cooking and preparation of food. High-ranking officials, provincial administrators, other notables, and their retinues began arriving in Addis Abeba a week or more before the occasion, trebling the population. The capital took on a generally festive atmosphere, and, in the market, trade in new clothes was brisk.

The *geber*, or feast, began at 9:00 A.M., in the huge modern hall Menilek had built in 1897 to replace an old-fashioned, outsized tent. From a dais at the hall's front, the emperor presided over as many as eight seatings each day, inviting noblemen to join him as they ceremonially greeted and paid him homage. Since public display required moderation and sobriety, the dignitaries therefore departed as quickly as did the ten thousand to fifteen thousand commoners who flowed into and from the hall at intervals regulated by palace guards. They ate their fill of chicken and meat stews, bread, and the raw beef (*brindo*) so beloved by Ethiopians. At around 4:00 P.M., the emperor left, and the day's feasting was officially over.

Menilek presided over his last geber on 11 September 1909, by then mortally ill from syphilis. He had been ailing since 1904 and had taken steps to ensure the continuity of the state. On 25 October 1907, he announced the formation of Ethiopia's first cabinet and quickly used the new Ministry of Justice to establish an appellate court system in the provinces. The number of cases forwarded to the emperor for final appeal was sharply reduced, relieving him of a terrible burden. Moreover, the new courts were structurally independent of provincial administration, and scribes recorded case proceedings, making it difficult for local dignitaries to intervene once the litigation was appealed to the crown. The provincial appellate system represented a significant imposition of imperial authority in the countryside.

Menilek also considerably strengthened individual rights to property. On 4 October 1908, he decreed a new and immediately popular inheritance law. Hitherto, all goods and property had belonged to the emperor, who could give or reclaim them at his pleasure. In reality, of course, property was heritable, but the state always had the right to confiscate wealth upon the death of the owner, and arbitrary actions by rapacious provincial and local officials was not unknown. The new legislation formalized inheritance by will. Except for capital cases or treason, goods no longer could be confiscated at the whim of the state. The change reflected Ethiopia's changing economy and was certainly inspired by the need to safeguard and to transfer capital generationally.

Beyond such reforms, the emperor established the office of prime minister, which he gave to Fit. Habte Giorgis, who was also the minister of war and the country's most prominent general. Menilek also instituted a crown council comprising leading noblemen, ranking church officials, and government ministers. This organization became important in February 1908, when the emperor suffered a stroke that severely incapacitated him. The government fell to the crown council, and, as its chairperson, Empress Taitou concentrated so much power into her hands that she became the de facto head of state. As long as Menilek was clearheaded enough to voice support for her activities, no one openly opposed her decisions. Notwithstanding her experience, intelligence, and ability, Shewa's power brokers were not ready to permit a woman to exercise sovereignty in her own right.

In August 1909, they influenced Menilek to designate Ras Tesemma Nadaw, an empire loyalist, as regent plenipotentiary for Menilek's grandson and heir-designate Lij Iyasu (1896–1935). On 28 October 1909, the emperor suffered a massive, almost mortal, stroke, which left him paralyzed and speechless. The government quickly called out troops to keep order, and decreed a dawn-to-dusk curfew. While Taitou's situation was inherently weak, she maneuvered deftly to obtain supporters, even permitting Dej. Tafari Makonnen (the future Haile Sellassie I), a youth of seventeen, to be nominated governor of Harerge, the strategic, rich eastern province. She was unable, however, to win over the governors of the important southern provinces or to strengthen her allies in the north. Her machinations nevertheless exacerbated an already confused situation, seriously compromising the new regime. Administrators and governors refused to take responsibility for new measures, to make decisions, to obey orders, or even to answer letters from the palace. Menilek's living death and the empress's continued meddling eroded the authority of centralized government in Ethiopia.

Ras Tesemma, in the early stages of an illness that claimed his life within a year, was apathetic in face of the assertive Taitou. She meanwhile was tampering with the crown council and the ministries, replacing Menilek's men with her own sycophants. She also sought to control diplomatic relations, thereby forcing the powers tacitly to recognize her supreme authority. While the Europeans were busily discussing their refusal to deal exclusively with Taitou, Menilek's men finally bestirred themselves to end the empress's brief reign.

On 21 March 1910, a group of military and civil officers condemned the empress for meddling in government. They marched on the residence of Abuna Mattewos and demanded release from their oath of fidelity. They then went to Ras Tesemma and won his cooperation, and the next morning Fit. Habte Giorgis followed his example. In a meeting in one of the capital's churches, both men prudently admitted negligence in failing to control the empress and vowed their support for removing her from power. After much discussion, the two leaders were instructed to inform Taitou that subsequently she would have no duties apart from caring for Menilek. The empress protested vigorously, arguing in vain against her detractors.

Her departure from government did not improve its administration. The new leadership insisted that business be handled by Menilek's ministers, but the latter understood neither their roles nor the concept of collective responsibility. Instead, the ministers discerned their roles in traditional terms and acted as governors seeking their fortunes, yielding decisions on the basis of gratuities and favoritism. Neither the ailing Tesemma nor the young and inexperienced Lij Iyasu were able to control the situation, and, without close leadership, government functioned in familiar, personal ways. The phenomenon was especially galling to the European diplomats and foreign businessmen who constantly pressed the bureaucracy for concessions and institutional decisions. For the Ethiopians, however, it was business as usual.

Lij Iyasu by now had taken Menilek's place at the palace's feasts, and he traveled around the town under the red parasol reserved for the sovereign. Various potential pretenders to the crown had been imprisoned; most of Taitou's appointees had been purged; and Lij Iyasu had divorced her niece, his child bride of little more than a year. Meanwhile, strategic Begemdir was consigned to Ras Wolde Giorgis, hitherto the strongman of the south, who moved his powerful army northward. In cooperation with Ras Mikail in Welo, Taitou's allies were completely neutralized, making Ethiopia's heartland safe for Iyasu. Finally, the young men who had led the coup against Taitou were rewarded with posts in southern Ethiopia recently vacated by Wolde Giorgis's lieutenants. By the end of 1910, the regency regime was completely in power, although Ras Tesemma's authority remained unfulfilled as he slowly succumbed to syphilis.

In February 1911, he suffered recurrent paralytic attacks reminiscent of Menilek's pathology. By the end of March, both regent and emperor lingered on in shattered bodies, barely conscious of their surroundings. When Tesemma was lucky enough to die, on 10 April 1911, the sixteen-year-old Iyasu took the opportunity to claim personal rule, and the ministers obliged by reorganizing themselves into a regency council under the prince's presidency. The youth was hardly ready to govern: during his adolescence, he had mostly abandoned the classrooms of the *gibbi* (Menilek's palace) for the capital's bars and brothels. Undoubtedly bright, he was, however, ignorant about running an increasingly complex administration. He had a short attention span, and he lacked political common sense, if not a grand vision. His idée fixe was a society in which religious and ethnic affiliations did not matter, a goal that contradicted the political situation in the empire. His insensitivity to this fundamental reality was left unchallenged by his advisers, a congeries of amusing but sycophantic courtiers.

They and their master bored easily, and so were always on the outlook for diversions. Iyasu was often gone from Addis Abeba, taking long journeys into the countryside, where he hunted and visited his subjects and sought to construct a political coalition independent of the men who had built and sustained Menilek's empire. He disregarded the permanency of the old emperor's new capital, now connected by modern communications to the provinces and the outside world, and which required the full-time services of a leader prepared to cope with the modern age.

Bereft of its head, the central government deteriorated during 1911–1913, but provincial governments remained as strong as their leaders, in some cases powerful enough to ignore orders and to evade taxes. Dej. Tafari Makonnen, from his vantage in Harerge, did not join in humiliating Iyasu's government. Cousins several times removed, he and the prince had grown up together in Menilek's palace, and before taking up his governorship, Tafari had solemnly vowed not to exploit his "Solomonic" blood line to compete for the imperial crown. Yet, he reckoned that Iyasu's lackadaisical attitude toward administration was responsible for the central government's decline.

Ethiopia's ruling class grew increasingly uneasy as World War I began, and Iyasu began a dalliance with Islam and also with the Central Powers. The heir believed that the defeat of the Allies might allow Ethiopia to push Italy out of Eritrea and Somalia. He therefore sought an alliance with the Seyyid Muhammed Abdullah (d. 23 November 1920), the so-called Mad Mullah, who long had pursued an anticolonialist war in Somalia. Since the seyyid ipso facto followed an anti-Ethiopian line in Ogaden, many believed that Iyasu's policy was treasonous. Moreover, the empire's high officials viewed with extreme distaste the prince's efforts to integrate Muslims into the administration. Iyasu was, however, convinced that his policy would reduce the empire-state's chronic unrest and benefit the economy. His important task was nation building, not imperial exploitation, but his method threatened those who ran Menilek's state, among them Dej. Tafari, the governor of largely Muslim Harerge.

Deciding the province was an excellent venue for his new policy, Iyasu expected little interference from Addis Abeba, whose impotent ministers, with the notable exception of Fit. Habte Giorgis, now owed their jobs and wealth to him. Furthermore, by 1915, Iyasu had replaced many of Menilek's provincial administrators with his own appointees. A good many disappointed and unhappy politicians were living out their frustrations and rancor in the capital, a place Iyasu disdained and largely ignored. Yet, with the proper incitement and leadership, the old elite could have mounted a potent rebellion.

On 13 August 1916, Iyasu removed Tafari from Harerge, reassigning him to the less important province of Kefa. Instead of taking up his new post, the dejazmach remained in Addis Abeba, where he had been since May. There, rumors circulated that Iyasu favored a victory by the Central

Powers, that he intended to rid the Horn of colonialism, and that he was arming non-Christians against the Europeans. On 12 September 1916, the Allies gave substance to the gossip by sending a note to the Foreign Ministry seeking an explanation for Iyasu's belligerency and announcing an arms embargo against Ethiopia.

Iyasu's many enemies feared that his continued leadership would plunge Ethiopia into war with the Allies and also lead to civil strife. At a meeting of aristocrats on 27 September 1916, the heir was accused of apostasy and of internal subversion on such insubstantial grounds that the abun refused to excommunicate him. When the prelate was shouted down, his second-in-command, obviously a party to the conspiracy, repeated the flimsy indictments and, on his own authority, excommunicated Iyasu as an unbeliever and ended his abortive but interesting reign.

NINE

Ras Tafari, to 1930

Circumstantial evidence reveals Tafari as a leading figure in the crisis that led to Iyasu's dethronement: there is no other explanation for his immediate promotion to ras and his nomination as heir apparent and regent to the new monarch, Empress Zawditu (b. 1876; r. 1916–1930), Menilek's daughter. Tafari's candidacy did not prevail easily, another indication that he had been a potent force in the coup. Behind closed doors, the ministers convinced themselves that Tafari's inexperience and youth would make him malleable, and they decided therefore that they would help Zawditu to govern and Tafari to administer. They then set about consolidating the new government's authority.

In Harer, the coup had gone awry, and, on 8 October, Iyasu had escaped into the Ogaden desert. From Welo, Negus (his rank since 1914) Mikail indicated displeasure with his son's situation, arguing that the lad might have been a trifle rash in some of his policies but that dethronement was an unnecessarily harsh punishment. Instead of debating with Addis Abeba, he should have moved on the city, which during the week was lightly defended. The king's excellent 100,000-man army would have easily taken Menilek's gibbi, where, since 30 September, Zawditu now resided. Two weeks later, 50,000 soldiers protected the new regime, of which 35,000 were along Shewa's northern frontier. The rulers of southern and western Ethiopia understood that the fight was about their power and had responded so enthusiastically that by 21 October the government's army greatly outnumbered its enemy.

On 26 October, after maneuvering several days for the best tactical positions, the two forces faced each other at Segele, about 40 miles north of Addis Abeba. Early the next day, Negus Mikail opened one of Ethiopia's more important historic battles, which he lost by noon, defeated by more men, better arms, and a superior general, Fit. Habte Giorgis. After the king was captured, his camp was taken intact, including tons of ammunition and arms. They had been intended for Iyasu's army, but the prince reached nearby Ankober too late to help his father. He immediately directed his 6,000 men toward the lowlands and thence to sanctuary in Welo.

Iyasu remained a dangerous threat to the new government, free to broadcast his subversive view of equality of opportunity for all Ethiopians, regardless of race, religion, caste, and way of life. The governors of the southern conquered provinces were especially hostile toward Iyasu, as their economic interests required a servile population to exploit. Zawditu's regime stood for socioeconomic orthodoxy and therefore well represented its supporters. In terms of the sweeping economic changes stimulated throughout Africa by the world economy, the new government, as orchestrated by Ras Tafari, would mediate commercial growth but maintain Menilek's political economy. Indeed, the coup against Iyasu was an effort to maintain the social hierarchy that had first resurrected the old empire and then had expanded beyond its previous frontiers.

At her coronation on 11 February 1917—the first in Ethiopian history attended by official European representatives—Zawditu pledged to rule justly through her regent. Her choice of words disclaimed an active role in government, and even at public occasions, Tafari was the more visible of the duo. Yet, she was not a strictly honorary ruler, since her position at the apex of the hierarchical Ethiopian state required arbitrating the claims of competing factions. Zawditu had the last word, a capability that sometimes irritated Tafari but which he respected and tried to manipulate.

Still, the ras carried the burden of daily administration, often an exercise in futility. His position was weak, his personal army poorly equipped, and his finances limited. He had little leverage to withstand the combined influence of the empress, the minister of war, and the more important provincial governors. He had to consult so widely that reform was consistently thwarted, and only the more innocuous measures became policy. Inevitably, he took the long view: foreseeing the increasing importance of Addis Abeba as Ethiopia's political, commercial, and communications center, he early began to place partisans in the municipality, especially in the financial departments. He always had understood the centrality of Shewa in Ethiopia's political renaissance and so formed a political alliance with Ras Kassa Hailu (later leul ras; 1881–1956), the province's most important political figure, who also realized that national survival required reform. Finally, Tafari acted as foreign minister, not only personifying Ethiopia to the foreigners but also convincing them and their governments that he was irreplaceable and deserved their full support. So, from the beginning of the new government, Tafari outlined the nature of his long career: he would concentrate on Addis Abeba, Shewa, and foreign affairs, around which he would build his authority.

His first policy was financial aggrandizement, to fuel his quest for personal power. He received funds from Ethiopians wanting jobs, favorable government decisions, or favors; from Europeans seeking concessions; from Asian business partners; from Harerge, where he had many investments in plantations and commercial firms; and from various financial organs of the central government, where he had placed his devotees. With others, he established the Société Éthiopienne de Commerce et d'Industrie, which became the government's main business agent and yielded great profits. Europeans thought Tafari corrupt and venal, though his behavior was completely understandable in traditional terms, since he redistributed the proceeds of his ventures to Addis Abeba's poor, including the soldiery. By so doing, he became the leader of the urban masses, themselves a new phenomenon in Ethiopian politics.

In 1918, life in the capital was difficult, largely because the war had isolated Ethiopia from its traditional buyers and suppliers, and the city's workers could no longer find employment in transport, construction, and day labor. Misfortune also dogged thousands of soldiers, who claimed to have been cheated out of salaries and food by their officers, who, in turn, blamed the ministers for having embezzled funds. The military men met and authorized a committee to seek redress. On 20 March, the nameless leadership called for the dismissal of the entire council of ministers and the transfer of power to a regency council composed of Zawditu, Habte Giorgis, and Tafari.

During the next few days, after a number of demonstrations, the committee placed the ministers under house arrest, and a reluctant Zawditu agreed to exile the men to their home provinces. Throughout the crisis, Tafari maintained ignorance about the conspiracy, and he later wrote that he had opposed the dismissals as untraditional. Always a good self-propagandist, his disclaimers cannot be taken seriously, since the ministers' exit left him in sole charge of running the government. Tafari was above all a player from behind the scenes, manipulating actors and events to his advantage. His political goals—as in this case, control of the government—were always obvious, even if he concealed his tactics.

With the ministers gone, Tafari named directors to the various departments of government. He appointed an obscure, but partisan, palace official to posts and telegraphs and directed him to expand the system. The postmasters and telegraph-telephone operators would be the ras's eyes and ears, able quickly to communicate provincial news to the capital. He selected one of his supporters as the empire's treasurer and others as *nagadrases* (officials in charge of markets) in Addis Abeba, Dire Dawa, Welega, Walamo, and Ankober. He provided stipends for each appointee in lieu of traditional fees, beginning the salariat so characteristic of modern, bureaucratic Ethiopia. His reforms not only increased the flow of information to the capital but also added significantly to the revenues remitted to the central government.

After the influenza epidemics of 1918, Tafari set about establishing a viable foreign policy. Given Ethiopia's colonial encirclement, the new government sought to guarantee the country's security; and, given its domestic situation, it required modern weaponry to be stronger than any combination of the more powerful provincial lords. It was, however, unable to break the European arms embargo: Italy, which still coveted Ethiopia, was totally opposed to any weapons procurement that might strengthen the Addis Abeba government. London generally was content with the status quo, since the Colonial Office believed that new weapons for Ethiopia would lead to a cross-border arms trade which would only worsen security in adjacent British holdings. Alone, Paris could do little, and so, in 1918, the Allies refused Ethiopia's offer to declare war against the Central Powers in return for a role in the peace talks and new weapons.

Ethiopia had a serious image problem in Europe. To Western eyes, the government was corrupt from top to bottom. The central administration was slow to achieve consensus, and Europeans mistook the indirection for inefficiency. Much of the apparent lethargy stemmed from a lack of qualified personnel willing to make decisions. To remedy the bureaucracy's backwardness, Ras Tafari immediately set about recruiting the newly educated for government service, but there were few schools, and the transition to a new breed of official, the *Young Ethiopian*—efficient, modern, and patriotic—was inevitably slow. On principle, the new men would do away with such archaic practices as slavery.

Historically, Ethiopians had exploited slaves as domestics or as farm laborers, frequently under gang conditions, or to proclaim wealth and status. As long as Ethiopia was autarkic, the available agricultural surplus could support the mass of slaves. The intrusion of the world economy in the late nineteenth century and the subsequent growth of cash crops in southern Ethiopia transformed the situation. During the 1920s, Ethiopian agriculture, especially in coffee, became increasingly profitable, rendering the exploitation of slaves uneconomic in terms of opportunity costs. Moreover, feudal lords suddenly became interested in transforming rights over gabbars into rights over land. They entered into economic alliances with each other and the Asian traders who mediated capitalism in Ethiopia. In short, the feudal nobility transformed itself into an oligarchy more interested in profit than pageantry.

Slaves were manumitted to take their place alongside subsistence agriculturists as sharecroppers in Ethiopia's developing market economy. This natural process was occurring when criticism of Ethiopia's social system developed overseas. It was difficult for Europeans to appreciate that capitalism in Ethiopia was defeating slavery when they saw an apparently thriving institution. As Ethiopia's best public relations man, Tafari claimed that his edict of 1918 banning the slave trade was a turn toward ultimate abolition. He patiently explained that he would have to educate his countrymen to see slavery as a social problem, since the government was trying to destroy a historic institution that many believed benefited both slave and owner. The process leading to liberation would be long and difficult, and the final stages had to be linked to economic growth in order to absorb the energies and talents of the hundreds of thousands of freedmen. Westerners, however, wanted quick action, and so the edict of 1918 won few friends in Europe.

Neither did goodwill missions sent, in 1919, to the United States and to Europe to congratulate the victors of World War I and to seek participation in the peace negotiations. Tafari's long-term policy was to wrap Ethiopia in the League of Nations' cloak of collective security. The ras was entirely enthusiastic about President Wilson's notion, which seemed a perfect answer to Ethiopia's security needs. He also believed that membership in the league would extricate the nation from the domination of the Tripartite powers and open it to other countries such as the increasingly powerful United States. Opposing his worldview was Fit. Habte Giorgis, who deeply abhorred foreign connections and who believed in *Fortress Ethiopia*. When, during a crisis in August 1919, the empress opted for internationalism, Tafari's political stature grew.

In January 1921, his position improved with the capture, in Tigray, of Lij Iyasu. The ras nonetheless lacked the overwhelming might needed to impose nationwide reforms and to keep the imperialists at bay. For Tafari, membership in the League of Nations, which would provide Ethiopia with unquestioned sovereignty under international law, was the only way to challenge the Tripartite powers' arms embargo. The first movement in that direction came in July 1923, when the league, thanks to a French maneuver, requested information about the slave trade directly from Ethiopia.

The Quai d'Orsay reasoned that the moment might be right for Ethiopia to seek membership and so informed the Addis Abeba government. From 23 to 29 July, day and night, meetings were held at the gibbi with officials and advisers appearing before the council of the realm. A majority seemed to favor entry into the league, although Tafari played the devil's advocate, raising the greatest number of objections related to Ethiopia's internal problems. He thereby rather deftly turned the decision into a high-level plebiscite on Ethiopia's modernization, although many of the old guard agreed only because they truly thought that entry would win renewal of the arms trade. On 1 August 1923, Tafari officially requested that Geneva consider Ethiopia's application for admission at the fall meeting of the assembly.

During the deliberations, the Ethiopian delegation did not have an easy time about the arms question and slavery. Italy derided Ethiopia as unable to control its domestic life according to "civilized" standards, a view echoed by the more sanctimonious British. Tafari thereupon cabled Rome and London, seeking explanations for the obvious hostility. Since they both had important interests in Ethiopia, they toned down their attacks. Meanwhile, the African candidate had become the cause célèbre of many of the league's lesser powers, who, with France, worked out a scheme that would simultaneously satisfy the criticisms and also maintain Ethiopia's national sovereignty.

The strategy required Dej. Nadaw Abba Welo (later ras; d. 1929), Addis Abeba's representative, to agree to statements pledging Ethiopia not to undertake an arms trade in Africa and ultimately to ban the status of slavery and the internal slave trade. To the crown council at home,

Nadaw recommended adoption of the disclaimers, since their language did not undermine Ethiopia's sovereignty and would destroy the logic of the opposition's arguments. In Addis Abeba, the statements were carefully studied and accepted as given, enabling Ethiopia to enter the league by unanimous vote on 28 September 1923. Tafari was elated, truly believing that membership secured Ethiopia from imperialism and that he could now attend to economic and social development.

In 1924, Ethiopia was, by any standard, a backward country. Its economy was based on a traditional agriculture that yielded grain, coffee, and pulses, and hides and skins were important export items. There were virtually no roads then, and trade was drawn to Addis Abeba to take advantage of the railway to the sea. Hidden in a forest of eucalyptus, Ethiopia's capital had a population of as many as one hundred thousand, who were all served by two modern hotels, two cinemas, two hospitals, and numerous drinking houses. There were approximately twenty-five hundred Europeans, mostly Greeks and Armenians, and possibly a thousand Asians, the last especially important since their capital and connections in East Africa and Aden were quickly making Addis Abeba an important participant in a growing regional commodities market. By its general nature, therefore, the Ethiopian capital was becoming a primate city, attracting an innovative and relatively cosmopolitan population.

Not surprisingly, therefore, Tafari believed that townspeople could adapt to change more easily than rural dwellers, and he concentrated "progress" in Addis Abeba, where he could supervise the process. In 1921–1922, he imported two printing presses and undertook the publication of Amharic-language books and tracts. In 1923, the ras began the important weekly newspaper *Berhanena Selam*, which provided news, homilies, sermons, propaganda, and advice for the increasingly aware urban population. By 1924, the capital's rudimentary educational system had touched several thousand people, but not enough for a country whose advancement required a cadre educated in Western ideas. In 1925, the ras established and financed the quasi-secondary Tafari Makonnen School, which by the end of the year enrolled 160 boys and youths. The ras's ideas about progress were almost strictly European, and in 1924 he decided to travel to the West to gain direct knowledge of its technology and education. He also had reason to believe that he might be able to regain a coastal port for Ethiopia, the goal the crown council set for the trip.

On 16 April 1924, Tafari and a large retinue left Addis Abeba on the first leg of their journey to Europe. The itinerary took the travelers, on 24 April, to Jerusalem for a week-long stay, during which the pious Tafari prayed, saw the sights, and then negotiated an agreement permitting Ethiopians priests to say mass at the Greek Orthodox monastery on Mount Golgotha. Then it was on to Egypt, where the Ethiopians had a wonderful time visiting all the tourist attractions. On 9 May, the delegation left Africa behind for France, arriving in Paris on 15 May, to a grand welcome. Regrettably, however, it soon became clear that the Quai d'Orsay was prepared to provide hospitality but no safe harbor for the Ethiopians.

After days of social events and tourism, a frustrated Tafari finally asked his hosts about Ethiopia's access to the sea. He was told that the French minister in Addis Abeba had exceeded his instructions by agreeing even to consider the matter and that any cession would be difficult to arrange in face of the well-organized colonial lobby. When Tafari rejoined that he would try London and Rome, the French ridiculed the possibilities as impractical and dangerous to Ethiopia's sovereignty. As it turned out, the Italians offered a possible ninety-nine-year lease at Aseb in return for communications concessions that would have opened Ethiopia, first to economic infiltration and then to military invasion. As for Great Britain, its prime minister scarcely knew where Ethiopia was, and his staff was so racist that it could not contemplate a valid idea by a black man.

Tafari was dejected by his inability to negotiate a sovereign access to the sea for Ethiopia, but he had learned much from his travels and was eager to return to Ethiopia to apply his new knowledge. When the ras arrived in Addis Abeba on 4 September, the ruling elites sniggered about the mission's failure and grumbled about its high costs. The city's masses did not concern themselves with criticism but enthusiastically welcomed Tafari as the first Ethiopian prince ever to have visited Europe.

Meanwhile, Paris grew uneasy that the ras, in umbrage about the free port, might divert Ethiopia's trade away from Djibouti. In March 1925, in compensation, it strongly supported Ethiopia's appeals in Geneva that it be accorded equality with other members to purchase weapons. Leading a coalition of lesser powers who resented any limitation of sovereignty, France managed to have Ethiopia excluded from arms prohibitions normally prescribed for Africa. Belgium immediately sold one hundred machine guns to Ethiopia, followed quickly by deals with Switzerland and Czechoslovakia. Thus, the trip to Europe bore indirect results through the agency of the league, which also was important in strengthening Ethiopia's claims to sovereignty in 1925–1926.

On 14 December 1925, Rome and London exchanged letters supporting a British-built dam on Lake Tana and Italy's right to construct a railway from Somalia to Eritrea through an exclusive economic zone in the west of Ethiopia. The two powers declared that the undertakings accorded with the provisions of the Tripartite Treaty of 1906, although some officials in the British foreign office appeared embarrassed about negotiating with Italy as if the Addis Abeba government did not exist. The two powers had of course been gulled by the conventional wisdom that there was no state in Ethiopia; that the central administration could not control the provinces, and that the country would soon dissolve into anarchy. Neither London nor Rome was attentive to the traditional excellence of Ethiopian diplomacy or with France's continuing need to restore its prestige in Addis Abeba.

When the Quai d'Orsay learned about the Anglo-Italian initiative, it was quietly jubilant, since the agreements clearly violated Ethiopia's territorial and sovereign rights as defined in the charter of the League of Nations. France unabashedly advised Tafari that the letters sharply altered his nation's political and territorial status in international law. The Ethiopian leadership was outraged, vowed never to recognize the arrangement, and took the matter to the league as a derogation of the sovereign equality of a member state. Addis Abeba blamed the whole affair on Rome, and *Berhanena Selam* waged the first media campaign in Ethiopian history against Italy. Shortly, responsible officials in Rome and London backed away from the extreme claims accepted in the letters and so advised Geneva and Addis Abeba. The Ethiopian government was satisfied that the clarifications safeguarded its sovereignty, and the issue was dropped. Membership in the League of Nations had shielded Ethiopia from the intrigues of the great powers and had given Tafari another triumph. From his experience in 1925–1926, the ras concluded that the league could protect his nation from external threat.

With the death of Habte Giorgis in December 1926, there was no longer any powerful voice for Ethiopian isolationism. Indeed, his demise changed the political landscape, especially in the south, which the fitawrari had dominated for decades. In the region's coffee-growing areas, considerable economic development had occurred, and the old feudal overlords—both settler and indigenous—had become landlords, transforming the traditional agriculturists into sharecroppers or rural proletarians. By the 1920s, the metamorphosis was so complete that the south had become Ethiopia's most important money earner. Nationally, ownership of money had become essential for power in Ethiopia's political economy, and control over southern trade added greatly to the strength of the emergent national oligarchy headed by Tafari.

Whether they were central government officials or provincial rulers, the new men exploited the produce shipped either from the towns that had evolved from Menilek's strategic posts or from new centers built near coffee-growing areas. The townspeople also required food, and their demand stimulated local production, permitting far greater returns than could be obtained from the usual two-party exchanges of small traditional markets. In the south, therefore, enough substantial centers of demand emerged to stimulate regional production, endowing such hitherto subsistence commodities as grain, ensete, and meat animals with the potential of cash crops. Any surplus was shipped, along with coffee, to Addis Abeba.

During 1926–1927, the capital boomed. The money supply grew sharply, imports and exports doubled, and another thirty-five thousand people came to seek work. Many were employed in coffee-sorting warehouses or in tanning plants; others became day laborers who manhandled packaged commodities from warehouses to the railway station for export to Aden and Djibouti for shipment elsewhere. The aristocracy invested in commerce and real estate in the capital, where property values soared. They and an emergent commercial and bureaucratic bourgeoisie began building stone-walled, tin-roofed, and square modern houses that they furnished with locally made or imported European-style furniture. The wealthy among them and many Europeans purchased automobiles, some three hundred of which circulated in the city in 1927, symbolizing Ethiopia's increasing involvement in the world economy.

There were similar signs of growth in the countryside, where local officials built roads and improved communications for the sake of trade. They also facilitated the penetration of Greek, Indian, Arab, and Armenian merchants, who ranged widely buying primary commodities and selling finished products, especially low-cost textiles. From Addis Abeba, the foreigners operated a rudimentary banking system that facilitated financial transactions. Coffee, hides, and other commodities became so profitable that Ethiopia's provincial rulers began thinking in national terms, wanting a strong central government to protect their economic interests.

Tafari, of course, worked hard to strengthen his administration and

Ethiopia's sovereignty. He consistently refused Europeans capitulary rights, arguing instead that Ethiopia's own legal traditions permitted "civilized" judgments. He slowly succeeded in stabilizing the frontier with Kenya, where anarchic hunters, hitherto the shock troops of Ethiopian expansionism, had to be transformed into disciplined border officials. In Ogaden, the government began to establish and occupy posts to the discomfort of the Italians, who had stations located in Ethiopian territory. Tafari delayed complaining about the incursions, since in 1928, he negotiated an agreement with Rome that apparently strengthened Ethiopia's security.

The Italians, however, regarded the twenty-year Treaty of Friendship and Arbitration of 2 August 1928 as a vehicle for Ethiopia's economic penetration. Addis Abeba obtained a free zone at Aseb, Italy a road connection from the Eritrean frontier to Dese, and both pledged to take problems to the League of Nations for arbitration and conciliation. Rome, however, never intended the league to interpret its relations with Addis Abeba. It aimed to ensure a vital economic hinterland for Somalia and Eritrea, by associating the two impoverished colonies with Ethiopia's obvious growth and modernization. On the other side, Addis Abeba never wanted the Italian road from the sea, a natural invasion route, to be built. Tafari signed the treaty to obtain Italy's long-term pledge of peace and friendship and a mechanism for conciliation and arbitration. The unstated agenda was too clever by half, since Ethiopia's refusal to abide by the stipulations of the 1928 agreement led to frustration and then to bitterness in Rome. Denied peaceful penetration, Italy ultimately would turn to war.

It was not the only policy that backfired. Tafari sought to break Europe's economic dominance of the Ethiopian economy by seeking new and less dangerous trading partners. He turned inevitably to India, Japan and the United States: by 1927–1928, the first two accounted for most of Ethiopia's imports and the last took most of the country's exports of hides and coffee. France, which traditionally had been a major trading partner, retained only 4 percent of the import market. The Quai d'Orsay reacted by reviewing France's role in Ethiopia and concluded that its interests there had become worthless, even though its intervention had safeguarded Addis Abeba's international rights. If France's investments in Djibouti and the railway could be guaranteed, then Paris might be able to barter its position in Ethiopia for substantial Italian concessions elsewhere. France's alienation was perhaps inevitable, given Ethiopia's economic policies, but foresight in Addis Abeba and sensitive diplomacy might have retained an important ally. The myopia was also present in negotiations with London about a Lake Tana dam.

Logic demanded that Tafari permit Britain to develop enough interests in Ethiopia to want to protect both its investments and Addis Abeba's sovereignty. Yet, when London proposed a barrage on Lake Tana to improve the Blue Nile's flow for irrigating Sudan's cotton-growing Gezira region, Tafari's reaction bordered on xenophobia. To get the project moving, London finally agreed that a private American company should do the work. Thus, Britain had no real interests to safeguard in Ethiopia beyond ensuring that the Blue Nile not be impeded. Tafari's strategy of reducing the importance of the Tripartite states thus divested Ethiopia of important protection. The unanticipated consequences revealed that in international relations his hand then lacked the deftness so obvious in domestic politics.

Tafari had consolidated his hold over the provinces, leading in 1928 to conflict with the old order. Many of Menilek's appointees refused to abide by new regulations concerning issuing written receipts for taxes collected. Dej. Balcha (1862–1936) of coffee-rich Sidamo was particularly troublesome, since he and his lieutenants had greatly improved provincial administration, and they had cooperated with Indian traders to establish a relatively efficient marketing and credit system. The revenues Balcha remitted to Addis Abeba did not reflect accrued profits, however, and when many peasants complained that the governor's men declined to issue receipts, Tafari recalled him to Addis Abeba.

The old man came in high dudgeon and, insultingly, with a large army, but he found no support from either the empress, currently ailing from diabetes and liver complications, or the capital magnates, now mostly Tafari's men. The ras quickly convened a crown council, which voted to remove Balcha from Sidamo and to confiscate his property and wealth. On 18 February 1928, the old man's camp on the outskirts of Addis Abeba was surrounded; when the council's decision was read out, most of Balcha's army deserted, and its leader was forced to surrender. Dej. Balcha's various holdings were doled out to Tafari's men, among them his son-in-law Fit. Desta Demtew (later ras; 1892–1937), who became ruler of Sidamo.

In September, a group of palace reactionaries, including some of the empress's courtiers, made a final effort to be rid of Tafari. The attempted coup was tragic in its origins and comic in its end: Tafari and about a company of troops surrounded the ringleaders who had taken refuge on the palace grounds in Menilek's mausoleum, only to be encircled by Zawditu's guard, who were subsequently ringed by the regent's khaki-clad soldiers, well armed with newly imported rifles, machine guns, small cannon, and an obsolete but menacing tank. Modernity easily won the day over conservatism, and not surprisingly, on 22 September 1928, Zawditu elevated Tafari to a kingship with full powers. His coronation was on 6 October, an event that soured Ras Gugsa Wolie (1887–1930), the empress's erstwhile husband.

He stayed put in Begemdir, resentful of the central government, which had caused his separation from Zawditu and had banned his presence from Addis Abeba. Embittered and isolated, Gugsa was not a party to the economic and political changes sweeping the empire. Completely out of step with Tafari's progressivism, he scorned the young Ethiopians running the country, belittling their Western education as un-Ethiopian. The ras was also troubled about Tafari's use of foreign experts and advisers, reasoning that their presence wrongly indicated that Ethiopians were incapable of administering their increasingly complex country. As long as Gugsa remained aloof and noncontroversial, however, the government abided his criticism and contempt.

In early 1929, he failed, however, to put down an uprising among starving Muslim pastoralists and Christian farmers in arid and semiarid regions in Welo and Tigray. The people there suffered not only from drought and locusts but also from provincial and local officials who refused tax relief. The crisis quickly took on class, religious, and ethnic overtones: rich and poor struggled for resources, Muslims and Christians fought, and pastoralists battled for water holes and scarce pasturage. Gugsa proved unable to suppress the rebellion, and when he was called to Dese for consultations, he balked, since he believed that he would be made the scapegoat for the crisis.

As the ras considered his continuing misfortune, he focused his frustration on the hated King Tafari, pondered the disagreeable present and the more unpleasant future, and raised the flag of rebellion. Addis Abeba quickly reacted by proclaiming Gugsa an outlaw and immediately called up troops. When mediation failed, the imperial army moved northward to arrive in Dese in late February 1929. Its presence had a noticeably chilling effect, especially on Gugsa's men, many of whom quickly deserted, although the ras remained defiant. In mid-March, the imperial army, under Dej. Mulugeta Yigazu (later ras; 1865–1936), since

1926 the minister of war, marched on Gugsa's stronghold of Debre Tabor and unleashed its secret weapon, an aircraft equipped with bombs.

The biplane followed rebel movements and also terrorized Gugsa's remaining soldiers. On the morning of 31 March, the Imperial Ethiopian Air Force, in the guise of one plane piloted by a Frenchman, made three bombing runs over Gugsa's army. The ten thousand men broke and ran, leaving the ras unprotected on his prominent white charger: he drew fire, was shot several times, and killed. The empress never knew that her husband was gone, since she was unconscious when the news was announced in the capital on 1 April. King Tafari was by her side when she died early morning the next day from paratyphoid fever, complicated by diabetes and the strict Lenten diet. The abun conducted her funeral that night in Menilek's mausoleum, where she was interred. The next day, the crown council proclaimed Tafari emperor.

TEN

Haile Sellassie, to 1936

Tafari took his baptismal name, Haile Sellassie (Power of the Trinity), for his reign and adapted his personality to conform to his new status. He believed the sovereign embodied tradition as the symbol of the nation, and his posture stiffened, especially on the throne. He chose the heavy decorum of the Swedish court and surrounded himself with ceremony in which the form often defeated substance. He attributed his success to destiny and invoked the deity often as he strove to build a centralized government, a modern professional army, a national system of communications, and prominent public works in Addis Abeba. Though the emperor's metier was power, he also believed heartily in progress.

He undertook an ambitious road-building program to link the capital to every economically important province and to tie commercial centers into a national grid. He built several new schools in Addis Abeba and proclaimed his faith in Ethiopia's youth. Many of the graduates joined newly opened provincial offices of the Ministry of Finance and the Customs Service. The central government's growing ability to gain its fair share of provincial revenues, otherwise lost to local officials, permitted Haile Sellassie to marshal, even during the nadir of the Great Depression, sufficient resources to pay for his programs.

In his rush to reform, the emperor hired foreign advisers: he cleverly put an Englishman in the Ministry of Interior, to supervise the antislavery campaign, thus endearing himself to Britain's influential antislavery zealots. A Frenchman went to the Ministry of Posts, Telegraphs, and Telephones, an organization long associated with French training and techniques. By 1930, Ethiopia employed two French advisers, one Englishman, one American, one German, one Greek, and two Swiss. For short-term jobs in Europe, the government hired well-respected experts, such as the Frenchman Gaston Jèze, who guided Addis Abeba toward an arms-purchasing treaty with the Tripartite powers.

By 1929, Britain had come to believe that a strengthened Ethiopian state, with a reliable supply of modern weapons, might be able to control its frontiers. France agreed, and Italy was finally pressured into reconsideration, when Addis Abeba declared that purchases would be limited annually to £300,000–£400,000, spent mostly on rifles, rapid-fire weapons, light field pieces, and armored vehicles. Addis Abeba was concerned solely with internal security, and its procurement would not threaten adjacent colonies. The new arms treaty, signed on 21 August 1930, was a victory for Ethiopia, which the Tripartite powers treated for the first time as a fully sovereign state freely exercising its power to ensure its own domestic tranquility.

Now the emperor sought religious liberty, but failed. He wanted a native primate but settled for an Egyptian metropolitan when the see of Saint Mark agreed to consecrate five Ethiopian bishops to serve in the provinces. He was more successful when he tried to achieve national control over Ethiopia's currency. In 1929, the economy once again had suffered when the value of the Maria Theresa dollar tumbled along with silver's international price. To put an end to a specie that had a variable intrinsic value, Haile Sellassie decided to transform the Bank of Abyssinia, a government-chartered, private organization, into a currency-issuing state bank. Although largely moribund and capital-depleted, the bank's holding company, the National Bank of Egypt, insisted on a selling price of £190,000. The emperor emptied out his own pockets, swept the exchequer clean, and paid the price in two installments in time for the new Bank of Ethiopia to open for business on 1 July 1931.

Finally, Haile Sellassie began to regulate foreign activities by requiring entry visas for visitors, registration for commercial firms operating in Ethiopia, and the licensing of all lawyers appearing in the Special Court that handled cases between nationals and aliens. He was particularly rigid about insisting on the jurisdiction of Ethiopian courts, although the Tripartite powers stubbornly insisted that a mistranslated article in the

Franco-Ethiopian (Klobukowski) Commercial Treaty of 1908 gave them capitulatory rights. The Special Court always sought to accommodate its European clientele, but it operated as an Ethiopian institution, to the considerable distress of the prideful legations, whose racist members delighted in describing the government's law as savage and primitive.

Meanwhile, the emperor worked to reform the government. Ras Kassa's appointment to Begemdir heralded a new relationship between the sovereign and his agents because Tafari assumed the authority to name the mayor and head of merchants for Gonder. Their responsibilities over social and economic life considerably reduced the autonomy of the office of governor. Kassa's acceptance of a diminished role reflected his conviction—no less than Haile Sellassie's—that Ethiopian officialdom should place Addis Abeba's needs before personal ambitions in the process of building a modern state.

The emperor's coronation in November 1930 was designed to advertise his regime's progress. The new monarch determined to make the event a debut for the revitalized and renewed state he headed. This decision, made at a time of economic crisis, when most of the government's programs remained incomplete or unstarted, reflected the emperor's faith in his destiny and in the ability of his people. Haile Sellassie took charge of the preparations, supervising public works; helping to design coronation vestments, symbols of state, and uniforms; and collecting "donations" from noblemen and merchants toward the estimated £300,000 that the week-long extravaganza would cost. The bulk of the work was done in September–October, when activities were spurred in expectation of the arrival of thousands of official guests and visitors.

The city transformed itself, but most astonishing of all was the metamorphosis of the police and the Imperial Bodyguard, who shucked off their tatters and appeared in smart, new khaki uniforms. Miracles were everywhere: triumphal arches rose on the main thoroughfares, electric lines suddenly appeared, telephones were installed in strategic locations, streets were graded and paved overnight, and, in some cases, sidewalks were laid down. The preparations were completed in the nick of time, and many remarked about the capital's relative newness. Meanwhile the city had filled with representatives of the empire's peoples, and they spent much of their time at the railway station watching the emperor and other members of the royal family welcoming distinguished arrivals.

Shortly after dawn on 2 November, Ethiopian dignitaries in resplendent uniforms escorted foreign envoys to Saint George's Cathedral for the coronation. They made their way through streets decorated in green, yellow, and red, the national colors, and filled with people attired in their traditional best. At 8:00 A.M., the Empress Menen and Emperor Haile Sellassie entered a large tent from inside the cathedral, where they had kept a nightlong vigil. Chanting clerics led the couple to their thrones, and the ceremonies began. At 10:00 A.M., after much praying and reading from the Scriptures, Haile Sellassie was crowned, followed by the investiture of the crown prince, the empress, and the royal family. At the end of the ceremony, a visiting British naval band played the newly composed national anthem, a 101-gun salute was fired, and Ethiopia's great men made formal obeisance. Then the newly minted emperor and empress climbed into the state coach for a two-mile journey through Addis Abeba to show themselves to the people before taking a well-deserved rest.

The next week was spent in ceremonial events, feasts, and receptions. On 7 December, the city's masses were present at a huge military review held at the imperial parade grounds. The emperor, gorgeously uniformed as a field marshal, happily presided as tens of thousands of Ethiopia's warriors passed the pavilion in which he and his foreign guests sat. From time to time, an officer would rush up to the emperor and shout out or pantomime his feats of bravery against wild beast or enemy, while simultaneously declaiming his fealty. The self-praise was in Amharic, which was fortunate for Rome's envoy, since several of the older men recounted how many Europeans they had killed during the war of 1894–1896. Still, the Italians took comfort in seeing that only one oversized battalion of modern troops marched past. Armed with current rifles, light machine guns, and mountain howitzers, they and their khaki uniforms signaled the emperor's commitment to change, the demonstration of which was one of the coronation's objectives.

The ceremony and events had been unabashedly modern, although Ethiopian in execution, symbolizing the amalgam that Haile Sellassie sought to refine through his administration. The successful completion of the coronation demonstrated the government's ability to mobilize and organize its population and resources. The Addis Abeba regime became credible to the Europeans, whose presence at the coronation was evidence enough for Ethiopians that the world recognized their nation's sovereignty and independence, thereby confirming the correctness of Haile Sellassie's foreign policy since 1916. The emperor was quick to exploit his new stature by reforming his government.

He replaced a number of old-style administrators with Young Ethiopians: Makonnen Habte Wolde (1895–1960) became director general in the Ministry of Finance under another educated man, Bejirond Tekle Wolde Hawariat (1900–1969). For director of the Ministry of War, Haile Sellassie appointed the controversial Dej. Nasibu Zamanuel (d. 1936), often attacked as un-Ethiopian because he was a mission-educated Catholic, spoke Italian and French, and wore modish European clothes and uniforms. The emperor cared only for his efficiency and his reformer's zeal.

In sharp contrast was Blattengeta Herui Wolde Sellassie (1878–1938), the new Minister of Foreign Affairs, a gregarious intellectual who spent his life in the emperor's service. His advancement foreshadowed a significant development in Ethiopia's international relations, since the emperor hired a well-qualified adviser and authorized representation in London, Paris, and Rome. The more complex foreign relations required that the troublesome issue of slavery be resolved. Haile Sellassie appointed his nephew to the newly formed administration of Maji and Goldiya, adjacent to both Kenya and Sudan. The fierce slave raiding in the area had spilled across frontiers, antagonizing a generation of colonial officials. By selecting a close relative as governor, the emperor signaled the imminent renewal of Ethiopian authority in the borderlands.

On 16 July 1931, Haile Sellassie capped his reforms by promulgating a Japanese-style constitution, whose fifty-five articles enshrined the rule of law while acknowledging the emperor's ultimate power to delegate authority to other institutions such as a two-house parliament. After Haile Sellassie had signed the document, representatives of the country's ruling classes appended their endorsements. Never before had a monarch achieved such a broad national consensus, a theme of unity the emperor mentioned often in his speech inaugurating the document. Despite all its problems and assertions of imperial supremacy, the constitution was a progressive statement that established a framework for a modern government. Haile Sellassie stressed this theme and the need for national unity on 3 November, when he presided over the official opening of parliament.

The institutionalization of the modern national government gave the emperor the authority to move against an outstanding anachronism, Abba Jifar II of Jima. Menilek had guaranteed his autonomy in 1884 in return for an annual tribute. Haile Sellassie's government lost patience

20. Haile Sellassie opening parliament in 1934. Reprinted from Eric Virgin, *The Abyssinia I Knew* (London: Macmillan, 1936).

with the old man and trumped up charges that Jima was developing an army to challenge its authority. On 12 May imperial troops invaded, and in July 1932, the emperor's son-in-law, the newly elevated Ras Desta Demtew, was named governor, with Abba Jifar the titular ruler.

Next to fall was Ras Hailu of Gojam, who had made a great success of the new national economy. Not only had he shrewdly invested in real estate in the capital but he and his family also dominated Gojam's economy. Moreover, he had exploited his administrative autonomy by negotiating independently with the Italians, who came to believe that Ethiopia's rases might be bought. Rome was always willing to weaken the national government, and the emperor increasingly came to regard Hailu as a security risk. As the putative enemy of the state, the ras became a victim to be mulcted of his last dollar. The emperor detained him in the capital after the coronation, so there was little Hailu could do to save himself.

Hailu's economic policies had alienated many Gojamis, and a number came to Addis Abeba to voice their criticisms and to seek imperial intervention. Not surprisingly, Haile Sellassie sided with the plaintiffs, fining the ras tens of thousands of dollars for misgovernment. In one notable case of April 1932, the emperor penalized him MT$300,000 and also divested him of half of Gojam. Still at liberty, Hailu hatched a plot to free Lij Iyasu, then to betray him to the emperor, who would gratefully return what rightfully belonged him. The scheme was foolhardy and unworkable, and from the start it was a botched job. Lij Iyasu did manage to escape from Fitche, but the emperor quickly learned that Hailu was behind it all. When Iyasu was recaptured, the ras was consigned to jail, and the state confiscated the rest of his property and wealth.

By 1932, Haile Sellassie enjoyed unchallenged ascendancy in Ethiopia. He had constructed a central government totally reliant on the crown for policy and direction. His men in the provinces implemented imperial policy, backed by an increasingly effective army and air force. The aristocracy was with him, appreciating the prosperity guaranteed them by his nation building, but they were uncomfortable with his reserve, which the emperor brandished as a political weapon. Aloofness allowed him to maneuver among competing factions and to govern indirectly through a few well-chosen henchmen. He also controlled the flow of information by withholding news, manipulating reports, or distorting the truth. By so doing, he could easily respond to the barrage of competition caused by his behavior, here choosing one side, there the other, creating and dissolving a series of shifting coalitions. Throughout, Haile Sellassie maintained himself as the country's sole fount of authority, effective enough, so the Italians often observed, to lead his backward empire to modernity and international legitimacy.

During 1931–1934, the emperor was busy implementing schemes that augured well for the future. There was a whirlwind of activity: projects and planning fell into place for roads, schools, hospitals, communications, administration, and public services. Given Ethiopia's limited resources and educated manpower, projects were mostly privately financed: the emperor, the royal family, the aristocracy, the national and foreign bourgeoisie, all profited from investments in transport companies or toll-road construction consortia. By mid-1934, the Addis Abeba–Jima road had passed the Omo River and was growing daily; Harer-Jijiga was completed; and Mojo-Sidamo was finished and being extended to Mega. The government was laying down a strategic network of tracks in Ogaden; and Ras Desta Demtew had completed rough tracks from Sidamo to Moyale via Mega, making it possible for trucks to travel from Addis Abeba to Nairobi.

The combined effect was to open the country to the world economy: by 1932, revenues were pouring into Addis Abeba from export taxes applied to twenty-five thousand tons of coffee, triple the amount shipped in 1928, but given the depression, only one-third more in money terms; from the recently opened provincial offices of the Ministry of Finance; and from reorganized customs stations that applied new, higher tariffs. In response to the growing national economy, the government replaced the Maria Theresa dollar with paper currency and coins issued by the Bank of Ethiopia. Since the modern sector was largely located in towns, the government could effectively force traders to use the money.

In September 1933, the new bank banned the private import and export of the Maria Theresa dollars, finally freeing Ethiopia from the international silver market. Henceforth, when the value of silver changed, the Bank of Ethiopia could alter currency reserve requirements and sell its surplus dollars for foreign exchange. Given such control, the bank could raise funds to cover the government's short-term needs by issuing bonds and other bills against its reserves. The fiscal reforms helped the government to finance its military modernization.

In 1932, Addis Abeba informed the Tripartite powers that it would purchase approximately £150,000 worth of machine guns, rifles, and ammunition. The piddling amount nonetheless distressed the Italians, who were already disturbed by the modern military training under way in Addis Abeba and other towns. By early 1933, a Belgian mission had readied a 2,250-man imperial guard for rapid deployment in company strength to Gojam and other trouble spots. Later that year, Ethiopia's first two Saint Cyr–trained officers, three of the Belgians, and fourteen noncoms from the imperial guard left for Goba in Bale to train an internal security force for deployment along the frontier. Rome's military attaché in Addis Abeba complained that the new military center, 230 miles away from the nearest Italian outpost, threatened Somalia. For home consumption, he exaggerated Ethiopia's battle readiness, its weaponry, and its training. In fact, by September 1934—two months before the crisis with Italy began—only three thousand troops were trained and equipped for modern warfare, and it was not until December that five Swedish officers came to open a military academy.

After 1931, the Italians worked to create an environment in which they might be able to destroy Ethiopia's independence. The Addis Abeba government unwittingly assisted by sharply raising duties on luxury imports, most of which came from France. Officialdom in Paris immediately began reconsidering France's relations with Ethiopia and concluded that it might be time to transfer its interests there to the Italians. Rome had the resources to help build a modern Ethiopia, and the French hoped that involvement would dissipate Italy's nationalistic energies harmlessly and distract Mussolini from the intrigues and uncertainties of European great power politics. Except for the railway from Djibouti, France had no vital interest in the Horn of Africa.

Paris reasoned that Italy might be granted a free hand in Ethiopia in return for concessions in Tunisia, where Rome exercised an annoying extraterritorial jurisdiction over Italian nationals. Throughout 1931, France's hitherto cordial relations with Ethiopia grew cool, to the emperor's anxiety. In early 1932, Paris rebuffed his efforts to improve the situation, explaining to its minister in Addis Abeba that nothing could be permitted to disrupt France's inter-European relations. While France was in the process of abandoning Ethiopia to Mussolini, Haile Sellassie was confronting Italy by ordering his army to move into Ogaden to counter infiltration from Somalia.

As early as 1925, the Italians had taken control over a line of strategic water holes defined by the settlements of Geregube, Welwel, Warder, and Geladi. By late October 1926, the regularity of Italian patrols from these places had become obvious and had elicited an Ethiopian protest. In June 1927, Addis Abeba sent an expedition into the region, but it was subsequently recalled when talks began for the Italo-Ethiopian Treaty of 1928. During the negotiations, Mussolini refused to consider any textual references to delimitation of the frontiers between Somalia and Ethiopia, since he hoped to add to Italian holdings.

By 1932, the advance had been considerable, and the Italians had even built a road from Danot to Geladi over terrain that contemporary maps placed in Ethiopia. A clash was inevitable, since imperial forces aimed to establish government at all levels, to open administrative offices and markets at all important water holes and wells, and to build roads, especially between Jijiga, Degeh Bur, and Korahe. In early 1934, the Ethiopians neared the Italian outposts, eliciting a protest that the imperial forces had impinged on Italian territory, although Rome refused to define the extent of its holdings. The emperor decided therefore to use an imminent Anglo-Ethiopian frontier demarcation to reveal the extent of Italian infiltration into sovereign Solomonic territory.

Article 4 of the Italo-Ethiopian Treaty of 16 May 1908 stipulated that territories inhabited mainly by clans dominating the coast should fall within Mogadishu's sovereignty, which, according to the subsequently disputed Italo-Ethiopian Agreement of 1897, followed a line not more than 130 miles inland. In no way, therefore, could Warder and Welwel be considered Italian territory. The British were fully aware of the dispute and interested in learning the extent of Italian penetration, but not at the expense of a major row with Rome. On 22–23 November 1934, the Anglo-Ethiopian demarcation team reached Welwel and encamped close to the Italian perimeter, near the wells.

The Italian commander complained that the commission's arrival was a complete surprise and refused to deal with the Ethiopians as equals. That afternoon, when two Italian planes buzzed the mission's camps, the British decided to retire northwest to Ado and the Ethiopians to dig in. A war of nerves ensued, with both sides shouting insults and threats until the Italians, obviously acting under orders, attacked during the afternoon of 5 December. After two days of fighting against planes and armored cars—man against machine, the theme of the subsequent war—the Ethiopians were beaten, taking many casualties, and the survivors retreated.

In September 1934, Mussolini had decided to take Ethiopia, so the Welwel incident provided an excellent basis for further action, although it remains uncertain whether the Italians then wanted war. Ethiopia immediately called for arbitration according to the Treaty of 1928, which Rome refused, arguing irrationally that Ethiopia's *aggression* rendered Article 4 moot. When Italy insisted on a number of demeaning conditions to resolve the matter, Haile Sellassie looked to the League of Nations, complaining that Italian forces had no right being within Ethiopia's frontiers. Almost from the crisis's onset, there was little chance of a peaceful settlement because in December Mussolini decided on war as the best way to destroy Ethiopia's potential threat. In his opinion, Italy would have to act before mid-1937, when Germany would have regained sufficient strength to take the initiative in Europe. First, however, Italy had to seek France's neutrality in any adventure in the Horn of Africa.

During the past few years, Paris had been signaling its willingness to negotiate about Ethiopia. There had been some preliminary discussions and agreement in principle, which permitted Premier Pierre Laval and Mussolini to conclude a formal pact on 7 January 1935 that conceded France's disinterest in Ethiopia—*the free hand long sought by the Italians*—for abandonment of Rome's rights over its subjects in Tunisia and an ephemeral military alliance in case Hitler moved against Austria. As of January 1935, none of the other powers, whether alone or united, could have stopped Italy from its war in Ethiopia. Most observers, however, did not foresee that eventuality, since they reasoned that Ethiopia would make concessions rather than fight a major European power. They were not only ignorant of Ethiopia's historic refusal to abandon its independence but they also were mostly racists who considered blacks incompetent and irresponsible. They did not reckon on the steel spine of Haile Sellassie and his compatriots' deeply entrenched anti-Italian attitudes.

Rome, meanwhile, was calling up troops and otherwise preparing for war, while simultaneously proclaiming its peaceful intentions. In Addis Abeba, the emperor resisted the mounting evidence: he had neither sufficient money, weapons, nor enough trained troops to contain a modern force. True, he could call up a traditional Ethiopian levy of five hundred thousand men, but such a mobilization was, the emperor knew, an act of defeat. He could no longer rely on France, which in March 1935 had barred transshipment of war matériel from Djibouti, contrary to all relevant treaties. His only option was to continue to trust the league's promise of collective security.

In Geneva, the Ethiopians charged that Italy was using a small incident as a pretext for war. Rome stonewalled all accusations and, as a matter of policy, lied, dissimulated, and repeatedly sought to postpone all debate. Slowly, the Ethiopian government came to realize that the Italians would use the league's time-consuming procedures as a convenient blind to prepare for war. To say that the league was working against Ethiopia's interests would be generous. The council's major powers tried to force humiliating concessions on Ethiopia so that an appeased Italy might then serve the needs of continental politics. Neither France nor Britain understood that to accommodate Mussolini beyond a certain point

21. Haile Sellassie reviewing troops in 1935.
Reprinted from Geoffrey Harmsworth, *Abyssinian Adventure* (London: Hutchinson and Co., 1935).

would destroy the league's credibility, the plausibility of collective security, and the European balance of power.

The ruin became obvious at a meeting in Stresa in April 1935. The conference had two objectives: to return Germany to legitimacy and to demonstrate the solidarity of Britain, Italy, and France in European matters. Stresa was blithely unconcerned with the world's nooks and crannies, or even with the developing crisis in the Horn of Africa, to Mussolini's considerable surprise. The Italian twice asked whether the final statement about collective security and the inviolability of treaties applied solely to Europe. The silence signaled that Italy could go to war with its European rear covered, permitting Rome to become more bellicose in May, when the major powers banned arms sales to the belligerents, a measure that hurt only Ethiopia.

In Addis Abeba, the emperor remained calm as he planned for an unwinnable war. Wherever he went, his officers demanded weapons, munitions, food, armored cars, fuel, anything to use against the enemy. He doled out the little he had, but he and his more realistic generals knew that Ethiopia could not withstand a modern force supported by aircraft armed with poison gas. Diplomats in Geneva, London, and Paris hoped this obvious conclusion would soften Ethiopia's unwillingness to consider concessions to Italy. Haile Sellassie refused any deal, hoping that the great powers would come to their senses and intervene, realizing that Ethiopia's destruction would destroy the league. Meanwhile, he developed a defensive strategy that relied on hit-and-run tactics on the flanks and behind enemy lines to generate casualties and chaos and sap the Italian will to continue. Avoidance of positional warfare was a sound tactic, though it countered traditional Ethiopian military wisdom.

Meanwhile, appeasement was the order of day in Europe, where most statesmen avoided alienating Italy out of fear of Nazi Germany. London reasoned, furthermore, that it had no interests in Ethiopia worth intervention, and in France, Laval was committed to his Italian ally. The league therefore came up with solutions tending to favor the Italians, who, by early September had 200,000 men in the Horn and another 140,000 being processed for travel there. On 25 September, the emperor announced that Ethiopian troops would remain thirty kilometers from the frontiers to avoid incidents and pretexts for fighting. He nevertheless had signed a decree for general mobilization, which he kept locked in his desk, hoping against all reality for a diplomatic resolution to the crisis. He formalized the order on 2 October, when he learned that the Italians had crossed the frontiers into Awsa.

The next morning, a stream of Ethiopians and European journalists made their way to the emperor's palace in response to the thudding of Menilek's great war drum, the old way of calling up the army. When the booming stopped, the court chamberlain clearly and loudly read out the mobilization order to a sober crowd. Haile Sellassie called on his people to fight for their national existence and their religion, without which they would be like the serfs of Somalia and Eritrea. He advised his soldiers to be cunning and not to wear white, or attend mass. As the crowd broke up, the news circulated that the Italians had invaded Tigray and the war was on.

At 5:00 A.M., 100,000 Italian troops under Gen. Emilio De Bono had crossed the Mareb River in three formations along a sixty-mile front. The

Italian advance developed quickly because the border region was undefended, and Ethiopian commanders had orders to retire until mobilization would bring reinforcements. On 6 October, the Italians entered Adwa, after two days of bombing had shocked Ras Seyoum into a hasty retreat and the abandonment of large stocks of food and other supplies. The humiliation was followed by dishonor at Mekele, when Dej. Haile Sellassie Gugsa defected with 1,500 well-armed men. By 15 October, the Italians entered lightly defended Axum, which they garrisoned, and then slowly moved toward the Tekeze. On the Ogaden front, however, the Italians encountered stiff opposition.

Ethiopian troops at Korahe quickly learned to cope with air attacks by diving into deep trenches, and they had sufficient modern arms to thwart assaults on the ground and to inflict heavy losses. Their morale broke, however, when Gerazmach Afework, their valiant and intelligent leader, was mortally wounded on 5 November. Thereafter, the Italians soon dominated, although Gen. Rodolfo Graziani came to respect his enemy's fighting abilities. He therefore paused to regroup, to rethink his strategy, and to consolidate his rear before marching on the 60,000 men that Dej. Nasibu commanded in the Harer-Jijiga–Degeh Bur triangle. With the lull in fighting came a flurry of diplomatic activity to end the crisis.

On 7 October 1935, the council of the League of Nations formally found Italy an *aggressor*, thereby raising the issue of sanctions. The French blocked any but the most anodyne measures while Mussolini blustered that he would accept peace only if Ethiopia ceded Menilek's conquests, eastern Tigray, and Ogaden—in return for which he would graciously permit Haile Sellassie to follow Italian advice in ruling his rump state. The emperor answered by holding a massive military review during which all manner of troops marched past, including fierce provincial fighters armed only with sharpened sticks. From the parade ground, a quarter of a million Ethiopians marched northward to block the Italian advance.

On 18 November 1935, Geneva imposed relatively benign import and export sanctions on Italy, which Mussolini used to rally his people to the war. Restrictions on oil sales might have had some effect, but Paris complained that such an embargo was a military, not a civil, sanction. This sophism was matched by the efforts of Sir Samuel Hoare, the British foreign minister, and Premier Laval to forge an arrangement that would satisfy Mussolini without giving the appearance of rewarding aggression and placate Haile Sellassie without signifying that honor and territory had been lost. On 7 December 1935—six years before another day of infamy—the two men announced a scheme of territorial cessions and Italian economic primacy that added up to appeasement in new verbiage. Although never implemented—indeed it met with worldwide rejection—the Hoare-Laval plan's cynical disregard for Ethiopia's fate destroyed any chance of bringing the crisis to a just end.

In mid-December, Haile Sellassie decided to attack in Tigray to test Gen. Pietro Badoglio, the new Italian commander who had replaced the slow and careful De Bono. He ordered Rases Kassa and Seyoum to push forward frontally into Italian-occupied Tigray, while Ras Mulugeta would move eastward to outflank the enemy at Mekele and to cut his supply lines. The plan worked well enough to leave Ethiopians entrenched in Temben but failed to disrupt the Italian rear. While the rases could claim victory, Badoglio had stopped the attack on 21–22 December by using poison gas bombs, foreshadowing the devastating Italian attacks to come. The first massive use of this potent weapon fell, however, on the southern front against Ras Desta Demtew's army.

From mid-December, Graziani carried out an *active defense* so vigorously that it became an offense. The Italians bombarded Ethiopian forward positions with clouds of gas, causing immense casualties and massive desertions. By 6 January, Desta reported imminent disaster for his troops, now dug in on both banks of the Juba, sixty miles north of Dolo. Graziani's attack on 10 January turned into a rout: thousands of Ethiopians were killed, and the survivors fled into the countryside after abandoning their weapons and supplies. Unaware that he could march easily into Ethiopia's soft underbelly, Graziani halted his advance to consolidate his gains, allowing the emperor to send reinforcements. Haile Sellassie refused to join the criticism of his son-in-law, realizing that the defeat had been caused by modern weapons and tactics, not by lack of courage or soldierly ability.

On 28 November, the emperor had left Addis Abeba for Dese, where he established his headquarters. He worked from morning to night trying to construct a winning strategy. He was mostly a patient leader, who emanated sangfroid and detachment from the crisis surrounding him. He was personally courageous, often leaving shelter for his personal anti-aircraft gun to rattle away, perhaps, at Mussolini's son. The enemy daily bombed the supply lines from Dese north, which traumatized the local Oromo, who rebelled when the military requisitioned most of their food and animals. Try as he might, the emperor was unable to secure his army's rear, as insurgent strength kept pace with peasant frustrations.

From 10 February, the increasing instability stimulated a persistent Italian offensive, which used air power and poison gas to separate, flank, and destroy the Ethiopian armies one by one. Within a four-week period, Badoglio's forces conquered Ras Mulugeta at Amba Aradam, demolished Ras Kassa's army at a second battle in Temben, and defeated Ras Imru in Shire. The rapidity of the debacle confounded most observers, among them the emperor, whose small, elite army now stood between the Italians and Addis Abeba. Instead of following his own advice and waging guerrilla warfare while withdrawing to Addis Abeba, Haile Sellassie chose to march north with his rear guard and to fight an unwinnable battle at Maychew, in extreme southern Tigray, directly in the path of the Italian advance.

The terrain there was all wrong for an attack, but a victory would vindicate the emperor, and a defeat might permit a soldier's death, converting him from monarch to martyr. By now, Haile Sellassie had little to lose; he was angry and frustrated, deeply wounded by the national calamity and morally outraged by the devastating use of poison gas against Ethiopia's peoples. He decided on an act of defiance, throwing an estimated forty thousand well-armed men, including five thousand modern troops, against a rapidly concentrating Italian mass. Through intercepted messages, Badoglio learned of his enemy's intentions and prepared his forces accordingly. There was no surprise, therefore, when Ethiopia's last organized force in the north began advancing at 4:00 A.M. on 31 March 1936.

From the start, the attack was a disaster, though so hard fought that the Italians did not immediately pursue the retreating enemy. By the evening of 3 April, however, mounting Italian pressure forced the emperor and his escort to move southward or be captured. The retreat was a nightmare, since the vengeful Oromo shot stragglers with Italian-supplied rifles and otherwise harassed the survivors, and on 4 April the Italians opened a day-long air attack with bombs and gas that completely broke the remnants of the Ethiopian army. Haile Sellassie survived the day but was so affected that he suffered a breakdown, stopping at Lalibela to seek divine guidance and wisdom about Ethiopia's defeat. Back in the capital, a crown council was deciding that the emperor and his family should go abroad to symbolize Ethiopia's refusal to accept defeat.

When Haile Sellassie returned to Addis Abeba on 30 April, he met with the council and was forced to accept its logic that as long as the sovereign was free and unbowed, Italian rule in Ethiopia could have no legitimacy.

For the monarch to remain in the country chanced a humiliating capture, death, or, even worse, submission to the conqueror. At 4:00 A.M. on 2 May 1936, a special train carrying the imperials left the capital for Djibouti, where it arrived on 3 May. The next day, the emperor, his family, and ranking officials boarded a British war vessel for five troubled years of exile and self-doubt in England. They left behind a nation that fought on against the Italians.

ELEVEN

Haile Sellassie, to 1955

When Addis Abeba learned that the imperial family had gone into exile, law and order broke down. An enraged and frustrated mob rampaged through the city's commercial center killing, looting, and burning. The arrival of the Italians on 5 May ended the rage, and, on 9 May, Mussolini proclaimed the Ethiopian Italian Empire before an enthusiastic throng in Rome. On 11 June, Marshal Rodolfo Graziani was named viceroy of Ethiopia, replacing Marshal Badoglio, who left for Rome.

The victory, however, remained incomplete; before entraining, Haile Sellassie had named Ras Imru regent and had established a provisional government in western Welega. It commanded the relatively large forces of Ras Desta Demtew and remnants of the north's defeated armies. During the rains of 1936, while the Italians were trying to consolidate their hold on northern and central Ethiopia, Ethiopian forces mounted a series of local attacks in Welega and Shewa and also cut the rail line south of Addis Abeba. At the end of the rainy season in September 1936, nearly two-thirds of Ethiopia was still administered by the emperor's officials, but the Italians were planning campaigns to pacify Sidamo, Arsi, and Bale. By October, the Italians were reconnoitering in force, and the Ethiopians used hit-and-run tactics and only at night, when they had the advantage of surprise. The Italian command now classified their adversaries as *brigands*, to be shot immediately and not treated as prisoners of war, a policy that stopped Ethiopian soldiers from surrendering.

The fighting was therefore fierce, with neither side granting quarter. By November, however, the Italians were moving on Jima and Gore, coordinating ground attacks with air assaults in a virtual rout of the Ethiopian enemy. By December 1936, Ras Imru was captured and exiled to Italy; three sons of Ras Kassa were taken and publicly hanged as an object demonstration of Italian justice toward brigands; and Dej. Habte Mariam of Welega (who aspired to build an Oromo republic) submitted to the Europeans. In February 1937, the Italians had tracked down and killed old Dej. Gebre Mariam, who had fought at Adwa, and who was one of the emperor's men in Harer; Dej. Beyene Merid, governor of Bale and the emperor's son-in-law; and Ras Desta Demtew, another son-in-law. The Italians were implacable in their pacification, their definition of brigand serving to justify executing many of the emperor's governing class.

With the main units gone and many of the top officers dead, the war against the Italians transformed itself into an insurgency with a changing cast of characters and fighters, depending on circumstance and opportunity. The Italians had strategic control, dominating the cities, towns, and major caravan routes. However, from rural Ethiopia, wherever nationalism had been nurtured, came the *arbenyotch*, or patriots, to harry Italian outposts and patrols and sometimes to test the strength of garrisons in the larger towns. Never in their quinquennium of rule did the fascists feel secure in Ethiopia, and their anxiety came to border on neurosis.

During a ceremony at the Viceregal Palace (Haile Sellassie's former residence; now Ras Makonnen Hall of Addis Ababa University), on 19 February 1937 (Yekatit 12), two young Eritreans lobbed as many as ten grenades into a crowd of Ethiopian and Italian dignitaries attending Graziani. One Ethiopian was killed, an Italian general was seriously injured, but the viceroy suffered only superficial wounds. The confused Italian security guard responded by firing into a crowd of Ethiopian onlookers, whose deaths prefaced an Italian orgy of vengeful killing.

Shortly after the incident, the Italian command ordered all shops closed and shuttered, directed people to return home, and suspended postal and telegraphic communications. Within an hour, the capital was isolated from the world, and its streets were empty. During the afternoon, Addis Abeba's Fascist party voted a pogrom against the city's population. The slaughter began that night and continued into the next day.

22. Oromo patriot and family, near Kibre Mengist

Ethiopians were killed indiscriminately, burnt alive in their huts, or shot as they tried to escape. Italian truckers chased people down and then ran them over, or tied their feet to tailgates and dragged them to death. People were beaten and stoned until dead. Women were scourged, men emasculated, and children crushed underfoot; throats were cut, people were disemboweled and left to die, or hung, or stabbed to death. A relatively large percentage of the victims came from the traditional ruling class and the Young Ethiopians, although many of these had already formally submitted to Italian authority.

Since reprisals were not limited to Addis Abeba, the bloodletting became a national calamity. Altogether as many as ten thousand people died, not a large figure by World War II standards but enough to reveal the Italians as murderous racists. When, a few months later, European-officered Muslim Somali troops went to Debre Libanos and massacred monks and deacons supposedly implicated in the plot against Graziani, Christian Ethiopia recoiled in horror, and the patriots stepped up their attacks.

Given Ethiopia's great size and difficult topography, the occupation army of 150,000 was severely taxed by the increased activity. It could achieve local control during a campaign, but the guerrillas returned as soon as the main Italian force moved on. Although increasing numbers of hospital trains arrived at Djibouti to transfer the severely wounded to ships bound for Italy, the colonial government denied that their policy had led to a general rising and more fighting. Yet, during 1937, a planned reduction of the garrison to 67,000 troops was dropped, and by 1940–1941 the numbers grew to 250,000, of whom 75,000 were Europeans.

By mid-1937, it became clear that the policies of terrorism and repression had succeeded only in strengthening Ethiopian hostility, delaying development and settlement projects, and raising security costs. Rome therefore decided on conciliation, recalling Graziani in November 1937 and replacing him with the civilian Duke of Aosta (d. 1942). While the new viceroy continued attacking the insurgents in the north, he also offered them parole with honor and material benefits. In the south and the east, he attempted to drive a wedge between the largely colonized population, many of whom were Muslim, and the mostly Christian insurgents, drawn mainly from prewar settlers. The viceroy had some success, since many had never forgiven Menilek's conquest and the subsequent land alienation; and most detested high government taxes and the status of being second-class citizens in their own countries. The alienation of Ethiopian from Ethiopian was spurred by the administrative reorganization of Italian East Africa that included Tigray in *Eritrea*, placed Ogaden in *Somalia*, and divided the rest of the country into the provinces of *Galla and Sidama*, *Harer*, *Shewa*, and *Amara*.

Having destroyed historical links, the duke's regime played up Haile Sellassie's flight from the country and his impotence in exile. Propagandists argued that the insurgents could expect no help from Great Britain and France, especially after they recognized Italy's sovereignty over Ethiopia in April 1938 and signed treaties of *bon voisinage*. Meanwhile, the colonial government developed a road network permitting quick troop movements and organized Ethiopian *bande* (irregular) units to police the countryside. By early 1939, the insurgency languished as the government expanded its control over the new provinces and as the patriots ran out of arms and ammunition. By then, Haile Sellassie had become despondent at his inability to obtain assistance through international law and was investigating the possibility of submitting to the Italians in return for Shewa's throne.

In September 1939, however, the outbreak of the world war changed the geopolitical situation in Haile Sellassie's and Ethiopia's favor. Although the Italians were not immediately involved in the war, the patriots increased their activities. The most famous insurgent leader was Dej. Abebe Aregai (later ras; 1903–1960), once police chief of Addis Abeba, who directed the guerrilla movement in northern Shewa throughout the occupation. A master at ruse and ambush, he specialized in attacking along the Italian flanks. He never concentrated his forces, instead distributing his operations among fifty-men units that could easily live off the land without alienating the peasants. Try as they might, the fascists were unable to contain and destroy his forces.

Although similar tactics arose from the conditions of the insurgency, there was little coordination among the patriot leaders. Quite often, as in Gojam's case, guerrilla groups fought each other over such scarce resources as weapons and ammunition. Yet, the province was largely liberated territory, from where it was possible to communicate with the outside world through Sudan. Immediately after the war began, the emperor sent Lorenzo Taezaz (1900–1946), via Khartoum, to Gojam to reconnoiter. He did not find an Italian in the area immediately adjacent to the frontier but discovered a citizenry ready to fight for Ethiopia's liberation and the emperor's return.

When Italy declared war on the Allies on 10 June 1940, Haile Sellassie's pleas for assistance were finally answered by a suddenly solicitous British government that saw the liberation of Ethiopia as a way of securing the Suez Canal's Red Sea flank from the Axis. On 12 July 1940, London recognized the emperor as a full ally, and two weeks later he was in Khartoum. The Sudanese government was dismayed, since its 2,500-man army was no match for the enemy's 250,000 troops and two hundred war planes. Fortunately, the Italians attacked only across the Eritrean frontier toward Kassala, allowing the British to train an Ethiopian force to invade Gojam and join up with the patriots. Its commander was the idiosyncratic and charismatic Maj. Orde Charles Wingate (later major general; 1903–1944), who transformed the emperor's ragtag assortment of 1,670 Ethiopian exiles, European eccentrics, and Sudanese misfits into a highly trained and disciplined unit called Gideon Force. They would confront a colonial army suffering from a crisis of confidence.

23. The Italian fort at Maji

The Italians in East Africa were isolated from Europe, uneasy about the future, and fearful of Ethiopian revenge. As soon as the European soldiers discovered that the insurgents were receiving outside support from Sudan, their anxieties led to a devastating drop in morale. When Haile Sellassie entered Gojam on 20 January 1941, he and Wingate encountered an enemy already defeated by its own mass paranoia.

The fighting therefore had peculiar qualities. On the arrival of Gideon Force and accompanying patriots, the Italians fled into their fortresses for safety. Often there was the absurdity of several hundred men besieging several thousand—in Debre Markos, Gojam's capital, 300 surrounded 14,000. In due course and, occasionally after hard fighting, the Italians surrendered with great dignity and ceremony and were usually allowed the honors of war. The most famous names of the war—Keren, Debre Markos, Mega, Dembidolo, and Ambalage—represent not battlefields but forts. Meanwhile, the emperor was received enthusiastically by even the most cynical guerrilla leaders and tumultuously by the rank and file. He was their ruler, even if the British were establishing a military government for what they considered occupied enemy territory.

Haile Sellassie therefore ignored the Occupied Enemy Territory Administration (OETA) and insisted that his return to Addis Abeba on 5 May 1941, five years after the arrival of Badoglio, restored the nation's freedom. As Ethiopia's sovereign, he named seven ministers and quickly resurrected provincial and local governments, paying off debts incurred to insurgent leaders for their long struggle and buying continuing fidelity. The British blustered but had so few troops outside of the capital and major towns that they were forced to deal with the restored imperial administration. Though Sir Philip Mitchell (1890–1964), the head of

24. Abandoned Italian tractor in 1961

OETA, sought to integrate Ethiopia into British East Africa, his notion was quashed when the government in London refused to undertake new colonial adventures. Haile Sellassie was therefore relieved to sign the Addis Abeba Agreement of 31 January 1942, which acknowledged Ethiopia as a sovereign state, though it contained provisions that limited Addis Abeba's freedom of action.

The emperor immediately determined to reduce the potentially dangerous foreign influence by obtaining non-British advisers, by evading London's control over Ethiopia's finances and customs, and by ending the British military presence in Ogaden, Dire Dawa, and along the railway line. He turned to the United States, which he concluded would be the dominant postwar world power, and complained bitterly that the 1942 agreement contained clauses suborning Ethiopia's sovereignty. The American consul in Eritrea, where the United States had taken over various Italian bases as assembly points and distribution centers for lend-lease in the Middle East, heartily agreed. Washington consequently intervened, as much because of its anticolonialism as with an eye to Ethiopia's potential postwar strategic importance.

The U.S. government later facilitated Ethiopia's entry into the United Nations, and in 1943 it reopened its legation in Addis Abeba. As a gesture of goodwill, Washington offered Ethiopia a lend-lease treaty, signed on 9 August 1943; provided some arms and ammunition; and agreed to dispatch a technical mission to investigate and report on Ethiopia's needs. Early on, Addis Abeba raised the issue of access to the sea and was pleased by America's positive response.

Ethiopia used its developing relationship with the United States to negotiate a new, more favorable, treaty with Great Britain on 19 December 1944. Washington subtly warned the Foreign Office not to bully the emperor into any form of political dependency on Britain. Ethiopian sovereignty over Ogaden and other reserved areas was, there-fore, formally recognized, although the British remained in control. The continuation of one government administering all Somalis embittered the Ethiopian government, which feared the notion of "Greater Soma-lia" first engineered by the Italian enemy and now continued by an ostensible ally. To show his displeasure the emperor signed the treaty but refused its £3 million of assistance, complaining that it was insufficient compensation for the insult done to Ethiopia's sovereignty.

Meanwhile, Haile Sellassie's government had reimposed its authority over the country. National and provincial administrations were led by a carefully balanced group of newly elevated patriots, officers from Gideon Force, returned exiles, and ex-collaborators. Only in the most blatant cases, such as Dej. Haile Sellassie Gugsa, did the emperor move against Italian appointees, whose preferments and titles he generally confirmed. Haile Sellassie not only made the politically sensible decision he also ensured his administration enough experienced and educated personnel to replace those killed during the war and occupation.

When the emperor's authority was seriously challenged during these early days, he moved decisively against the dissidents. In 1943–1944, with British air support, Addis Abeba violently suppressed the Woyane insurrection, a serious peasant uprising in Tigray that had been sparked by maladministration, excessive taxation, official corruption, and conse-quent brigandage. The emperor did not ask about the justice of the case; it was enough that the rebels had challenged his administration. He was just as harsh against threats from individuals, especially from those who enjoyed their own popularity as patriot leaders, as in the case of Belai Zelleke, whom he had ennobled as a dejazmach and given a subprovince in Gojam to administer.

For reasons yet unclear, Dej. Belai had become insubordinate, loudly proclaiming that he was unwilling to serve a monarch who had deserted his country during its greatest travail. Even after he had been silenced and ordered to Addis Abeba, where his activities could be monitored, Belai remained alienated. With other noblemen, he organized a conspiracy that involved a number of the emperor's guard and that ended in bloodshed. After a show trial, the dejazmach was publicly hanged in the capital. The emperor was less harsh with Dej. Tekle Wolde Hawariat (1900–1969), an ardent nationalist and reformer who criticized the government for its favoritism and lack of democracy. For his candor, the dejazmach was detained for two-and-one-half years on the grounds of the imperial palace.

By the time of his release, Haile Sellassie had recreated the prewar political economy and relied on a bureaucratic class as the vehicle of control and change. The emperor's policies could now be implemented in a country where the Italians had conditioned several million to accept money wages and to respond to the market. During the colonial interval, demand for cotton, salt, kerosene, and the like strengthened, and new needs appeared for tools, machinery, technical equipment, trucks, spare parts, and petroleum products. The Italian period had spurred growth along lines already evident before the occupation. When Haile Sellassie and his followers returned to power, they found a familiar but more complex, larger, and better organized economy and infrastructure to exploit for the satisfaction of high wartime demand for Ethiopia's produce.

Following the prewar model, the new Ethiopian oligarchy—now composed of patriots, collaborators, and returnees—organized import-export institutions in cooperation with expatriate businessmen. The most important of the new organizations, an anonymous and private grain-exporting company, was housed unabashedly in the Ministry of Agriculture, clearly indicating, if not revealing, the monopoly's ownership. The company was so successful in buying low and selling high to the British that London considered its purchases in Ethiopia a form of subsidy. Yet, the profits went not to the government but to private persons, who also had shares in ventures that dealt in coffee, hides, and beeswax, much in demand in the Middle East. The elasticity of supply was high owing to the Italian-built road system. Even with worn-out transport, the exchange of goods between the interior and the capital was much quicker than before the war.

Peasants were eager to trade their produce for scarce cotton goods that the oligarchy supplied at exorbitant prices through the Ethiopian National Corporation, the private distributor invariably appointed by the Ministry of Commerce to handle the import and distribution of textiles.

The corporation was owned and operated by the imperial family, high government officials, and ranking members of the aristocracy. In 1944, the corporation returned a profit of between £1.2 million and £1.8 million, or 25 percent, approximately double the standard margin for most businesses in Ethiopia. The textiles were supplied through American lend-lease, and U.S. legation officials were horrified at the racket but were powerless to interfere, given the emperor's involvement.

Indeed, Washington viewed Haile Sellassie's adherence to the Allies and to the League of Nations as promoting the war effort among African-Americans. The U.S. State Department therefore supported a meeting on 13 February 1945 between the emperor and President Franklin Delano Roosevelt (d. 1945), in Egypt en route home after the Yalta Conference. Haile Sellassie considered the meeting a high point in his career and recognition of Ethiopia's regional importance.

The agenda he submitted to the president characterized Ethiopia's foreign policy goals until the revolution of 1974: (1) Ethiopian ownership over the railway to Djibouti; (2) free and unfettered access to the sea; (3) recovery of Eritrea; (4) war reparations from Italy; (5) military assistance to develop a small modern army; (6) and U.S. investments in development projects. The emperor sought nothing less than U.S. political support, American technology, and Wall Street finance. Meanwhile, he continued to establish his independence of action.

In early 1945, the Ethiopian government introduced a new currency and coinage; exchanged the East African shillings for sterling, adding to its already significant holdings; and once again retired the Maria Theresa dollar. The latter's demonetization made tons of silver available for export to Aden and resale. The handsome profits added to Ethiopia's already considerable foreign exchange surplus. There was sufficient money to finance the administration; to build schools in the capital and elsewhere; and to begin some development projects, among them a cotton- and wool-spinning complex, an agricultural development bank, and an industrial training center. The government also used its sterling reserves to purchase trucks, tires, machinery, and spare parts, but delivery was frustratingly slow as Britain tried to satisfy demand throughout its empire.

The British were also dilatory in providing equipment to the Ethiopian military. In early 1946, the imperial army numbered about twenty-seven thousand men, half of whom were irregulars. The emperor wanted four divisions totaling about forty-five thousand men, sufficient enough to reoccupy Ogaden and to garrison the whole country. The British training mission in Ethiopia was small, in keeping with the Labour government's concentration on domestic social programs and its inclination to divest itself of empire and hegemony. The British position in the Horn of Africa was irremediably weak, even if it appeared to Addis Abeba that London had every intention of retaining Ogaden as part of Greater Somalia, an arrangement that the Foreign Office believed was not only fair but which also would lessen regional tensions.

The Addis Abeba government viewed the scheme as anathema, in the same category as Italy's efforts to destroy Ethiopia's unity. It similarly abhorred the protonationalist Somali Youth League (SYL), which sought to incorporate all its confreres in Kenya, Djibouti, and Ethiopia into one ethnic state. By late 1947, most Somali policemen, soldiers, and officials were members, meaning that the SYL ran the protectorate for the British, a fact that determined Addis Abeba to regain Ogaden as soon as possible. The Ethiopian Foreign Ministry decided to use the exploratory drilling of the American Sinclair Oil Company as its cover.

Haile Sellassie had told the American minister that granting the concession to an American firm was a political act. When his government issued the Americans passes valid for one year's stay in Ogaden, the British had to cooperate under the provisions of the 1944 treaty. In response, the Jijiga branch of the SYL denounced Ethiopia's sovereignty in the region and Britain's acquiescence. When, in January 1948, an international commission arrived in Mogadishu to seek advice about Somalia's postwar disposition, the SYL questioned Sinclair's right to be in Ogaden, and some of its activists assaulted an American drilling team working near Warder. The British officer commanding the local gendarmerie was powerless to intervene, since all his men belonged to the SYL.

The incident served starkly to reveal London's weakness, and a mortified high command, knowing that improvement was impossible, advised immediate withdrawal from Ogaden and other reserved zones, thus terminating any British responsibilities for Sinclair and Washington. When the Foreign Office concurred, the Ethiopians were advised on 17 March 1948 that British troops would shortly be withdrawn from Jijiga. The Addis Abeba government quickly planned a new administration for Ogaden, which was in place by the end of September 1948. So striking was Ethiopia's diplomatic success that the emperor turned to involving the United States in his quest for Eritrea.

After its restoration in 1941, the Addis Abeba government repeated, at every opportunity, that Eritrea, then governed by a British military administration, had been an integral part of Ethiopia before being colonized and that retrieval would provide access to the sea and just compensation for wartime cruelties and losses. In Eritrea, the emperor's agents helped establish the "Patriotic Association for the Union of Eritrea and Ethiopia," popularly known as the "Unionist party." The organization was subsidized by the Addis Abeba–based "Society for the Unification of Ethiopia and Eritrea" led by Wolde Giorgis Wolde Yohannes (1902–1984), Minister of Pen and de facto the emperor's *chef de cabinet*.

The two groups sought the unconditional integration of Eritrea into Ethiopia, a goal resisted by a congeries of Christian and Muslim factions in the ex-colony. While disunity hurt their chances, the case for independence was lost when the Allies sent a fact-finding delegation (the "Four-Power Commission") to Eritrea. After a long visit, 12 November 1947 to 3 January 1948, the mission concluded that although the population generally opposed dividing the colony between Sudan and Ethiopia there was no national consciousness to nourish statehood and that Eritrea's backward agriculture, crude industrial base, and poor natural resources could not sustain independence. The commission therefore recommended some form of dependency, a decision ultimately referred to the United Nations, where the United States was the most influential power.

Washington's main concern in Eritrea was Radio Marina, an Italian facility in Asmera taken over by the U.S. military in 1942 and subsequently expanded and incorporated into a global network that gathered and beamed intelligence to the Pentagon. At seven thousand feet, Asmera was ideally sited in a latitude little affected by daily variations in weather or by seasonal changes, thus reducing the need for numerous frequency changes. Radio Marina was important to American security, and it was located in a region that Washington wanted to keep free of Soviet influence. Since Italy then had the West's largest Communist party, and it was possible that Marxists might rule in Rome, the United States refused to entertain any notion about returning Eritrea to Italy. The State Department regarded Mitsiwa, where American ships had docking and visitation rights, as the only port that could satisfy Ethiopia's demand for sovereign access to the sea. Since Addis Abeba had a strong preference for the West, American policymakers decided to support Ethiopia's claim to Eritrea, a move that was backed ultimately by Great Britain and other major powers.

Washington reasoned, however, that the ex-colony's recent history was different enough from the other Ethiopian provinces to warrant an autonomous government. Sponsoring a federal arrangement was the perfect American way of showing gratitude for Ethiopia's contribution of troops to the United Nation's effort in Korea, while mollifying Muslim and other Eritrean separatists. The federal arrangement minimally satisfied the Ethiopian government's aspirations and more directly involved the United States in the country's affairs.

Immediately after accepting the federal solution, Addis Abeba began pressuring the United States for military assistance. In June 1951, an American general arrived in Addis Abeba to assess Ethiopia's demand, and he hinted that once the Korean war was under control, aid would be forthcoming. The Pentagon agreed, responding to new geopolitical developments caused by Israeli independence, the Nasser revolution in Egypt, and the consequent growth of Soviet influence in the eastern Mediterranean. The State Department concurred, seeing in Ethiopia a stable ally in the Red Sea region. In October 1952, negotiations to formalize the status of Radio Marina, then called Kagnew Station (after the Ethiopian battalion that had returned from Korea in May 1952), provided the vehicle leading to the signature, on 22 May 1953, of a base and facilities agreement and a standard military assistance treaty regulating the delivery of weapons and other equipment and providing for a Military Assistance Advisory Group. By then, the United States was also deeply involved in Ethiopia's economic development.

Through 1950, Addis Abeba received Import-Export Bank loans amounting to over US$10 million to purchase cars, trucks, spare parts, machinery, and planes for Ethiopian Airlines, then under management by TWA. A plan developed in 1945 by a U.S. technical mission provided the blueprint for Ethiopia's economic development strategies until well into the 1960s. It comprised an integrated program that coordinated manpower, raw materials, and capital resources aimed at overcoming deficiencies in education, transportation, marketing, technology, and public administration. Since so many problems had to be faced at once, relatively few projects were targeted to ensure their success. Revised in 1947, the development plan recommended a three-year $11.7 million program to establish three industries: six meat-processing centers; six associated tanneries; and a cotton textiles complex capable of producing ten million pounds of cloth annually.

The first two industries would be able to satisfy international demand, earning valuable profits, whereas the last would substitute domestic production for imported goods and therefore save foreign exchange. The net revenues would soon be used to finance cement factories, a leather works, machine shops, and tire-manufacturing and coffee-grading and processing facilities. In the future would come a salt-refining complex, a potash plant, a chemicals company, a burlap and bagging mill, a soap factory, vegetable oil and sugar refineries, a shoe industry, and a wood products works. Associated throughout was a $10 million program of road building and education.

Little attention was given to agriculture beyond providing extension agents. It was assumed that Ethiopia's farmers would rapidly adopt the schemes that agents of development would recommend. The cultivators' labor and productivity would provide the capital to finance industrial, not rural, development in Ethiopia. The towns would be the stage for modernity, whereas the countryside would remain socially traditional.

To carry out modernization, Haile Sellassie was pushing forward to educate a devoted elite. He believed that the effects of education would transform his feudal empire into a modern state. The Ministry of Education admonished the population to send their children to school to learn how to improve Ethiopia and imposed a supplementary land tax in November 1947 to help provinces and localities pay for new schools and teachers. By 1950, Ethiopia's five hundred schools enrolled 52,965, a very small percentage of school-age children to be sure, but they were well taught and thoroughly indoctrinated with loyalty to the throne, respect for the country's traditions, and patriotism. When the Americans finally began to provide economic assistance, there was a cadre of eager and qualified Ethiopians ready to cooperate.

Until 1960, Washington's development programs were devoted to technical assistance administered under a Point Four Agreement signed on 15 May 1952. For the first few years, the U.S. assistance mission was a simple organization in which technicians were paramount. The Americans worked alongside their counterparts on projects defined by Ethiopian policymakers. The latter's piecemeal approach was in keeping with the previous scattered efforts at development, with immediate utility being the most compelling criterion for adopting a project. Much was achieved in agricultural, medical, vocational, and industrial education; in animal husbandry and breeding, coffee research, and forestry; and in road-building and other communications projects.

Ethiopian investment sustained 70 percent of U.S. Point Four efforts. The capital came from a burgeoning economy, which in 1953 and 1954, yielded a net surplus of about $50 million. The sale of coffee, the economy's mainstay, benefited from various crop disasters in Brazil and also from high world demand, especially from the United States. The increasing acceptability of Ethiopian coffee also owed much to new plantings, better care of coffee stands, improved sorting and cleaning of beans, and more thorough harvesting. Moreover, the improved road system was reliably delivering product to regional centers and thence to Addis Abeba, from where it was exported by rail. By the end of 1954, the United States had become the chief destination for Ethiopia's coffee and therefore *the* vital player in the country's economy, a fact recognized by the government's consistent appointments of Americans to head the State Bank.

Coffee also purchased expertise from non-American sources. A bevy of foreigners were helping to build Ethiopia's modern economy and its infrastructure. The British were deeply involved in the Commercial School that supplied graduates to business and government. The Czech government provided an ammunition factory and technicians to run it until Ethiopians were trained. France and Canada supplied teachers for the new University College of Addis Abeba, which graduated its first class in 1954. The Food Agricultural Organization of the United Nations sent experts for various research stations around Ethiopia; and the International Bank for Reconstruction and Development agreed to finance the rehabilitation of the country's telephone and telegraphic services. The Dutch, casting about for overseas ventures, obtained a sixty-year concession for sugar manufacturing in the Awash valley. Finally, the Swedes trained the air force and also ran the new Building College. And there were many expatriate Greeks, Armenians, Italians, and others who contributed by investment of cash or skills in the work of development, whether in Addis Abeba or in the countryside.

The United States nevertheless remained Haile Sellassie's preferred donor of military goods, capital, education, and technology, as he made abundantly clear during his triumphal visit there in May–June 1954. In a speech before Congress, the emperor modestly pointed out Ethiopia's achievements since 1947: a quadrupling of the country's foreign trade, currency, and foreign exchange holdings; an efficient national bank and the only dollar-based currency in the Middle East; a fourfold increase in school enrollment; and governmental stability in a part of the world noted for unrest. He referred to Ethiopia's fertile soils, its excellent climate, its abundant rainfall, and its energetic and productive population. He regarded Ethiopia as a land of opportunity, where American ingenuity and technical skills were welcomed.

The emperor also spoke of Ethiopia's unique position on the world's most important strategic line of communications, both by sea and radio. He advised that his country's Christian tradition oriented Ethiopia toward the West. Haile Sellassie reaffirmed Ethiopia's commitment to Western values and to the United States, a valued friend that had refused to recognize Italian sovereignty over Ethiopia. Yet, neither the U.S. government nor American capitalism eagerly poured millions into Ethiopia, either to make it into a bulwark of private enterprise or a bastion of democracy.

In the military sphere, American administrative machinery operated so slowly that by 1955 the Ethiopian government saw little new weaponry, although the Military Assistance Advisory Group was busily training the army. After complaints, Washington decided to provide a minimum annual aid program of US$5 million, plus direct sales of air force and naval equipment. That figure was finally met in 1959, when economic aid amounted to another US$5 million and technical assistance, US$4 million, totaling (including the military's $5 million) a relatively small US$14 million. The economic assistance was designed to supplement Ethiopia's ability to support a planned reorganization of the military into three divisions headquartered in Addis Abeba, Harer, and Asmera and to help build an infrastructure to support a modest but modern jet air force.

The increased assistance came when Ethiopian economic growth slowed. During the late 1950s, the international coffee market had been glutted by increased Latin American production, and Ethiopia's exports of cereals, oilseeds, and beans suffered from the closure of the Suez Canal and from increased competition in Africa. Industry and agriculture languished, trade was depressed, and the government drew heavily on its reserves to pay its bills. Recent high school and university graduates could not find jobs, and in Eritrea there was labor unrest, capped by a general strike in Asmera on 10 March 1958. Last but not least, a drought and famine struck Eritrea, Welo, Harerge, and Tigray, making it painfully obvious that agriculture suffered from a lack of investment.

The U.S. government was fully aware that the military programs reduced the amount of capital available for development programs but reasoned that any reduction might weaken Ethiopia's commitment to the West. In the summer of 1959, the emperor made a trip to the Eastern bloc and returned with over US$100 million in credits, an amount that stunned Washington. The Ethiopian government clarified that it would not use the credits if Western aid was forthcoming. With the imminence of Somalia's independence in 1960—a weak state that might fall under Soviet influence—Washington responded by offering more economic assistance, support for a new road-building program, and an expanded military program, thus increasing the rent for Kagnew Station. The American connection also permitted the emperor to supplement his personal power through the growth of the bureaucracy and the capital city.

TWELVE

Haile Sellassie, to 1973

The infrastructure of modern life in Ethiopia existed in the capital and in a few provincial centers. Elsewhere, modernity was limited to paying taxes and to purchasing a small range of imported goods. Many peasants were drawn into the market sector, but others were forced off their lands and pasturage and transformed into a rural proletariat by the establishment of large-scale plantations in the Awash and, later, in the Omo and Didesa valleys, by the increasing capitalization of coffee in Sidamo and elsewhere, and the spread of truck farming in Shewa and Arsi. Ethiopia's oligarchy invested heavily in agribusiness and with their profits helped to finance Addis Abeba's development.

Conforming to the emperor's views about modernization, investments in financial institutions, internal security, public works, education, and social services were concentrated in the capital. Indeed, the city's modern amenities attracted a cross section of Ethiopia's peoples, foreign merchants and capitalists, and an increasing number of European technicians, advisers, educators, and adventurers. By 1960, there were four large hotels and a score of others, a number of hospitals and clinics, many paved streets and large boulevards, hundreds of shops, tens of factories and warehouses, many government buildings and monuments, thirty or so embassies and legations, several movie houses, and hundreds of restaurants, bars, and night clubs.

25. Addis Abeba in 1970, city hall in the background

Most institutions of higher education were located in the capital, as were nine of the empire's twenty secondary schools. Of the country's 620 government elementary schools, 38 were in Addis Abeba, 125 were in Eritrea, and most of the remaining were in the north. Such imbalance was further complicated by the government's prejudice for its own official culture that stressed Amharic. The Oromo keenly felt this discrimination, since many believed that their taxes probably paid for the north's disproportionate number of clinics, orphanages, and other social services.

In 1960, the best life was to be had in Addis Abeba, but it remained better to be an agriculturist or urban dweller in the north than to live in a southern town; worst of all was to farm in the south, which meant land alienation, isolation from modern amenities, and increasing exploitation as the export economy grew. Thus, the modernity of the capital, Asmera, Harer, and perhaps two or three other urban centers appeared as a sharp contrast, a contradiction, to the experience of most Ethiopians. The incongruity was revealed clearly in the revised constitution of 1955, the emperor's gift to his people on the occasion of the twenty-fifth anniversary of his coronation.

The document grafted modern elements onto an essentially traditional monarchical system attempting to survive through adaptation. The emperor was left in a leading position, although finances and taxes had to be authorized by parliament, which could also question ministers and disapprove imperial decrees. The constitution introduced an elected lower house of parliament, a theoretically independent judiciary committed to the rule of law, the doctrine of separation of powers, a catalog of human rights, and the idea of bureaucratic responsibility to the people. The emperor's speech of promulgation on 3 November 1955 recorded his sense of constitutional achievement and of economic development.

Ranging over the previous quarter of a century, the emperor found much in which to take pride. Other than social and educational achievements, he cited expanded telephonic and telegraphic services, the highly successful Ethiopian Airlines, and the many new roads built during his reign. He believed that the new communications had greatly spurred commerce, permitting the national budget to grow from $5 million to over $100 million in 1955. The monies had been used to build an efficient administration that worked for Ethiopia's unity. The monarch claimed that his policies had wiped out feudalism and provided social mobility for all of his subjects.

The emperor's assessment did not appreciate that his country remained poor and backward even by African standards. He was not a relativist: he saw 240 medical facilities in 1955, whereas a quarter-century earlier there had been 48. Tens of thousands of children were actually in school, compared with the meager few thousands of 1931. Haile Sellassie was enough of a traditional figure that he could not grasp the reality of Ethiopia's problems as he witnessed and presided over changes that would have been unimaginable to Menilek II, during whose reign he had been born, reared, and educated. Others, especially from the educated military and bureaucratic elites, came to blame the emperor for the country's poverty and relative lack of infrastructure.

In 1955, the emperor began a period of personal rule, using the recently developed organs of the Addis Abeba government and a spate of newly educated returnees to consolidate his authority over the central administration. Among the ministers, he subtly established competing power factions, which allowed him to pick and choose between policies. Obtaining intelligence from a variety of networks, the emperor was able to respond effectively to a barrage of competition and to influence a series of shifting coalitions in the cabinet. Governmental efficiency suffered, and Haile Sellassie's intervention also nurtured sycophancy and worked against development and modernization.

The youthful returnees became disenchanted working for a regime in which personal loyalty to the emperor was the paramount consideration. They were watched by agents led by Lt. Col. Workneh Gebeyehu (1925–1960), the director of security in the Ministry of Interior. Workneh, however, slowly began to sympathize with the perception of the newly lettered that their superiors were ignorant, corrupt, and inefficient impediments to progress. He came to agree that the rising generation was fighting to change a traditional regime that compared poorly with the modern governments led by well-educated and progressive young Africans who shortly would lead their countries to independence. Ultimately, he joined the activists who clustered around Germame Neway (d. 1960), the intellectual leader of the coup of 1960.

Descended from middle-level functionaries in Menilek's court, and reared in comfortable and relatively modern circumstances in Addis Abeba and Shewa, Germame was a member of the emperor's expensively educated bureaucratic elite. After graduation from the capital's excellent Haile Sellassie I Secondary School, he went on to the United States for bachelor and master of arts degrees. While abroad, he was active in Ethiopian student politics; his master's thesis, "The Impact of White Settlement Policy in Kenya" (Columbia University, 1954), dramatically revealed the plight of Africans exploited and oppressed by a powerful elite. On return to Ethiopia, Germame was posted to the Ministry of Interior under Dej. Mesfin Seleshi (later ras; 1902–1974), the archetypal Ethiopian oligarch.

The minister had been governor of Kefa from 1945 to 1955, the years of the coffee boom, during which he had managed illegally to purchase thousands of hectares of prime coffee land. During the harvest, his agents forced peasants either to sell their beans to the governor or to ship their produce to market using his high-cost trucking service. In the capital, Mesfin marketed his coffee at great profit through the National Coffee Board, whose appointees he controlled. With his wealth, he purchased stock in the nation's fledgling industries and bought real estate in Addis Abeba, a wine estate in Shewa, and large tracts of prime farm land to the south of the capital. He was exactly the kind of opportunist the young educated elite abhorred, since he put profits before patriotism.

Germame believed that Ethiopia's economic stagnation could be broken only by the full participation of a population freed from exploitation and permitted, under wise leadership, to act in its own self-interest. When appointed governor in Walamo, he organized peasant-manned security organizations to monitor local police activities. He also distrib-

26. Imperial Bodyguard in ceremonial uniforms,
outside the Jubilee Palace, 1962

uted government holdings to the landless, which sharply reduced labor supplies, causing local landowners to seek Germame's recall. On return to Addis Abeba, he explained to the emperor that it had been his responsibility, as governor, to end the suffering of the starving landless. Unable to criticize such public idealism, Haile Sellassie sent Germame to administer the pastoral Somalis of Jijiga.

Although there were no property issues in the desert, Germame continued as a radical reformer. New wells were dug and old ones were improved; he established clinics and improved public health, built schools, and planned development schemes; and he held his officials strictly accountable for their actions. He quickly uncovered inertia,

corruption, and maladministration, greatly embarrassing provincial officials, who successfully demanded his recall to Addis Abeba. Germame
concluded from his experiences in Walamo and Jijiga that no progress
could be made until the existing political system was changed.

From 1958 to 1960, he politicized a small group of men who met
regularly at the home of Brig. Gen. Mengistu Neway (d. 1961), Germame's
brother and since October 1956 commander of the Imperial Bodyguard.
Both Neway brothers, Lieutenant Colonel Workneh, and other highly
placed individuals were devoted patriots who sought the country's
progress. They were fully aware of the ideological and material changes
sweeping the world and recognized the need for the development of an
Ethiopian infrastructure capable of sustaining dramatic growth. They
were repulsed by the apparent obstructionism of the imperial system and
agreed that the ruling oligarchs should be replaced by the educated elite.

Germame, Mengistu, and their small group of associates were planning an elitist coup, even if they justified their efforts in terms of national
salvation and the needs of the people. Unsure, however, about the latter's
support in a direct confrontation with Haile Sellassie, they decided to act
when he was on a representational trip to South America in December
1960. General Mengistu told his soldiers, the chosen instrument of the
coup, that the army and some notables had rebelled and that the
Bodyguard had to restore imperial authority. Mengistu, Germame, and
Workneh believed that their efforts to destroy the old regime would
quickly attract the support of most lettered Ethiopians and succeed.

They were to be disappointed. First of all, for security reasons, their
cabal lacked representatives from the army and key government ministries. Second, they had no real plan beyond taking Addis Abeba and
awaiting the acclamation of the people. Third, the emperor had such solid
support in the provinces that controlling the capital was insufficient to
gain victory. Fourth, during the coup's beginning on 14 December
1960, the organizers failed to arrest, among others, Gen. Merid Mengesha
(1912–1966), commander of the First Division and Dej. Asrate Kasa
(later ras; 1918–1974), vice president of the Senate, who quickly began
organizing loyalist opposition. They did, however, detain as hostages
ministers and members of the imperial family, including the empress and
the Crown Prince Asfa Wossen (1916–; since 1989, the self-nominated
Emperor Amha Sellassie I).

During the afternoon of 14 December, Asfa Wossen delivered a speech
on Radio Addis Abeba that summed up the rationale for the coup and its
aims. Presumably the crown prince was acting under duress, but there is

evidence that he was at least consulted about the speech and other matters. Whatever his involvement, for the first time in modern history an Ethiopian leader described the nation's social and economic problems in radical terms. Asfa Wossen alleged that a self-perpetuating minority exploited Ethiopia's peoples and stressed his conviction that the new leadership would work for progress and national unity.

A skeptical army nonetheless mobilized forces in the capital and in Asmera and called up units from around the empire. In Brazil, meanwhile, the emperor had been informed about the coup and prepared to return home. From the Genet Leul palace, where Mengistu and Workneh had taken their high-ranking prisoners and which was now the coup's headquarters, there was little activity and no news. Foreigners found it surprising that the Imperial Bodyguard had not yet deployed its regiments or that it had sent out few patrols to investigate what its adversaries were doing. Much was going on behind the scenes by telephone, however, and the rebel leadership still hoped to succeed without bloodshed. Their expectations were hourly becoming illusory.

The next day, 15 December, revealed that Bodyguard ineptitude and failure would lead to the coup's failure. During the night, General Mengistu had done nothing to improve his troops' tactical positions. The army, in contrast, was receiving reinforcements by air, railway, and road. General Merid and his staff had developed a reasonable plan of action and were forming up units before attacking the rebels. So impressive was the army's program that the hitherto neutral U.S. Embassy concluded the rebels could not succeed and decided to offer the loyalists advisory staff support.

That night, however, the students at University College listened to Mengistu speak glowingly about the coup's goals and decided that, for Ethiopia's sake, it must not fail. They voted to demonstrate in favor of the rebels and by so doing placed themselves in the center of the country's politics. Their manifesto contained unsophisticated ideas and analyses that were to develop into the articulate and defined ideology that undermined the emperor's position continuously thereafter. The students were mostly concerned about the exploitation of the poor to satisfy the needs of the wealthy and blamed the government for the failure of the educated to improve the lives of the broad masses. The new regime, the students claimed, would permit the intelligentsia to develop policies for modernization.

On the morning of 16 December, most of University College's

students marched from the campus[1] toward army headquarters, singing, waving placards, and yelling slogans. The onlookers hardly responded, foreshadowing the failure of the students to influence the army. Shortly before noon, the idealism of youth encountered the reality of a platoon of soldiers who ordered the students to turn back. The troops were so nervous that several Ethiopian academics intervened and convinced their pupils to return to campus. The student collapse signaled the end of the coup, now in its penultimate stage.

Meanwhile, the rebel leaders had sought to make a face-saving deal with the army, which refused several offers of mediation. Indeed, at 2:50 P.M., on 15 December, Merid ordered an attack, and gunfire sounded throughout the capital. In the late afternoon, one air force plane dropped leaflets signed by the patriarch denouncing the rebels and supporting the emperor, and another cracked the sound barrier, causing a terrifying sonic boom. That night, the emperor became directly involved in the mutiny's suppression, thanks to being permitted, en route home, to use the U.S. Air Force's international radio network to talk to loyalist leaders.

On the morning of 16 December, while Haile Sellassie was airborne, jets in Addis Abeba bombed and strafed enemy positions in coordination with ground attacks. Carrying a letter from General Merid warning that the army would fight until the last rebel was killed, the U.S. ambassador and two aides drove to the palace to mediate an end to the combat and the release of the hostages. While both matters were being discussed, the army attacked the palace, the Americans quickly left, and the rebels, out of despair and frustration, killed fifteen of their hostages. By the evening, the capital was secured, and the emperor was in Asmera, where he received a tumultuous welcome. The next afternoon, Haile Sellassie returned to Addis Abeba, to be greeted at the airport by Asfa Wossen, a number of happy generals and other loyalist leaders, the patriarch, high-ranking officials and aristocrats, and the U.S. ambassador and his military attachés.

While the emperor pondered the reasons for the attempted coup, his government was tracking down major and minor rebel figures. By 23 December, the Addis Abeba area had become much quieter, and firing had diminished as guardsmen surrendered in the city's suburbs and exurbs. Many had died, among them Colonel Workneh, who chose suicide rather than chance the emperor's justice. Loyalist forces relent-

---

1. Now the Faculty of Science.

lessly hunted the brothers Neway, who were brought to ground on Christmas eve near Nazret, some seventy kilometers south of Addis Abeba. After a shoot-out, Germame was dead and Mengistu seriously wounded but alive to face a court martial.

Haile Sellassie meanwhile was missing the point of the coup. For example, he attributed Eritrea's constancy as a mark of loyalty to the crown, instead of appreciating that the federated state's population might have regarded the crisis as an internal Amhara affair. In fact, there was much latent dissatisfaction in Eritrea because the central government had undermined its autonomy since the beginning of the federation. Courts, schools, and social services had slowly become organs of the imperial regime; the freedoms enunciated in the Eritrean constitution had been eroded; political parties had been stifled and leading personalities sent into exile; use of the Amharic language and other attributes of the official culture had been imposed on the population; the Eritrean flag had been suppressed; and, in 1960, the designation Eritrean *government* had been changed to Eritrean *administration*. Furthermore, though Eritrea had received more development funds than any other region in Ethiopia, the towns and industries sustained by the needs of the Italian colonial and British military regimes continued to deteriorate before Ethiopia's different national requirements. Though the emperor could be satisfied with Eritrea's current security arrangements, the long-term outlook was uncertain.

So, too, was the prognosis for Addis Abeba. Though the city's population had appeared apathetic, the coup had struck a responsive chord among the intelligentsia, the students, and obviously among a segment of the military. The new elites were interested in progress, and they wanted more authority within the government to implement change. The emperor, however, refused to acknowledge the need for reform and attributed the coup to a small group of willful men whose actions had shamed Ethiopia. Haile Sellassie pointed to the obvious fact that the coup had occurred in the capital, whereas the provinces had remained either peaceful or supportive of the crown. Finally, the emperor convinced himself that the goals of the coup were identical to the intent of his existing policies, and his new government, named in February 1961, reflected the status quo ante.

He made fifty-eight appointments, among them some able young officials, but gave the top positions to aristocrats or military men whose loyalty was undoubted. By ignoring the forces that had shaped and inspired the recent crisis, the emperor lost the support of the progressives with whom he had built the modern state. He was forced rather to rely increasingly on overt military power for authority and on the aristocracy and oligarchy for administrative support. Since the last two represented the property-owning classes, Haile Sellassie was unable to implement significant land reform, in the absence of which the intelligentsia and the students, at first quietly and then stridently, opposed the regime. The monarchy gradually lost its credibility and its authority, especially as Ethiopia became embroiled in conflicts in Eritrea and with Somalia.

The Mogadishu government became independent on 1 July 1960, its very flag a challenge to the Ethiopian nation-state. One of the tips of its five-pointed star represented the Somali-inhabited Ogaden.[2] The Addis Abeba government sought to accommodate the pastoralists, and the emperor toured the region in 1956, reminding his subjects that they were members of the greater Ethiopian family. In 1957, the government allocated $7 million (E$2.50 = US$1.00) for Ogaden's development and opened several schools that, however, taught in Amharic, the national language, mostly unknown to the Somalis. A few years later, Addis Abeba named Somali advisers to the Amhara governor of Ogaden and appointed Somali governors to three of the four subgovernments and to the twenty-three district administrations. The efforts of the Ethiopian government could not, however, overcome the pull of Somali nationalism.

Ogaden's schooled young men were particularly attracted to the idea of Greater Somalia, and they began to organize clandestine organizations. They heeded Radio Mogadishu's constant calls for liberation, preparing themselves for an armed struggle. They found a pretext in February 1963, when the Ethiopian government sought to introduce a head tax to help sustain development efforts. The Somali nomads vigorously resisted the tax, even killing some Ethiopian officials. Guerrilla war commenced immediately, and the Somali state supported the insurgents.

From June 1963, Somali rebels attacked isolated police and military positions, which the government yielded, leaving the nationalists in tactical control of much of Ogaden. The Ethiopian army reinforced administrative centers and sent out motor patrols, many of which the rebels ambushed to obtain arms. The army's poor showing gave the nationalists the confidence necessary to expand their activities in the fall

2. Britain did not leave the Haud until 1954.

of 1963, but their hit-and-run tactics failed to weaken Ethiopia's strategic control. The situation changed, however, when Somalia openly joined the struggle and, in November 1963, signed a military assistance pact with the Soviet Union, which undertook to equip a twenty-thousand-man Somali army.

The shocked Ethiopians decided to suppress the insurrection before the Somalis had time to build up their forces. The American-equipped Third Division moved into Ogaden in full strength and in mid-January 1964 attacked Somali border posts and adjacent towns to warn Mogadishu to cease supporting the rebels. Instead, the Somali government declared an emergency and moved its army to the frontier. Initially, the Somalis did well against the Ethiopians, but advantages in numbers and especially in air power won the day for Addis Abeba. When the Somalis failed to obtain support from other African states or from its Soviet protector, Mogadishu negotiated a cease-fire effective 6 March 1964.

The imperial high command was nonetheless plunged into gloom, first by the successes of the guerrillas and, second, by the poor performance of the army. Moreover, the fighting had revealed the fundamental problem of the empire-state, that of the rights of the nationalities. Had Mogadishu made good its claims to represent people living within Ethiopia, the emperor and his advisers reckoned that other ethnic groups might have sued for national rights and destroyed the nation's unity. More ominously, the Soviet Union had arrived to destabilize the Horn of Africa, a threat that galvanized the Ethiopian government to seek more American assistance. Gen. Merid Mengesha, since 1961 the minister of defense, told the American ambassador that Ethiopia faced its gravest threat and needed more and bolder weapons.

Already in the throes of the costly Vietnam War, Washington was not easily moved. It did not believe that Ethiopia's economy could bear the internal costs of an enlarged military effort. The State Department therefore suggested that the Ogaden problem, and others like it, could be solved through socioeconomic development and by the grant of self-rule. Washington was ready therefore to support development projects in the provinces, to speed up the delivery of weapons already authorized, and to provide relatively inexpensive logistical and training support for counterinsurgency warfare and to bring the Ethiopian army to its operational strength of forty thousand. That number, the Pentagon reckoned, could contain the Somalis and the growing insurgency in Eritrea.

In July 1960, a group of mostly Muslim exiles living in Cairo announced the establishment of the Eritrean Liberation Front (ELF). Its manifesto asserted the necessity of an armed struggle to obtain Eritrea's rights, although the organization remained militarily ineffective until 1962, when fighters—mostly lowland Muslim pastoralists—organized themselves to attack isolated posts and settlements in the remote Gash and Baraka regions. Meanwhile, for fund-raising, the ELF established branches among Eritreans living in the Middle East and, for more efficient fighting and intelligence operations, cells back home. Although loosely structured, the Eritrean groups related to the organization in Cairo, which was also searching for a champion among the Arabs.

The Syrians were attracted to the idea of supporting a largely Muslim rebellion in a country tied to the United States and Israel. In mid-1963, shortly after the Eritrean Assembly had been forced to vote to end the federation and fully to join the province to Ethiopia, Damascus agreed to provide military training for thirty Eritrean students, and in 1965 it took another group, who were followed every two years or so by others. By 1966, about one thousand fighters were active in Eritrea, mostly in the western lowlands, where they disturbed but did not seriously disrupt Ethiopia's control. They and the leadership in Cairo tended to see their efforts in pan-Muslim terms, but by the end of the 1960s, rising nationalist agitation in Eritrea's Christian highlands changed everything.

The disaffected Christians were led by former students who had benefited from the expanded educational opportunities made available in Eritrea and elsewhere by the central government. They had reacted sharply to Addis Abeba's efforts to subvert the federation, being especially aggrieved in the early 1960s when Amharic replaced Tigrinya, the home tongue of most Christians, and Arabic, revered by the Muslims, as the language of instruction in the primary schools. The Eritrean intelligentsia regarded imposition of Amharic as a sinister impediment to building a successful career. Besides English, Eritreans now had to learn another foreign language to succeed in government schools and to gain access to the university in Addis Abeba.

Once there, the Eritreans constituted the largest non-Amhara group, and they were among the more politically conscious. Given their reservations about Ethiopian rule in Eritrea, they quickly took to the radicalism that dominated Addis Ababa University[3] after 1965. The general

---

3. In 1962, a number of small institutions of higher education were amalgamated to become Haile Sellassie I University; it was renamed after the revolution of 1974.

Ethiopian student movement viewed the world and its problems increasingly in terms of the struggle of progressive forces against world imperialism, led by the United States. To the Ethiopian student, Haile Sellassie was an agent of reaction, who allowed Ethiopia to be exploited for the benefit of the United States and its allies. Internally, they identified the oligarchs as the enemy of the people, pointing to the huge profits they made from sharecropping and other forms of capitalistic agriculture. They put forward the idea of giving land to the tiller and limiting property size and rights, really wrongheaded notions for an economy that, during the 1960s and early 1970s, was prospering and developing capital through commercial agriculture.

True enough, the students were witnessing an economic process that caused social crisis as the elites enclosed common pasturage, limited access to water, evicted inefficient producers, and forced tenants to pay exorbitant rents in money or shares. And it was not only the oligarchs that benefited but also the bourgeoisie, which purchased land for truck farms and plantations to exploit the demand for Ethiopia's coffee, beans, cattle, sheep, and grain. Radiating from Addis Abeba was a zone of economic development that grew annually, dislocating the traditional farmer. Peasant anxieties about land dispossession were loudly repeated by the students, who abhorred the realities of unequal economic growth and opted instead for the theoretical egalitarianism of unproved Marxist-Leninist models of development.

Meanwhile, the Soviets were busily arming Somalia, which had become by 1970 the most militarized state, per capita, in the Horn of Africa, sustaining twenty thousand troops on an expenditure of US$30 million. Ethiopia's armed forces remained between forty-five and fifty thousand, with the budget devoted to the military actually declining from US$66 million, about 20 percent of a total budget of US$317 million, in 1970, to US$62 million, or 14 percent of a US$456 million budget, by the revolution. Addis Abeba managed to contain the Eritrean guerrillas and to check the Somalis with relatively modest outlays and was able, therefore, to devote more of its gross national product, US$2.69 billion in 1970, to economic development programs. The imperial regime may have wanted to spend more on the military, but its chief arms supplier, the United States, had decided as a matter of policy not to permit Ethiopia an offensive capability and therefore provided money and arms for internal security and for frontier defense. In the early 1970s, the emperor's high command became restive about the Somalis as the

27. Haile Sellassie presiding over university graduation, 1966

Eritrean problem came to absorb a third of the army's effective strength.

During the late 1960s, the radical politics of Sudan and South Yemen facilitated arms deliveries to Eritrean fighters. There were more combatants, also, thanks to newly established ELF cells in Asmera that recruited Christian students.[4] With them, the anti-Ethiopian movement grew strong enough to mount successful attacks on Eritrea's administrative and economic infrastructure. The government slowly responded, finally asking the Israelis to organize counterinsurgency commandos composed of Christian peasants. The imperial government's decision corroborated Syria's view that Ethiopia was merely an anti-Arab outpost of the West, and with other Arab states Syria increased assistance to the ELF, which, in turn, more vigorously pursued the armed struggle.

In December 1970, the government declared a state of emergency in parts of Eritrea and replaced the civilian governor, Ras Asrate Kasa, with a general. Thereafter, a military solution was applied to Eritrea, costing the government much support in the highlands and stimulating the establishment of a new organization, the Peoples Liberation Forces, which recruited among the Christian urban petite bourgeoisie and the peasantry.

The government also used force in Bale and Sidamo between 1963 and 1970 to put down a rebellion among Oromo farmers and Somali herders. Their struggle against new land and animal taxes inevitably became involved with the politics of Greater Somalia, a circumstance that caused the government in late 1966 to order the army to intervene. By then, the rebels controlled southern Bale and southeastern Sidamo and were attacking northern districts at will, though the Somalis and Oromo were disunited and did not even attempt coordination. Broadcasting to both groups, Radio Mogadishu stressed the need for Muslim unity against the Amhara, including the Oromo in the framework of Somali nationalism. The Oromo remained unconvinced, and in early 1967 the army, now two brigades strong, had little difficulty in pacifying the rebellion in Sidamo. Bale, however, was a different case, and the soldiers had to coordinate with the air force in order to destroy flocks and deny water holes to the Somalis. By early 1970, the rebellion sputtered out, and the emperor visited the region to inform the people that their taxes would henceforth be invested in development projects.

---

4. Among them were future leaders of the more radical and more secular Eritrean Peoples Liberation Front.

The Eritrean and Bale challenges revealed that the Ethiopian government had not undertaken social and economic programs sufficient to win the allegiance of the people. There were no political parties that could generate competing agenda for action, and parliament remained very much under the control of landlords. It was impossible for the institution seriously to consider bills that reformed land tenure, controlled rents, or levied taxes on the rich. By default, therefore, force became the only tool of social control, partly because the emperor had grown reliant on the military but also because his government was inherently weak.

From 1961 to 1966, Prime Minister Aklilu Habtewold (1912–1974) presided over thirteen ministers who reported daily to the emperor. Thereafter, the ministers were given authority over their units and met as a cabinet under Aklilu, who saw the emperor for approval or disapproval of policies and actions. The emperor retained the power to appoint and dismiss his prime minister, who, however, was permitted to name his own cabinet. Although the Council of Ministers enjoyed a theoretical independence after 1966, the emperor continued to treat it as a body to coordinate and deal with the myriad administrative details created by a growing bureaucracy. As long as Haile Sellassie provided strong leadership, the government functioned adequately, but his refusal to devolve real power did not permit Aklilu and others to become responsible policymakers. They remained the tools of an emperor increasingly dependent on the military for power.

Yet some in the armed forces, especially junior officers, were alienated from the monarchy. The sharpest critics included a group of highly intelligent, unforgiving officers compelled to join the army in the 1950s and early 1960s when the government decided to upgrade the officer corps. Others, especially in the army and air force, had taken night courses at Addis Ababa University and had become infected with student radicalism. And not a few, including Mengistu Hailu Mariam (1935–), Ethiopia's dictator from 1977 to 1991, had gone abroad for advanced training and quickly apprehended how backward Ethiopia really was. As had the leaders of the 1960 coup, the three types of dissidents blamed the government for being more interested in emperor worship than in development.

Included in their indictment was the military high command, which had been recruited into the ruling elite through land grants and other favors. Since the Ethiopian military then operated largely on the company or battalion level, the junior officers often had served in the empire's trouble spots, seeing firsthand the misery that had resulted from the government's policies. Throughout the sixties, therefore, the emperor's base of power subtly eroded.

Meanwhile, Ethiopia's economy seriously deteriorated, greatly hindering the growth of bureaucracy and development programs, both important to the city-dwelling bourgeoisie. The first shock came in 1967, when the Suez Canal was closed in the aftermath of the Six-Day War between Israel and Egypt, raising the prices of imported goods and Ethiopia's exports, generally causing inflation, and sharply reducing the government's revenues from tariffs and duties. Thanks to high international commodity prices in 1972 and an excellent harvest, the economy rebounded, but by then the government was having serious trouble funding the growing counterinsurgency in Eritrea, development programs, and education. The failure to provide more schools, classrooms, and teachers demoralized the urban elites, which wanted better futures for their children. The provinces attached sinister connotations to Addis Abeba's inability to improve education opportunities in the countryside and in non-Amhara regions.

Ethiopia's economy experienced another jolt in 1973, when oil prices went sharply upward in the wake of the Yom Kippur War, providing the immediate background to the coup of 1974. This time, however, the situation was greatly worsened by drought and famine in overpopulated and overfarmed northern Shewa, Welo, and Tigray. The attendant crisis of 1973–1974 revealed that the emperor's government was neither humane nor competent enough to meet the obvious needs of millions of its impoverished subjects. Addis Abeba's inaction, indeed its preliminary denial of the facts, became an international scandal that strongly aroused the dissidents and stimulated others, especially among the capital's bourgeoisie, to become socially active. The politically aware junior officer corps soon understood that a paralyzed government presented an opportunity for fundamental change and quickly intervened, at first indirectly, and then openly. Seen as society's paladins, the men in uniform drew growing support as they purposefully destroyed the ancien régime. The monarchy had created a new Ethiopia that it could not govern; the nation required new men and new ideas. On 12 September 1974, Haile Sellassie I, the Elect of God, was deposed by the military, and Ethiopia moved into an entirely new period.

THIRTEEN

The Revolution, to 1977

By 1973, it was clear that the power behind the throne was the army. Most Ethiopia watchers believed the military would take over once the emperor died, though they all assumed the continuance of the monarchy and, by implication, the society and political economy of the old regime. Haile Sellassie had himself opened the way for the soldiers by failing to create the institutions necessary for popular government, by refusing quickly to name a new heir when Crown Prince Asfa Wossen suffered a massive stroke in January 1973, and by impeding the development of a leadership independent of the crown. Moreover, during the 1970s, Haile Sellassie's once imposing mental powers had started to slip toward senility, helping to explain his lack of effective response to the events of the slowly evolving coup that began in early 1974.

The phenomenon was sparked by the ecological disaster in northern Ethiopia and in lowlands in Harerge, Bale, Sidamo, and Gamo Gofa. By 1973, the peasants had exhausted their reserves, sold off their goods to purchase food, and even eaten seed grain. Desperate and starving, hundreds of thousands left their homesteads and made for the towns, where they hoped the government would provide relief. In their reports, fearful provincial administrators obscured the magnitude of the tragedy, and, in Addis Abeba, officials at first denied the existence of the famine and did not even inform the emperor.

Meanwhile, hearsay about the dead and dying circulated in the capital, as truck drivers recounted the horrendous scenes they had seen in the ravaged provinces. Educated Ethiopians quickly criticized the government's inertia, student militants ascribing the inaction to the antipeople nature of the regime. Although famine long had been a feature of Ethiopian life, the lack of a national relief mechanism was a scandal, matched only by the government's ban of all news about the calamity, which it formally denied until May 1973. The admission was forced by the findings of an ad hoc committee of Haile Sellassie I University professors, who traveled to Welo in April 1973 and returned with pictures and a report describing the ruination they had seen.

Responding to the mounting criticism, the government established an emergency committee, which struggled to contain the crisis by mobilizing internal resources. Although much was accomplished, it could not overcome profiteering, corruption, and the refusal of local and provincial government to waive taxes, and it was unable to divert grain exports to relief agencies. The international media reported such official callousness, which the Ethiopian government rejected as misinformed and exaggerated. Yet, worldwide press and television coverage brought badly needed relief supplies into the country and helped to contain the famine in 1974, a year that opened with two related economic crises.

The first stemmed from the sharp increase in the cost of petroleum products caused by the closed Suez Canal and the second from related inflation in the prices of finished goods and food, which rose 20 percent and 80 percent, respectively. Sensing people's irritation, students in Addis Abeba and elsewhere began agitating against the government, which in late January recklessly imposed a 50 percent hike in the cost of petrol, while refusing an offsetting increase in taxi and bus fares. Addis Abeba's cabbies were irate, and on 18 February they went on strike to reverse the price rise, underscoring their determination by forcing the capital's buses off the roads. Their action was coordinated with a teachers' strike for greater pay and more job security and against a government plan[1] requiring many of them to teach in provincial posts. The students, meanwhile, kept up their pressure, going out on strike, taking to the streets, and stoning expensive private cars. By 19 February, with a meeting of the foreign ministers of the Organization of African Unity imminent, the streets of Addis Abeba had become unsafe.

1. The so-called *Educational Sector Review.*

On 21 February, the government announced that the army had been given full authority to deal with the crisis. Two days later, Haile Sellassie toured the market area, meeting with the people and defusing the tense situation. When he went on the air that evening, he delivered a platitudinous and rambling speech, in which, however, he announced a drop in the cost of gasoline and the imposition of price controls on basic essentials. The monarch warned that the military henceforth would apply strict measures in cases of civil disturbance, and on Monday, 25 February, it appeared that Addis Abeba had returned to normal. The scene now shifted from civil to military unrest.

In mid-January, noncommissioned officers in Negele had arrested their officers, sought the emperor's intervention to ameliorate their dreadful living conditions, and then badly handled the general sent to investigate the matter. A month later, in Bishoftu (Debre Zeyt), the enlisted men at air force headquarters demanded improved working conditions and higher pay. At this point, the government decided to raise military salaries, so that when the next event occurred in the capital on Sunday, 24 February, it was prepared. The emperor himself went to First Division Headquarters to handle a small mutiny and satisfied the soldiers' grievances by promising to improve their living conditions and by pointing to a military pay raise of approximately 20 percent (a private would receive about E$100, or US$40, monthly) announced that morning.

Though a good salary, its announcement did not head off a crisis in Asmera, which began on 25 February when the men detained their commanders and took control of all communications, the banks, and important public installations. While declaring their loyalty to the throne— characteristic of the soldiers until the coup's final stage—they sought greater pay, better food, and more freedom to proffer their criticisms through the chain of command. The mutiny's noncommissioned leaders also pointed to the frustrations of fighting an insurgency with inadequate supplies and armaments and suggested that a political accommodation be considered. The recommendation was more than the emperor could bear, and he refused Asmera's demands. On 27 February, from the balcony of his palace, Haile Sellassie told a hastily convened meeting of supposedly loyalist soldiers that the country could not afford another military pay raise, that enemies were coordinating an attack on Ethiopia's unity, and that they should do their patriotic duty by obeying their officers.

The appeal to patriotism was ignored as garrisons throughout the country joined the insurrection. The students, meanwhile, had continued their agitation, now calling for the end of the monarchy, land reform, the disestablishment of the Orthodox church, and for free speech and other civil rights. Since 1960, the regime had relied on the military to retain its primacy, and when the capital's soldiers joined the insurrection, Haile Sellassie's government became vulnerable to its ideological enemies. Rumors began circulating that the soldiers wanted to be rid of the cabinet, and Aklilu Habtewold, the prime minister, reasoned that the crisis might ease if he and his ministers resigned. At 8:00 P.M. on 27 February, the nightly television news told its stunned audience about the cabinet's unprecedented action.

The next morning, events quickened: troops took control of Addis Abeba and began to arrest the old ministers. Army helicopters overflew the city and dropped leaflets from various units that pledged soldierly loyalty to the emperor while urging the uncommitted police and Imperial Bodyguard to join the revolutionary movement. At the palace, Haile Sellassie was listening to his advisers and to the day's hearsay. Unable to learn much about the military movement, the emperor decided on a new pay structure for the soldiers and on the young aristocrat Endalkatchew Makonnen (1926–1974) for prime minister to satisfy the army's rumored craving for new blood in government.

Educated at Oxford, Endalkatchew had served the emperor in a variety of positions and was qualified for the job he undertook. His cabinet mostly represented the elite educated after the war. With an average age of forty-seven, 75 percent of the cabinet had bachelor's degrees or better and spoke one or more European languages. They generally came from Addis Abeba or Shewa and had connections to the crown, the aristocracy, or to the landed gentry. They represented neither the empire's heterogeneity nor the aspirations of the soldiers. Endalkatchew's first press conference on 1 March proved a disaster, since his thoughtful answers were often drowned out by thousands of chanting students calling for his resignation and for Aklilu's death.

On 4 March, the reform cabinet was sworn in, and the new prime minister began his efforts to restore order and to reestablish the regime's legitimacy. He worked in a hostile environment in which the students continued agitating for radical change, and even the timid Confederation of Ethiopian Labour Unions (CELU) threatened a general strike if demands for minimum wages and better working conditions were not met. Endalkatchew, however, believed that reform would win the day, and on 5 March he pressured the emperor to accept changes that would have transformed Ethiopia into a constitutional monarchy. That evening his subjects heard Haile Sellassie report that he had ordered a revision of the 1955 constitution which would make the prime minister responsible to parliament and guarantee greater civil rights for the people. While momentous in terms of the emperor's reign, the concessions revealed how remote Haile Sellassie and Endalkatchew were from the current political reality.

The CELU's general strike began the next day, as if to demonstrate the people's disdain of the government. This action, and others that followed, denied the regime the time needed to fulfill its promises. Its energy was dissipated in coping with demonstrations by workers, students, teachers, government officials, Moslems, and Orthodox priests, each of them accompanied by pamphlets that demanded reforms. They contained few references to Marx, Lenin, or to socialism. None asked for executions, few assailed the emperor directly, but many called for due process of law against corrupt officials and the ex-ministers. Military leaflets attacked high-ranking officers as a class but generally made the same points as had the civilian tracts. The soldiers were especially adamant about bringing about change with a minimum of bloodshed and stood strongly for national unity.

The military, meanwhile, was politicizing itself. The original mutineers were noncommissioned officers, joined early by junior commissioned officers. Their quick successes revealed that, without the cooperation of the military, the government was impotent. This realization led radical officers and men to contemplate the possibility of revolutionary political changes. Nameless at the time, they certainly conformed to the model represented by Mengistu Haile Mariam: idealistic, committed, calculating, shrewd, ruthless, and patient. Such men realized that they would have to discredit the monarchy before they established a revolutionary regime, and they would have to subvert any progressive changes made by Endalkatchew's government.

After March, the direction was toward revolution, although from March to May the prime minister and the emperor continued along the road of reform. Believing that the turmoil would be short-lived, they developed ideas and plans for change. On 26 March, Haile Sellassie announced that a special commission would be appointed to investigate charges of corruption leveled against individuals in and out of government. He also announced a rise in minimum pay for the nation's poorest laborers and named a new commission to study, and make recommendations to improve, working conditions. On 9 April, Endalkatchew's cabinet issued a comprehensive statement outlining its plans to reform taxes and land tenure; to accelerate the pace of development, especially in the countryside; and to narrow income disparities. The document described Ethiopia's problems as a national crisis and pledged the government's unremitting efforts to improve the life of the people and to maintain national unity and the country's traditions. Several weeks later, Endalkatchew announced the end of press censorship, to allow the people the information necessary to debate the great national questions facing Ethiopia.

In the interim, the army was being infused with fully developed Marxist-Leninist ideas by homegrown ideologues or by returnees from self-imposed European and American exile. Very few of the soldiers questioned how appropriate Marxism was for Ethiopia's preindustrial economy; rather, the ideas were swallowed whole by the more militant and socially conscious officers and men. They wanted the emperor's deposition and a military government prefatory to elections for a truly democratic state. They were unable to convince many of their more conservative colleagues, who formed a faction led by Endalkatchew's relative, Col. Alem-Zewd Tessema, commander of the airborne unit. The colonel assumed radical positions, claiming that his group would ensure that reforms were carried out. Yet, he cooperated with the government in putting down insurrections in the air force and gaining Endalkatchew's entrance into various barracks where he could recruit supporters for the government's program.

On 18 April, the prime minister met with two thousand noncommissioned officers and men at Fourth Division Headquarters. He was criticized for allowing the old ministers the freedom to continue influencing the emperor. Desperately needing military cooperation, Endalkatchew decided to detain most of the previous government's leading administrators, and he asked Alem-Zewd to gain Haile Sellassie's permission. The emperor consented only after being assured that the former officials would enjoy due process of law. The old regime dutifully gave itself up to Endalkatchew and the soldiers, little realizing that the prime minister used them to gain political points and that the emperor was helpless to protect them.

Given Haile Sellassie's impotency and Endalkatchew's obvious dependence on Alem-Zewd, the radicals decided to push ahead on their program leading to a democratic republic. The leadership comprised twelve to sixteen officers, mostly graduates of the Holetta Military Academy, which accepted recruits from the ranks. They were united in criticism of the government's continuing failure to make meaningful reforms, and they asked Ethiopia's military organizations to send delegates to Addis Abeba in late June for an important meeting to discuss the country's future. Their message was so seductive that, on 22 June, Alem-Zewd lost control over his own organization and even over his own paratroopers.

On 27–28 June, the military representatives constituted themselves as the Coordinating Committee of the Armed Forces (in Amharic, *derg*, or "committee"). During its meetings, a number of officers rose to speak, but none was more eloquent than Maj. Mengistu Haile Mariam, of Harer's Third Division, who became the Coordinating Committee's chairperson. He brought order to the boisterous proceedings and gave shape to the derg's demands. He told his colleagues that nothing was more important than the unity of the military and the nation, and he may have introduced the still potent slogan Etiopia Tikdem, or "Ethiopia above all." The derg ordered the arrest of the old regime's leading magnates and dignitaries, including the powerful Ras Asrate Kasa. Unwilling to order the Imperial Bodyguard to intervene, and thereby cause civil strife, the emperor was powerless to stop the derg, and so was Endalkatchew, whose government now fell apart as some of its more prescient members resigned and went into exile.

The months of July and August were filled with bile for the increasingly feeble emperor. He heard the derg's often repeated statements of loyalty, while watching it destroy the monarchy's foundations. Although he often refused to sanction the Coordinating Committee's orders, his veto was ignored. He watched helplessly while the men-in-uniform arrested trusted old friends and advisers, dismantled the institutions that he had established and through which he ruled, and forced Endalkatchew from power on 22 July.

His replacement was the Oxford-educated Mikail Imru (1926–), whom the derg manipulated from the outset. It had organized itself into eleven committees to supervise public life and to fine-tune the revolution it had decided to sponsor. Mikail really had no opportunity to follow an independent policy, but he provided a cover of legitimacy for the derg's decisions. The military quickly revealed that it would oppose all civilian initiatives aimed at ending the crisis. When on 7 August the Constitutional Commission, itself a result of the derg's pressure, reported that it would recommend a liberal-democratic constitutional monarchy, the derg showed almost complete disinterest and would not allow the document to be made public. Moreover, it continually sought to turn the Anti-Corruption Commission toward its long-term goal of ridding the country of the monarchy.

That much became clear throughout the first half of August as the derg artfully and carefully neutralized the last institutions that supported and maintained the monarchy. Cut from the emperor was his Imperial Bodyguard, his private cabinet, his crown council, his special court, and his advisers. In the palace, Haile Sellassie's retainers daily observed all the formalities surrounding the imperial presence, but otherwise the court was an empty place devoid of power, with its main inhabitant virtually under house arrest. In parts of the palace, where the old emperor could no longer go, members of the derg were reading through files for information to use to destroy Haile Sellassie's worrisome charisma.

During the second half of August, publications in the capital printed lies about the size of the emperor's fortune and the profits his estates and businesses produced, and half-truths about the comfort and privilege in which the imperial family lived. The royals and the entire ruling class were characterized as corrupt, blamed even for the high number of prostitutes and bars in the capital. The emperor and his men were described as interested only in power and wealth, not the welfare of the people. The climax to the campaign of vilification came on the evening of 11 September, when the capital's television station broadcast two shows, one contrasting the lives of the people with the comforts afforded the emperor's dogs, and the other, a doctored version of the previous year's BBC show on the famine, which interspersed pictures of the tragedy with shots of the lavish life led by the imperial family and the aristocracy.

The next day, with Addis Abeba cut off from the world and under curfew, a small group of officers went to the palace and, at 6:00 A.M., summoned Haile Sellassie. He appeared in full uniform and, with great dignity, stood proud and erect while a nervous officer read out a proclamation of deposition. The old man declared his acceptance, if it were for the good of the people, and he was escorted outside, where an awaiting vehicle and small escort took him to Fourth Division Headquarters. Within the hour, Radio Addis Abeba reported that Ethiopia had been freed from Haile Sellassie's oppression by a Provisional Military

Administration Council (PMAC)—the descendants of the Coordinating Committee—that had abolished parliament and suspended the constitution.

The new administration, still popularly called the derg, was led by Gen. Aman Mikail Andom (1924–1974), much revered because he had won the war against Somalia in 1964, had pushed for democratic reforms, for which he had been shunted aside into the Senate, and had cooperated with the military from the beginning. Indeed, he had been minister of defense in Mikail Imru's cabinet and had had a key role in the unfolding bloodless coup. That he was an Eritrean was another asset, since the crisis in the north had to be resolved before the government could redirect funds to economic development. Although head of state and government, minister of defense, and chief of staff, he was not made chairman of the Coordinating Committee. Once again, the de facto ruler was isolated from the real source of power and authority.

In Addis Abeba, meanwhile, many students, returnees, and labor unionists continued agitating for a civilian regime. The dissidence masked serious policy differences among the military, which had a number of difficult problems to resolve: (1) the duties of the head of state and government; (2) the fate of the detainees; (3) the Eritrean crisis; (4) land reform; and, of course, (5) the organization of the new government. General Aman and a number of conservative officers took a moderate approach to these questions, whereas the leadership in the derg, headed by Mengistu, wanted radical solutions. In November, Aman became frustrated at the Coordinating Committee's disregard of his recommendations about conciliation in Eritrea and a return to the federation, about due process for the prisoners, about freeing the imperial princesses, and about the establishment, through a referendum, of a democratic republic. To pursue his program, he joined a conspiracy of anti-derg soldiers and a few at-large imperial generals and aristocrats.

He made the mistake of discussing plans on his tapped telephone, and the evidence of Aman's complicity was offered to a hastily arranged meeting of the derg on 22 November. The decisions made that day represented a victory for the hard-liners, who opposed the moderate positions espoused by Aman. They believed that the quick establishment of a republic would end the revolution before it had begun; that, for nationalist reasons, it was wrong to yield to the liberation movements in Eritrea; and that officials from the old regime should be executed without trial. In a fiery speech, Mengistu instructed his audience to look to the future: Ethiopia needed land reform, national unity, and revolution.

Reactionaries, he declared, had infiltrated the derg, and they were conspiring with remnants of the old regime to restore the status quo ante. The PMAC thereupon voted Aman out of office, and that night, when he resisted arrest, he was killed in the ensuing melee. Shortly thereafter, at a hastily arranged meeting, Mengistu insisted on summary justice for the detained former officials, whose deaths would be reported the next day along with the announcement of Aman's execution. Mengistu argued that the Ethiopian people sought revenge and that the revolution needed a bold statement of intent.

Although there was opposition to the suddenness of the action, none had the courage to oppose the arbitrary and capricious proceedings that resulted in the condemnation of fifty-nine men, including generals, cabinet officers, aristocrats, and members of the royal family. The subsequent execution, regarded as a massacre by many Ethiopians, shocked the nation and also the world, both of which had believed in the bloodless coup. The event revealed that a ruthless military regime controlled Ethiopia and that it would not build on the foundations of the old order. Instead, tempered with blood, the Coordinating Committee would follow its own path.

On 20 December, the government issued its Declaration of Socialism, which foresaw a one-party state, public ownership of the main sectors of the economy, and collective agriculture. The document called for national unity and equal opportunity for all ethnic, religious, cultural, and religious groups. The new year saw the nationalization of private financial institutions and, in February 1975, most of Ethiopia's industry, including all of the foreign-owned companies. So far, the military had followed a standard African revolutionary process, replacing one elite with another. Although foreigners were uneasy about the regime's radical rhetoric and about its commitment to human rights, few believed that the military would continue to move left, especially since the declaration also specified that Ethiopia's foreign policy would remain unchanged, leaving the country allied to the conservative United States.

Yet, the government needed a great popular success to rally civilian support and also required a national consensus in order to mobilize men and matériel to confront the worsening military situation in Eritrea. Shocked by Aman's death, the army there remained in its forts, while the secessionists stepped up their activities and liberated area after area. To garner the hearts and minds of the majority Oromo people, leftist members of the derg, led by Mengistu, conceived of a radical land reform

28. Military review, 20 December 1974, for the
Declaration of Socialism; Gen. Taferi Benti, head of state,
taking the salute

to redress the land expropriations that had occurred during the reigns of
Menilek and Haile Sellassie. Fulfilling the revolution's leading motto,
Land to the Tiller, would destroy the political economy of clientage and
sharecropping predominant in southern Ethiopia since the 1920s and
stop the development of capitalistic agriculture radiating in all directions
from Addis Abeba.

29. Students in the uniform of the Development through Cooperation Campaign, waiting to march past the reviewing stand, 20 December 1974

On 4 March 1975, the derg issued Proclamation No. 31, which nationalized all rural land, permitted farming households usufruct over as many as ten hectares, and established the Peasant Association (PA) as a new mass organization and as an organ of government. Each PA would be allocated an eight-hundred-hectare area, and its membership of farmers meeting in a general assembly would elect its own leadership. With wide local powers, PAs replaced the old regime's subdistrict administrations; they were given their authority over internal security and economic life and were also made responsible for the equitable redistribution of land within their jurisdictions.

To expedite the changes, the derg cleverly decided to use high school and university students and staff on the Development through Cooperation Campaign (the *zamacha*). The youth helped to implement the land reform and in establishing the PAs but occasionally had to be restrained from pushing forward to collectivization and meting out revolutionary justice to ex-landlords and displaced officials of the old regime. Student response to the zamacha showed that the younger, educated civilian population was more radical than the government. Yet, it was not in the countryside but in the cities where the contradiction was played out.

On 26 July 1975, the government issued Proclamation No. 27, which nationalized urban land but allowed individuals the ownership of one house and the use of as many as five hundred square meters for residential purposes. Additional dwellings were confiscated, and rents were sharply reduced, especially for low-income families. The proclamation also provided for the establishment of neighborhood organizations, or *kebelays*, the urban equivalent of the peasant associations. The kebelay collected all rents on small homes and used the proceeds to finance social services for its members. The latter included all adult persons who lived within the precincts of the kebelay, and they elected a policy committee responsible for the organization's functions. Almost from the outset, the government tried to manipulate election results in order to control the urban centers.

In Ethiopia's towns and cities lived the nation's politicized classes, comprising a mixed bag of students, labor unionists, teachers, bureaucrats, returnees, and even street boys and other members of the lumpen proletariat savvy to urban life. The last had swelled the ranks of the many demonstrations that punctuated the old regime's slow demise, in the process becoming a major political factor. In 1975–1976, however, their immediate importance receded in the face of the ideological squabbles that dominated relations between the military and the intelligentsia, now organized into Marxist-Leninist parties that carried on pedantic and semiotic warfare in the media, seeking backing for their finely honed theoretical positions.

The Ethiopian Peoples Revolutionary party (EPRP) and the All-Ethiopia Socialist Movement (Amharic acronym, MEISON) came to represent the two main lines of radical thought. MEISON was dominated by French-trained intellectuals led by Haile Fida (presumed executed in 1978), who believed in self-determination within Ethiopia for minorities and nationalities. They arrogantly believed that the derg could be so thoroughly tamed to socialism as to transfer power to the party. Since MEISON stood forthrightly for Ethiopian unity, the military decided to use its ideas for its own purposes. MEISON members therefore had a crucial role in developing the rural and urban land reforms, provided reliable men for important government posts, and helped to establish in December 1975 the important Yekatit '66 Political School for training cadres and the Provisional Office of Mass Organizational Affairs (POMOA) for politicizing Ethiopia's broad masses.

MEISON's theorists were largely responsible for the Program of the

National Democratic Revolution (NDRP), which provided a political agenda. Its issuance in April 1976 was mostly Mengistu's doing, as he and his allies in the derg continued to push the country leftward. Its bold commitments to "scientific socialism" and a vanguard proletarian party alienated Washington just as it helped convince Moscow that events in Ethiopia were progressing along a properly revolutionary path. Written in terms familiar to the Eastern bloc, the NDRP accorded nationalities autonomy within a united Ethiopia; declared class war on bureaucratic capitalism, feudalism, and imperialism, the enemies of the broad masses; provided for comprehensive economic development following a central plan guided by socialist principles; gave the armed forces a paramount role in safeguarding the nation's territorial integrity; and projected the establishment of a people's democratic republic.

The new state was to emerge after a period of dialogue among political organizations formed by farmers, the national bourgeoisie, and proletarians, the last of which were to take a leading role. Political coherence would lead to the formation of a larger organization, to which the derg would transfer power. Meanwhile, the POMOA would facilitate the political process and otherwise help to create a stable environment for the creation of the People's Democratic Republic of Ethiopia.

The top-down management of the revolution greatly distressed the EPRP, whose members were mostly locally schooled or educated in the United States. They sought to accord the peasantry and the proletariat immediate political primacy under a dictatorship of the working classes. In the EPRP's thinking, the military deserved no transitional role and should immediately return to the barracks to prepare itself to accept civilian authority. They regarded the military as opportunists who had stolen their programs, ideas, and ideology. The EPRP sought a state based on elections and popular authority, even at the expense of state sovereignty. The party accepted the theoretical right of nationalities to secede from Ethiopia, although it preferred to see the empire's peoples construct a state based on respect for cultural autonomy.

In May 1976, in light of the NDRP, the derg offered discussions with Eritrea's progressive movements, in effect trying to split the Marxist-oriented Eritrean Peoples Liberation Front (EPLF) from the more conservative Eritrean Liberation Front (ELF). By then, the EPLF held the upper hand in its internal struggle for power, and its war against Addis Abeba was going well. The government's twenty-five thousand men were fighting a holding action in eastern Eritrea, having abandoned the west to the insurgents in 1975. During the rainy season of 1976, the EPLF rejected the derg's *demarche* and besieged virtually all of the army's strong points. The government responded by organizing a whimsical "Red March" on Eritrea by untrained and poorly armed peasants who had been promised land for their efforts. The campaign proved a military disaster as the disciplined Eritreans turned their modern weapons on the hapless peasants.

The political consequences were as severe, since the newly formed Tigrayan Peoples Liberation Front (TPLF) regarded the Red March as evidence of the regime's refusal to consider provincial autonomy and joined with the EPLF in turning back the campaigners. Throughout 1977, the situation worsened as the TPLF threatened Addis Abeba's control over the vital highway north to Asmera and as the EPLF took most of eastern Eritrea, leaving only the major centers in government hands. In Addis Abeba, the intelligentsia watched with alarm as the government persisted in its efforts to solve a political crisis with military means. The ranks of the EPRP swelled with urban dwellers who believed that civilians might have more success with the EPLF, a view that some in the derg held. In July 1976, moderate officers, led by Maj. Sisay Habte, mounted an abortive coup against Mengistu. Its failure led the EPRP to mount an urban guerrilla war, which it began on 12 September, during the parade celebrating the second anniversary of Haile Sellassie's dethronement.

As the violence grew, members of the derg once again voiced reservations about the obvious failures of the government to end the fighting in Eritrea and to defeat political opponents. In December 1976, a coalition voted to reduce Mengistu's executive powers, and in late January 1977, Gen. Tafari Bente, Aman's successor as head of state, made a speech in which he called for negotiations with the Eritreans and with the civilian opposition. On 3 February, Mengistu and his hard-core supporters unilaterally arrested General Tafari and five of his closest allies. Using trumped-up evidence, Mengistu accused them of plotting with the EPRP to oust him and to suppress MEISON and forced a reluctant mass meeting of the derg to condemn the men, who were promptly executed. On 12 February, the derg declared Mengistu head of state and its chairman, making him the revolution's solitary leader.

He decided to break the EPRP by giving kebelays wide police powers to be exercised by revolutionary guards chosen from among the lumpen proletariat. When he declared a "Red Terror," the guards undertook class warfare against the comparatively well-educated and economically secure members of the EPRP and its student allies. During 1977, the year it took to break the EPRP, anarchy reigned in Addis Abeba, in the major urban centers, and even in the countryside. Unspeakable horrors were perpetrated on a largely defenseless civilian population for the sake of dogmatic purity, the broad masses, democracy, national integrity, and civilian rule. The government, however, had the urban masses, history, and guns on its side and finally wore down the EPRP, in the process killing, or forcing into exile, thousands of Ethiopia's best-educated and idealistic young people. The Red Terror was so traumatic that subsequently there was virtually no overt civilian opposition to the PMAC. Indeed, the Somali attack in July 1977 won the government and Mengistu considerable nationalistic support.

By then, Mengistu and his men were building a people's militia trained by North Korea and supplied by the Soviet Union, which the derg had courted from the outset of its rule. Mengistu believed that the USSR's revolutionary history of national reconstruction was more in keeping with Ethiopia's political goals than were the traditions of American capitalism and bourgeois liberalism. He therefore sent members of the derg and thousands of other key military personnel to the Soviet Union and its allies for military and political training. By 1975–1976, Moscow was convinced that the Ethiopian revolution would lead to the establishment of an authentic Marxist-Leninist state, and it prepared to transfer its interests from inherently weak Somalia to Ethiopia, the Horn of Africa's leading state. Meanwhile, it continued to supply Mogadishu with weapons, while simultaneously promising Mengistu military aid on condition that he break off the alliance with the United States.

The American connection, already eroding in the last years of Haile Sellassie as space-borne satellites rendered obsolete the American communications center outside of Asmera, attenuated as the Carter administration took a strong "human rights" stance against Ethiopia. Furthermore, even though Washington had increased its military assistance, the new government reckoned it was insufficient to guarantee internal security and to resolve the crisis in Eritrea. Mengistu decided therefore to close down the American military mission and Kagnew Station in April 1977, an event followed in May by a secret agreement with Moscow to supply Ethiopia's military needs.

The situation in Eritrea was now so desperate that the government stripped the southern command of troops to reinforce its beleaguered

30. Eradicating the past in Addis Abeba. Photograph by Susan Drabik.

garrisons in Asmera, Aseb, and Mitsiwa, leaving the Somalis with overwhelming local military superiority. Thanks to Soviet military assistance, Mogadishu had enough supplies to wage a six-month war and mustered 35,000 men and 15,000 Ogadeni fighters in the Western Somali Liberation Front (WSLF), 250 tanks mostly fitted with 105-mm guns, 300 armed personnel carriers, 200 mobile artillery, 50 MiG fighters, and a squadron of Il-28 bombers.

The buildup during the sixties had been undertaken implicitly to serve the goal of reuniting all Somalis. President Siad Barre's government therefore found Ethiopia's weakness irresistible and decided on war. The few Ethiopian soldiers in scattered Ogaden garrisons could do little during May–June 1977 to counter the WSLF's attacks and were completely defeated by the Somali army, in the guise of WSLF volunteers, which crossed the disputed frontier on 23 July. Within a week, key towns in eastern Ogaden were in Somali hands, including the air base at Gode.

Now in a difficult position, the Soviets recommended a "Socialist Federation" for Ethiopia, Somalia, and South Yemen to resolve their conflicts. The scheme revealed both Moscow's slavish devotion to ideology and its ignorance of the passionate issues of religion and

31. Slogan from 1977–78

nationalism that characterized international relations in the Horn of Africa. Meanwhile, the invasion progressed, and by September 1977, Mogadishu controlled 90 percent of Ogaden and had followed retreating Ethiopian forces into non–Somali-inhabited regions of Harerge, Bale, and Sidamo. This aggression rankled the Soviets, who from the outset had warned Siad Barre not to advance beyond Ogaden. Moscow consequently suspended all military aid to the aggressor, began openly to deliver weapons to Addis Abeba, and reassigned Soviet military advisers from Somalia to Ethiopia.

Meanwhile, the North Koreans were training a people's militia in the use of the Soviet weapons that daily flooded in. The derg recruited tens of thousands of peasants, largely from among the Oromo agriculturists, who had gained most from the land reform. The propaganda of mobilization stressed the historic role of the masses in retaining Ethiopia's freedom and territorial integrity and pointedly termed Adwa a people's victory. On 25 June 1977, the elements of the new militia, 80,000 strong, marched in Addis Abeba before a cheering populace, amazing European observers. For Mengistu, the creation of the militia was a great achievement, and during the next ten months another 240,000 men were trained and sent off to fight Ethiopia's wars.

The militiamen fought well enough to give Ethiopia's battered regular army time to regroup and to restore its chain of command. The derg recalled imperial officers purged in 1974, regaining logistical and technical services in which the old army excelled and making the war a patriotic issue that crossed political and class interests. By late September, the battle lines had hardened around Dire Dawa and Harer, and the Somali army lost its momentum and began exhausting its supplies and all hope of remaining victorious. The ensuing war of attrition inevitably favored Ethiopia, which had forty million inhabitants to Somalia's four million. Every day, Addis Abeba's soldiers became better armed, whereas Siad Barre was unable to entice the United States into resupplying his troops. A friendless Somalia made a sharp contrast with Ethiopia, which had become an internationalist cause célèbre, not only receiving weapons and other assistance from the Socialist bloc but also enjoying the services of 13,000 Cuban and 4,000 South Yemeni soldiers. The latter helped to train the Ethiopians in the use of Soviet tanks, and the former helped to contain and finally expel the Somalis.

In mid-January 1978, Somalia ordered its last offensive, which was smartly beaten back by the completely reequipped Ethiopian army and its thousands of new fighters. Addis Abeba counterattacked on 23 January 1978, and a week later, after satisfying advances, a confident Mengistu called on Mogadishu to withdraw from Ogaden or suffer a calamitous defeat. Try as it might, the Somali government could not gain international support for its position, since every other country in Africa and the major powers supported the notion of the inviolability of Africa's frontiers as negotiated by the colonialists. By late February, after weeks of artillery shelling, a combined Ethiopian and Cuban force broke through softened Somali lines on the road to Jijiga, and the town fell on 5 March. A few days later, Barre broadcast the withdrawal of all Somali forces from Ogaden. On 23 March 1978, Radio Addis Abeba announced that the government had regained control over all Ogaden military posts and administrative centers.

While concentrating on the more important Somali threat, government troops still held on in Eritrea. With the Ethiopians preoccupied elsewhere, EPLF and ELF fighters had tightened their hold over the province, making an insurgent victory appear inevitable. The internal politics of the Eritrean insurgency intervened, however, on Addis Abeba's behalf. The largely Muslim ELF was active in the lowlands and sought to implement a moderate program of reform. The EPLF, on the other hand, was a radical organization that aimed to create a modern secular state guided by scientific socialism. As liberation from Ethiopia came closer, the two organizations began to look to the future, cooperation broke down, and the historic moment bypassed the Eritreans. The instant occurred at Mitsiwa.

Working separately, the ELF and the EPLF had by October 1977 pushed the Ethiopians from Akordat and had taken control of the Mitsiwa-Asmera road. On 9 December, when the government tried to clear the artery, the EPLF countered so effectively that it broke through the army's line of defense around Mitsiwa, took the water works, and occupied the mainland part of the town. With the Ethiopians isolated on Mitsiwa Island, the EPLF decided to attack without ELF support. Twice, the Eritrean command sent its men across three dikes strongly defended by Ethiopian infantry. The Eritreans died in the thousands and left the field to the Ethiopians, seemingly proving that they could not fight a concerted and organized campaign against their enemy. The victory boosted the morale of the Ethiopian army sufficiently to enable it to hold on until the war against Somalia was over in early 1978. The government then moved massive reinforcements into Eritrea and won back most of the province by the end of the year, although the EPLF managed to hold on in the Nacfa area, which offered easily defensible mountainous terrain.

Meanwhile, in Addis Abeba, Mengistu had managed to wipe out virtually all organized civilian opposition, including MEISON. The latter had willingly cooperated with the derg in suppressing the EPRP, its political rival, in order to build its own power base among the peasant associations and kebelays. Once the EPRP was gone, however, Mengistu realized that MEISON's activities threatened the derg, which by now had established its own socialist party, Abyot Seded (revolutionary flame). The new party's existence underlined the military's resolve to meet its own ideological needs and signaled its frustration with civilian resistance to its rule. In July–August 1977, with the Red Terror a success, military ideologues took control of the POMOA and the Yekatit '66 Political School, both largely staffed by MEISON members, and the government passed decrees placing both organizations firmly under its control. Though they went into hiding, MEISON's top leaders were soon apprehended and executed, and only a few managed to leave the country. Many secondary figures, however, joined Abyot Seded and subsequently became important government officials.

In contrast, Lt. Col. Atnafu Abebe, the derg's deputy chairman, found that he could not condone all the killings in the name of Marxism, an ideology he considered alien to Ethiopia's political traditions. At the derg's third congress in November 1977, he made a speech vilifying the

Red Terror and socialism, which, he declared, would be impossible to establish in Ethiopia during his lifetime. He ridiculed the notion of a workers' party in a largely peasant country and condemned the alliance with the USSR as alienating Ethiopia from its longtime Western allies who, besides weapons, had provided capital and technology. He called for moderation in politics and international relations and for reconciliation among Ethiopia's warring factions. Atnafu misread his popularity within the derg, and he completely misunderstood the attraction of the Marxist vision that now conditioned the derg's thinking. In response, Mengistu termed his old colleague in arms a reactionary, a view that the military council sustained. When, over the next few days, Atnafu refused several times to recant, Mengistu had him summarily executed on 13 November 1977.

By early 1978, Mengistu had defeated the Somalis, the Eritreans, civilian dissidents, and opposition within the derg. In each case, he had used the force supplied by the Soviets and exercised by a congeries of Ethiopians, who for one reason or the other supported him, or Ethiopia, or socialism, or all three. Yet, the very consolidation of the new government's rule left behind a legacy of disunity, since the military subsequently never attempted political solutions to the problems left behind by the Haile Sellassie regime. The derg thus maintained the authoritarian nature of government in Ethiopia, its own actions rendering nugatory its much vaunted Program of National Democratic Revolution.

FOURTEEN

The Failure of the Revolution, to 1991

In the decade following Mengistu's consolidation of power, the continuing insurgencies in Eritrea and Tigray diverted resources from his regime's social and economic agenda. For a time the government tried more or less peaceably to win over the hearts and minds of the Eritrean people and was having some success, especially in the Christian highlands. By late 1981, however, Mengistu grew impatient and decided, characteristically, on a massive campaign to take the province's Sahil district, where the Eritrean Peoples Liberation Front was heavily fortified in the Nacfa region.

The Red Star Campaign, as it was called, was intended as much as a program of economic development as an act of war. Before too long, however, the military effort became paramount, undermining the campaign's other goals. From Asmera in January 1982, Mengistu personally planned the campaign and then commanded the 200,000-man Ethiopian army. Before too long, the government's soldiers converged on Nacfa, and, through hard fighting, forced a gap in the Eritrean lines. At the last minute, the EPLF was saved by a political decision to allow Mengistu's old division to move up and take the town. By the time the Ethiopians had repositioned themselves, the EPLF had restored its lines, and the advance quickly stalled. Thereafter, the momentum switched to the EPLF, and the entire campaign bogged down, leaving Mengistu without his victory and 11,000 Ethiopian deaths in vain. Nacfa became the symbol of Eritrean indomitability, revealing the need for a political settlement between the government and the EPLF.

Compromise, however, was not in the regime's political vocabulary. Working from a Marxist-Leninist text, the government sought to transform Ethiopia into a command state inhabited by a disciplined people. To accomplish its goal, the government replaced the royalist ideology with *scientific socialism* and the emperor's elites with a new party. On 18 December 1979, Mengistu announced the formation of a Commission for Organizing the Party of the Working People of Ethiopia (COPWE). Its objectives were to spread Marxism-Leninism and to build a party prefatory to the establishment of a People's Democratic Republic of Ethiopia.

COPWE's structure and organization gave enormous power to its unspecified chairman, who also mediated between the commission, whose membership he controlled, and the government. During its first years, the commission built about sixty-five hundred cells, drawing much of its membership from the military and most of its leadership from the derg. It drew charges of sexism because of its few women participants and allegations of domination by the old rulers because of its many Amhara adherents. Indeed, notwithstanding the propaganda surrounding the evolution of COPWE into a nationally representative party, it remained more typical of the army than of the nation. By January 1983, when COPWE held its Second Conference, its regional leaders were all military, and its membership was composed largely of civil servants, soldiers, and teachers, with workers and peasants a distinct minority.

For his tool of change, Mengistu wanted a disciplined and loyal organization to repair the disorder and individualism that he and his ideological advisers believed had retarded Ethiopia's development. By 1980, the leadership was beginning to realize that it would take more than slogans and new administrative structures to reshape Ethiopia. The government, through COPWE, asserted control over virtually every organ of authority and power, especially the All-Ethiopia Trade Union (in 1986, changed to Ethiopia Trade Union) and the peasants' associations and kebelays. It established such new organizations as the Revolutionary Ethiopia Women's Association, the Revolutionary Ethiopia Youth Organization, and the Working People's Control Commission, the last ostensibly a check against official abuse and corruption. In fact, the mass organizations were not intended to have a life of their own or to influence and inform government but were designed as instruments political cadres could use to establish socialist programs.

There is no question that the government intended to establish a command economy. In 1974–1975, it had nationalized most of the country's industry, which languished subsequently because of a dearth of capital, technicians, spare parts, and raw materials. Heavy-handed and often confused central planning in the 1980s did little to ameliorate the shortages, and the few industrial projects undertaken by Ethiopia's socialist allies were either inappropriate or too expensive to operate. The rhetoric of Mengistu's socialism scared off Western investors, and Ethiopia remained starved for capital throughout the revolutionary period. In fact, the government was so doctrinaire that it squandered its limited resources on propping up inefficient state farms and in sponsoring forms of collective agriculture.

After the revolution, peasants' associations quickly dominated the countryside, largely replacing the local government. By 1980, a relatively peaceful year throughout the country, about seven million households were organized into 23,506 associations. As COPWE extended its authority, the PAs lost their autonomy and were transformed into organs of the central government. The peasants came to regard their leaders as little more than government tax collectors and propaganda agents. The average cultivator paid more taxes in money, services, and in kind than he or she ever did under the Haile Sellassie regime. No amount of roads, clinics, and schools could offset peasant grievances about compulsory sales of crops to parastatal firms at below-market prices and about unpaid labor on local development projects.

Though the land reform was carried out fairly and was mostly popular, it did not yield surplus land for redistribution. The imperial elites had not themselves cultivated latifundia but had extracted surplus from tenants. Since the latter largely retained their rights of usufruct and the few mechanized plantations became state farms, there was no reorganization of the mode of production and therefore no increased efficiency in the exploitation of land. Since the peasantry was located in associations and everyone had the right to farm, pressure on land increased. Subsequent redistribution led to smaller plots, overcultivation, land degradation, and declining yields.

Instead of investing in fertilizer, high-yield seeds, labor, expertise, and tractors to increase production among the peasants, the government throughout the 1980s devoted 60 percent of these scarce resources to state farms and collectivized Producers' Cooperatives (PCs), hoping to make the latter an attractive possibility for peasants. Yet, by June 1984, only about 4 percent of Ethiopia's total arable land was collectivized, an even smaller percentage of cultivators were involved, and yields on producer cooperatives were less than farms organized more loosely in peasants' associations. To obtain the foodstuffs necessary for Ethiopia's cities and towns, the government created the Agricultural Marketing Corporation (AMC), a powerful parastatal.

The AMC regulated the domestic food trade by establishing quotas for the PAs, PCs, and national farms and by setting prices that varied from province to province depending largely on productivity and availability of transport. The AMC was never able, however, to convince the PAs and PCs to deliver their full quotas of grain at below-market prices. To reduce the likelihood that peasants would smuggle their produce to Ethiopia's cities and towns, where prices were high, the AMC built checkpoints at provincial frontiers and at strategic points along the main roads. The net effect was to fragment the national economy and to reduce the peasants' incentive to produce. There was a consequent drop in crop yields, forcing the government to rely on the state farms' relatively high-cost grain to feed the cities. For the rest of the country, however, little surplus remained to store against an emergency, and the AMC's policies impeded the delivery of grain into needy areas. The disaster of the new regime's agricultural policies was soon revealed.

When the rains failed during July–September 1983, a new famine was signaled for 1984. The projection was withheld from Mengistu and other top leaders, since they were preparing for the revolution's tenth anniversary and the establishment of the Workers' Party of Ethiopia (WPE). Told only about successes and triumphs, the leadership believed that its policies had fostered a period of prosperity and achievement. Throughout the remainder of 1983, however, concerned officials in the government's Relief and Rehabilitation Commission (RRC) leaked Ethiopia's bad news to the international press, nongovernmental relief organizations, diplomats, and visiting foreign delegations. Although a great deal of sympathy was generated, there was no general alarm, since the Ethiopian government had not acknowledged the country's plight, even after the short rains failed in February 1984.

By then, approximately ten thousand people were dying weekly in Welo, and the RRC was close to exhausting its resources. In March, its commissioner, Dawit Wolde Giorgis, sent a full report to Mengistu and other top officials, seeking the regime's acknowledgement of the famine so that international relief could be mobilized. Receiving no reply, Dawit raised the matter during a long meeting devoted to a grandiose and completely unrealistic ten-year plan to be unveiled during the September celebrations. Mengistu responded that drought and famine were temporary setbacks along the road to economic success laid out in the proposed economic blueprint. Even when in April 1983 Dawit was able to force some of his colleagues to acknowledge the gravity of the situation in the north, the government was unwilling to divert resources, money, and attention away from the tenth-anniversary celebrations; and it certainly was not going to admit the existence of a famine worse than the one that had shattered Haile Sellassie's reign.

While one-sixth of Ethiopia's peoples were threatened with death and were fleeing their homes to seek food, the government prepared an expensive extravaganza to showcase the establishment of the new WPE. Before the event, the regime's media described only the prosperity and freedom that Mengistu and socialism had brought to Ethiopia. It lambasted the West for its imperialism, while praising its Eastern allies, especially the Soviet Union, for their help and support. The RRC's dilemma was thereby made worse, since the European Economic Community and the United States held the grain surpluses, whereas the Soviet Union was facing its own shortages, and the other Warsaw Pact nations had little extra to donate to the starving Ethiopians.

Meanwhile, the peasants kept dying, and the regime resolutely refused to take responsibility. In June and July 1984, while Addis Abeba was drilling to prepare for a massive parade on 12 September, the rains again failed, transforming disaster into cataclysm. By July, it was obvious that Welo, Sidamo, Harerge, Shewa, Tigray, and Gonder provinces were the worst hit, and each had its refugee camps, some of whose names—Korem, Ibnat, Alemata—recall the death and despair of the period. Even in Addis Abeba, there were signs of famine, as the capital's poor found it difficult to pay the increasingly inflated prices for food and lined up for bread and other commodities at hastily established distribution centers.

For the most part, however, September's foreign visitors saw nothing but a clean, well-appointed capital city, bedecked in celebration of the revolution's tenth anniversary. Most knew, however, about the famine, since the Western press was reporting news from Ethiopia in terms of a government callous enough to ignore the needs of its starving citizens by spending its limited revenues to celebrate an obviously hollow revolu-

32. Feeding camp at Bati, July 1985

tion. During the four-day gala, there were pomp and ceremony, banquets, and parades. The guests, mostly from the Eastern bloc, dutifully observed the events and clapped in the new order.

In the recently constructed Congress Hall, the Workers' Party of Ethiopia was called into being, and a central committee was elected, which named a politburo. The latter unsurprisingly picked Mengistu Haile Mariam as the WPE's general secretary, commander in chief of the armed forces, and chairman of the Council of Ministers. In a five-and-one-half-hour acceptance speech, Mengistu described past achievements and future plans, never once mentioning the famine.

At the end of September, however, when the general secretary finally turned his attention to the crisis, the RRC needed ninety thousand tons of grain monthly to feed famine victims. The politburo became involved, and the Western media were permitted access to the stricken areas. In late October, two BBC television reports from the camps at Korem and Mekele were broadcast worldwide, galvanizing an international relief effort. Though many Western powers remained critical of the Marxist-Leninist direction of Mengistu's government, they divorced politics from the plight of the Ethiopian people and made available vast amounts of

33. Survivors, Bati, July 1985

surplus grain. By mid-1985, the worst part of the crisis was over, thanks to the international assistance that the RRC efficiently distributed.

Meanwhile, the Addis Abeba government determined to move people from the drought regions to the west and south, where supposedly surplus lands were available. The idea of resettlement was on historically firm ground, and even the Haile Sellassie government had projected easing overpopulation in the overfarmed north by moving people to Sidamo. The new regime, however, went about the population shift as if it were a military campaign, not a humane program. Worse, the government did not have the necessary resources or infrastructure to provide proper housing, tools, medical treatment, or food for the refugees. By 1986, it had moved six hundred thousand people, but many had been forced to go, families had been broken up, and sick and old people had died during the trip. The government was criticized as callous and the new settlements as unworkable, uneconomic, and a drain on Ethiopia's limited resources. The regime responded that resettlement served the long-terms needs of an afflicted people, but admitted in 1987 that wiser planning and better use of resources might have improved the program.

After 1985, Addis Abeba embarked on villagization, another expensive and controversial program, to change the highlands' historic patterns of settlement from scattered hamlets located near water and fields to concentrated dwellings clustered along the main communication lines. The authorities argued that villagization derived from the need to provide modern services to Ethiopia's rural population and that government was not resettling people but merely making their communal activities easier. Skeptics charged, however, that a rural people organized in villages alongside roads made for a more easily exploitable and controlled population. They pointed out that the government had neither the manpower nor the resources necessary to provide the new villages with social, educational, and health services. In fact, as late as 1990, most villages lacked the promised amenities because of the resource-draining civil strife in Tigray and Eritrea.

After 1982, the EPLF continued to wage low-level war, sapping the morale of government garrisons. It openly cooperated with the Tigrayan Peoples Liberation Front in February 1983 when the government launched a two-front campaign into Tigray from Eritrea and Welo. Rather than stand against Mengistu's heavily armed soldiers, the TPLF retreated from the province's cities and towns toward remote and more easily defensible mountain sanctuaries. They adopted hit-and-run tactics and were assisted by the EPLF, which harried the enemy from the rear. The government, however, maintained strategic control over Tigray and even managed to break lines of communication between the EPLF and the TPLF.

There was a lull in large-scale warfare until early 1984, when a regrouped EPLF launched a spectacularly successful attack against Tesenay, capturing armored vehicles, fuel, weapons, and ammunition. In March, the Eritreans used the armor to spearhead a campaign against the government's posts to the east of Nacfa. One after the other they fell, demoralizing thousands of soldiers, who fled into Sudan or surrendered to the rebels. The success emboldened the EPLF to start agitating among a peasantry increasingly alienated by the central government's harsh counterinsurgency tactics and to undertake guerrilla operations to the south of Asmera. Though the government's military situation had deteriorated greatly, Mengistu refused either to give quarter or to attempt compromise. Instead, his government stepped up recruitment to bolster the armed forces and asked Moscow to speed delivery of more tanks and ground support aircraft.

During the famine, Mengistu used proffered food aid as a weapon against his enemies, whom he considered bandits. He refused to allow relief supplies to enter rebel-held territory, in effect seeking to starve partisans of the TPLF and EPLF into submission. Also not blameless, the two organizations were using whatever food they acquired to raise revenues, to gain adherents, and to force international recognition of their status as quasi-sovereign authorities. In fact, neither the government nor the movements were willing to put aside their long-held positions and refused all attempts to arrange a modus vivendi to make food available to the needy. The EPLF and TPLF continued raiding, and the Ethiopian command carried on bombing.

In August 1985, almost immediately after the famine crisis was past, the government successfully launched a major campaign in Eritrea, pushing the EPLF from positions occupied in June and July. The Eritreans maintained they once again had decided on a tactical withdrawal to keep strength and equipment intact. In Tigray, the government continued its strategic control of towns and roads, although in mid-August the TPLF showed optimism about its future by founding the Stalinist Marxist-Leninist Arm of Tigray. In Addis Abeba, meanwhile, the regime was also demonstrating confidence by constructing a new constitution for Ethiopia's many peoples.

Unveiled in early June 1986, the draft constitution was mostly centrist in orientation. The document gave the new national assembly (the Shengo) broad authority, nevertheless, to establish autonomous regional and administrative assemblies with specified powers, including the ability to tax. There was, however, no distinct reference to the concept of self-determination for nationalities or to the right of secession from Ethiopia. The draft assigned the Workers' party the leading role in society and government, even if its chairman did not need to be the country's president. The latter, necessarily a party member, was elected by the Shengo to a five-year term and enjoyed wide powers over military and civil activities.

For the next two months, the draft was distributed widely and was discussed at kebelay and peasants' association meetings, in army units, factories, and government offices, and even by émigré groups. In August 1986, when the 343-person drafting committee reviewed the criticisms, it proposed ninety-five, mostly cosmetic, changes to the original document, which was then sent for acceptance to the Workers' party central committee. The final document once again avoided the central questions of self-determination for national groups and regional autonomy, but did increase the powers of the presidency over all organs of government.

On 1 February, the government held its much heralded referendum even in most towns and cities in Tigray and in southern Eritrea, although the EPLF complained that the voting was carried out at gunpoint. Nationwide, the constitution was approved by 81 percent of the registered voters. In elections in June, the government allowed Ethiopians in each constituency of the Shengo to vote from among three carefully selected candidates. On 10 September 1987, the old government dissolved itself, and the new parliament inaugurated the People's Democratic Republic of Ethiopia (PDRE), most of whose leading members were retained from the military administration. On that day, Mengistu Haile Mariam, now the PDRE's president, swore to defend his nation's freedom and unity, to promote socialism, to foster equality among nationalities, and to work for Ethiopia's progress and prosperity. He did not mention autonomous regions nor hint at compromise with the nation's long-standing dissidents. These oversights did not reveal strength, as events a few months later would reveal.

In December 1987, the EPLF broke through the Ethiopian lines before Nacfa and pushed its enemy back twenty kilometers. The defeat demoralized the long-serving Ethiopian soldiers, who had been told by the political cadres that the new republic, with its autonomous zones, quickly would win over the rebels. The Eritrean victory revealed, on the contrary, that the war would continue. When government soldiers refused to go out on routine patrols, Mengistu flew to Eritrea in February 1988 to deal with the unrest. During meetings, Mengistu reacted sharply to suggestions that a political solution be sought by ordering the execution of one general and by dismissing and arresting other commanders. The rank and file continued to lose hope.

They fought badly at Af Abet, southeast of Nacfa, when the EPLF launched a large-scale attack in mid-March 1988. One government division was destroyed as a unit, and approximately ten thousand soldiers were killed or captured. Worse, the EPLF captured fifty tanks, several batteries of rocket launchers, artillery, and large stores of small arms, munitions, and fuel, allowing the organization to flesh out its twelve brigades and eighteen thousand fighters, and it was emboldened to negotiate an agreement of military coordination with the TPLF. The Ethiopian command consequently decided to retire from now untenable positions in western and north-central Eritrea and to concentrate its forces at Keren. The government blew up installations, destroyed stores, and withdrew civil servants to Asmera. By April, the EPLF could fairly claim to have liberated northern Eritrea.

Meanwhile, the government moved troops from northern Tigray into

Eritrea, allowing the TPLF to attack and overrun garrisons along the road near the Eritrean frontier. In late March, with captured heavy weapons and munitions, the TPLF successfully ejected the army from Axum, Adwa, and Inda Silase, confiscating even more and better weaponry and supplies from the retreating troops. The bulk of government forces fell back on Mekele, the provincial capital, to regroup and prepare a counter-attack. Mengistu, meanwhile, reached an agreement on 20 March 1988 with President Siad Barre of Somalia to retain the political status quo in Ogaden, allowing the Ethiopian 100,000-man garrison there to be redeployed to Eritrea and Tigray.

No major military action occurred during the rest of 1988, although there was desultory fighting in Eritrea and Tigray. Both the EPLF and the government claimed to be ready for negotiations, but Addis Abeba's offer of autonomy was not acceptable to a movement that continued to seek independence. Mengistu stubbornly clung to moribund Stalinist notions about nationalities, just as he retained statist economic policies rapidly being discredited in the Soviet Union.

Indeed, during a visit to Moscow in July 1988, Mengistu was told that Soviet support depended on substantial economic and political liberalization, and he was advised to seek a negotiated solution in Eritrea. President Gorbachev thereupon rejected Mengistu's request for additional military assistance. The Ethiopian then went to China, where he was cautioned to abandon his reliance on the cult of personality, doctrinaire agricultural policies, and even his Maoist-style uniforms. Thus, by the end of 1988, the government's political and military position was much worse than at the year's beginning, and there was no hope for the massive infusion of arms required to defeat the EPLF and the TPLF.

The economy was not faring any better. The government proclaimed its intention to expand the demoralizing villagization program and to speed the socialization of production in the countryside. Since 1974, agricultural production had declined at an average annual rate of 0.4 percent, whereas population had grown consistently at 3 percent. State farms accounted for only 3 percent to 4 percent of total crop production, and only half the land at the government's disposal had been placed under cultivation. Trade and industry had stagnated since the revolution. The only figure that had grown enormously was the $1,500,000,000[1] spent

1. After the revolution, the PMAC replaced the foreign-word dollar with the Ethiopian word *birr* (literally, silver), long used for the silver Maria Theresa dollar. Its value against the U.S. dollar remained at B2.07 until 1992, when it was devalued to B5.00.

for arms in 1988, representing 54 percent of government revenue. Servicing of Ethiopia's international debt took $530,500,000 in 1988, up from 1974's modest $51,400,000. The country, in effect, was bankrupt.

In February 1989, the economic constraints and the lack of weaponry forced the government to evacuate Tigray in face of humiliating military defeats and to withdraw its garrison at Humera, on the TPLF's main supply line from Sudan. The scale of the disasters soon became known as the wounded flooded into the capital and as the government drafted younger and younger males. Morale in Addis Abeba dropped, and ranking officers began to discuss Mengistu's removal.

The highly efficient, East German–trained security services soon learned a conspiracy was in the making, and Mengistu countered by retiring potentially disloyal but competent senior generals and by promoting trusted but untried colonels as replacements. By changing his commanders, Mengistu simultaneously weakened the army's fighting ability and disrupted the plotters' capacity to coordinate their efforts. A scheme nonetheless went forward, timed to begin when Mengistu left for East Germany on 16 May 1989. After seeing their president off at the airport, the three highest-ranking conspirators returned to the Ministry of Defense to begin the operation. Their action triggered responses by the security apparatus, which quickly ended the attempted coup. Many generals were killed, others were jailed, and hundreds of field grade officers were detained, demoralizing and confusing an already discouraged army.

Mengistu was forced to reorganize his high command, air force and army headquarters, the defense ministry, and even the leadership of the second army in Eritrea, whose officers strongly supported the coup. Interestingly, the EPLF decided not to attack Asmera, whose defense might have rallied support for Mengistu as the guardian of Ethiopia's territorial integrity. Instead, the Eritrean movement worked to rid Ethiopia of Mengistu by supporting the TPLF's efforts to cobble together a broad antigovernment coalition called the Ethiopian Peoples Revolutionary Democratic Front (EPRDF).

This effort yielded little until the EPRDF, largely composed of the TPLF and its creation, the Ethiopian Peoples Democratic Movement, pushed deeply into Gonder and Welo provinces in September 1989. Observers were surprised at the strength of the thrusts, which seriously threatened the cities of Dese and Gonder, because they misunderstood the depth of antipathy the largely peasant fighters felt for the government. The latter labeled the TPLF tribalist and denounced its support of the seccesionist EPLF. Mengistu made it appear that Ethiopia had only two choices: unity under his highly centralized regime or political anarchy and the nation's destruction. Meanwhile, the EPLF followed the politics of status quo in Eritrea, preferring to let Tigray and its allies weaken the central government.

In late 1989, Mengistu sought ways out of his dilemma. He resumed relations with Israel, more or less bartering the Beta Israel for unspecified military assistance. He began a new recruiting campaign, to strengthen his army by two hundred thousand men, and he distributed arms in parts of Gonder and northern Shewa to give local Amhara the means to resist the Tigray. He also sought to manipulate new droughts in northern Welo, eastern Tigray, and Eritrea to his advantage.

With about 1.8 million people at risk, his control over the main ports and the roads would help maintain his government's international position as Ethiopia's only sovereign force; and he could use access to the food as a weapon against his Tigrayan and Eritrean adversaries by forcing peasants to come to government-controlled feeding stations. At the least, Ethiopia would receive trucks and other forms of help from the nongovernmental organizations accredited to the Addis Abeba government.

The EPLF responded on 9 February 1990 by mounting a successful assault on the road linking Asmera to the coast and by following up with a surprise attack on Mitsiwa. At the port, the Eritreans used speedy patrol boats to attack and destroy the small Ethiopian fleet, most of which was in harbor for the naval academy's annual graduation day. So unprepared and disorganized were the Ethiopians that the city easily fell to the EPLF. This victory cut the major supply lines of the Ethiopian second army, already isolated by the TPLF, which controlled the major road link from Ethiopia; broke the Ethiopian stranglehold on supplies entering the country; and demonstrated that the Addis Abeba government no longer was able to provide relief for stricken areas in Tigray and Eritrea.

When the government moved troops from Welo by air transport via Addis Abeba, to shore up its lines in Eritrea, the TPLF advanced against Debre Tabor. There, it won a major victory, taking thousands of prisoners, cutting the Addis Abeba–Gonder road, and putting Gojam at risk. From this point on, Mengistu was doomed to defeat, though he tried to evade fate. On 5 March, he announced the end of socialism in Ethiopia,

34. Bomb damage, Mitsiwa, December 1991

the replacement of the elitist Workers' party with the more open Ethiopian Democratic Unity party, and the demise of the command economy. Critics immediately censured his program as irrelevant to the politics of the military crisis.

The reforms, however, were consequential in the provinces: many people abandoned the regime's villages for their old homesteads, and farmers quickly dismantled collectives and redistributed land and capital goods. Regaining control over their lives, peasants ejected or ignored party and government functionaries, and in several cases killed recalcitrant administrators. The net effect was to weaken the Mengistu regime in the countryside, especially in southern Ethiopia, where suddenly the long-dormant Oromo Liberation Front became active. The United States, meanwhile, had decided that Mengistu's regime soon would be ousted and began talking to the EPLF, giving the latter an international status it long had sought. When Isayas Afeworki, the EPLF's general secretary, appeared in Washington in May 1989, he was received by high-ranking officials at the State Department and by important congressional leaders, signaling the beginning of the end of the U.S. policy supporting Ethiopia's territorial integrity in terms of Addis Abeba's definition of national unity. In 1990, the U.S.–EPLF connection strengthened, and Isayas met in Khartoum with American diplomats.

35. The imperial palace in Mitsiwa, bombed by government planes.
Photograph by Paul Henze.

During 1990–1991, the EPLF and TPLF-EPRDF continued to win victory after victory. By May 1991, EPRDF forces controlled Tigray, Welo, Gonder, Gojam, and about half of Shewa, encircling Addis Abeba. Mengistu continued to tinker with his government and its ideology but to no great effect. For example, as late as 26 April 1991, in response to recommendations made by the Shengo, he reconstituted his government, replacing hard-liners with more liberal officials, and agreed to begin discussing with opposition factions the possibility of a cease-fire. Predictably, the EPLF, TPLF, and the EPRDF rejected negotiations, insisting that Mengistu had to resign before peace could be contemplated seriously.

The EPRDF had, by now, taken on a unique importance as a largely peasant movement. Its fighters comprised countrymen from every ethnic and linguistic group in Ethiopia, a characteristic that frightened the urban bourgeoisie in Addis Abeba and other cities. They had conformed to the long-standing official culture of the government and were accustomed to controlling the economy and the nation's administration. Though they

36. Triumphal arch in Asmera, celebrating the successful war against Ethiopia

grumbled about Mengistu, they had posed no threat to his regime, and by 1991 they regarded him as perhaps the only person who could keep the country from breaking apart, even as they accused him of having brought Ethiopia to ruin. Beyond such a paradox, the urban elites also feared the advent of "peasant power" and the loss of their authority over what they regarded as a rabble. They depicted the EPRDF leadership as ill-educated Marxists, refusing to believe the words of Meles Zenawi, the EPRDF leader, that he sought a democratic Ethiopia with a prosperous mixed economy.

The EPRDF's and EPLF's refusal to talk placed enormous pressure on Mengistu, whose presence in Ethiopia blocked progress to a cease-fire. By mid-May, it was obvious that the army did not have sufficient morale, manpower, weapons, munitions, and leadership to stop the enemy's advance on Addis Abeba. Without any maneuvering ground left, Mengistu fled Ethiopia on 21 May 1991, without informing his closest confidants and advisers. He made his way to Zimbabwe, where President Robert Mugabe offered sanctuary and security. On 28 May 1991, the EPRDF marched into Addis Abeba and took power. By 3 June, Meles Zenawi's men controlled most of the country, except for Eritrea, where the EPLF was in charge.

What can the new rulers learn from Ethiopia's long history? They can take heart that, notwithstanding the most extreme cases of secession and governmental weakness, the country reunited. There is no escaping the

37. Eradicating the past in Asmera: the word *Ethiopia* has been removed

essential wholeness of Ethiopia's highlands and environs. The two have functioned as an economic unit historically, and there seems little reason to think that modern politics can disrupt that long-standing pattern.

A sovereign Eritrea has to retain economic access to the Ethiopian hinterland, especially if Asmera builds a light manufacturing economy. Eritrea has always been a net exporter of people to Ethiopia, from where much of its food has been imported. This truth manifested itself during Axumite times and has been a fact throughout history. The economic symbiosis has not necessarily been reflected in the area's political allegiances. Although the coastal strip was for long periods not under its sovereignty, Ethiopia always used Mitsiwa as one its main ports.

The need for access to the sea remains paramount for Ethiopia, now suddenly landlocked. For Addis Abeba to divert its produce to non-Eritrean ports would mean that Mitsiwa and especially Aseb would wither as commercial centers. There is therefore a clear need for a relationship between Ethiopia and Eritrea that goes beyond the normal bilateral relations of neighbors. Over time, the two nations will have to forge a new political relationship reflecting economic realities.

Ethiopia also will have to create a new official culture reflecting the nation's diversity. In recent history, the state has been identified with the Semitic-speaking, Christian population, and since World War II, specifically with the dominant Amhara culture. For the non-Christian, non-northerner, the cost was assimilation into an alien culture. As Ethiopia became ethnically conscious in the seventies and eighties, the country's nationalities came to regard acculturation as surrender to a ruling minority. In part, the rise of the TPLF was a response to the derg's denial of provincial and cultural autonomy and the apparent continuation of Amhara political domination.

More recently, the Oromo and other groups have strongly asserted their national rights. If Ethiopia is to survive as a corporate body, its peoples must feel that their cultures and languages are being safeguarded by the government. Cultural and political autonomy must be respected as a matter of right. Otherwise, the state will split apart as the minorities compete for power.

There must also be economic compromise. The Ethiopian economy had begun to prosper in the 1960s and early 1970s, thanks to a vigorous capitalist agriculture. The growth caused considerable social unrest as peasant farmers were thrown off their land or forced to sell out as proprietors put together parcels of land to create plantations or large truck farms. The military regime regarded that consolidation as inequitable and exploitative, and its land reform brought economic development to an abrupt halt. Moreover, the government assumed broad responsibility for the economy and, through a variety of parastatal organizations, sought also to become purchasing agent, jobber, wholesaler, and transporter. These activities devastated the Ethiopian economy, leading to undevelopment. If recent history teaches anything, it is that the government must abandon the command economy, liberate the peasants to work out their own destinies, and facilitate the market.

Finally, Ethiopia always has functioned best in an expanded version. After resolving ethnic and regional divisions, Addis Abeba should discuss greater political and economic cooperation with its neighbors. First, Djibouti and Ethiopia are vital to each other. Logic demands that some sort of political relationship be negotiated between hinterland and port. Second, the historic connections between Ethiopia and Eritrea are obvious and unassailable; instead of being explained away, they ought to be stressed and reinterpreted so that the two polities can work out a joint destiny. Third, Ethiopia should open discussions with Somalia for regional planning, since no clear economic boundary separates them. The two peoples must undertake regional economic development, especially irrigation and water diversion and conservation projects, that transcends the straight-line frontiers. Somali nomads have ignored the borders for generations; government must now come to understand the futility of such artificial separation, especially as there is a pressing need to address long-term ecological and climatic concerns.

Last, the various governments and movements that now claim the Horn of Africa must relearn the lost art of compromise. In the future, Ethiopia, Eritrea, Somalia, and Sudan will have only themselves to blame for their destinies because they no longer will be able to point an accusatory finger at the great powers. Historically, Ethiopia and its neighbors have lived together fruitfully when ideological or ethnic concerns have been muted. When, however, religion, politics, or economic factors have become dominating and unbalancing, the entire region has fallen into mayhem. Should the region split apart, the Era of the Ministates will make the Age of the Princes appear as a golden epoch! It may take several generations before the logic of geography and history works to recreate the larger political and economic sphere necessary for a better future. In the end, Ethiopia will rise again.

FIFTEEN

The New Rulers, to 1995

The Tigrayan Peoples Liberation Front (TPLF) is one of the forebears of the Ethiopian Peoples Revolutionary Democratic Front (EPRDF), which, after the fall of Mengistu's regime in May 1991, organized and led the Transitional Government of Ethiopia (TGE) from 1991 to 1993. The TGE, in turn, established the Federal Democratic Republic of Ethiopia (FDRE), now governed by the EPRDF. The TPLF derived from the Marxist-inspired student movement of the 1960s and 1970s, when many non-Amharas experienced an ethnic patriotism in face of the state's official culture. The Tigrayan students in particular felt demeaned that their historic tongue was considered tribal, whereas Amharic enjoyed national status. It mattered little to them that even the Tigrayan emperor, Yohannes IV, used Amharic as his court language or that Amharic was the more important literary language. They felt marginalized by their Christian Amhara cousins, even though the Tigray had participated in Emperor Menilek's empire building and in Emperor Haile Sellassie's efforts to establish a nation.

In the early 1970s, most Tigray students concluded that it would be best to destroy the Amhara rulers and their Tigrayan allies by implementing a class-based revolution in which people also would have ethnic equality. Some students organized the Tigray National Organization

(TNO) to overthrow the province's traditional rulers and engage in a national liberation struggle, since one of the competing student ideologies held that Ethiopia's different nationalities should enjoy the right to self-determination. The TNO located itself in the towns and sought its allies among teachers, bureaucrats, and other urban professionals. When it became clear in 1975–1976 that the national military government opposed ethnic sovereignty in favor of a unitary regime, the TNO and Tigrayan students in Addis Abeba decided that it was time for an armed struggle against the garrison fascists.

Being strong nationalists as well as committed Marxists, the young men decided to politicize the countryside, where most Tigrayans lived, and to wage class warfare against the provincial nobility led by Ras Mengesha Seyoum. On 18 February 1975, at Dedebit in the insalubrious west-Tigray lowlands, sixty-five kilometers from Sheraro, they transformed the TNO into the Tigrayan Peoples Liberation Front, emulating the successful Eritrean Peoples Liberation Front (EPLF) next door. Of the original thirty-seven members, eleven started the armed struggle with a mixed bag of weapons, nine went to the towns to agitate and recruit—among them Meles Zenawi, later president of the TGE and prime minister of the FDRE—and seventeen went to Eritrea for military training with the EPLF.

The EPLF hoped to use the new organization as a cat's-paw against the Eritrean Liberation Front (ELF), which was active in the Sheraro-Badme area where many Eritrean farmers had migrated. Otherwise, the EPLF ignored the Tigray group, underestimating, as would the derg, the strength it would draw from its commitment to the peasants and the countryside.

The military regime's land policies seriously distressed Tigray's farmers, who had suffered a badly organized and unfair land redistribution, new taxes, the time-consuming and mind-numbing meetings of mass organizations, and the forced sale of much of their produce to the government at below-market prices. Moreover, farmers' household economies were jeopardized by the derg's prohibition against working in the towns and by the ban on hiring agricultural laborers. Given the decreasing ability of the province's exhausted land to support a growing population, over 200,000 Tigrayans annually had sought periodic work in commercial centers or followed cash crop harvests around Ethiopia. Now that these practices were prohibited, the standard of life in the average household deteriorated.

Tigrayans also had been alienated by the apparently senseless assassination of leading members of the imperial regime in November 1974 and by the death of the aged emperor in August 1975, which was widely considered in the province to be murder. Merchants and traders were antagonized by the many and often absurd regulations that the derg imposed on commerce and transport. Tigrayans generally were outraged at the absolute prohibition of any expression of regional or ethnic identity as counterrevolutionary.

Given Tigrayan discontent, TPLF members were seen as local heroes. Small groups of fighters traveled throughout Tigray, exhorting the peasants to oppose the derg's oppression, which they declared worse than the excesses of the old regime. The units moved quickly, as much for the sake of security as to give the impression of a larger organization. In the towns, activists clandestinely distributed tracts and pamphlets that lauded Tigrayan particularism and compared their ethnic-centered approach to the stance of the Ethiopian Peoples Revolutionary Party (EPRP), which was pushing for a pan-Ethiopian socialist regime. They also castigated the liberal Ethiopian Democratic Union (EDU) led by Ras Mengesha, their chief provincial adversary. In both cases, the TPLF had the stronger appeal, especially since it described itself in terms of the populist Woyane movement, which had fought for the rights of Tigray's peasants in the 1930s and 1940s. Indeed, at the TPLF's inaugural Fighters Congress held in Agame on 18 February 1976, the first anniversary of the front, its entire membership of 170 approved the Manifesto of the TPLF, which asserted that the organization's first task was to establish an Independent Democratic Republic of Tigray.

While the manifesto's language is clear, and it obviously represented the membership's collective will, current TPLF apologists clarify that the document also stipulated that secession and independence were to preface socialism and communism in Ethiopia. They also point out that independence as the organization's primary goal was repudiated at a subsequent Party Congress, although it was not then publicly announced. The lack of transparency on this point led to problems with the EPLF, which maintained that only polities with a colonial background could claim independence, and with Ethiopian patriots, who regarded the TPLF as secessionist. In any case, the TPLF never wavered in its support for the principle that Ethiopia's nationalities had the right to self-determination up to and including independence.

Many Tigrayans continued to believe, therefore, that in face of an oppressive Ethiopian state, the TPLF stood for the province's separation and independence.

First, however, the TPLF had to undermine the old order's hold over the peasantry. The Teranafit, a loose but strongly patriotic organization comprising local nobility and farmers, had emerged in the chaos surrounding the end of the old order. It supported Ras Mengesha, whom the derg had deposed as Tigray's governor; opposed the land reform, standing for traditional land tenure based on rights of kinship; and championed the church, whose properties had been confiscated and whose clergy were suddenly impoverished. Led by a congeries of local nobles, thousands of fighters from populous and historic western Tigray, especially Agame, joined the new group. Since, in 1976, the TPLF did not have the firepower to confront the Teranafit, it mounted a propaganda campaign designed to reveal its adversary as reactionary and itself as revolutionary, standing for equitable land reform and democratic rights.

Meanwhile, Ras Mengesha had organized the EDU, which claimed a pan-Ethiopian membership, advocated democratic government, stood for national unity, and supported the Teranafit. Given Mengesha's popularity, the peasants were confused about where to place their allegiance until the petty nobles and their retinues proved to be hooligans who raped, pillaged, and looted. In contrast, the tightly disciplined TPLF men never confiscated goods or crops; always paid for what they wanted; refrained from alcohol and even consensual sex; helped people with plowing, seeding, weeding, and harvesting; and were invariably concerned with the welfare of the Tigrayans. Borrowing from Mao, the TPLF leadership harshly judged members' crimes against the peasants, meting out summary executions or prison terms.

The TPLF's political goal was to win the complete trust of the Tigrayans and then to establish mass organizations mostly devoted to raising political awareness among the peasantry. At first, the TPLF governed through administrative committees, with members elected from among the populations of a number of hamlets, and eventually through use of more formal *baitos,* or peasant associations, with wide-ranging powers. In EDU-held areas, landlords and nobles remained in charge, and the people remained generally unaware of the larger political issues competing in Tigray. Their loyalties were not to a cause but often to very local leaders, for whom they fought well against the

TPLF when civil strife broke out. In 1976–1977 they forced TPLF fighters to retreat into sanctuaries to study and rectify their military inadequacies.

The front came to realize that units of sixty to one hundred fighters could best reconnoiter the countryside and attack EDU encampments. The TPLF hit hard to inflict as much damage as possible, but in face of stubborn defense, the fighters would suddenly withdraw to prepare for action elsewhere. These tactics not only discombobulated the enemy but also convinced the peasantry that the TPLF was a wide-ranging fighting force. Moreover, as people increasingly came to understand the TPLF's peasant-based program, they turned away from Ras Mengesha's men. When the last battle of the war against the EDU began on 4 November 1979, western Tigray was ready to heed the new rulers. The TPLF now turned to confront the Ethiopian Peoples Revolutionary Party, which controlled large parts of the eastern Tigray.

As a doctrinaire Soviet-style Marxist organization, the party believed that power should be wielded by the intelligentsia in alliance with the politically volatile working class, and not with a peasantry presumed politically supine. When the military regime chased the EPRP out of Ethiopia's major towns, its members had sought sanctuary in the remote mountainous regions of Welo, Gonder, and Tigray. The EPRP came to dominate the border region of Agame, adjacent to Eritrea, from which it could access the coast for supplies through liberated territory and obtain help, if needed, from the EPLF.

From its rural bases, the EPRP hoped to attack and weaken the derg so that it could pursue the urban warfare that formed the basis of its strategy. The differences between the EPRP and the TPLF could not have been more stark. The front was solely based in Tigray and was not only Marxist but also nationalist and peasant-oriented in the style of the Chinese Communist Party. It was active in the countryside because it believed the province's biggest problems were concentrated there. EPRP leaders tended to regard their TPLF counterparts as parochial country bumpkins and narrow nationalists, more interested in military struggle than the correct political ideology.

In late 1978, the TPLF's approach yielded important support from the peasants of Agame's Sobia district, who, after a series of meetings, decided that their compatriots shared their culture and best understood the province's problems. When the EPRP refused to leave the district and began terrorizing the community into submission, the

TPLF responded, in December 1979, by transferring veterans from the east and soon winning an important string of victories that drove the EPRP out of Agame and Tigray. The victories proved once again that the TPLF's emphasis on ethno-nationalism and its close affiliation with the peasantry was the correct line to take in Tigray.

Meanwhile, a war with the Eritrean Liberation Front (ELF) was developing. By 1977, the ELF was blocking the TPLF's land reform program in the western awraja of Shire, claiming that Eritrea's boundaries there extended beyond the line negotiated between Ethiopia and Italy. The ELF, mainly dominant in southwest Eritrea, also had established itself in the western Tigray districts of Sheraro-Badme, where many Eritreans had migrated. In 1979, when the TPLF had defeated the EDU and the EPRP, it began to implement a major land reform that weakened the ELF's hold over the area. With that, the beleaguered ELF started a propaganda campaign characterizing the TPLF as occupying Eritrean territory and evicting Eritreans. Whether by chance or by design, the TPLF campaigned against the ELF in November 1979, at a time when the EPLF also fought to destroy its rival. The end result was that the ELF was not only pushed out of Sheraro-Badme but also from southwest Eritrea into Sudan.

A scant four years after its establishment, the TPLF had won the hearts and minds of Tigray's peasants and, always outarmed and outnumbered, had fought and defeated the EDU, the EPRP, and the ELF, serious ideological and military adversaries. The TPLF's success stemmed from its careful attention to the needs of Tigray's countryside, its élan and high morale, and its political discipline. As a bottom-to-top organization, the TPLF's members spent much of their time meeting with the peasants and explaining various policy options to them.

By comparison, the EPLF was effective primarily because of its military organization and the tightly hierarchical nature of its leadership. Top-to-bottom reform was administered by a cadre responsive to the EPLF central committee and politburo. The front's goal was to restructure society and traditionally distinct political regions into a unitary government, as outlined in an eclectic National Democratic Program adopted at its First Organizational Congress on 31 January 1977. A fusion of Afro-Marxist ideas and secular nationalist aspirations, the program claimed the province's independence by right of having been an Italian colony.

By making this argument, which became increasingly multilayered and complex as the struggle with Ethiopia continued, the Tigrayans of the Eritrean highlands had to exclude their brothers across the Mareb, because inclusion would have weakened their political arguments and goals. The EPLF had to mitigate talk of cultural affiliation by asserting that, historically, the Tigrayans of Eritrea and Ethiopia had lived separately, which had led to differentiation even before the coming of Italian colonialism. Such a claim was, of course, ahistorical, since church students studied with famous teachers in Eritrea and Tigray, devout Christians visited famous shrines in both areas, and trans-Mareb Tigrayans worked, traded, socialized, and intermarried with one another. Meles Zenawi, Ethiopia's prime minister, and Isayas Afeworki, Eritrea's president, have mothers who came from Eritrea and Tigray, respectively. Still, the EPLF worked hard to convince the world that Tigrayans in Eritrea were different from those in Tigray.

While Italian colonialism had not greatly affected life in the Eritrean countryside, the town-dwelling population had been transformed into a more or less modern workforce. Interestingly, Italian propaganda had asserted that Eritrean Tigrays were smarter, more moral, and better disciplined than their benighted brethren in Ethiopia. Since most people like to believe themselves superior, this baseless claim did not die with the end of Italian colonialism in 1941. Instead, the Eritrean elite, even the students at Haile Sellassie I University in Addis Abeba, stressed their superiority. They even maintained that their way of speaking Tigrinya was purer and more original than that spoken across the Mareb. They were contemptuous of the Ethiopian Tigrayans, especially those from Agame, about whom they told crude and tasteless jokes. EPLF leaders, many of whom were ex-HSIU students who should have known better, were caught up in an arrogance that consistently led them to underestimate their TPLF brothers.

Although the EPLF never acknowledged that the TPLF assisted it in the war against the ELF, the Tigrayan front permitted 3,000 of its men to fight alongside the Eritreans at the crucial battle for Nakfa, during the Red Star Campaign of 1981. TPLF leaders reasoned that destruction of the EPLF would leave them vulnerable to Ethiopian pressure on two sides and easily whipsawed into submission. A tactical alliance with the Eritrean front was a practical necessity, even though the Tigrayans disliked the EPLF's top-down approach to government and its tendency to fight a conventional war against the common enemy. Preferring hit-and-run tactics to reduce the number of casualties, the TPLF undertook positional warfare only as a final option.

From time to time, however, as in northern Welo in 1983 and increasingly throughout the decade, the TPLF integrated its fighters with the local defense militias to defeat large government units, astounding not only the high command in Addis Abeba but also the EPLF leadership. By 1983, the TPLF was taking enough weapons from the Ethiopian army to equip its men adequately and begin training its own fighters, thus growing independent of the EPLF.

The two fronts obviously differed over military strategy against the Ethiopians, the nature of their commitment to grassroots democracy, and the types of government they would establish. Moreover, the Tigrayans fought to safeguard their national heritage within Ethiopia, whereas the EPLF struggled for the opportunity to establish a new tradition within an independent nation-state. In October 1985, the TPLF publicly questioned the nature of the EPLF's relationship to the Eritrean masses and repeated its view that a truly democratic movement would necessarily respect the right of nations and nationalities within its political jurisdiction to self-determination up to and including secession. Seriously offended, the EPLF broke military and political relations with its trans-Mareb cousin, closed down the TPLF's radio station, and refused Tigrayan relief organizations the right of free passage across Eritrea to supply depots in Kassala.

Ethiopia was then suffering one of its periodic famines, made worse in Tigray by the derg's strategy to starve the peasants out of their commitment to the fighters by interfering with food production and sales, periodic markets, and the delivery of relief supplies. The EPLF's simultaneous break from the TPLF entirely aggravated the situation and sparked questions about the rationale and timing of the break. Ironically, the Eritreans appeared to be cooperating with the Ethiopian enemy and were apparently unconcerned with the great distress they caused to the malnourished people of Tigray. In response, the TPLF mobilized 100,000 of its peasant supporters to build a direct road to Gederef that bypassed Eritrea, and the leadership looked beyond the EPLF for allies.

The TPLF moved further from its insular Tigrayan roots toward a more generalized approach to intra-Ethiopian politics under a new umbrella organization, the Marxist-Leninist League of Tigray (MLLT). The new organization, founded on 25 July 1985, was established within the TPLF by moderates, such as Meles Zenawi, to cooperate with other national organizations in a united front to reform Ethiopia along ethnic lines. The MLLT remained a shadowy organization, even as its members soon came to dominate the front's mass organizations and top positions.

In 1987, with the famine well over, the reformed TPLF exploited a string of EPLF victories in the Sahil to take the war to Welo and Begemdir, thereby denying the derg overland access to Eritrea. The Tigrayan successes and the huge Eritrean victory at Af Abet, in mid-March 1988, led the next month to the reestablishment of the tactical alliance between the TPLF and the EPLF. When the TPLF then proposed to negotiate some political and other differences, including the question of the frontiers, the EPLF persuasively argued for a settlement after the derg's defeat, which appeared imminent.

The government had moved troops from western Tigray to Eritrea's central highlands in order to defend Keren and Asmera, and the TPLF attacked remaining garrisons and forced the enemy from eastern Tigray, in effect liberating the province although Mekele, Tigray's capital, remained occupied. Although the derg counterattacked in September 1988, forcing the TPLF to withdraw from the towns, the front continuously harassed the army, which fell apart under the pressure. The military was finally defeated in a series of battles in February and March 1989 and retreated from the province, leaving behind enough matériel for the TPLF to transform its fighters into a conventional force ready for positional warfare.

With the endgame in sight, the TPLF began to organize itself politically for the future. Seeking to recruit ethnic-based parties for a governing coalition, it was first attracted to the largely Amhara Ethiopian Peoples Democratic Movement (EPDM), which had splintered off from the increasingly isolated EPRP. In 1981, at its founding congress, the EPDM had used Marxist language to describe the oppression of the country's nationalities by Amhara governing elites. Reasoning that ethnic conflict was the root of Ethiopia's problems, it adopted a program to solve the question of nationalities on the basis of equality of peoples. When the TPLF and the EPDM began talking seriously in the mid-1980s, they found that they shared political principles and goals, and that they could cooperate to destroy the derg under the banner of the TPLF-organized Ethiopian Peoples Revolutionary Democratic Front (EPRDF). The amalgamation occurred in 1989, giving the lie

to the Mengistu regime's propaganda that the TPLF sought to dis-
unite Ethiopia.

The Oromo Liberation Front (OLF) remained aloof from the coalition, since it regarded Tigrayans and Amhara as historical oppressors,
collectively the enemy of the people it represented. Reacting to this
attitude, the EPRDF decided to work with the Oromo Peoples Democratic Organization (OPDO), which did not condemn whole nationalities as exploiters but, eschewing ethnic chauvinism, castigated only
the ruling classes. The OPDO also opted for a future within Ethiopia
because it reasoned that, with ethnic equality, the larger the economy,
the greater the opportunities for the Oromo. The EPRDF strengthened the organization by transferring some of its Oromo members
from the EPDM—most notably Dr. Negaso Gidada, the FDRE's first
president—and its small affiliate, the Ethiopian Democratic Officers
Revolutionary Movement (EDORM), composed of ex-prisoners of war
from the campaigns of 1988 and 1989. Feeling that it had established
itself as a strong multinational organization, the EPRDF launched a
southern offensive with 15,000 to 20,000 fighters, mostly from the
TPLF and the EPDM. By late October, Gonder and Dese were under
siege, and so wary was Mengistu that he transferred two divisions from
Asmera to Addis Abeba, just in case the capital needed defending.

At this point many Tigrayans questioned the need to continue
fighting, since the province was now free. Meles, elected chairman of
the TPLF and EPRDF in 1989, convened mass organizations to explain the front's goals and praxis to the people and to obtain popular
support. At the many meetings held through early 1990, culminating
in a month-long conference in Mekele, Meles and his colleagues argued
that unless the government were completely destroyed, Tigray would
be bombed continuously; and the priests maintained that the unity of
the Orthodox Church demanded that Tigray help free Ethiopia from
atheistic Marxism.

With the goal of Ethiopia's liberation now firmly embedded in
Tigrayan consciousness, Meles visited London and Washington in
February and March 1990, where he reportedly renounced Marxism-
Leninism, committed the EPRDF to a free-market economy, and undertook to introduce democracy in Ethiopia. These commitments satisfied
the State Department, and when Meles did not demur to Eritrea's
claims of independence, U.S. officials scrapped the long-standing policy of supporting the inviolability of Ethiopia's frontiers. When they

were able to assure Isayas about Eritrea's separate future—he also had made a trip to Washington—the end was in sight for Mengistu's government. Moreover, both Meles and Isayas had charmed and impressed American policymakers, who, without much serious reflection, placed them in the category of progressive young leaders who would construct true African democracies in the near future.

During the first third of 1991, the Addis Abeba regime suffered defeat after defeat and was forced to ask the United States to sponsor a peace conference that would preface a transitional government. On 21 May 1991, with the capital virtually encircled by the EPRDF army, Mengistu fled to Zimbabwe. On the morning of 28 May, just hours before the parley convened in London, the acting president of Ethiopia, General Tesfaye Gebre Kidane, informed the American embassy that he had lost control over what remained of the army. Since the city's police force was mostly at the front, and only the unarmed traffic officers were on the streets, the U.S. State Department worried that Addis Abeba might fall into anarchy, looting, and devastation.

Herman Cohen, then the assistant secretary of state for Africa, also knew that the EPRDF army (EPRDA) had halted just outside Addis Abeba not because it was unable to enter the city, but because Meles reasoned that delay might facilitate decision making and peace talks in London. The United States government now considered that the fate of Addis Abeba hung in the balance and, in keeping with the facts on the ground, asked the EPRDA to enter the city to ensure law and order. When Cohen announced the U.S. action, the hapless PDRE delegation withdrew from the London meetings in protest. The EPLF, EPRDF, and OLF deputations agreed to meet shortly in Addis Abeba to negotiate a charter for a two-year transitional period, then returned home to pursue separate goals. The OLF was engaged in a serious political struggle with the OPDO for political power in Oromia; the EPLF needed to set up the Provisional Government of Eritrea (PGE), declared on 29 May 1991; and the EPRDF sought authority over the central government in order to create an interim national administration.

On 3 June, Meles Zenawi announced that the new authorities controlled virtually the entire country. The still-intact government military units had surrendered, and 300 leading figures, including thirty generals from Mengistu's government, had given themselves up as meekly as had the members of the Haile Sellassie regime. Many Ethiopians, however, abhorred the new government's view of national secession, manifested in the loss of Eritrea, and the return to being a landlocked country. For Ethiopian expatriates and for members of the old ruling classes—including Amhara, Oromo, Tigray, and others—the notion of government based on ethnic lines dangerously undermined unity based on an official culture or a common identity. They were unable to understand how any new multiethnic state could hold together, and their anxiety was not assuaged by the national conference held in Addis Abeba from 1 to 5 July 1991.

It was a carefully organized and orchestrated event, attended by 500 delegates from twenty-four nationality movements (virtually all of which had actively opposed the derg and the PDRE), representatives from the university and the union movement, and the EPLF, which attended as an observer. Not present were organizations that had fought the TPLF, such as the Workers Party of Ethiopia (WPE), the EPRP, and the EDU; the Coalition of Ethiopian Democratic Forces (CEDF), an umbrella alliance of various exile groups; and Tigrayan groups that opposed the TPLF. While the exclusions worried many Ethiopians, especially those in the diaspora, others (including western observers and diplomats) were impressed that the proceedings were televised live and in their entirety. At the conference, many of the nationality movements voiced their dismay at having been treated as second-class citizens by Ethiopia's ruling elites and expressed their strong support for a government based on ethnic, not individual, rights. They said very little, however, about the restructuring of the country along ethnic lines, leaving it to the government to act by proclamation.

The conference did adopt a National Charter to see Ethiopia through the two-year transitional period agreed to in London. It established a multinational council, or parliament, in which the EPRDF held thirty-two seats, its supporters twelve, and the OLF twelve, with the remainder held by a variety of ethnic organizations. It also stipulated that national office be shared by members of different nationalities, and the council chose Meles Zenawi, Tigrayan, as president; Fekadu Gedamu, Gurage, as vice chairman of the council; Tesfaye Habbiso, Kembata, as secretary of the council; and Tamrat Layne, Amhara, as prime minister. When the OLF complained that Tamrat's position should have gone to an Oromo, cabinet posts were very carefully distributed among six Oromo, six Amhara, two Tigray, one Afar, one Somali, one Kembata, one Harari, one Wolayta, one Gurage, and two others. Nevertheless, the EPRDF dominated the council and the government, since its members filled the offices of president and prime minister and held the ministries of defense, foreign affairs, and the interior. EPRDF forces also assumed responsibility for national security after the PDRE's army was demobilized. In virtually every way, Meles and company were in charge—except in Eritrea.

As worked out in advance by the EPLF and the EPRDF, the conference agreed that Eritrea could not be forced to remain in Ethiopia, and, like other nationalities, the province should enjoy the right of self-determination up to and including independence. It was decided that the Eritreans would vote their preference in a referendum within two years but, in the meanwhile, would govern themselves and maintain a permanent delegation in Addis Abeba, which would be an embassy in all but name. During the interim, Ethiopia would have free access to the sea through Aseb, and joint Ethio-Eritrean committees would be established to oversee security, economic and social activities, and the unhindered circulation of services, commerce, and people.

The schema of relations was worked out between Ethiopia and Eritrea as independent entities, a sign of the EPRDF's recognition that the ex-Italian colony was de facto the sovereign master of its own destiny. Isayas Afeworki commented that as far as he was concerned, Eritrea was already independent and the referendum was merely a necessary legal formality. Moreover, shortly before the Addis Abeba conference, the EPLF established border posts and began expelling non-Eritreans in sensitive positions. The process devolved into a mass banishment of resident Ethiopians, unprotested by Addis Abeba, which made the government complicit in the abuse of its own people.

For many Ethiopians, the Addis Abeba conference confirmed what they characterized as the U.S. "giveaway" of Eritrea. They overlooked the major role in the creation of Eritreanism played by the ineptitude and wrong-headed policies of the Mengistu regime; they ignored the fact that the EPLF had made good its claim to independence through blood; and they rejected the reality in Eritrea and the facts on the ground. They were also due for a shock in November 1991, when the Transitional Government of Ethiopia (TGE) issued a provisional regional map that had been agreed to by the EPRDF and the OLF on 18 October 1991.

The map divided Ethiopia into twelve provinces *(kilils)* based on ethnicity as defined by the dominant mother tongue. For example, largely Oromo-speaking areas were mostly placed in Oromia, within which special non-Oromo speaking areas might be designated. The Gurage, Kembata, and Hadiya surprised the mapmakers by opting to unite as one kilil with Amharic as its language. Tigray ceded its eastern desert to the Afar Kilil but took a big slice of Begemdir and the rich Setit-Humera farming lands, where generations of Tigrayans had worked as migrant laborers. While the map more or less followed language zones, political and administrative needs left many non–mother tongue speakers in somebody else's kilil. Such inclusions more commonly affected the Oromo—Ethiopia's largest ethnicity—than others and enraged more militant members of the OLF, who believed that diminishing the size of Oromia and its population was an EPRDF political goal.

Ever since the London conference, the two fronts had been estranged: first because the meeting had concentrated on internal security without any consideration of internal colonialism, and second because the OLF was locked in an intense political struggle with the EPRDF-affiliated OPDO. The OLF had proved heavy-handed in the south and southeast, intimidating non-Oromo, undertaking ethnic cleansing, and prohibiting its compatriots from cooperating with the central government. Meanwhile, the OPDO had been busy at the grassroots level, capturing local government positions, not permitting the OLF to register its voters for the elections of 21 June 1992, and persecuting opposing candidates and their supporters out on the hustings.

When fighting broke out, it appeared that the situation might devolve into civil war or lead to the breakup of the government. In Mekele, on 15 April 1992, the EPRDF, the OLF, and a small team of U.S. mediators met to try to resolve the problems in the south and southeast. The belligerents agreed to stop fighting, the OLF promised to return soldiers to their barracks, and the government undertook to withdraw excess forces. Within twenty-four hours, however, in western Harerge, the cease-fire broke down in a welter of mutual recriminations.

As the fighting continued, bridges were destroyed, roads mined, trains attacked between Awash Station and Dire Dawa, and cadres on both sides were killed or kidnapped. There was some strife between Oromo and Amhara, but it mostly originated from the OLF's and OPDO's preelection political maneuvering. When the situation grew chaotic, the OLF petitioned the Council of Representatives to postpone the elections until order was restored. On rejection, the OLF withdrew from the electoral process and the TGE, and ordered its fighters to leave their official cantonments to protect the Oromo people from the oppressor, in this case the ruling party. The move was unwise since the more disciplined, battle-hardened, better-armed national (EPRDF) army then entered the south and southeast with the goal of ensuring internal security. Within a few months, 20,000 OLF fighters, supporters, and sympathizers had been captured or detained and the organization neutered as a fighting force. Since it had abandoned its role in the government, the OLF was no longer politically influential, and the field was left to the OPDO.

The elections went ahead on 21 June 1992, but were seriously flawed. First, the withdrawal of the OLF was followed by those of several other parties, including the All-Amhara Peoples Organization (AAPO), reducing the number of people involved in the election process. Second, the government had failed to organize local election committees, leaving authority to the EPRDF or its affiliates, who frightened and alienated the electorate and opposition parties. Third, ballots and registration cards were not delivered on time, and people were not educated about how to vote. Fourth, violence against non-EPRDF candidates and parties was widespread, and in OLF-dominated areas, EPRDF hopefuls suffered from attack. Often the government's security forces, composed largely of EPRDF fighters, acted against the opposition. It was no surprise, therefore, that the ruling coalition ran away with the election. The TGE stood by the results, and Meles proclaimed his satisfaction that he now had greater moral authority to be president.

Though officials in Washington had grumbled about the election process, shortly before voting day, the U.S. State Department had negotiated an aid package of $95 million, with a total of $800 million promised over the following few years. The United States government, much to the disgust of expatriate Ethiopians, was signaling its willingness to accept even a very limited form of democracy, as long as there was movement in that direction. Washington was opposed to further disunity in the Horn and was ready to support the new Ethiopia and the very new Eritrea as long as they ensured law and order. U.S. officials regarded Eritrea as Ethiopia's natural outlet and Ethiopia as Eritrea's natural hinterland. Agreeing with EPRDF officials, the State Department believed that the logic of complementarity would push Eritrea to rejoin Ethiopia, notwithstanding the imminence of the

1993 referendum, which many critics claimed offered the limited choice of independence or nothing. However imperfect Meles and Isayas were, the United States believed that the two men would introduce free-market economies that would facilitate the development of democracy. Even then, that hope appeared baseless.

In November 1991, the TGE passed a New Economic Policy (NEP) that impressed many westerners, especially the World Bank, with whom Addis Abeba was negotiating a Structural Adjustment Program (SAP). According to the World Bank, Ethiopia's annual per capita income of $120 was declining. General growth during the previous decade had averaged only 1.6 percent and only 1.2 percent for agriculture, which accounted for an estimated 70 percent of the economy. Social services, the World Bank found, were poor in quality, had an urban bias, and were deteriorating. Poverty in Ethiopia had an absolute, grinding quality that eroded human and capital resources and caused enormous environmental damage as the poor extracted remaining resources from the land.

Instead of liberating the peasants from their dependence on nature and the small land allotments to which they were entitled, the TGE continued the previous regime's policy of state landownership. Meles's government argued paternalistically that with freehold tenure, the peasants would sell their plots and flood into the cities without any way to support themselves and their families.

Wanting to avoid social crisis, the EPRDF disregarded the probability that market forces would lead to larger and more economic forms and the capital so desperately needed for the nation's economic development. In 2000, therefore, the countryside remained populated by tattered, malnourished, impoverished people similar to those one saw in 1961. There was evidence, however, of considerable growth along the roads, where villages, small in the 1960s, had become sizable towns, and places such as Lekemti, Shashamane, Dese, and Fenote Selam had grown into cities. Truck-borne trade in cash crops such as coffee, hides, grains, oil seeds, legumes, and chat had made the difference between the countryside and the roadside.

Thus, the NEP must be regarded as a palliative, intended to avoid social dislocation for as long as possible and to impress naive foreigners with the regime's commitment to a free-market economy. The policy stipulated that the government be active in economic areas not subject to the market, such as defense and energy, mining, public utilities, and communications, although it did not explain why the last sectors should not be privatized. By 2000, energy, public utilities, and communications were excessively expensive, inefficient, and unable to meet demand, causing power blackouts, water shortages, and inadequate connectivity to the Internet.

The NEP outlined the state's primary function as the builder of an infrastructure with sufficient services, skilled manpower, and facilities to attract investment. Regrettably, neither the TGE nor the FDRE has been able to fulfill these needs, and many potential investors have learned that they cannot rent or lease property for their enterprises nor can they secure sufficient electricity for their machinery, a guaranteed supply of raw or imported materials, experienced and disciplined workers, adequate banking and credit facilities, and modern communications. However good their ideas, many potential investors leave Ethiopia in frustration when they realize that the government is not serious about economic change and modernization that might disrupt the political economy it has built.

Meles and company have consistently controlled the economy from the ruling heights or through an oligarchy carefully chosen for its political reliability. The Ethiopian economy is certainly more open to small enterprise than it ever has been, giving Addis Abeba and the towns and cities along the roads a bustling appearance; but virtually all large-scale business is in the hands of a favored few, whose cooperation is necessary for the success of any foreign investment. Moreover, the government intervenes freely in the economy. In July 2000, it raised prices for fuel without referencing parliament, the business community, or consumers; it meddled in the sale of Agip to Shell, two private organizations; it interfered with the sugar market; and it ordered importers to use the government-owned and expensive Ethiopian shipping line. So much for Ethiopia's free-market economy!

Eritrea's economy also was tightly controlled by the ruling EPLF, which monopolized business and production through twenty-six party-dominated holding companies. This arrangement accorded well with a political system that was not only authoritarian and centralized in nature but that allowed a small group of ex-guerrilla leaders to impose their unitary national idea on the country. The leadership followed a strategy of nation building from above and, naturally enough, created an interventionist government that permitted the development of neither political pluralism nor a free-market economy. Furthermore,

Eritrea remained tied to the birr, Ethiopia's demand for its goods, and the need to repair a war-damaged infrastructure. The Asmera government would begin to particularize its own identity and economy only after the impending referendum, which would give Eritrea recognized international status.

The referendum, held from 23 to 25 April 1993, phrased the issue in such a way as to lead to the affirmation of independence, which was approved by 99.8 percent of the electorate, comprising 872,000 in Eritrea and 330,000 outside. Of the latter, 154,000 were in Sudan, 57,700 in Ethiopia, with the remainder in Arabia, Europe, and the United States. Even if the referendum had included an option for a renewed relationship with Ethiopia, it is doubtful, given the history of the original federal period (1952–1962), that it would have garnered much support. Yet, on 25 April, a pleased Isayas told a press conference that close economic ties with Ethiopia might lead to the negotiation of a confederation. He also remarked that he stood for a multiparty political system and democracy, but that some years might pass before either could be attained, since the government first had to ensure stability.

On 19 May, Isayas decreed the formation of a Government of Eritrea (GOE), which consisted of a National Assembly whose members included the EPLF central committee, thirty delegates from provincial assemblies, and twenty others, including ten women, all chosen by the ruling party. The assembly enjoyed supreme power as the legislative body and had the authority to adopt a constitution. It elected the president–head of state, who thereupon became the assembly's moderator, and named and controlled the Council of State, or cabinet. Chaired by the president–head of state, the latter comprised all ministries and was responsible to the assembly, whose legislative power it held when the assembly was not in session. The Government of Eritrea Decree also stipulated that a permanent regime, organized within a maximum of four years, would then operate under a constitution drawn by a commission to be established by the assembly and composed of EPLF and ELF members and independent experts. They were to design an egalitarian, multiparty democratic state that respected human rights but eschewed religious, ethnic, and regional parties.

On 24 May 1993, the second anniversary of the EPLF's entry into Asmera, Isayas formally declared Eritrea's independence before the heads of state of the adjacent countries, including Meles, whose government was among the first to recognize the new sovereignty. Its territory was defined on the basis of *uti possidetis* and according to the frontiers established by the Italian colonial state, including those undisputed boundaries agreed upon with Ethiopia in the treaties of 10 July 1900 and 16 May 1908. According to two Ethio-Eritrean conventions of 18 April 1992, Aseb and Mitsiwa had the status of free ports for the transit trade.

On 21 January 1993, Eritrea negotiated a commercial accord with Ethiopia that included free trade and mutual commercial ventures. Then, on 20 July 1993, the two countries concluded agreements of cooperation in foreign affairs, defense, and security; resources, energy, and transport; and social relations, especially in education. The signatories confirmed their earlier commitments to the unhindered movement of people and goods and to the free ports of Aseb and Mitsiwa. Finally, to oversee relations, they established a Mixed Commission. Composed of the Ethiopian prime minister, the two ministers of foreign affairs, and the two ambassadors, the commission would meet as needed to solve problems transmitted to it by political, economic, and social committees, which were formally established on 22 September 1993. Two further committees on security and technical cooperation were initiated on 2 November and 18 December 1993, respectively.

Meanwhile, the TGE's ready acceptance of Eritrean independence subjected the EPRDF to much criticism at home and abroad, especially by overseas Ethiopians. The government's close cooperation with Asmera and the revision of Ethiopia's administrative zones by ethnicity led many to believe that Meles wanted to weaken the central government so that it would never be able to reverse Tigray's autonomy and Eritrea's independence. Others took the radical line that Meles sought the breakup of Ethiopia in favor of a Greater Tigray; or that the TPLF was repaying what it owed Isayas and the EPLF for their help against the derg.

As evidence of complicity between Meles and Isayas, they noted that Asmera had not offered to compensate Ethiopia for the state and economic infrastructure left behind, for cargoes appropriated in Aseb and Mitsiwa, or for property abandoned by an estimated 200,000 Ethiopian deportees. In reality, however, trying to figure out such a valuation not only would have stimulated Eritrean demands to compensation for war damages, but also would have led to a highly contentious debate that would have exacerbated relations at a time when healing required calm and reason.

The critics were ignorant of the difficult relations between the two over the years and the continuing contradictions in their approaches to state organization and policies. In fact, Meles acted as a statesman when he decided not to raise the issue of division of assets, and his leniency toward Eritreans in Ethiopia signaled his hope that Asmera might, in the near future, restore some type of political relationship with Addis Abeba. Yet, the integration of an Eritrean unitary state that officially ignored the particularism of its citizens would not have succeeded in an Ethiopian federation based on ethnicity.

Meanwhile, in Ethiopia, the Meles government was pushing forward its political agenda, and there were complaints from around the country that the fourteen ethnically based, regional governments discriminated in favor of their own kind. There were problems with government land policies, and urban businessmen found land-lease a tenure too insecure to make long-term capital investments. In the countryside, farmers complained that land allotments were being made on the basis of political loyalty, as in the old, bad Mengistu days. Political considerations aside, there was not enough land to fill the needs of Ethiopia's growing population, in 1994 approximately 55 million, 90 percent of whom were cultivators.

In Addis Abeba, meanwhile, people were horrified when, in January 1993, the police suppressed student demonstrations against Eritrean independence by indiscriminately charging, and firing into, the crowd, killing a still-disputed number of protestors. On the convenient but specious grounds that they had incited student violence, the government then dismissed forty-two Addis Ababa University professors, among them many of the institution's most productive researchers and scholars, its top administrators, and its best teachers. Since most of the purged were Amhara—a number active in the All-Amhara Peoples Organization and the Ethiopian Human Rights Organization (EHRO)—the government's action, unprecedented in the annals of the university and illegal in its system of governance, was regarded by the urban intelligentsia and by expatriate groups as a form of ethnic-academic cleansing. Cynicism about the EPRDF's publicly expressed commitment to human rights grew at home and abroad when, in December 1993, the government arrested seven delegates from expatriate organizations as they deplaned in Addis Abeba to take part in an Opposition Conference. This crisis of trust was accompanied by a refrain of reports that cadres were pressuring street boys not to sell certain newspapers and magazines, and also by the jailing of a number of journalists, an activity in which Ethiopia was second only to Turkey. The government was charged with having transgressed the Proclamation on Freedom of the Press of 21 October 1992, which outlined a number of loosely drawn sins against the state and its nationalities.

Such was the background to elections on 5 June 1994 for a Constituent Assembly (CA) and the approval of a new constitution, which was to complete the work of the transitional government. A Constitution Drafting Commission (CDC) had been proclaimed on 18 August 1992 by the TGE's Council of Representatives. Under the chairmanship of Kifle Wodajo, a former foreign minister and ambassador of the Haile Sellassie regime, the commission comprised twenty-nine members organized into panels on (1) human rights, (2) government structure and division of powers, and (3) social issues, such as languages and citizenship. The CDC held meetings and consultations throughout 1993 and brought scholars, lawyers, and jurists to Ethiopia to educate the public in the arcane business of constitution making. In November 1993, it printed a booklet reflecting constitutional views that conformed to the EPRDF's fixed idea about the paramountcy of ethnicity.

In early 1994, the CDC organized a series of meetings to obtain the views of people at the regional, district, kebelay, and peasant-association levels. The discussions, however, were dominated by EPRDF cadres, allowing the commission to deliver, on 8 April 1994, a draft constitution based on the notion of ethnic federalism. In the subsequent debate in the Council of Representatives, Meles spoke strongly in favor of the constitution, the unanimous approval of which cleared the stage for the Constituent Assembly elections of June 1994, the last important act of the TGE.

Nongovernmental commentators have agreed that the elections were fraudulent, especially since most opposition parties abandoned the campaign when their candidates were harassed, their offices closed, and their supporters persecuted and beaten. The EPRDF cadres forcibly ensured voter turnout and security so that election day went off without discernible violence or obvious irregularities. The EPRDF and its associated parties won 484 out of 547 contested seats, and many of the successful independents were surrogates for the front. The CA met on 28 October 1994 to begin the process of transforming the draft constitution into Ethiopia's legal charter.

On 8 December 1994, the assembly voted for ratification with no significant changes and scheduled an election for 7 May 1995 to choose a National Assembly that, in turn, would declare the Federal Democratic Republic of Ethiopia (FDRE). Once again, main opposition groups did not participate, and most of the fifty-nine political parties registered for the election were ethnically based organizations of the ruling coalition. The EPRDF won 483 seats in the parliament and over 90 percent of the votes. It also took control over the seven elected regional councils, although in the Afar, Somali, and Harer areas, the election was delayed owing to internal unrest.

In the countryside, cadres got out the vote by threatening to reconsider land and fertilizer allotments. The peasants were concerned about the high costs of fertilizer and other inputs, since they never seemed to be able to harvest any cash from their efforts. They worried also about the decreasing availability of oxen for plowing. Above all, they criticized the cadres for telling them what to do and how to vote and for never seeking their advice or opinions—so much for the EPRDF's much-advertised bottom-to-top politics.

Thus, the peasants participated in the election, but not with any expectation that the government would address their cares. Their perception that power holders always tried to control them was similar to the urban dwellers' belief that they needed to conform politically or they would lose their jobs or perquisites. To many Ethiopians, the EPRDF's rhetoric of democracy did not seem very different from the message of socialism preached by the derg. Even though most people were therefore cynical about the EPRDF regime, the fact that the government lacked the mean character of the previous regime made them feel more secure in their private lives.

Indeed, on the face of it, the new constitution would seem to ensure a decent future for Ethiopians. It provides for a federal multi-party system of government based on ethnicity according to language. The preamble begins with "We, the Nations, Nationalities, and Peoples of Ethiopia" and proclaims the country to be "A Nation of Nations," just as the Solomonic dynasty's emperor was "The King of Kings." The federal union is composed of nine states based on "the settlement patterns, identity, language, and consent of the people concerned." The constitution places sovereignty with Ethiopia's various ethno-linguistic nations, which elect delegates to a two-chamber parliament that includes the House of Peoples Representatives and the House of

Federation, in which each nation is entitled to at least one member and additional members for each million of population. As the core institution of the Nation of Nations, the House of Federation is empowered to interpret the constitution and to decide matters of grave concern, such as the right to secession, for which there are detailed sets of implementing procedures. In such matters, the Council of Constitutional Inquiry, comprising legal experts chaired by the chief justice of the Federal Supreme Court, assists the House of Federation.

The constitution makes Amharic the federal vernacular, although it proclaims that all Ethiopian languages enjoy state recognition. Ownership of rural and urban land is vested "in the state and in the peoples of Ethiopia . . . and [is] not subject to sale or to other means of transfer." Religion and state are declared separate. Prime ministers are to be elected from among members of the House of Peoples Representatives for terms of five years, like the members of parliament, and they hold almost unlimited power as long as they retain the majority. The federal state is divided into legislative, executive, and judicial branches, a model followed by the ethnic units over which the central government wields considerable reserved powers. The judiciary is ostensibly independent but in fact relies on political, legislative, and executive organizations for its authority.

Chapter 3 of the Constitution specifies the "Fundamental Rights and Freedoms" enjoyed by the Ethiopian people. The fifteen articles defining "Human Rights" include the usual guarantees for life, liberty, security of person, privacy, and religious freedom. "Democratic Rights," described in sixteen articles, provide for conventional freedoms of thought, opinion, expression, assembly, association, and movement. Chapter 3 imposes clear limits on the power of government, but, as with so many Ethiopian decrees, laws, and constitutions over the nation's history, it is a statement of intention.

Political reality and the fear of losing power continue to override idealism in a country bereft of human resources, government infrastructure, communications, and political will. Even if the last were firmly in place, the central and national bureaucracies and the police can, and do, find many ways to defeat constitutional restraints; perhaps because the EPRDF sponsors a parallel system of governance through party activists, for whom retention of state power takes precedence over the rule of law. There is thus a major contradiction between the EPRDF's rhetoric of democracy and constitutionalism and its actions.

On 24 August 1995, the House of Peoples Representatives, in which the EPRDF held 493 seats, voted overwhelmingly for the new constitution and the new government. President Meles Zenawi of the TGE became prime minister of the FDRE; and the largely ceremonial presidency went to Dr. Negaso Gidada, a historian and academic who had left the OLF for the EPDM and the OPDO, since he believed Oromia would prosper only in a united Ethiopia. The ruling front held eight out of seventeen posts in the new Council of Ministers, which was composed of one Tigrayan, four Amhara, four Oromo, two Gurage, and one each from Hadiya, Kembata, Somali, and Wolayta. Five assistant ministers were Tigrayan, however, and they had direct access to Meles.

The TGE's Amhara prime minister, Tamrat Layne, became deputy prime minister and minister of defense in the new cabinet. Most of his senior officers, a number of whom had been to staff schools in the United States, were Tigrayan. Tamrat and his generals were directed to make the military more representative of Ethiopia by demobilizing the bulk of the army's Tigrayan fighters, several thousands of whom were to join the police. The air force, which in July 1995 had become operational again with forty MiG fighters and two dozen Mi24 gunships, was to rebuild to its former strength of 1989–1990. Nobody seemed to know how the government would pay for the new aircraft.

Since 1992, however, the EPRDF government had benefited from a peace dividend of high growth rates, which encouraged the World Bank to provide $4 billion in loans and grants, one-third for balance of payments and the remainder for investment in social services, roads, and other infrastructural improvements. The World Bank's confidence, in turn, encouraged Britain, France, and Italy to provide credits for needed imports and to contemplate financing major mineral and hydro-electric projects. Meanwhile, the TGE had deregulated agricultural marketing and transport and reduced military expenditure to 10 percent of the budget. Virtually alone in Africa, Ethiopia managed to maintain a strong local currency and to limit inflation to about 10 percent. It tightly controlled the budget deficit, money supply, and government borrowing. The government also improved economic co-ordination between its ministries and the regional governments, most of which had proved incapable of administering the small capital budgets allocated to them by Addis Abeba.

These economic achievements were matched by social accomplishments often ignored by the TGE/FDRE's critics, especially those living outside of Ethiopia. By 1995, people and goods moved freely in the country, and foreign observers and officials could come and go as they pleased, since the government believed there was nothing to hide and behaved as if there were no security problems. Nongovernmental organizations, now often run by Ethiopians, were widespread and involved in development and social welfare efforts in many parts of the country. The independent media had learned to live with the government, and vice versa, and daily provided valuable and critical information about the state of the country. As never before, the individual citizen could read about the achievements as well as the miscarriages of justice, corruption, the state of the roads, trade in the countryside, educational problems, economic difficulties, and the like; and rarely did the media, even government-owned outlets, puff up political figures.

In the towns, but also in very remote rural areas, necessary consumer goods were available, and prices were lower than during the previous regime. Constitutional protections, while flawed, did provide individuals a basis for seeking justice, and mass organizations had lost their coercive powers. The government could argue that it was doing well by the Ethiopian people and that life would improve as its programs succeeded. The progress was, however, to be interrupted by the outbreak of an unlikely and fratricidal war with Eritrea.

SIXTEEN

Peace and War, to 2000

In Eritrea, meanwhile, the EPLF, now known as the Peoples Front for Democracy and Justice (PFDJ), was having trouble making the transition from a liberation movement to a political party. In 1994–1995, for example, the government refused to explain its dismissal of 10,000 or so civil servants and 40,000 fighters when it would have been easy to justify the action in budgetary terms. The PFDJ was criticized for monopolizing all key positions in government and filling them with its members regardless of whether they had the necessary qualifications and skills. The party's control over the economy was also a subject of complaint. In 1994, the PFDJ separated its assets from those of the government, leaving it in control of most major companies. In fact, the party was Eritrea's main economic force and was willing to finance new companies for a 51-percent stake.

In the traditional sector, the government owned the land, and priority, during periodic redistributions, was given to PFDJ members and supporters. Elsewhere, the administration suppressed traditional bottom-up institutions in favor of top-down organizations dominated by cadres—often young, invariably not from the area—who were now responsible for making the land allocations. The PFDJ also reduced administrative regions from ten to six, explaining the change as a way of saving money even as it ensured the party's political hegemony throughout the country. Akele Guzay, a historic Christian district that nonetheless had supported the largely Muslim ELF, disappeared, and the Afar people, also present in Ethiopia, were divided to be ruled in the new Red Sea and Mitsiwa regions. The reforms disregarded ethnic, religious, and regional loyalties, as did Eritrea's constitution, which was ratified on 23 May 1997 but remained unimplemented as late as the end of 2001.

Taking the opposite approach, Addis Abeba was working to achieve ethnic balance. For example, by mid-1996, almost one-third of the Tigrayan fighters in the Ethiopian army had been retired or transferred to the police, making room for men from other ethnic groups or even from Mengistu's army. Eight new brigadier generals had been named from the EPRDF ruling coalition, among them two each from the TPLF, the OPDO, the Amhara National Democratic Movement (ANDM, formerly the EPDM), and the Southern Ethiopian Peoples Democratic Front (SEPDF). Although authority in the high command still favored Tigrayan officers, Tsadkan Gebretensae, the deputy defense minister, was promoted to major general, and his successor as chief of staff, Brigadier General Yemane Kidane, a member of the TPLF central committee, was charged with reorganizing the army to reflect Ethiopia's ethnic composition.

The Eritreans, meanwhile, were formalizing their military structure with pay tables and ranks. In May 1996, President Isayas named twenty-two brigadier generals, three colonels, and a number of lieutenant colonels in Keren, where a United States training team was stationed. Ironically, the Americans were teaching the Eritreans about training insurgents, in this case southern Sudanese, to fight a guerrilla war. In response, Khartoum had pushed the ELF and other antigovernment Muslim groups to attack civilian targets in western Eritrea. Although little mischief was done, the authorities in Asmera were forced to move tank and infantry units to the frontier.

Eritrea, Uganda, and Ethiopia composed one unit in America's worldwide defense against Islamic radicalism. In the Horn of Africa, Ethiopia's population of 60.9 million made it the leading player, but Meles worried that his political opponents would unleash their Muslim adherents against the federal state. He therefore used some of his American military assistance against the Somali Al-Itahad al-Islami (Islamic union, AIAI), which in 1995 mounted several bomb attacks in the Ogaden and attempted to assassinate Abdul Majid Hussein, a cabinet minister and the leader of the Ethio-Somali Democratic Movement. In response, Meles ordered his army into Somalia to destroy AIAI bases along the frontier, and he sent truckloads of American-supplied weapons to opposition movements. At the same time, he tried to conciliate the Oromo, whose leadership was mostly Muslim.

In June 1997, at talks with the OLF held in Germany, the EPRDF tabled a memorandum that would have permitted the OLF, dignity intact, to rejoin Ethiopia's political life. The government agreed to recognize the OLF as a legitimate political party and to permit it to open offices throughout Oromia and elsewhere, to have a radio station and a small army under its control, and to hold a referendum on independence within four years. The deal broke down because the federal government refused to transfer power in Oromia from the OPDO to the OLF, claiming, not unreasonably, that internal politics was best left to competition between the two parties. The OLF subsequently withdrew from the negotiations, believing that the United States would never permit an honest referendum because Oromia's secession would mean the destruction of Ethiopia and of Washington's strategy to contain radical Islam. It was not to be the OLF, however, but Isayas's Eritrea that was responsible for the ruination of America's policy in the Horn of Africa and its hopes for a new African leadership.

Most observers were blind to the friction between Ethiopia and Eritrea that had developed after 1993, as Asmera worked to give substance to its sovereignty. Achieving true autonomy was, of course, an impossible endeavor, but during the long war against Ethiopia, astute EPLF propagandists convinced themselves and much of the world that an independent Eritrea could be self-sufficient and even thrive in the modern global economy. Since Eritrea did not have the resources for autarchy in any form or fashion, Asmera sought to augment the country's internal product through trade, the provision of services, and manufacturing. The government assumed that it would be able to acquire from Ethiopia necessary raw materials, access to its huge markets, and cooperation.

From 1992 to 1996, Eritrea sent an average of 66 percent of its manufactured products to Ethiopia and was able to import cereals, industrial raw materials, timber and other wood products, cotton, sugar, oil seed, tobacco, iron ingots, corrugated iron sheets, and yarn and thread. According to the 1997 report of the International Monetary Fund, Eritrea's mean annual food consumption was 400,000 metric tons, of which it produced about 180,000 metric tons, with the rest coming from Ethiopia. Since all transactions were made in Ethiopian currency, which both countries used, there was no problem with the balance of payments and no need to expend scarce hard currency.

North of the border, Eritreans were treated as citizens and often held important government positions. They engaged in domestic trade and services and were deeply involved in trucking and communications. As businessmen, they were able to obtain bank loans and letters of credit without discrimination. Since Asmera subsidized the exchange of birr for dollars—in other words, it ran a black market in currency—it repaid in cheaper birr. Eritrean merchants also had an advantage in purchasing exportable Ethiopian products, such as coffee, which they illegally sent home for transshipment. Eritrea thus enjoyed political independence while simultaneously profiting from being part of a larger economy.

Ethiopians, on the other hand, were not certain that the economic relationship was benefiting them. Since there were no financial barriers between the two countries, Eritreans easily evaded Ethiopian taxes by disguising earnings and sending home birr profits and remittances. Loans to Eritreans dried up bank liquidity, drove up interest rates, and made obtaining credit generally more difficult. Some Ethiopians regarded the thousands of Eritreans who worked in the public sector as taking jobs that should have gone to their compatriots. Most Ethiopians were irate that they did not have the same access to Eritrea as Eritreans enjoyed to Ethiopia. If they wanted to obtain a license to run a business or a work permit or to make business investments, they had to find Eritrean surrogates willing, for a price, to let their names be used.

Businessmen and government officials in Addis Abeba grew increasingly skeptical of Eritrea's goodwill toward Ethiopia. When Asmera began to squeeze as much profit as possible out of the Aseb and Mitsiwa ports, it ignored official Ethiopian complaints that price changes should have been negotiated in the Joint Economic Committee and then referred to the Mixed Commission. Cartage and hauling fees kept rising, surcharges were applied to bulk imports, and docking and stevedore rates grew. Furthermore, as experienced Ethiopian managers were replaced with untried Eritreans, efficiency decreased and turnaround time increased, raising shipping costs and forcing consumer prices upward.

By 1996–1997, when Asmera made an estimated one billion birr from its ports, Ethiopian businessmen turned increasingly to the port at Jibuti, where fees were lower. They also purchased the lower-cost petroleum products that were offered by the port city's newly installed ultramodern minirefinery. The obsolete and high-cost refinery in Aseb suffered a deep drop in business and profits.

As these two major sources of Asmera's income began to erode, the Ethiopian economy experienced a weakening of the international coffee market and a loss of export income. In order to fulfill the requirements of various structural adjustment programs, the Addis Abeba government needed to squeeze as much as it could from the banking system, from the import/export trade, and from international currency transactions. It therefore began to regulate commerce and money as never before, further decreasing the flow of revenue to the Eritrean government. In August 1997, with only remittances from expatriate nationals as a reliable source of funds, Asmera announced that it would introduce its own currency, the nakfa (N).

Asmera forwarded to Addis Abeba a memorandum proposing the new money's parity with the birr and its free circulation on both sides of the border. Ethiopia did not respond until late October 1997, when it rejected the proposal and unilaterally declared that trade would be conducted, as between any two sovereign states, with formal clearances in hard currency. The FDRE's decision destroyed Asmera's profitable transit and currency trades, further undermining an already weakened economy. By the time the nakfa became Eritrea's sole legal tender in December 1997, the Ethiopians had issued a new set of birr notes to block any possibility of Asmera's redeeming the old currency. For Eritreans, Addis Abeba's actions constituted an unfriendly act, made worse by the new birr note's small inset map that seemingly placed parts of Eritrea in Tigray. Many in Asmera believed that the map revealed sinister Ethiopian ambitions, characterized after May 1998 as Tigrayan expansionist intentions.

After 1991, along what had become a de facto international frontier, there were occasional local and small-scale disputes of a type common in farming communities that work on both sides of a boundary. Many problems occurred at plowing times, when peasants clashed over the exact limits of their fields. Local officials usually resolved the differences, but between 1993 and 1996 some claims were taken to higher levels. In August 1997, after a serious conflict over the Bada region of

38. Money to die for

the southern Eritrea/northern Afar depression, Isayas wrote to Meles, suggesting the establishment of a Joint Border Commission, the first meeting of which took place in Asmera on 13 November 1997. Commission members decided to set up a technical subcommittee comprising experts from both countries to examine and report on the border problems. In the meantime, both sides agreed to retain the status quo and to take steps to reduce the possibility of future clashes.

There were a number of disputed areas along the six hundred-mile frontier: Badme and its environs; Humera in the west; Tsorona and Zalembessa north of Adigrat; Altiena and Irob; Bada in the Afar depression; and Bure on the road to Aseb. Eritrea based all of its claims on the colonial frontiers as they existed under Italian rule; and Addis

Abeba countered by citing the lines specified by the Italo-Ethiopian treaties of 10 July 1900 and 16 May 1908, which had never been challenged. The difficulties derived from the period, 1952 to 1991, when Eritrea was ruled from Addis Abeba and the old international boundaries were disused. Solutions to administrative problems were then based on common sense. For example, the Altiena area appears on most maps as part of Eritrea, but, as it was populated by Christian Irob people, it was governed as part of the Tigrayan Irob region. For a sovereign Eritrea, however, administrative convenience was secondary to retaining Altiena as the gateway to the important salt trade from the Afar depression and to controlling Bada, which enjoyed decent soils and good rainfall, both in short supply in the new nation.

The Badme situation was also complicated by Eritrea's erstwhile status as part of Ethiopia. In the early twentieth century, sparsely settled with Kunama people, Badme attracted Tigrinya-speaking farmers from both Eritrea and Tigray. In the 1960s, Ras Mengesha ignored provincial boundaries and administered Badme as part of Tigray's Shire district. After the revolution of 1974, the Kunama cooperated with the Mengistu regime and fought against both the EPLF and ELF, the latter of which had come to dominate the area. To further complicate the situation, the TPLF allied with the EPLF in 1981 to oust the ELF and take over Badme, which it controlled from Sheraro, its base in undisputed Tigrayan territory. After 1991 Tigray continued to administer Badme town, which had grown so large that even its location was disputed. Yet, Eritrea did not protest, because it was focused on consolidating its authority more generally.

The point that emerges from even a factual recounting of the situation is the lack of clarity in the frontier claims. They needed to be negotiated politically by people who could compromise on the issues. The use of force would not easily solve the problems, unless one side could be forced to concede to the other's demands, which was not the case. The circumstances surrounding the meeting of the Joint Border Commission in Addis Abeba on 8 May 1998 revealed an Ethiopia content with negotiations and an Eritrea losing patience with the political process. By then, the Regional Education Board of Tigray had issued a map that showed disputed areas as part of the kilil. The Eritreans were reminded of the birr minimap and interpreted both as part of a TPLF plot to create the Greater Tigray of its 1976 manifesto.

At first, Asmera appeared willing to negotiate the frontier issues, since its delegation was led by Defense Minister Sebhat Efrem. Both sides reported that the first meeting went well, even though on 6 May, armed Eritreans had appeared at a number of points around Badme and, when challenged, claimed that the area belonged to Asmera. The commission agreed that the armed units would withdraw into uncontested Eritrean territory and that the status quo ante would be restored until a final settlement was reached. Sometime between the end of the meeting and the next day, 9 May, when the group was scheduled to reconvene, Isayas made the decision to use force. By the morning, to the surprise of an Ethiopian escort sent to fetch them, members of the Eritrean delegation had left their hotel and returned to Asmera. On the morning of 12 May 1998, after three days of fruitless but intense telephone negotiations, tank-supported Eritrean forces took Badme and its environs.

The next day, the Ethiopian parliament formally condemned the aggression, demanded an immediate withdrawal, and warned that Addis Abeba reserved its right to defend the nation. At the end of May, the Ethiopian command probed the Eritrean lines on the Altiena front, which yielded little military importance; then in early June they fought at Zalembessa for control of the town and the main road to and from Eritrea. By the end of the fighting in mid-June, Eritrea held the town, blocking any possible enemy movement north, but Ethiopia controlled the road, preventing further Eritrean advances south.

On 5 June, two waves of Ethiopian MiGs attacked the airport at Asmera, killing one person but otherwise doing little but symbolic damage. About an hour later, two Eritrean planes appeared over Mekele and hit a number of nonmilitary targets, killing forty-seven civilians, among them ten children whose school was bombed, and wounding 153 people including a number of youngsters. The incident caused a great outcry in Addis Abeba and elsewhere and embarrassed the Eritreans, who explained that the casualties resulted from error. The next morning, when Ethiopian planes returned to bomb Asmera airport, once again causing little damage, diplomats went into action and negotiated a suspension of raiding for thirteen hours after 5:00 P.M. to permit the air evacuation of 2,000 foreign nationals.

On 11 June, Eritrean aircraft once again bombed civilian targets in Mekele, killing four and injuring forty. Since the raids on both sides seemed to have little to do with the contested frontier regions, international criticism convinced Meles and Isayas to agree, as of 15 June, to a cease-fire in the air. The truce was welcomed by Asmera as the beginning of the end of the war, but the Ethiopian Foreign Ministry issued a communiqué stating that the agreement did not lessen Ethiopia's intention to defend its sovereignty. Nevertheless, the air armistice closed the fighting's first phase, and, with the beginning of the long rainy season, a lull set in, during which both sides rearmed even as the international community tried to influence them to negotiate a peace agreement. The former was easier than the latter, since the world was awash with surplus Soviet weaponry.

During the remainder of the year, Eritrea spent $90 million for six Russian jet fighters and four helicopter gunships, plus $150 million for small arms and antiaircraft missiles. Ethiopia's bill was $500 million for twelve assorted fighter-bombers, ten helicopter gunships, ten self-propelled artillery pieces, and small arms. The differential in expenditures can be explained by Ethiopia's need to attack, against which Eritrea would defend from the safety of its heavily fortified trenches.

Isayas fundamentally believed that his soldiers were better trained and more motivated than their Ethiopian adversaries. He regarded them as invincible as they hunkered down in their burrows and bunkers. When propaganda officers took foreign diplomats and journalists to see the fortifications, they slyly likened them to those that had frustrated Mengistu's army at Nakfa. The foreigners duly reported that the Ethiopians would not be able to pierce the fortifications, and that any such effort would end in massive defeat.

Addis Abeba ignored these prophecies and refused any peace plan that left Eritrea in control of contested territories; and Asmera sought a solution based on military occupation until its claims were realized through international mediation. In August, Eritrea rejected an Organization of African Unity (OAU) peace plan that called for both a withdrawal to the positions occupied before 6 May and the stationing of UN peacekeepers until the frontier line could be negotiated. By October, Eritrea was inclined to accept an international observer force, perhaps demilitarization, but not withdrawal, whereas Ethiopia demanded the return to the status quo ante before it would enter into talks. Both sides claimed to be willing to give the OAU a chance to negotiate a satisfactory cease-fire before they would return to warfare.

Meanwhile, over half a million small farmers and nomads who had been displaced on both sides of the contested frontier required rehousing and food assistance. Another 70,000 people were forcibly deported—about 50,000 from Ethiopia to Eritrea and the rest in the other direction. The story is very complex, full of contradictions, and has been reported in the rhetoric of the warring parties or in the didactic of international human rights agencies. The Ethiopian government used the cover of the war to cleanse the bureaucracy of Eritreans in powerful and sensitive jobs and to eliminate those who had voted in the referendum, held Eritrean identity cards, or had been known to send money to the Asmera government. These people were considered ipso facto security risks, as were those who could manipulate the economy in any way, who worked in trucking, communications, and education, and who held positions in embassies, NGOs, and UN agencies. The deportations represented a rejection of Meles's very generous pro-Eritrean policies, and, as such, they were undertaken in a broad sweeping process that disrupted many innocent lives.

Among those deported were people who had one Eritrean parent, who had lived all their lives in Ethiopia, who did not speak any Eritrean languages, had Ethiopian spouses and children, held Ethiopian passports and identity cards, and who regarded themselves as true Ethiopian patriots. The deportations themselves were accomplished in the harshest possible way. People were not permitted to settle their affairs or to take much with them; they were jammed into buses without adequate food or water and unceremoniously dumped at the frontier. After they had gone, their property and goods were confiscated and sold or auctioned off to pay alleged tax arrears or bank loans. The deportations interrupted generations of intimacy, and it will be a long time before Eritrea and Ethiopia again refer to each other as fraternal countries.

On the Eritrean side, the process of deportation was subtler. Before the crisis, an estimated 100,000 Ethiopian long-term residents and migrant laborers worked in Eritrea, 35,000 in Aseb and the others mostly in Asmera, Mitsiwa, and Keren. Even before the war began, many Ethiopians had lost their jobs because import/export firms decided to divert cargoes to lower-priced Jibuti. Competition from the cost-efficient minirefinery at Jibuti had also caused the shutdown of Aseb's obsolete refinery, which resulted in more Ethiopians losing their jobs. The war accelerated the decline of Aseb and the unemployment of Ethiopians living there, and thousands elsewhere suffered arbitrary dismissals. Without work and income, most became destitute and homeless, unable to pay their debts or purchase exit visas. It was not until the Asmera government rescinded these requirements, a truly merciful action, that the International Red Cross was able to return 22,000 to Ethiopia by the end of January 1999.

By then, the Ethiopians were losing patience with the peace process. The mediators refused to understand that in Addis Abeba's view, Ethiopian territory had been invaded and the crisis was about national sovereignty. Outsiders persisted in an evenhanded approach, since they regarded the war as much ado about nothing, given the largely insalubrious terrain at stake. In fact, the war was being fought over hegemony in the Horn of Africa, and it was a struggle that Ethiopia dared not lose. In the hope of stirring up the ethnic cauldron that many Eritreans imagined Ethiopia had become, Asmera conspired with the EPRDF's opponents and blamed the war on the TPLF, not on the Ethiopian government. Specifically, Asmera accused the Marxist-Leninist League of Tigray of wanting to either establish a Greater Tigray or destroy the Eritrean social experiment. Ethiopia's various national groups ignored such absurd claims and remained true to the federal union.

When the country's kilils responded positively by contributing men and money to the war effort, the Addis Abeba government discovered that nationalism was intact, giving the lie to long-standing criticism, especially from expatriate Ethiopians, that the FDRE's ethnic policy would lead to disunity and destruction. In fact, as the crisis deepened, the EPRDF's critics came to support if not the government then the war effort. In this, they responded as Ethiopians to the historic fact that the Italians twice had invaded from Eritrea through Tigray to destroy Ethiopia's sovereignty and unity. Since the Eritreans made their Italian colonial heritage the etiological basis of their claim to independence, Ethiopians regarded them as latter-day imperialists. After World War II, Haile Sellassie had fought to regain the ex-Italian colony in part to protect against Eritrea's again being used as a base from which to launch an attack on Ethiopia. For similar reasons, in the 1950s Haile Sellassie had sought to recruit Somalis into a confederal state to block the possibility of invasion from that direction. A political relationship was never achieved, and, in 1977, Siad Barre followed General Rodolfo Graziani's invasion route of 1935–1936 into Ethiopia.

When Addis Abeba realized that the foreign peacemakers did not understand the war's real issues and that Asmera would not return to the status quo ante, the Ethiopian army attacked with overwhelming force at Badme on 23 February 1999. The Eritrean command had assumed that Meles's forces would follow Mengistu's tactics by attacking head-on. Instead, the Ethiopian high command concentrated artillery, armor, and manpower at two points along a sixty-kilometer front and, over two days, blasted through the Eritrean lines using tanks as bulldozers. Thousands of Ethiopian soldiers rushed through the gaps, rolled up the flanks, fired into the trenches, and broke the enemy, who fled before them. So overconfident were the Eritreans that they had prepared only one trench line in defense, and they therefore had no fortifications to fall back upon and no reserves closer than Barentu, across the Mareb River.

The Eritrean retreat was so chaotic that the victors could have marched far into Eritrea—some say to Asmera—had they wanted to. But, after advancing only twenty kilometers to take the Baduma plains, the Ethiopians stopped, a fact that contradicts Eritrea's later charge that Addis Abeba sought its reintegration into Ethiopia. The defeat at Badme was not masked by Asmera's usual claims that it was redeploying its troops, because on 27 February Eritrea officially accepted the OAU plan to end the war, commenting that its withdrawal from Badme showed its good faith. Although the Eritreans claimed that Ethiopia had lost tens of thousands of men in "human wave" attacks, the Addis Abeba command denied using such tactics. As General Tsadkan later explained, "Some journalists have painted a very ugly picture of the Ethiopian defense force, portraying us as a mass of flesh with no brain" (*The Monitor,* 13 August 2000). In fact, the Eritreans also took heavy casualties, and thousands were taken prisoner as the trenches failed them.

Ethiopia celebrated its victory, accused the Eritreans of trying to buy time to reorganize and rearm, and suggested that if Isayas were really sincere, he should withdraw his army from all of the disputed territory as the OAU plan proposed. There was some truth in the Ethiopian charge of Asmera's hypocrisy: in late May and June, the Eritreans counterattacked—killing more young people—but failed to regain Badme. There was also some later violence, but the remainder of 1999 was given over to international efforts to negotiate an end to the war. Both Addis Abeba and Asmera wanted to settle the conflict, but neither side was willing to admit defeat or wrongdoing. They turned facts on their head to prove their blamelessness, often reducing rationality to absurdity.

In December 1998, both governments had received the Organization of African Unity Proposal for a Framework Agreement for a Peaceful Settlement of the Dispute between Eritrea and Ethiopia, which was based on the United States–Rwanda plan of May 1998. It was not a document that favored the Eritrean position, which is probably why Asmera later balked over the details. The proposal called for the immediate cessation of hostilities and an end to antagonistic propaganda. It stipulated that Eritrean forces in Badme, its environs, and along the entire frontier return to the positions they occupied before 6 May 1998 "as a mark of goodwill," but without prejudice to the final demarcation. After the final settlement, "the legitimate authority [would] immediately exercise full and sovereign jurisdiction over the territory . . . recognized as belonging to them." Once sovereignty had been decided, there would be a subsequent investigation into the events of 6 May 1998 and other incidents that might have contributed to misunderstanding. The two belligerents agreed to determine modalities for the implementation of the Framework Agreement and to establish a joint committee under the auspices of the OAU and the UN, which would begin working on the signature of the Framework Agreement.

On 12 December 1998, the Eritrean government handed the visiting OAU secretary-general a list of Issues . . . Concerning the Framework Document. Asmera requested clarifications about virtually every important item in the Framework Agreement and basically asserted that all the disputed territories were Eritrean to begin with. The Isayas government therefore questioned why its forces and administration had to be withdrawn, since the least investigation would reveal the Eritrean character of the areas under contention. Asmera's logic was ignored in the Modalities for the Implementation of the OAU Framework Agreement on the Settlement of the Dispute between Ethiopia and Eritrea, which reaffirmed that the belligerents would return to the positions held prior to 6 May 1998. The Framework Agreement was accepted by the warring parties at the OAU summit in Algiers in July 1999.

Not so the Technical Arrangements for the Implementation of the OAU Framework Agreement and Its Modalities, which Addis Abeba rejected as unhelpful to the restoration of the situation that existed before 6 May 1998. Meles complained that the document seemed to accept Asmera's sophistry that the various OAU arrangements related only to Badme and its environs, which had been liberated by Ethiopian forces, and not to still-occupied territories. He showed contradictions between certain provisions of the Framework Agreement and Modalities Document. For example, the Technical Arrangements Document would have delayed the redeployment of forces and created authoritative external bodies that would have restricted the sovereignty of the restored civilian administration. In a letter of 13 August 1999, Meles requested that the OAU make the Technical Arrangements Document conform to the Framework Agreement and Modalities Document. The OAU response of December 1999 was opaque and repetitious and was probably a factor in the Ethiopian decision to restore the status quo ante by returning to military force.

Meanwhile, the Eritreans had declared a general mobilization, stopped issuing exit visas to men under the age of forty, and conscripted previously exempt able-bodied males who worked for embassies and foreign concerns. In this way, the government found 40,000 to 60,000 new soldiers to replace those who had died or were wounded at Badme and on other fronts. Asmera also purchased six obsolete MiG-21s, not being able to afford more expensive Sukhoi 27s or MiG-29s. Financing the war had deepened Eritrea's trade deficit to 60 percent of its 1998 GDP, or $464 million, and the country's banks had halted the issuance of letters of credit to finance consumer imports. Isayas had run short of money, since his sole remaining reliable source of revenue came from Eritreans living in the diaspora, and they had already been squeezed hard. Nonetheless, in December 1999, Isayas toured Europe to gather more funds.

His Ethiopian adversaries had been able to double their military expenditures, compared to previous figures, by using emergency funds in the federal budget, revenue accruing from the sale of state-owned companies, "voluntary" contributions from patriotic Ethiopians throughout the country, and surplus from the Petroleum Products Stabilization Trust. A small but growing amount of money was coming from the diaspora, especially from Ethio-Americans, who increasingly supported the war effort. The Ministry of Defense bought sixty Russian armored vehicles, six advanced Sukhoi 25 fighter-bombers, and at least twenty Russian-built helicopter gunships to maintain Ethiopia's air superiority. To fly these aircraft, Meles mobilized a group of pilots who had been jailed since 1991, incidentally because of war crimes against Eritrea.

Having waited long enough for a diplomatic solution, the Ethiopian government attacked Eritrean-occupied areas on 12 May 2000. The subsequent campaign led to a swift and sure victory that surprised many who believed in the tensile strength of the Eritrean army. The execution of the new campaign was as well planned and prepared as the attack on Badme in February 1999. The success there had led the Ethiopian command to redouble its training efforts, and recruits were drilled into their roles by battle-experienced junior officers and noncoms. They were, of course, taught to follow orders, but they were also given permission to use their own judgment if a situation called for independent action. Their bodies and stamina were developed for fighting in mountainous terrain through a rigorous program of physical education. Finally, they were sent to the front lines, where they were drilled into their jobs with the enemy target before them.

From the middle of 1999, in order to respond quickly to battlefield emergencies, Ethiopia had reorganized its chain of command and included Mengistu-army specialists in logistics, intelligence, and tactics to cope with the arrival of newly purchased equipment. In planning operations, commanders at various levels carefully studied their objectives with consideration for the terrain and possibilities of engagement. Since Meles had declared that Ethiopia probably would not return to war until after its May general elections, surprise was an important factor in the attacks.

The surprise factor was not merely a matter of timing but also of place. Eritrean commanders expected any offensive to concentrate on the central Zalembessa front, and they therefore stationed 60 percent of their best forces and mechanized and artillery units there. Instead, on 12 May, the Ethiopians attacked the relatively undermanned and poorly defended western front and then, after five or six days of success, feinted eastward. When the Eritreans began shifting men and matériel toward the defense of Mandefera, the Ethiopians, on 23 May, wheeled and attacked in force along the central Zalembessa-Tsorona front, making for the ends of the trench lines where there were fewer defenders and heavy weapons. Commando units moved swiftly on the right flank, using the cover of darkness to advance beyond Altiena and thereafter climbing 3,000 meters to reach the trenches at Aiga, one of the high points commanding the Zalembessa-Senafe plateau. Another contingent continued on to take terrain closer to Senafe, and a third, including a mechanized detachment with bulldozers, cleared a road

39. Center of Zalembessa when recovered on 26 May 2000.
Courtesy of Larke Mariam Demessie.

to Altiena for artillery and tanks to position themselves to bombard Eritrean posts northeast of Zalembessa,

Meanwhile, at Aiga, the Eritrean line quickly cracked when the trenches were attacked from the left and right flanks and then from behind in coordination with armor, artillery, and air strikes. The Ethiopians moved quickly since fresh troops were continuously flooding through the flanks. By the afternoon of 23 May, the trenches east of Tsorona and at Mai Alba were under Ethiopian control, and the Ethiopian foreign minister predicted the crumbling of the central front by the next day. As usual, Asmera dismissed the forecast by claiming to have repulsed every Ethiopian attack.

The next day, 24 May, the fighting turned into an Eritrean rout, and in the evening, Ethiopian commanders reported the imminent collapse of the enemy army, since their soldiers now controlled Zalembessa's rear and had completely liberated Irob. Repeated Eritrean counterattacks failed, but Asmera claimed that the Ethiopian army and air force had been so badly mauled that their strength was "severely degraded." This type of propaganda continued throughout the day of 24 May, but at midnight, Asmera admitted defeat by claiming that "for the sake of peace" it would comply with the OAU request for redeployment, which was *the* Eritrean explanation for its withdrawal from Badme.

The Ethiopian success stemmed from its use of mobile warfare, which the TPLA had developed against Mengistu's heavy infantry. The then muscle-bound Ethiopian soldier could not have maneuvered or feinted, and he was defeated time and again by Eritrean fighters in the trenches, redoubts, and bunkers of Nakfa. The fortifications had sustained the EPLF's resistance at crucial times, and Isayas instinctively had returned to their use in constructing his defense of the contested areas. Whereas the newly flexible Ethiopian command structure gave individual units the freedom to decide the best tactics for taking their objectives, Eritrean forces were micromanaged on the battlefield by Isayas, who bypassed his own chain of command, just as Mengistu had done. The Eritrean army was therefore not very adaptable, and when the fighting did not go as planned, nobody took authority and the command structure broke down. Hundreds of Eritreans died in aimless retreat and thousands were taken prisoner.

On 27 May, the Ethiopian command turned to the eastern end of the Eritrean line, attacking Bure on the ground and Aseb by air. By now, it was clear that Eritrea had everything to gain by withdrawing. To drive this point home, Ethiopia demonstrated its military superiority on 29 May by bombing the military airport in Asmera and destroying a nearly completed power plant in a Mitsiwa suburb. On 31 May, Meles Zenawi called for a meeting of the diplomatic corps to report that his army had verified that the disputed areas, including Bada in the east, were clear of Eritrean troops. In Addis Abeba's opinion, the war was over, and the FDRE had sent a delegation to Algeria, whose president, Abdelaziz Bouteflika, was the current OAU chairman, to open proximity talks with Eritrea and negotiate a formal cease-fire. Meles assured his listeners that Ethiopia had no claims to make on undisputed Eritrean territory. He added, however, that Ethiopian troops would remain in position around Zalembessa until Addis Abeba received ironclad international assurances that Eritrean forces would not return until the question of sovereignty was settled.

The discussions in Algiers went on until 10 June 2000, when diplomats initialed a Proposal of the OAU for an Agreement on Cessation of Hostilities of the Federal Democratic Republic of Ethiopia and the Government of the State of Eritrea. The proposal was put into effect on 17 June in Algiers, when both foreign ministers, looking dyspeptic, publicly signed it and, with a beaming President Bouteflika as witness, hesitantly shook hands. As negotiated, the proposal reaffirmed the Framework Agreement and Modalities Document and did not mention the Technical Arrangements Document much criticized by Ethiopia.

The proposal called for an immediate cessation of hostilities and guaranteed free movement for a peacekeeping mission to be deployed by the UN under the auspices of the OAU. On 10 August 2000, Kofi Annan, secretary-general of the UN, recommended a UN Mission in Ethiopia and Eritrea (UNMEE) of up to 4,200 personnel, including 220 military observers, three infantry battalions, and support units. The mission was to monitor the cessation of hostilities and the redeployment of Ethiopian troops, ensure the observance of security commitments made by both sides, and oversee a temporary security zone. A Military Coordination Commission, composed of representatives of the two parties and chaired by the leadership of the UN peacekeepers, was to supervise the UNMEE's work.

Ethiopia pledged to leave positions that were taken after 6 February 1999 and those that were not under Ethiopian administration before 6 May 1998. The Ethiopian withdrawal was to be completed within two weeks after the deployment of the peacekeeping mission, which would verify the movement. Thereafter Eritrean civil administration, including police and local militia, could return to prepare for the arrival of the population. In order to reduce tension and to establish "a climate of calm and confidence," Eritrean forces were to respect a "zone of separation," referred to as a "temporary security zone," and remain twenty-five kilometers out of "artillery range" from redeployed Ethiopian units.

The lack of reference to the Technical Arrangements Document revealed who had won the political war, and the establishment of the temporary security zone within Eritrea evidenced who had prevailed on the ground. The objectives set by the Ethiopian government in May 1998, when the Eritreans had occupied the disputed territory, had been fulfilled, regrettably not through jawing but through warring. In order to force Asmera to accept the OAU arrangements, the Ethiopian army had to push its Eritrean foe from its entrenched position. Isayas claimed to have withdrawn for the sake of peace, when it was fighting that forced him to sophistry.

The rationalizations continue, and in the fall of 2000, Eritreans began repeating that they won the war since their army had kept the

Ethiopians from occupying Asmera and from taking Aseb. These were never Ethiopian objectives, but Asmera has reverted to the same kind of thinking that bemused Saddam Hussein into claiming that he had won the Gulf War. If Eritrea continues to behave with such disregard for reality, the war between the two countries will never end. As I have often written, and it is one of the thoughts with which I finished the first edition of this book, people in the Horn of Africa find it difficult, almost impossible, to compromise, and it is only through accommodation and peace that development will be able to relieve the suffering of the broad masses.

Epilogue

On 11 May 2000, the International Monetary Fund released an abstract of Eritrea summarizing economic statistical data reported by the Asmera government through 1999. The figures revealed an economy in crisis, even without considering the impact of the war. Since 1997, overseas remittances had declined, the GNP had shrunk to the level of 1996, and external debt had tripled, reaching $225 million, about one-third of the GNP. Although Eritrea reported a growth rate of 3 percent in 1999 it was almost entirely due to a rise in government spending on the war and was of no lasting value. There is not much of a multiplier effect in the purchase of military hardware, supplies, and services, especially if scarce hard currency is being expended.

Eritrea has always had deficits, but in 1998 and 1999, according to the IMF statistics, the negative figures became truly horrific. In 1998, the deficit was N1.6 billion ($200 million) and in 1999, a whopping N2.6 billion. These figures are 27.3 and 37.4 percent of the GNP, respectively, and approximately 50 percent of the gross domestic product. The IMF figures show that the 1999 deficit exceeded total government revenue and external grants combined and was more than twice the country's earnings.

40. The Shida monument of the distinctive sandals worn by all EPLF fighters, commemorating the tenth anniversary of Eritrea's independence, in Asmera 2001. Courtesy of Professor Richard Greenfield.

Eritrea reported its defense expenditures as 62 percent of its budget in 1998 and 61 percent in 1999, huge by any standard and probably underestimated since some military costs were likely hidden in the categories of "general spending" or "capital spending." Government debt had grown 250 percent since 1997, accounting for 60 percent of Eritrea's total debt and indicating a national credit problem. Inflation in 1998 was at 16.6 percent, and investment had dropped from N851 million in 1996 to N362 million in 1999. The IMF statistics revealed a country that was already in deep economic crisis before the war exacerbated these long-term trends.

Eritrea's rulers must shape the country's future within the economic realities and also must respect Ethiopia's demonstrated unity and its large patriotic population. Judging from Eritrea's interactions with its neighbor between 1991 and 1996, a viable future lies in its close cooperation with Addis Abeba and Ethiopian institutions. Addis

Abeba must not hinder the development of the Eritrean economy, and it must permit its neighbor to compete on an even playing field, even with its own nationals. The two countries have to build a new political relationship. Eritrea's sovereignty must be redefined with consideration for Ethiopia's access to the sea, which would revive Mitsiwa and Aseb, and Eritrea's need to participate in the Ethiopian economy. It is necessary that the agreement be sensitive to Addis Abeba's leading role in banking, import and export, and currency. Both sides need to develop and use joint economic planning and institutions so as to eliminate the need for unilateral actions. I suggest the Canadian-American model in which both economies function together but both polities remain separate and sovereign.

During the recent hostilities, both warring factions freely used internal subversion as a weapon, which they must eschew for the future. Eritrea might again try working with Ethiopia to end strife in the Horn and thereby gain the peace dividends of renewed trade, the growth of capital, and economic development. Addis Abeba and Asmera should cooperate in creating a common market that also includes Sudan, Djibouti, Somalia, Somaliland, and Puntland. Traders, farmers, nomads, migrants, and refugees have ignored the frontiers for years, and it would be advantageous for the governments to recognize this fact by having legal and open borders. Maybe the birr, nakfa, franc, shilling, and pound should be replaced by a common currency, which Asmera and Addis Abeba ought to have introduced in 1998. If neither Ethiopia nor Eritrea can commence the process of accommodation, then Northeast Africa is in for a generation of upset and strife that will retard economic and political development, impoverish the people, and keep the Horn of Africa in chaos. The way out of this dilemma is for Eritrea to be permitted to build an economy and for Ethiopia to play its central role in the Horn of Africa. These goals require a new bilateral arrangement for the long term, one that perhaps should have been negotiated before the referendum of 1993. Once this type of document is signed, the region's way will be clear for the transition from anarchy to peace.

Maps

Place names mentioned in the text generally appear only once in the maps, and not necessarily as the maps are ordered. The reader looking for a particular place name should therefore consult all the maps.

1. Ethiopia in 1994

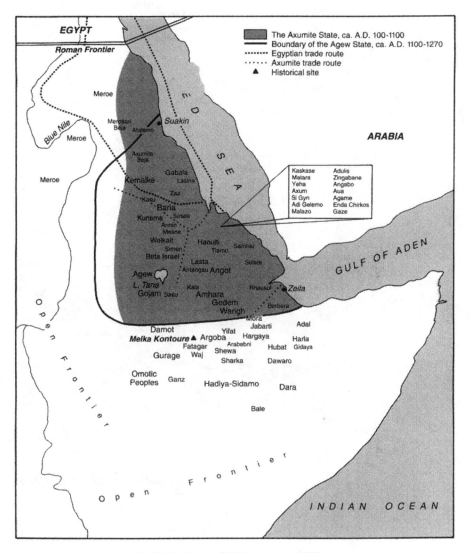

2. Ethiopia, ca. 2800 B.C.–A.D. 1270

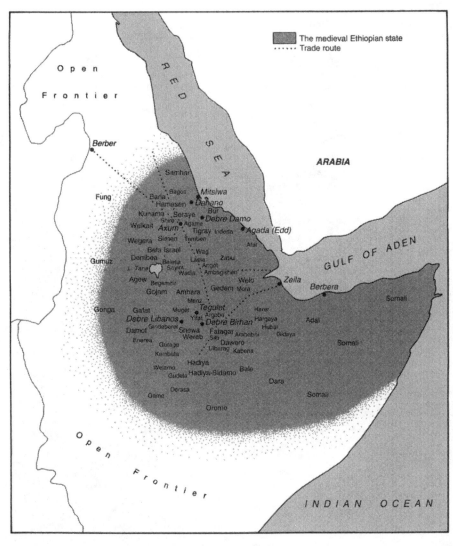

The medieval Ethiopian state
Trade route

Open Frontier

RED SEA

ARABIA

Berber

Fung

Samhar

Bagos *Mitsiwa*
Baria *Dahano*
Hamasen
Kunama Seraye Bur
Shire Agame *Debre Damo*
Walkait *Axum* Tigray Inderta *Agada (Edd)*
Wegera Simen Tembien Afar
Beta Israel Wag
Dembea Lasta Zabul
L. Tana Balesa Sayint Angot
Agew Wadla Ambase-chem
Begemdir Wag Welo
Gojam Amhara Gedem Mora Zeila
Berbera
Menz
Gatat Muger *Tegulet* Harar
Debre Libanos Yifat Argobs Hargaya
Girdeberet *Debre Birhan* Hubai
Damot Snewa Fatagar Sah Arababni Gidaya
Enerea Wereb Dawaro
Gutage Libareg Kabena
Kembata
Welamo Hadiya Bale
Gudela Hadiya-Sidamo Dara
Derasa
Gamo Somali
Oromo

GULF OF ADEN

Somali

Adal

Somali

Gumuz

Gonga

Open Frontier

INDIAN OCEAN

3. Ethiopia, 1270–1524

4. Ethiopia, 1600–1855

5. Ethiopia, mid-twentieth century

Population Affected by
Food Shortage 1980–1983

- Above 65 percent
- 33 to 65 percent
- 11 to 32 percent
- 10 percent or less
- Nomadic areas (no data)
- —— Approximate limit of cropping areas
- • Shelter for affected population

6. Ethiopia, areas of drought and food shortage, 1973–1990

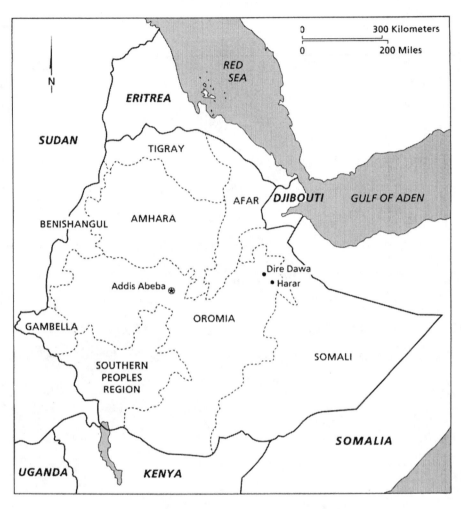

7. Ethiopia by ethnic region. Courtesy of Theodore M. Vestal,
Ethiopia: A Post–Cold War African State (Westport, Conn.: Praeger, 1999).

8. Eritrea by region. Courtesy of Kjetil Tronvoll, *Mai Weini,*
A Highland Village in Eritrea (Lawrenceville, N.J.: Red Sea Press, 1998).

9. The killing fields: disputed areas and battlefields.
Adapted from Patrick Gilkes and Martin Plaut,
War in the Horn: The Conflict between Eritrea and Ethiopia
(London: Royal Institute of International Affairs, 1999).

Glossary

Note: I have rendered place names as they are presented in the most recent maps published by the Ethiopian Mapping Agency. I have also used the spellings *Menilek* and *Haile Sellassie*. The former conforms better to the Amharic spelling and is steadily winning favor. The latter was the spelling used by the emperor's palace and by the university that bore his name. Finally, I have tried hard to make Amharic sounds conform to English spellings without the confusion of diacritics and linguistic symbols. I hope I have succeeded more than I failed.

AAPO	All-Amhara Peoples Organization.
abba	Literally, "father"; a priestly title.
abba dula	Literally, "father of war"; a high-ranking Oromo officer.
abuna, abun	Metropolitan of the Ethiopian church; a title also given to Ethiopia's suffragan bishops.
Abyot Seded	Literally, "revolutionary flame"; one of the socialist parties of the early derg period.

AIAI   Al-Itahad al-Islami (Somali Islamic union).

alaka   Teacher-leader; a priestly title.

alakenat   In eighteenth- and nineteenth-century Gonder, a device endowing one individual with property and power in trust for the next generation.

amba   A flat-topped mountain, difficult of access; a natural fortification.

amoleh   A salt bar used as money.

ANDM   Amhara National Democratic Movement (formerly the EPDM).

arbenyotch   The patriots who fought against the Italian occupiers.

asrat   Agricultural tax.

ato   Literally, "sir"; now "Mr."

awraja   The largest subprovincial unit of government ("administrative region" is the current term for province).

bahr negash   "Ruler of the seas"; the Ethiopian governor who ruled the Red Sea coast.

baito   Tigrinya for peasant association.

balambaras   Commander of a fortress; a title of nobility equivalent to baronet.

ballabat   Literally, "one who has a father"; a local-level official who mediated between the people and the government.

bande   Irregular military units.

bejirond   Treasurer.

Beta Israel   Modern designation for Ethiopian Jews (Falasha).

bitwoded, bit.   Literally, "beloved"; a title of nobility equivalent to earl.

blatta, blattengeta   A title given to learned men and councillors.

brindo   Raw beef.

CA   Constituent Assembly.

CDC	Constitution Drafting Commission.
CEDF	Coalition of Ethiopian Democratic Forces.
COPWE	Commission for Organizing the Party of the Workers of Ethiopia.
dejazmach, dejaz., dej.	Literally, "commander of the gate"; a title of nobility equivalent to count.
derg	Literally, "committee"; a term almost exclusively associated with the regime that governed Ethiopia from 1974 to 1991.
EDORM	Ethiopian Democratic Officers Revolutionary Movement.
EDU	Ethiopian Democratic Union.
EHRO	Ethiopian Human Rights Organization.
ELF	Eritrean Liberation Front.
EPDM	Ethiopian Peoples Democratic Movement. *See also* ANDM
EPLF	Eritrean Peoples Liberation Front.
EPRDF	Ethiopian Peoples Revolutionary Democratic Front.
EPRP	Ethiopian Peoples Revolutionary Party; a socialist organization active during the early derg period.
etchege	The administrative head of the Ethiopian church.
Falasha	*See* Beta Israel.
FDRE	Federal Democratic Republic of Ethiopia.
Feta Negast	"Law of the kings."
fitawrari, fit.	Literally, "leader of the vanguard"; a title of nobility equivalent to viscount.
gabbar	Literally, "farmer"; in southern Ethiopia, it had serflike connotations.
gada	Oromo generational-grade form of government.
gasha	A nonstandard measure of land, between thirty and fifty hectares.
geber	A feast.

gerazmach, geraz.	Literally, "commander of the left"; a title of nobility equivalent to baron.
gibbi	Any large structure such as a palace or a villa; a term associated with Menilek's grand palace in Addis Abeba.
GOE	Government of Eritrea.
gult	A fief.
Habasha	Common usage for "Ethiopian."
itegue	Empress.
jarsa biyya	Oromo elders.
k'allu	*See* qallu.
karra haimanot	"Knife creed"; the belief that Christ had two births. *See also* sost lidot.
kebelay	A post–Haile Sellassie unit of urban government equivalent roughly to a U.S. precinct.
Kebre Nagast	"The glory of the kings"; the pastiche of legends describing the origins of the Solomonic dynasty.
kenyazmach, kenyaz.	Literally, "commander of the right"; a title of nobility equivalent to baron.
ketema	In the nineteenth century, a strategic village; now the word for town or city.
kibat	Unction of the Holy Ghost.
kilil	National region, similar but not identical in meaning to *kifle ager,* or province.
korro	A lieutenant of the ballabat.
koso	A purgative.
lij	Literally, "child"; a title reserved for the children of the high-ranking nobility.
luba	Oromo warrior.
makwanent	The high nobility as a body.
MEISON	All-Ethiopia Socialist Movement; a party active in the early derg period.

nagadras, nag.	Literally, "chief of the merchants" with authority to levy and collect market taxes and customs.
nakfa (N)	Eritrean unit of money.
NDRP	Program of the National Democratic Revolution.
neftennya	Literally, "one who owns a gun"; associated with soldier-settlers in southern Ethiopia to whom the government granted rights over land and people.
negus	King; title of a few provincial lords of high birth or special merit granted by the negus negast, "king of kings," or emperor.
negus negast	"King of kings"; emperor.
NEP	New Economic Policy.
OLF	Oromo Liberation Front.
OPDO	Oromo Peoples Democratic Organization.
PDRE	Peoples Democratic Republic of Ethiopia.
PFDJ	Peoples Front for Democracy and Justice, the postwar term for the EPLF.
PGE	Provisional Government of Eritrea.
qallu	Oromo official.
ras	Literally, "head"; a title of nobility equivalent to duke.
SAP	Structural Adjustment Program.
SEPDF	Southern Ethiopian Peoples Democratic Front.
seyyid	Teacher, a learned one.
Shengo	Parliament.
shifta	Outlaws; brigands.
sost lidot	"Three births"; the belief that Christ had three births. *See also* karra haimanot.
tewahdo	Term associated with the belief in the inseparability of Christ's human and divine natures.
TGE	Transitional Government of Ethiopia.

TNO	Tigray National Organization.
TPLF	Tigrayan Peoples Liberation Front.
UNMEE	United Nations Mission in Ethiopia and Eritrea.
wagshum	The sovereign of Wag (Lasta).
weyna dega	The high highlands.
WPE	Workers Party of Ethiopia.
woizero, woiz.	Literally, "lady"; now used for "Mrs."
zamacha	Word associated with military campaigns or expeditions.
Zamana Masafent	The "Age of the Princes," roughly 1750 to 1850.

Select Bibliography

Chapter One

Butzer, Karl. "The Rise and Fall of Axum, Ethiopia: A Geo-archeological Interpretation." *American Antiquity* 46 (1981).

Ehret, Christopher. "On the Antiquity of Agriculture in Ethiopia." *Journal of African History* 20 (1979).

Fattovich, Rodolfo. "Remarks on the Pre-Aksumite Period in Northern Ethiopia." *Journal of Ethiopian Studies* 23 (1990).

Hudson, Grover. "Language Classification and the Semitic Prehistory of Ethiopia." *Folia Orientalia* 18 (1977).

Johanson, Donald C., and Maitland A. Edey. *Lucy: The Beginnings of Humankind*. London: Grenada, 1981.

Kaplan, Steven. *The Monastic Holy Man and the Christianization of Early Solomonic Ethiopia*. Wiesbaden: Franz Steiner Verlag, 1984.

Kobischanov, Yuri. *Axum*. University Park: Pennsylvania State University Press, 1979.

Lewis, Herbert S. "The Origins of the Galla and the Somali." *Journal of African History* 7 (1966).

Marrassini, Paolo. "Some Considerations on the Problem of the Syriac Influences on Aksumite Ethiopia." *Journal of Ethiopian Studies* 23 (1990).

Michaels, Joseph W. "The Axumite Kingdom: A Settlement Archeology Perspective." In *Proceedings of the Ninth International Congress of Ethiopian Studies*, vol. 6. Moscow: Nauka, 1988.

Munro-Hay, Stuart. "The Rise and Fall of Aksum: Chronological Consider-
ations." *Journal of Ethiopian Studies* 23 (1990).
Sergew Hable Sellassie. *Ancient and Medieval European History to 1270.* Addis
Abeba: United Printers, 1972.
Taddesse Tamrat. "Reflections of Feudalism in Aksumite Documents." In
Proceedings of the Annual Seminar of the Department of History, AAU, 1983.
Addis Abeba: Addis Ababa University Press, 1983.

Chapter Two

Braukamper, Ulrich. "Islamic Principalities in Southeast Ethiopia between the
Thirteenth and Sixteenth Centuries." *Ethiopianist Notes* 1 (1977).
Huntingford, G. W. B. "The Lives of Saint Tekle Haymanot." *Journal of
Ethiopian Studies* 4 (1966).
Kaplan, Steven. *The Monastic Holy Man and the Christianization of Early
Solomonic Ethiopia.* Wiesbaden: Franz Steiner Verlag, 1984.
Levine, Donald N. "Menilek and Oedipus: Further Observations on the Ethio-
pian National Epic." In *Proceedings of the First U.S. Conference on Ethiopian
Studies, 1973,* edited by Harold G. Marcus. East Lansing: Michigan State
University, African Studies Center, 1975.
Martin, B. G. "Mahdism, Muslim Clerics, and Holy Wars in Ethiopia, 1300–
1600." In *Proceedings of the First U.S. Conference on Ethiopian Studies, 1973,*
edited by Harold G. Marcus. East Lansing: Michigan State University, African
Studies Center, 1975.
Merid Wolde Aregay. "Population Movements as a Possible Factor in the
Christian-Muslim Conflict of Medieval Ethiopia." *Symposium Leo Frobenius.*
Munich: Pullach, 1974.
Taddesse Tamrat. "Some Notes on the Fifteenth-Century Stephanite 'Heresy' in
the Ethiopian Church." *Rassegna di Studi Etiopici* 22 (1966).
———. "The Abbots of Däbrä-Hayq, 1248–1535." *Journal of Ethiopian Studies*
8 (1970).
———. *Church and State in Ethiopia, 1270–1527.* Oxford: Clarendon Press,
1972.
———. "A Short Note on the Traditions of Pagan Resistance to the Ethiopian
Church (Fourteenth and Fifteenth Centuries)." *Journal of Ethiopian Studies*
10 (1972).
———. "Processes of Ethnic Interaction and Integration in Ethiopian History:
The Case of the Agaw." In *Proceedings of the Ninth International Conference
of Ethiopian Studies,* vol. 6. Moscow: Nauka, 1986.
Yeshaq, Archbishop. *The Ethiopian Tewahedo Church: An Integrally African
Church.* New York: Vantage, 1989.

Chapter Three

Bartnicki, A., and J. Mantel-Niećko. "The Role and Significance of the Religious Conflicts and People's Movements in the Political Life of Ethiopia in the Seventeenth and Eighteenth Centuries." *Rassegna di Studi Etiopici* 24 (1969-1970).

Berry, Laverle Bennette. "The Solomonic Monarchy at Gonder, 1630-1755: An Institutional Analysis of Kingship in the Christian Kingdom of Ethiopia." Ph.D. diss., Boston University, 1976.

Braukamper, Ulrich. "Oromo Country of Origin: A Reconsideration of Hypotheses." In *Ethiopian Studies: Proceedings of the Sixth International Conference, Tel Aviv, 1980*, edited by Gideon Goldenberg. Rotterdam: Balkema, 1986.

Chihabed Din Ahmad. *Histoire de la conquête de l'Abyssinie*. Vol. 2. Translated by René Basset. Paris, 1897.

Guidi, Ignatius, trans. and ed. *Historia Gentis Galla* by Bahrey. In *Scriptores Aethiopici*. Vol. 3 of *Corpus Scriptorium Christianorum Orientalium*. Paris, 1907.

Merid Wolde Aregay. "Southern Ethiopia and the Christian Kingdom, 1508-1708, with Special Reference to the Galla Migrations and Their Consequences." Ph.D. diss., School of Oriental and African Studies, University of London, 1971.

———. "Society and Technology in Ethiopia, 1500-1800." *Journal of Ethiopian Studies* 17 (1984).

Mohammad Hassan. *The Oromo of Ethiopia: A History, 1570-1860*. Cambridge: Cambridge University Press, 1990.

Perret, Michel. "Les partis à la cour de Gondar en 1769." In *Proceedings of the Eighth International Conference of Ethiopian Studies*, vol. 2, edited by Taddesse Beyene. Huntingdon, England: ELM Publications, 1989.

Tekle-Tsadik Mekouria. "Histoire abrégé de Haylou Esheté (Degiaz-matche)." In *Proceedings of the Eighth International Conference of Ethiopian Studies*, vol. 2, edited by Taddesse Beyene. Huntingdon, England: ELM Publications, 1989.

Trimingham, J. S. *Islam in Ethiopia*. New edition. London: Frank Cass, 1965.

Chapter Four

Asfa-Wossen Asserate. *Die Geschichte Von Šawa (Äthiopien), 1700-1865*. Wiesbaden: Franz Steiner Verlag, 1980.

Abir, Mordechai. *Ethiopia, the Era of the Princes: The Challenge of Islam and the Re-unification of the Christian Empire*. London: Longmans, Green and Co., 1968.

Crummey, Donald. "Doctrine and Authority: *Abuna* Salama, 1841-1854." In *IV Congresso Internazionale di Studi Etiopici*, vol. 1. Rome: Accademia Nazionale dei Lincei, 1974.

————. "Society and Ethnicity in the Politics of Christian Ethiopia during the Zamana Masafent." *International Journal of African Historical Studies* 8 (1975).

————. "State and Society: Nineteenth-Century Ethiopia." In *Modes of Production in Africa: The Precolonial Era,* edited by D. Crummey and C. C. Stewart. Beverly Hills: Sage Press, 1981.

————. "Family and Property amongst the Amhara Nobility." *Journal of African History* 24 (1983).

————. "Three Amharic Documents of Marriage and Inheritance from the Eighteenth and Nineteenth Centuries." In *Proceedings of the Eighth International Conference of Ethiopian Studies,* vol. 1, edited by Taddesse Beyene. Huntingdon, England: ELM Publications, 1988.

Guluma Gemeda. "The Process of State Formation in the Gibe Region: The Case of Gomma and Jimma." In *Proceedings of the Second Annual Seminar of the Department of History, AAU,* vol. 1. Addis Abeba: Dept. of History, Addis Ababa University, 1984.

Merid Wolde Aregay. "Society and Technology in Ethiopia: 1500–1800." *Journal of Ethiopian Studies* 17 (1984).

Mohammed Hassan. *The Oromo of Ethiopia: A History, 1570–1860.* Cambridge: Cambridge University Press, 1990.

Rubenson, Sven. *King of Kings: Tewodros of Ethiopia.* Addis Abeba: Oxford University Press, 1966.

Shiferaw Bekele. "The State in the *Zamana Masafent:* An Essay in Reinterpretation." In *Kasa and Kasa,* edited by Taddese Beyene, Richard Pankhurst, and Shiferaw Bekele. Addis Abeba: Book Centre of Addis Ababa University, 1990.

Tekle Tsadik Mekuria. *YeEtiopiya Tarik KaAtse Lebna Dengel Eska Atse Tewodros* (History of Ethiopia from Emperor Lebna Dengel to Emperor Tewodros). Addis Abeba: Ministry of Education, 1968.

Chapter Five

Caulk, Richard A. "Menelik and the Ethio-Egyptian War of 1875–1876: A Reconsideration of Source Material." *Rural Africana* 11 (1970).

————. "Firearms and Princely Power in Ethiopia in the Nineteenth Century." *Journal of African History* 13 (1972).

————. "Armies as Predators: Soldiers and Peasants in Ethiopia, c. 1850–1935." *International Journal of African Historical Studies* 11 (1978).

Crummey, Donald. "The Violence of Téwodros." *Journal of Ethiopian Studies* 9 (1971).

————. *Priests and Politicians.* Oxford: Clarendon Press, 1972.

————. "Orthodoxy and Imperial Construction in Ethiopia, 1854–1878." *Journal of Theological Studies* N.S. 29 (1978).

Darkwah, R. H. K. *Shewa, Menelik, and the Ethiopian Empire.* London: Heinemann, 1975.

Marcus, Harold G. "Menilek II." In *Leadership in Eastern Africa: Six Political Biographies*, edited by Norman Bennett. Boston: Boston University Press, 1968.

———. "Imperialism and Expansionism in Ethiopia from 1865 to 1900." In *Colonialism in Africa*, vol. 1, edited by Lewis Gann and Peter Duignan. Cambridge: Cambridge University Press, 1969.

Rubenson, Sven. *King of Kings: Tewodros of Ethiopia*. Addis Abeba: Oxford University Press, 1966.

———. *The Survival of Ethiopian Independence*. London: Heinemann, 1976.

———. "Meqdela Revisited." In *Kasa and Kasa*, edited by Taddesse Beyene, Richard Pankhurst, and Shiferaw Bekele. Addis Abeba: Book Centre of Addis Ababa University, 1990.

Zewde Gabre-Sellassie. *Yohannes IV of Ethiopia: A Political Biography*. Oxford: Clarendon Press, 1975.

Chapter Six

Bahru Zewde. "The Historical Context of the Dogali Encounter." In *The Centenary of Dogali*, edited by Taddesse Beyene, Taddesse Tamrat, and Richard Pankhurst. Addis Abeba: Institute of Ethiopian Studies, Addis Ababa University, 1988.

Bairu Tafla, ed. *A Chronicle of Emperor Yohannes IV, 1872–1889*. Wiesbaden: Franz Steiner Verlag, 1977.

Caulk, Richard A. "The Occupation of Harar: January 1887." *Journal of Ethiopian Studies* 9 (1971).

———. "Religion and the State in Nineteenth-Century Ethiopia." *Journal of Ethiopian Studies* 10 (1972).

———. "Minilik II and the Diplomacy of Commerce: Prelude to an Imperial Foreign Policy." *Journal of Ethiopian Studies* 17 (1984).

Erlich, Haggai. *Ethiopia and Eritrea during the Scramble for Africa: A Political Biography of Ras Alula, 1875–1895*. East Lansing: Michigan State University, African Studies Center, 1982.

Marcus, Harold G. *The Life and Times of Menelik II: Ethiopia, 1844–1914*. Oxford: Clarendon Press, 1975.

Rubenson, Sven. "The Protectorate Paragraph of the Wichale Treaty." *Journal of African History* 5 (1964).

———. *The Survival of Ethiopian Independence*. London: Heinemann, 1976.

Tesema Ta'a. "Prologue to the Ethio-Sudanese Frontier." In *Kasa and Kasa*, edited by Taddesse Beyene, Richard Pankhurst, and Shiferaw Bekele. Addis Abeba: Book Centre of Addis Ababa University, 1990.

Zewde Gabre-Sellassie. *Yohannes IV of Ethiopia: A Political Biography*. Oxford: Clarendon Press, 1975.

Chapter Seven

"La Bataille d'Adowa d'après un récit abyssin." *Revue française de l'étranger et des colonies et exploration* 21 (1896).

Guébrè Sellassié. *Chronique du règne de Ménélik II, roi des rois d'Ethiopie.* Translated by Tèsfa Sellassié and annotated by Maurice de Coppet. 2 vols. Paris: Librairie Orientale et Américaine, 1930 and 1932.

Hussein Ahmed. "The Life and Career of Shaykh Talha b. Ja'far." *Journal of Ethiopian Studies* 22 (1989).

Marcus, Harold G. "The Black Men Who Turned White: European Attitudes toward Ethiopians, 1850–1900." *Archiv Orientalni* 39 (1971).

———. *The Life and Times of Menelik II: Ethiopia, 1844–1914.* Oxford: Clarendon Press, 1975.

Pankhurst, Richard. "Firearms in Ethiopian History." *Ethiopia Observer* 6 (1962).

———. "Menelik and Addis Ababa." *Journal of African History* 2 (1969).

Prouty, Chris. *Empress Taytu and Menilek II: Ethiopia, 1883–1910.* London: Ravens Educational and Development Services, 1986.

Rossetti, Carlo. *Storia diplomatica durante il regno di Menelik II.* Turin: Società Tipografica—Editrice Nazionale, 1910.

———. *Italia ed Etiopia dal Trattato d'Uccialli alla Battaglia di Adua.* Rome: Istituto per l'Oriente, 1935.

Rubenson, Sven. "Adwa 1896: The Resounding Protest." In *Protest and Power in Black Africa,* edited by R. Rotberg and Ali Mazrui. New York: Oxford University Press, 1970.

Zaghi, Carlo. *Crispi e Menelich nel diario inedito del conte Augosto Salimbeni.* Torino: Ilte, 1956.

Chapter Eight

Bairu Tafla. "The Political Crisis in Tigray, 1889–1899." *Africa* 34 (1979).

Ege, Svein. "The First Ethiopian Cabinet: Background and Significance of the 1907 Reform." In *Proceedings of the Eighth International Conference of Ethiopian Studies,* vol. 1, edited by Taddesse Beyene. Huntingdon, England: ELM Publications, 1988.

Guébrè Sellassié. *Chronique du règne de Ménélik II, roi des rois d'Ethiopie.* Translated by Tèsfa Sellassié and annotated by Maurice de Coppet. 2 vols. Paris: Librairie Orientale et Américaine, 1930 and 1932.

Marcus, Harold G. "The Foreign Policy of the Emperor Menelik, 1896–1898: A Rejoinder." *Journal of African History* 7 (1966).

———. "Motives, Methods, and Some Results of the Unification of Ethiopia during the Reign of Menilek II." In *Proceedings of the Third International Conference of Ethiopian Studies, Addis Ababa, 1966,* vol. 1. Addis Abeba: Artistic Printing Press, 1969.

————. "Some Reflections on the Development of Government and Taxation in Southern Ethiopia around the Turn of the Century." In *IV Congresso Internazionale di Studi Etiopici*, vol. 1. Rome: Accademia Nazionale dei Lincei, 1974.

————. *The Life and Times of Menelik II: Ethiopia, 1844–1914.* Oxford: Clarendon Press, 1975.

Mahetema Sellassie Wolde Maskal. *Zikre Neger.* Addis Abeba: Nassanat Printing Press, 1948.

Prouty, Chris. *Empress Taytu and Menilek II: Ethiopia, 1883–1910.* London: Ravens Educational and Development Services, 1986.

Rémond, Georges. "L'agonie de l'empéreur Ménélik." *Le Correspondent* 244 (1911).

Sanderson, G. N. "The Foreign Policy of the Negus Menelik, 1896–1898." *Journal of African History* 4 (1964).

Shiferaw Bekele. "Some Notes on the Genesis and Interpretation of the Tripartite Treaty." *Journal of Ethiopian Studies* 18 (1985).

Vanderheym, J. G. *Une expédition avec le négous Ménélik.* Paris: Librairie Hachette, 1896.

Chapter Nine

Arce, Laurent d'. *L'Abyssinie: Étude d'actualité (1922–1924).* Avignon: Librairie Aubanel Frères, 1925.

Haile Sellassie I. *Haywatayna Yeitiopia Armaja.* Vol. 1. Addis Abeba: Berhannena Selam Printers, 1973. Edited and translated by Edward Ullendorff as the *Autobiography of Emperor Haile Sellassie I: "My Life and Ethiopia's Progress," 1892–1937.* Oxford: Oxford University Press, 1976.

Herui Wolde Sellassie, Blattengeta. *Biographie: Sa Majesté Hailé Sélassié.* Addis Abeba: Berhannena Selam Printing Press, 1930.

Kebede Tessemma. *YeTarik Mestawasha.* Addis Abeba: Artistic Printing Press, 1953.

McCann, James. *From Poverty to Famine in Northeast Ethiopia: A Rural History, 1900–1935.* Philadelphia: University of Pennsylvania Press, 1987.

McClellan, Charles. *State Transformation and National Integration: Gedeo and the Ethiopian Empire, 1895–1935.* East Lansing: Michigan State University, African Studies Center, 1986.

Mahetema Sellassie Wolde Maskal. *Zikre Neger.* Addis Abeba: Nassanat Printing Press, 1948.

Marcus, Harold G. *The Life and Times of Menelik II: Ethiopia, 1844–1914.* Oxford: Clarendon Press, 1975.

————. "The Infrastructure of the Italo-Ethiopian Crisis: Haile Sellassie, the Solomonic Empire, and the World Economy, 1916–1936." In *Proceedings of the Fifth International Conference of Ethiopian Studies,* edited by Robert Hess. Chicago: University of Illinois, Chicago Circle, 1979.

———. "Genesis of an Ethiopian Monarch, 1916–1918." *Horn of Africa* 3 (1980–1981).

———. *Haile Sellassie I: The Formative Years, 1892–1936.* Berkeley and Los Angeles: University of California Press, 1987.

Chapter Ten

Badoglio, Pietro. *The War in Abyssinia.* London: Methuen Publishers, 1937.

Baer, George. *The Coming of the Italo-Ethiopian War.* Cambridge: Harvard University Press, 1967.

Bahru Zewde. "Economic Origins of the Absolutist State in Ethiopia." *Journal of Ethiopian Studies* 17 (1984).

———. "The Concept of Japanization in the Intellectual History of Modern Ethiopia." In *Proceedings of the Fifth Seminar of the Department of History.* Addis Abeba: AAU Printing Press, 1990.

Boca, Angelo del. *The Ethiopian War, 1935–1941.* Chicago: University of Chicago Press, 1969.

Haile Sellassie I. *Haywatayna Yeitiopia Armaja.* Vol. 1. Addis Abeba: Berhannena Selam Printers, 1973. Edited and translated by Edward Ullendorff as the *Autobiography of Emperor Haile Sellassie I: "My Life and Ethiopia's Progress,"* *1892–1937.* Oxford: Oxford University Press, 1976.

Marcus, Harold G. "Disease, Hospitals, and Italian Colonial Aspirations in Ethiopia, 1930–1935." *Northeast African Studies* 1 (1979).

———. "The Embargo on Arms Sales to Ethiopia, 1916–1930." *International Journal of African Historical Studies* 16 (1983).

———. "France's Abandonment of Ethiopia to Italy, 1928–1936." In *Ethiopian Studies Dedicated to Wolf Leslau,* edited by A. J. E. Bodrogligeti and S. Segert. Weisbaden: Otto Harrasowitz, 1983.

———. *Haile Sellassie I: The Formative Years, 1892–1936.* Berkeley and Los Angeles: University of California Press, 1987.

Moore, Robert W. "Coronation Days in Addis Ababa." *National Geographic* 59 (1931).

Steer, George L. *Caesar in Ethiopia.* London: Hodder and Staughton, 1936.

Virgin, General Eric. *The Ethiopia I Knew.* London: Macmillan, 1936.

Chapter Eleven

Baer, George. *Test Case: Italy, Ethiopia, and the League of Nations.* Stanford: Hoover Institution, 1976.

Boca, Angelo del. *The Ethiopian War, 1935–1941.* Chicago: University of Chicago Press, 1969.

Cumming, Sir Duncan. "The U.N. Disposal of Eritrea." *African Affairs* 52 (1953).

Haile Sellassie I. *Haywatayna Yeitiopia Armaja.* Vol. 2. Addis Abeba: Berhannena Selam Printers, 1974. Edited and annotated by Harold Marcus and translated by Ezekiel Gebissa as *My Life and Ethiopia's Progress*, vol. 2, East Lansing: Michigan University Press, 1994.

Jandy, Edward C. "Ethiopia Today: A Review of Its Changes and Problems." *Annals of the American Academy of Political and Social Sciences* 306 (1956).

Marcus, Harold G. "Insurgency and Counter-Insurgency in Ethiopia, 1936–1941." In *Challenge and Response in Internal Conflict*, vol. 3, edited by D. M. Condit et al. Washington, D.C.: American University Center for Research in Social Systems, 1968.

———. *Ethiopia, Great Britain, and the United States, 1941–1974.* Berkeley and Los Angeles: University of California Press, 1983.

———. "American Security and Ethiopia, 1948–1953." In *Proceedings of the Seventh International Conference on Ethiopian Studies*, edited by Sven Rubenson. Uppsala: Scandinavian Institute for African Studies; Addis Abeba: Institute of Ethiopian Studies, Addis Ababa University; and East Lansing: Michigan State University, African Studies Center, 1984.

Mockler, Anthony. *Haile Selassie's War.* New York: Random House, 1984.

Norberg, Viveca Halldin. *Swedes in Haile Selassie's Ethiopia, 1924–1952.* Uppsala: Scandinavian Institute for African Studies, 1977.

Perham, Margery. *The Government of Ethiopia.* 1st edition. London: Faber and Faber, 1948.

Sbacchi, Alberto. *Ethiopia under Mussolini.* London: Zed Books, 1985.

Spencer, John H. *Ethiopia at Bay.* Algonac, Mich.: Reference Publications, 1987.

Steer, George. *Sealed and Delivered.* London: Hodder and Staughton, 1942.

Chapter Twelve

Addis Hiwet. *Ethiopia, from Autocracy to Revolution.* London: Review of African Political Economy, 1975.

Balsvik, Randi Rønning. *Haile Sellassie's Students: The Rise of Social and Political Consciousness.* East Lansing: Michigan State University, African Studies Center, 1985.

Bereket Habte Sellassie. *Conflict and Intervention in the Horn of Africa.* London: Monthly Review Press, 1980.

Clapham, Christopher. *Haile Selassié's Government.* London: Longmans, Green and Co., 1969.

Cohen, John, and Dov Weintraub. *Land and Peasants in Imperial Ethiopia: The Social Background to a Revolution.* Assen: Van Gorcum, 1975.

Cohen, John, and P. H. Koehn. *Ethiopian Provincial and Municipal Government: Imperial Patterns and Post-Revolutionary Changes.* East Lansing: Michigan State University, African Studies Center, 1980.

Erlich, Haggai. *The Struggle over Eritrea: War and Revolution in the Horn of Africa.* Stanford: Hoover Institution, 1983.

Gebru Tareke. *Ethiopia: Power and Protest.* Cambridge University Press, 1991.

Gilkes, Patrick. *The Dying Lion.* New York: St. Martin's Press, 1975.

Jordan Gebre-Medhin. *Peasants and Nationalism in Eritrea.* Trenton, N.J.: Red Sea Press, 1989.

Lefebvre, Jeffrey A. *Arms for the Horn.* Pittsburgh: University of Pittsburgh Press, 1991.

Marcus, Harold G. *Ethiopia, Great Britain, and the United States, 1941–1974.* Berkeley and Los Angeles: University of California Press, 1983.

———. "Somalia and the Decline of American Interest in Ethiopia, 1963–1969." In *Proceedings of the Second International Conference on Somali Studies,* edited by Thomas Lobban. Hamburg: Universität Verlag, 1985.

Markakis, John. *Ethiopia: Anatomy of a Traditional Polity.* Oxford: Clarendon Press, 1974.

Spencer, John. "Haile Sellassie: Triumph and Tragedy." *Orbis* 18 (1975).

Chapter Thirteen

Addis Hiwet. *Ethiopia, from Autocracy to Bourgeois Dictatorship.* N.p., 1976.

Erlich, Haggai. *The Struggle over Eritrea: War and Revolution in the Horn of Africa.* Stanford: Hoover Institution, 1983.

Farer, Thomas J. *War Clouds on the Horn of Africa.* 2d ed. New York: Carnegie Endowment for Peace, 1979.

Halliday, F., and M. Molyneux. *The Ethiopian Revolution.* London: Verso, 1981.

Henze, P. B. "Arming the Horn...." In *Proceedings of the Seventh International Conference of Ethiopian Studies,* edited by Sven Rubenson. Uppsala: Scandinavian Institute of African Studies; Addis Abeba: Institute of Ethiopian Studies, Addis Ababa University; East Lansing: Michigan State University, African Studies Center, 1984.

———. *The Horn of Africa, from War to Peace.* New York: St. Martin's Press, 1991.

Lefort, Rene. *Ethiopia: An Heretical Revolution.* London: Zed Books, 1983.

Legum, Colin. *Ethiopia: The Fall of Haile Selassie's Empire.* London: Collins, 1975.

Markakis, John, and Nega Ayele. *Class and Revolution in Ethiopia.* Nottingham: Spokesman Books, 1978.

Mesfin Wolde Mariam. *Rural Vulnerability to Famine in Ethiopia.* Addis Abeba: Addis Ababa University Press, 1984.

Ottaway, David, and Marina Ottaway. *Ethiopia: Empire in Revolution.* New York: Africana Publishing, 1978.

Ottaway, Marina. "Land Reform in Ethiopia, 1974–1977." *African Studies Review* 20 (1977).

———. "Democracy and New Democracy: The Ideological Debate in the Ethiopian Revolution." *African Studies Review* 21 (1978).

Pliny the Middle Aged [pseud.]. "The PMAC: Origins and Structure." Part One. *Ethiopianist Notes* 2 (1978–1979); Part Two. Northeast African Studies 1 (1979).

Shepherd, Jack. *The Politics of Starvation.* New York: Carnegie Endowment, 1975.

Sherman, R. *Eritrea: The Unfinished Revolution.* New York: Praeger, 1980.

Ståhl, Michael. *Ethiopia: Political Contradictions in Agricultural Development.* Stockholm: Rabén and Sjögren, 1974.

Chapter Fourteen

Africa Confidential, 1980–1991.

Alemayehu Lirenso. "Villagization: Policies and Prospects." In *Ethiopia: Options for Rural Development,* edited by Siegfried Pausewang et al. London: Zed Books, 1990.

Alemneh Dejene. *Peasants, Agrarian Socialism, and Rural Development in Ethiopia.* Boulder: Westview Press, 1987.

Amare Tekle. "Continuity and Change in Ethiopian Politics." In *The Political Economy of Ethiopia,* edited by Marina Ottaway. New York: Praeger, 1990.

Brüne, Stefan. "The Agricultural Sector." In *Ethiopia: Options for Rural Development,* edited by Siegfried Pausewang et al. London: Zed Books, 1990.

Clapham, Christopher. *Transformation and Continuity in Revolutionary Ethiopia.* Cambridge: Cambridge University Press, 1988.

Dawit Wolde Giorgis. *Red Tears.* Trenton, N.J.: Red Sea Press, 1989.

———. "The Power of Decision-Making in Post-Revolutionary Ethiopia." In *The Political Economy of Ethiopia,* edited by Marina Ottaway. New York: Praeger, 1990.

Dessalegn Rahmato. *Agrarian Reform in Ethiopia.* Trenton, N.J.: Red Sea Press, 1984.

Harbeson, John. *The Ethiopian Transformation: The Quest for the Post-Imperial State.* Boulder: Westview Press, 1988.

Keller, Edmond J. *Revolutionary Ethiopia.* Bloomington: Indiana University Press, 1988.

Markakis, John. *National and Class Conflict in the Horn of Africa.* Cambridge: Cambridge University Press, 1987.

Mulatu Wubneh. "Development Strategy and Growth of the Ethiopian Economy: A Comparative Analysis of the Pre- and Post-Revolutionary Period." In *The Political Economy of Ethiopia,* edited by Marina Ottaway. New York: Praeger, 1990.

Pankhurst, Alula. "Resettlement: Policy and Practice." In *Ethiopia: Options for Rural Development,* edited by Siegfried Pausewang et al. London: Zed Books, 1990.

Pankhurst, Helen. *Gender, Development, and Identity: An Ethiopian Study.* London: Zed Books, 1992.

Taye Mengistae. "Urban-Rural Relations in Agrarian Change: An Historical Overview." In *Ethiopia: Options for Rural Development,* edited by Siegfried Pausewang et al. London: Zed Books, 1990.

Chapter Fifteen

Abu Girma Moges. "Ethiopia: Recent Fiscal Developments and Emerging Concerns." In *Ethiopia in Broader Perspective,* vol. 2, edited by Katsuyoshi Fukui, Eisei Kurimoto, and Masayoshi Shigeta. Kyoto: Shokado, 1997.

Africa Confidential, 1991–1995.

Alemseged Abbay. *Identity Jilted or Re-Imagining Identity: The Divergent Paths of the Eritrean and Tigrayan Nationalist Struggles.* Lawrenceville, N.J.: Red Sea Press, 1998.

Andargachew Tiruneh. *The Ethiopian Revolution, 1974–1987: A Transformation from an Aristocratic to a Totalitarian Autocracy.* Cambridge: Cambridge University Press, 1993.

Fasil Nahum. *Constitution for a Nation of Nations: The Ethiopian Prospect.* Lawrenceville, N.J.: Red Sea Press, 1997.

Goy, Raymond. "L'indépendence de Érythrée." *Annuaire Français de Droit Internationale* 39 (1993).

Haile-Selassie, Teferra. *The Ethiopian Revolution, 1974–91.* London: Kegan Paul, 1997.

Hammond, Jenny. *Fire from the Ashes: A Chronicle of the Revolution in Tigray, Ethiopia, 1975–1991.* Lawrenceville, N.J.: Red Sea Press, 1999.

Iyob, Ruth. *The Eritrean Struggle for Independence: Domination, Resistance, Nationalism, 1941–1993.* Cambridge: Cambridge University Press, 1995.

Kinfe Abraham. "Ethiopian History Revisited: Power Conflict in National Integration and Foreign Intervention." Addis Abeba: Ethiopian Institute of Politics and International Relations, 2000.

Marcus, Harold, and Kevin Brown. "Ethiopia and Eritrea: Nationalism Undermines Mass and Technology." In *Ethiopia in Broader Perspective,* vol. 2, edited by Katsuyoshi Fukui, Eisei Kurimoto, and Masayoshi Shigeta. Kyoto: Shokado, 1997.

Medhane Tadesse. "EPRP versus TPLF, 1975–78." Paper presented at the graduate history seminar at Addis Ababa University, Addis Abeba, June 1994.

———. *The Eritrean-Ethiopian War: Retrospect and Prospects.* Addis Abeba: Mega, 1999.

Mesfin Araya. "Issues of Hegemony in Post-Independent Eritrea." In *Ethiopia in Broader Perspective,* vol. 2, edited by Katsuyoshi Fukui, Eisei Kurimoto, and Masayoshi Shigeta. Kyoto: Shokado, 1997.

Ottoway, Marina. "The Ethiopian Transition: Democratization or New Authoritarianism." *Northeast African Studies* 2, no. 3 (1995).

Poluha, Eva. "Conceptualizing Democracy: Elections in the Ethiopian Countryside." *Northeast African Studies* 4, no. 1 (1997).

Shimelis Bonsa. *Survey of the Private Press in Ethiopia: 1991–1999*. Addis Abeba: Forum for Social Studies, 2000.

Sorenson, John. *Imagining Ethiopia: Struggles for History and Identity in the Horn of Africa*. New Brunswick, N.J.: Rutgers University Press, 1993.

Tucker, Stevens P. "Ethiopia in Transition, 1991–1998." *Writenet* (April 1998).

Vestal, Theodore M. *Ethiopia, A Post–Cold War African State*. Westport, Conn.: Praeger, 1999.

Young, John. *Peasant Revolution in Ethiopia: The Tigray People's Liberation Front, 1975–1991*. Cambridge: Cambridge University Press, 1997.

Chapter Sixteen

Addis Tribune (Addis Abeba), 2 June 2000.

Africa Confidential, 1995–2000.

Amnesty International. *Ethiopia and Eritrea: Human Rights Issues in a Year of Armed Conflict*. London: International Secretariat, 1999.

Biles, Peter. "Drive to Victory." *BBC Focus on Africa* 11, no. 3 (July–September 2000).

Brook Ahmed. "Economic Indicators of the Effects of the War on the Ethiopian Economy." *Capital* 2, no. 81 (25 June 2000).

Eritrean Ministry of Foreign Affairs. "TPLF: Subtle Campaign to Deceive Public Opinion." Asmera, 1999.

Ethiopian Economic Association. *Economic Focus* 1, no. 6 (December 1998).

Ethiopian International Institute for Peace and Development. *News and Networking Bulletin*. Addis Abeba: Ethiopian Economic Association, 2000.

Gilkes, Patrick, and Martin Plaut. *War in the Horn: The Conflict between Eritrea and Ethiopia*. London: Royal Institute of International Affairs, 1999.

Henze, Paul. "Eritrea's War against Ethiopia." Washington, D.C., 2000.

Indian Ocean Newsletter, 1998–2000.

———. *Eritrea's War*. Addis Abeba: Shama Books, 2001.

Last, Alex. "Defiant in Defeat." *BBC Focus on Africa* 11, no. 3 (July–September 2000).

Mellessee Wolde Sellassie. *Deporting Eritreans from Ethiopia, A Lesson to the World*. Asmera: Sabur Printing Service, 2000.

Milkias, Paulos. "Ethiopia and Eritrea at War; Saga of Triumph and Tragedy at the Dawn of the Millennium." *Horn of Africa* 17, nos. 1–4 (December 1999).

The Monitor (Addis Abeba), 30 May 2000, 24–25 June 2000, 4 July 2000, 12–13 August 2000.

The Reporter (Addis Abeba), 31 May 2000, 7 June 2000, 14 June 2000.

Research and Documentation Center of Eritrea. *Ethiopia's War on Eritrea*. Asmera: Research and Documentation Center of Eritrea, 1999.

The Sun (Addis Abeba), 18 May 2000, 1 June 2000.

Walta Information Center. *Dispatches from the Electronic Front: Internet Responses to the Ethio-Eritrean Conflict*. Addis Abeba: Walta Information Center, 1999.

Index

Abba dula, 56
Abba Jifar II, of Jima, 56, 81, 84, 134–135
Abdullahi, Emir, of Harer, 83, 84
Abdullahi, Khalifa, of Sudan, 102
Abdul Majid Hussein, 246
Abdul Resul, 55, 81
Abebe Aregai, Ras, 151
Abreha, Gen., 9–10
Absolutist state, 77
Abyot Seded (Revolutionary Flame) Party, 200
Abyssinia, 38, 40, 45, 48, 49, 66, 67, 68
Abyssinia, Bank of. *See* Banking
Access to the sea, 122, 123, 156
Adal, 26, 29, 30, 31, 32
Adal, Ras, of Gojam. *See* Tekle Haimanot, King (Negus) of Gojam
Adari, xvii
Addis Ababa University, 175, 189, 227, 231; mass dismissal of professors in 1993, 240; student radicalism and activism at, 175–176, 179, 182, 185, 221, 240

Addis Abeba, xvii, 32, 65, 85, 91, 107, 108, 109, 110, 113, 114, 116, 117, 119, 120, 132, 145, 147, 162, 206, 222, 231; boom of 1926–1927, 125; demonstrations of 1974, 182, 184; Haile Sellassie's return to, 152; National Conference of 1991, 232–233; in 1960, 164, 165 fig. 25; rebellion of March 1918, 118
Aden, 13, 70, 122, 125
Aden, Gulf of, 35
Adigrat, 98
Administration, modern, 137
Ado, 139
Adulis, 5, 9, 11
Advisers, foreign, 77, 128, 130–131, 152, 161. *See also* Ilg, Alfred
Adwa, 69, 72, 74, 91, 98, 143, 212
Adwa, Battle of: between Italy and Ethiopia, 98–99, 108, 148; between Yohannes IV and Wagshum Gobeze, 72
Aedisius, 7
Af Abet, Battle of, 211, 229
Afar, xvii, 26, 30, 54, 74

Afar-Saho, 34
Afework Woldesemiat, Dej., 143
African-Americans, 156
Afro-Asiatic languages, 3
Agame, 5, 54, 224, 225, 226; Sobia district, 225
"Age of the princes." *See* Zamana Masafent
Agew (country, language, and people), 6, 10, 11, 12, 32, 38
Agew Midir, 57
"Agew" Neguse. *See* Neguse Welde Mikail
Agreement on Cessation of Hostilities of the Federal Democratic Republic of Ethiopia and the Government of the State of Eritrea, 262–263. *See also* Ethio-Eritrean campaigns of 1998–2000
Agribusiness, 164, 176, 190–191
Agricultural Marketing Corporation, 205
Agriculture, 3, 4, 160, 204–205, 212; Ministry of, 155
Ahmad Badlay, 26
Ahmade, Dej., of Welo, 56
Ahmad ibn Ibrihim al-Ghazi, Imam, 31, 32, 33, 34
Aiga, 261
Airborne unit, 186
Aircraft and aviation, 128, 159, 166, 171, 174, 178; imperial air force, 161, 162; Italian, 142, 144, 145
Akele Guzay, 5, 74
Akilu Habtewold, 178, 184
Akordat, 200
Alakenat, 49
Alemata, 206
Alem-Zewd Tessema, Col., 186, 187
Alexandria, Sea of, 7, 8, 8n, 9, 24, 58, 131. *See also* Christians: and Monophysite theology
Ali I of Yeju, Ras Bitwoded, 52, 56
Ali II of Yeju, Ras, 57, 58, 59, 60, 61, 66
Aligaz, Dej., of Yeju, 56
Al-Itahad al-Islami (Islamic union, AIAI), 247
Aliyu Amba, 55

All-Amhara Peoples Organization (AAPO), 235, 240
All-Ethiopia Socialist Movement (MEISON), 193, 194, 195, 200. *See also* Provisional Military Administration Council and its successors: Yekatit '66 Political School; Provisional Office of Mass Organizational Affairs
All-Ethiopia Trade Union. *See* Ethiopia Trade Union
Allies, 156
Almoulqah, 5
Altiena, 251, 252, 259, 260, 261
Alula, Dej., of Yeju and Gojam, 56
Alula, Ras, 81, 83, 84, 85, 89, 91, 94
Aman Mikail Andom, Gen., 189, 190
Amara, 150
Amba Aradam, Battle of, 145
Amba Chara, Council of, 63
Amba Jebeli, Battle of, 63
Ambalage: Battle of (1895), 96; siege of (1941), 152
Amda Siyon, Emperor, 19, 21
Amhara National Democratic Movement (ANDM). *See* Ethiopian Peoples Democratic Movement
Amhara people, xvi, 38, 47, 51, 53, 65, 70, 178, 214
Amhara region, 32, 37, 47, 51
Amharic language, xvii, 3, 19, 165, 172, 175
Amoleh. See Salt and salt bars
Angot, 11
Animals, meat, 125
Ankober, 55, 68, 117, 119
Annan, Kofi, 261
Annuak, xvii
Antioch, 14
Antonelli, Count Pietro, 78, 85, 87, 89, 91, 93
Aosta, Duke of, 150
Arabia, 9, 10, 28, 54, 55
Arakil Nubar, Bey, Governor of Mitsiwa, 74
Araya Sellassie, Ras, 80, 86
Arbenyotch (patriots), 148, 149, 150, 151

Arendrup, Soren, Pasha, 74
Aristocracy, 137, 156, 172
Ark of the Covenant, 18
Armed forces: imperial, 156, 179–180, 183–186, 198–200; revolutionary, 196, 198
Armenia and Armenians, 23, 43, 122, 125, 161
Arms embargo, post–WW I, 119, 121, 123, 131
Arsi, xvii, 37, 78, 147, 164
Art, 12, 13, 17, 28
Aseb, 75n, 123, 126, 197, 239, 249–250, 255, 262, 264
Asfa Wossen, Meridazmach, 169, 171, 181
Asmera, 85, 87, 89, 158, 162, 197, 200, 229, 230, 255, 262
Asrate Kassa, Ras, 169, 178, 187
Atbara, 8
Atnafu Abebe, Lt. Col., 200–201
Atnatyos, Abuna, 72
Attetegab, Woiz., 59
Aurelian, Emperor, 39
Australopithecus, 1
Austria, 140
Automobiles, 125
Awash River and Valley, 2, 22, 31, 55, 65, 79, 161, 164
Awash Station, 234
Awsa, 31, 55, 74, 142
Axum, xvi, xviii, 4–10, 19, 42; Church of Mary, 72; town, 24, 56, 69, 143, 212
Ayshal, Battle of, 62, 66
Azebo Oromo, 53

Bada region, 250–251
Badme, 222, 226, 251, 252, 260. *See also* Kunama
Badoglio, Gen. Pietro, 144, 145, 147, 152
Baduma plains, 257
Baeda Mariam, Emperor, 29
Bahrey, 37
Bahr Negash, 27
Baitos. See Tigrayan Peoples Liberation Front: mass organizations

Balcha, Dej., 127
Bale, 26, 32, 37, 137, 147, 148, 198; peasant uprising in 1963, 178–179
Ballabat, 105
Balla Warka, 67
Bande, 150
Banking, 107, 125, 127, 131, 137
Baraka, 175
Baratieri, Gen. Oreste, 96, 97, 98, 99
Barettuma moiety, 35
Bartolomewos, Abuna, 23
Basso market, 55, 56
BBC, 188, 207
Beans, 162, 176
Beeswax, 155
Begemdir, 11, 23, 32, 39, 44, 49, 51, 52, 54, 56, 57, 68, 70, 72, 73, 86, 87, 89, 94, 113, 132
Beja, 6, 8
Bekaffa, Emperor, 45
Belai Zelleke, Dej., 154–155
Belgian military training mission, 137
Beni (Bela) Shangul, 105
Berbera, 54
Berhanena Selam, 122, 124
Berta, xvii
Beshlo River, 11
Beta Israel, 22, 38, 42–43, 214
Beyene Merid, Dej., 148
Bezabeh, Ras, 80
Birr, 238, 249, 250, 251 fig. 38
Biru Goshu, Dej., of Gojam, 58, 60, 63
Bitwoded, 29
Bogos, 73, 75, 81, 82, 83, 87,89
Bono, Gen. Emilio de, 142, 144
Borena, xvii, 34, 37, 105
Borena moiety, 35
Bourgeoisie, national, bureaucratic, and foreign, 137, 155, 176
Bouteflika Abdelaziz, president of Algeria, 262
Brancaleone, Niccolo, 28
Britain and British, xix, 70, 71–72, 73, 82, 83, 85, 101, 105, 107, 121, 123, 124, 130–131, 140, 142, 146, 151–152, 154, 158; Anglo-Ethiopian campaign

Britain and British *(continued)*
　(1941), xiii; military assistance, 157;
　OETA, 152, 153
Building College (Addis Abeba), 161
Bure, 251, 262
Byzantine traders, 9
Byzantium, 7, 9, 10

Cabinet government, 110, 112, 179,
　184
Caleb, Emperor, 9
Canada, 161
Capitalism, 107, 120, 124, 125, 164,
　176, 191; bureaucratic, 194
Capitulary rights, 126. *See also* Special
　Court
Caravan trade, 8, 55, 56, 107
Cash crops, 120, 125, 164
Cavalry, 26
Central powers, 114
Chalcedon, Council of, 8
Chelenko, Battle of, 84
Chercher, 31
Chilga, 46
Chinese Communist Party, 225
Cholera, 93
Christians, xvi, xvii, 7, 10, 14, 19, 22,
　23, 24, 25, 29, 32, 37, 38, 39, 40, 44,
　55, 58, 83, 86, 105, 128; and Mono-
　physite theology, 43, 44, 47, 51, 53,
　58, 59, 63, 64, 66, 76
Christian Topography (Indicopleustes), 6
Coalition of Ethiopian Democratic Forces,
　(CEDF), 232
Coffee, 40, 49, 54, 56, 94, 120, 122, 124,
　125, 127, 137, 155, 161, 162, 164,
　167, 176
Cohen, Herman, 231
Collective security, 120, 141
Commerce, Ministry of, 155
Commercial School (Addis Abeba), 161
Commission for Organizing the Working
　People of Ethiopia (COPWE), 203,
　204
Communications, modern, 107, 113, 119,
　136–137, 161, 166, 188, 207. *See also*

Posts, Telegraphs, and Telephones,
　Ministry of; Railway: Addis Abeba–
　Djibouti
Confederation of Ethiopian Labour
　Unions (CELU), 184, 185
Confession of Faith (Emperor Galawedos),
　39
Conglomerate state, 28, 29
Constituent Assembly, 241–242. *See also*
　Constitution: of 1994
Constitution: of 1931, 143; 1955
　revision, 17, 165–166; 1974
　suppression of, 188; of 1987,
　210–211; of 1994, 242–243
Contemporary history, xii
Coordinating Committee of the Armed
　Forces *(derg)*, 187, 189, 201. *See also*
　Provisional Military Administration
　Council and its successors
Corvée, 19
Cotton, 155
Council of Ministers. *See* Cabinet
　government
Coup of 1960 (abortive), 169–172;
　background of, 167–168
Coup of 1974, 184–189; background of,
　179–183
Coup of 1989 (abortive), 213
Court protocol, 130
Courts, provincial appellate, 111
Crafts, 43, 49
Crispi, Francesco, 92, 93, 96, 97
Crown council, 111, 122, 127
Cuba, 199
Cushitic languages and speakers, xvii, 3, 34
Customs service. *See* Finance, Ministry of
Czechoslovakia, 123, 161

Da'amat, Kingdom of, 3, 4
Dabarki, Battle of, 61, 71
Dahlak Islands, 27
Damot, 19, 20, 21, 22, 46, 51
Danot, 138
Darge, Ras, 67, 68
Dawaro, 20, 21, 26, 32
Dawit I, Emperor, 23, 24

Dawit III, Emperor, 45
Dawit Wolde Giorgis, 205, 206
Debre Abay, 57
Debre Beg, 67
Debre Birhan, 26, 28, 29, 66, 67
Debre Bizen, Monastery of, 23
Debre Damo, Monastery of, 8
Debre Libanos, 44, 149
Debre Markos, 152
Debre Tabor, 58, 61, 62, 71, 129; Battle
    of, 214
Dedebit, 222
Degeh Bur, 139, 143
Dembea, 44, 60, 61, 63
Dembidolo, 152
Deportees and refugees, from Ethio-
    Eritrean campaigns of 1998–2000,
    254–256
Deresge, Battle of, 64
Dereso, Ras, 80
Derg, 187, 189, 200, 223, 228, 231;
    counterattack in Tigray (1988), 229;
    massacre of 23 November 1974, 222
Dese, 126, 128, 129, 144, 213, 230, 236
Desta Demtew, Ras, 127, 135, 144, 147,
    148
Development, social and economic: 122,
    156, 159–160, 161, 166, 186; and
    1974 coup, 179, 180, 192
Development through Cooperation
    Campaign, 192
Dhu Nuwas, 9
Didesa valley, 164
Dinder River, 61
Dinkenesh, 1n
Dire Dawa, 2, 107, 119, 153, 199, 234
Djibouti, 107, 108, 123, 125, 146, 157
Dogali, Battle of, 83, 85
Dori, Dej., of Yeju, 57
Droughts, 128, 180, 181, 214. *See also*
    Famines
Dysentery, 86

East Africa, 122
Economy, command, xix, 204
Economy, national , xix, 105, 107, 110,

111, 114, 117, 120, 122, 126, 135,
    137, 155, 159, 161, 164, 176;
    breakdown of, 212–213; deterioration
    after Arab-Israeli war of 1973, 180,
    181; fragmentation under PMAC,
    205; importance of southern Ethiopia
    to, 125; Italian period's effect on, 155.
    See also Banking; Capitalism
Economy, political, 5, 11, 19, 25, 28, 29,
    43, 48, 49, 52, 56, 65, 117, 120, 125,
    155, 191
Economy, world, 77, 107, 117, 120, 125,
    137, 161. *See also* Merchants, Indian
Education and schools, 107, 120, 122,
    130, 136, 156, 160, 162, 165, 180,
    181. *See also* Young Ethiopians
    (Abyssinians) and educated elites
Efrata, 67
Egigayahu, Woiz., 66
Egypt, 5, 13–14, 20, 26, 27, 59, 61, 69,
    73, 81, 82, 83, 123; campaigns in
    Ethiopia, 74–75; National Bank of,
    107, 131
Ella Amida, Emperor, 7
Ella Asbeha, Emperor, 9
Elleni, Queen, 29
Embabo, Battle of, 80
Endelkatchew Makonnen, 184, 185, 186,
    187
Enerea, 40, 48, 56
Ensete, xvii, 125
Entoto. *See* Addis Abeba
Eritrea, xvi, xvii, xviii, xix, 23, 24, 27, 38,
    49, 73, 85, 87, 91, 96, 108, 114, 124,
    126, 150, 162, 165, 173; anti-
    Ethiopian agitation in, 174–175;
    destruction of the federation by Haile
    Sellassie's regime, 172; economics
    and development, 237, 246–247,
    248–249, 250, 265–267; EPLF takes
    Mitsiwa, 214; expatriates, 249, 258;
    expulsion of Ethiopians in 1991, 233;
    General Aman's policy toward, 189;
    the government's deteriorating
    situation in 1977, 196–197; Govern-
    ment of Eritrea Decree, 238–239;

Eritrea *(continued)*
    insurgency and counterinsurgency,
    180; the Mengistu government
    successfully counterattacks (1978),
    199–200; military policy, 247;
    national politics, 246–247; northern
    part liberated, 211; PMAC's
    deteriorating position in, 190;
    PMAC's efforts at negotiation with
    insurgents, 194; postwar Ethiopian
    policy toward, 156, 157–159; Red
    March, 195; Red Star Campaign,
    202–203, 227; referendum, 233,
    235–236, 238; revolt against the
    Italians, 95–96; state of emergency
    declared, 178; warfare in, xii, 209,
    210–212, 229, 259–264. *See also*
    Addis Ababa University; Ethio-
    Eritrean campaigns of 1998–2000;
    Ethiopia: relations with Eritrea;
    Frontiers: between Eritrea and Ethio-
    pia; Italy and Italians: reorganization
    of Italian East Africa
Eritrean Liberation Front (ELF), 175, 178,
    194, 199–200, 222, 226, 227, 252
Eritrean Peoples Liberation Front (EPLF),
    178, 194, 195, 199–200, 202–203,
    211, 212, 215–216, 231, 232, 233,
    246; cooperation/differences with
    TPLF, 222, 223, 225, 226–228, 229,
    251; Sahil campaign (1987), 229;
    victory at Af Abet, 229
Etchege (highest Ethiopian church official),
    44, 58, 59, 72
Ethio-Eritrean campaigns of 1998–2000:
    air war (May–June 1998), 253–254;
    arms purchases, 254, 256, 259,
    262–264; at Badme (1999), 260;
    Eritrean general mobilization, 259;
    Ethiopian blitzkrieg of May 2000, xii,
    259–262; peace proposals and
    negotiations, 253, 256, 259, 262–264;
    propaganda and strategy, 254,
    256–257, 259, 261–262; refugees and
    deportees, 254–256
Ethiopia, Bank of. *See* Banking

Ethiopia, present-day. *See* Federal
    Democratic Republic of Ethiopia
Ethiopian Airlines, 159, 166
Ethiopian Democratic Officers Revolu-
    tionary Movement (EDORM), 230
Ethiopian Democratic Union (EDU),
    223, 224–225, 226, 232
Ethiopian Human Rights Organization
    (EHRO), 240; human rights, 243
Ethiopian National Corporation, 155–156
Ethiopian Peoples Democratic Movement
    (later the Amhara National Democratic
    Movement), 229, 247
Ethiopian Peoples Revolutionary
    Democratic Front (EPRDF), xi, 213,
    214, 216, 217, 231, 232, 233, 234,
    235, 236; southern campaign of 1989,
    229–230
Ethiopian Peoples Revolutionary Party,
    193, 194, 200, 225, 226, 232
Ethio-Somali Democratic Movement
    (ESDU), 248
Ethiopia Trade Union, 203
Ethnicity, xi, xii, 221, 222, 223, 225, 226,
    228, 229, 230, 232, 233, 239, 240,
    241, 243, 244, 246–247, 255, 256;
    language, 221, 227, 233–234; right
    to independence, 222, 223, 226,
    232
Ethno-history, xii
"Etiopia Tikdem," 187
Eucalyptus, 122
European Economic Community, 206
Ewostatewos, Abba, 22, 23
Ewostathians, 23, 24, 25, 43, 44, 47
Ezanas, Emperor, 7, 8

Falasha. *See* Beta Israel
Famines, 93, 108; and food aid as political
    weapon, 209–210, 214, 228; of 1984,
    205–208, 228; of 1973–1974, 181
Fashoda, 101, 105
Fasil, Dej., of Damot, 51, 52
Fasilidas, Emperor, 40, 41, 43, 44, 72
Fatagar, 26
Fazughli (region), 10, 40

Feasting *(geber)*, 110
Federal Democratic Republic of Ethiopia
(FDRE, present-day Ethiopia), xi, 221,
245; Constituent Assembly and new
constitution, 242–243; demonstration
of 1993 against Eritrean independence,
240; economics and development,
235–237, 240–241, 242–245,
247–249; elections of June 1992,
234–235; elections of June 1994, 241;
elections of May 1995, 242; and
expatriate Ethiopians, xii, 232, 239,
242; freedom of the press, 241, 245;
land tenure, 222, 236, 242; military
policy, 243, 246; National Charter of
July 1991, 232–233; national politics,
232–235, 241–245, 247–248;
relations with Eritrea, 230–231, 233,
235–236, 237–240, 251, 253–254,
248–264, 267; student movement,
221. *See also* Ethio-Eritrean campaigns
of 1998–2000; Frontiers: between
Ethiopia and Eritrea
Federalism, xi
Fekadu Gedamu, 232
Fenote Selam, 236
Feudalism, 11, 19, 20, 25, 28, 37, 38, 43,
44, 48–49, 50, 56, 77, 105; transition
to capitalism, 120, 124
Filipos, Abba, 23, 24
Finance, Ministry of, 130, 134, 137
Finfinni (region), 65
Firearms, 32, 33, 34, 39, 46, 53, 54, 55,
58, 61, 63, 66. *See also* Weaponry,
modern
Fitche, 136
Food Agricultural Organization, 161
Foreign Affairs, Ministry of, 134
Four Power Commission, 158
Fourth Division, 186
France and French, 82, 83, 101–102, 105,
121, 123, 124, 141, 161; foreign pol-
icy of 126–127, 138, 143; geopolitical
concerns of, 95, 101; pact with Italy,
140. *See also* Railway: Addis
Abeba–Djibouti

Frontier Demarcation Commission of
1934, Anglo-Ethiopian, 139
Frontiers, 126; between Eritrea and Ethiopia, 225, 226–227, 228–229, 230,
238–239, 250–253, 258–259, 263
Frumentius, 7, 8
Fung of Sennar, 39

Gabriel, Abuna, 24, 25
Gada system, 35–38, 106
Galawedos, Emperor, 34, 39
Galla and Sidama. *See* Italy and Italians:
reorganization of Italian East Africa
Gallabat, 74
Gama, Christopher da, 43
Gamo Gofa, 104
Gash, 175
Gayint, 16
Geber (feasting), 110
Gebre Egziabeher, Dej., 106
Gebre Mariam, Dej., 148
Gebre Medhin, Wagshum, 68
Gebru, Dej., of Simen, 53, 56
Gedem, 67, 79
Ge'ez, 4, 8
Geladi, 138
Gera, 48, 56, 81
Geregube, 138
Germame Neway, 167–168, 172
Germany, 141, 142, 213
Gezira scheme, 127
Gibe Region and basin, xvii, 45, 48, 49,
54, 56, 79
Gideon force, 151, 152, 154
Girar, 27
Gishan, Amba, 28
Gishe, 67
Goba, 137
Gobana, Ras, 79, 80
Gobeze, Wagshum (self-proclaimed
Emperor Tekle Giorgis II), 72, 73
Gode, 197
Gojam, xvi, 19, 22, 32, 37, 38, 39, 43,
44, 47, 54, 56, 57, 59, 61, 63, 65, 70,
74, 75, 76, 80, 86, 89, 94, 135, 151,
152, 216

Gold, 11, 19, 40, 94, 105

Goldiya, 134

Golgotha, Mount, 123

Goma, 48, 56

Gonder province, 206, 213, 214, 216

Gonder town, xii, xvi, xvii, 40, 44, 45, 46, 49, 51, 52, 54, 56, 57, 58, 59, 60, 61, 63, 66, 70, 73, 79, 86, 213, 230

Gonga states, 45, 48

Gordon, Gen. Charles George, 81

Gore, 148

Goshu, Ras Bitwoded, of Amhara, 51, 52

Goshu Zewde, Dej., of Gojam, 57, 59, 60, 61–62

Government, modern, 110, 111. *See also* Cabinet government

Government of Eritrea. *See* Eritrea

Grains, 122, 125, 162, 176

Graziani, Rodolfo, field marshal and viceroy, 143, 144, 147, 150

Greek language, 7, 8

Greeks, 9, 43, 122, 125, 161

Guard, imperial, 132, 137, 170

Gudit, Queen, 11, 11n

Gudru, 80

Gugsa, Ras Bitwoded, of Yeju, 52, 53, 56, 57

Gugsa Wolie, Ras, of Begemdir, 128

Gult (fiefdom), 19, 20, 50

Guma, 56, 81

Gundet, Battle of, 74

Gura, Battle of, 74–75

Gurage, xvii, 55, 65, 76

Gur Amba, Battle of, 61–62

Habte Giorgis, Fit., 108, 111, 112, 114, 117, 118, 121, 124

Habte Mariam, Dej., of Welega, 148

Hader, 1

Hadiya, 19, 20, 21, 29, 32

Haile Fida, 193

Haile Malakot, King of Shewa, 65, 66, 67

Haile Mariam, Dej., of Simen, 53, 56, 57

Haile Sahle Sellassie, Meridazmach, 68

Haile Sellassie, Emperor, xvii, xviii, xix, 112, 114, 116, 117, 177 fig. 27, 221,

231, 256; attempted coup against, 127–128; death of, 223; detention of former cabinet members, 86; development ideas and programs, 122, 128, 130; elevation to imperial throne and coronation, 130, 132–133; elevation to kingship, 128; in exile, 146, 150–151; failures as a ruler, 181; foreign policy of, 119, 120, 121, 125–126, 133, 134, 156; government and administration of, 127, 130, 132, 134, 166, 179; introduction of reforms by, 185, 186; 1924 trip to Europe, 123; political enfeeblement and dethronement of, 179, 187, 188–189; political strategy and behavior of, 118, 125, 130–131, 136; postwar restoration of government by, 151, 152, 154; response to attempted coup of 1960, 169, 171–173; as seen by student radicals, 176; twenty-fifth-anniversary assessment of achievements, 166; visits to foreign leaders, 156, 161–163; at war with Italy, 140, 142, 144–146. *See also* Court protocol; Young Ethiopians (Abyssinians) and educated elites

Haile Sellassie Gugsa, Dej., 143, 154

Haile Sellassie I Secondary School, 167

Haile Sellassie I University. *See* Addis Ababa University

Hailu, Ras, of Gojam, 135

Hailu Wolde Giorgis, Dej., of Kwara, 59

Hamasen, 74, 91

Hamitic-Semitic languages, 3

Haoulti, 4

Harerge, xvii, 31, 37, 94, 112, 114, 118, 198

Harer town, xvii, 54, 55, 56, 74, 83, 84, 96, 116, 143, 162, 199

Hargigo, 85

Hejaz, 6

Herui Wolde Sellassie, Blattengeta, 134

Hewett, Admiral Sir William, 82

Hides, 54, 94, 122, 155

Hitler, Adolf, 140

Hitmulo, 85
Hoare, Sir Samuel, 143
Hoare-Laval Agreement, 143–144
Hoe agriculture, xvii
Holetta Military Academy, 138, 187
Homo species, 1–3
Hospitals, 107, 136
Human rights. *See* Ethiopian Human
    Rights Organization (EHRO)
Humera, 213, 251
Hussein, Saddam, 264

Ibnat, 206
Idaga Hamus, 97
Ilg, Alfred, 77, 78, 109
Ilubabor, 105
Imperial family, 137, 156
Import-export bank loans, 159
Imru Haile Sellassie, Ras, 145, 147,
    148
Inda Silase, 212
Inderta, 54
India, 126
Indian Ocean, 35, 46
Indians, 43. *See also* Merchants, Indian
Indicopleustes, Cosmas, 6
Indirect rule, 94
Influenza epidemics of 1918, 119
Inheritance Law of 1908, 111
Interior, Ministry of, 167
International Bank for Reconstruction and
    Development, 161
International Monetary Fund (IMF), 248,
    265
International Postal Union, Ethiopia's
    entry into, 107
Irob, 252, 261
Iron bars, 7
Isayas Afeworki, 215, 227, 231, 233, 236,
    238, 239, 247, 248, 251, 253, 254,
    259, 262, 263
Islam and Muslims, xvii, xviii, 10, 11, 19,
    20, 21, 25, 26, 27, 28, 29, 30, 31,
    32, 35, 37, 38, 43, 47, 48, 49, 52,
    53, 55, 56, 57, 58, 69, 73, 76, 81,
    83, 128, 149, 247–248; Lij Iyasu's

relations with, 114; Somali propa-
    ganda about, 178; Tewodros's fear of,
    69–70
Ismail, Khedive, 74, 81, 82
Israel, Kingdom of, xvi, 18
Israel, Republic of, 159, 175, 178, 214
Issues . . . Concerning the Framework
    Agreement, 258. *See also* Ethio-
    Eritrean campaigns of 1998–2000
Italian East Africa. *See* Italy and Italians
Italian Geographic Society of Rome, 75
Italy and Italians, xix, 75–76, 78, 82, 83,
    84, 87, 89, 91, 95, 114, 123, 124,
    126, 144, 145, 161; anti-Ethiopian
    sentiments and propaganda, 121,
    124, 137–138; declaration of Ethi-
    opian Italian Empire, 147; defeat
    of, 152; First Italo-Ethiopian War,
    96–99, 133; pacification of Ethiopia,
    148, 149, 150; post–WW I policy,
    136, 138, 139; reorganization of
    Italian East Africa, 150; Second
    Italo-Ethiopian War, 140–146. See
    also *Arbenyotch* (patriots); League
    of Nations; Somaliland, Italian
    (Somalia)
Ivory, 3, 5, 8, 11, 19, 54, 81, 94
Iyasu, Lij, 111, 112, 114, 115, 116, 117,
    121, 136; character of, 113
Iyasu I, Emperor, 42, 44, 45
Iyasu II, Emperor, 46
Iyoas, Emperor, 46, 47, 51

Japan, 106, 126
Jared Abun, Sultan (of Adal), 31
Jarsa biyya, 35
Jebeli Amba, 63
Jeldessa, 31
Jema River, 11
Jerusalem, 17, 26, 123
Jews and Judaism, 9, 18
Jèze, Gaston, 131
Jibuti, 250, 255
Jifar I, Abba, of Jima, 56
Jijiga, 139, 143, 157, 168, 199
Jima, 48, 56, 80, 81, 148

Joint Border Commission (of Ethiopia and Eritrea), 251
Juba River, 144
Justice, Ministry of, 111

Kagnew Station, 159
Kaskase, 4
Kassa, Dej., of Tigray. *See* Yohannes IV, Emperor
Kassa Hailu. *See* Tewodros II, Emperor
Kassa Hailu, Leul Ras, 118, 132, 144, 145, 148
Kassala, 151
Kebelays (neighborhood organizations), 193, 195, 200, 203
Kebre Negast, 17, 18, 38
Kefa, 45, 48–49, 80, 104, 114, 167
Kembata, 32
Kenya, 105, 134, 157
Kerelos, Abuna, 58
Keren, 89, 152, 211, 229, 255
Kerosene, 155
Ketema, 105, 125
Kibat. *See* Christians: and Monophysite theology
Kinfu, Dej., of Kwara, 57, 59
Koman, xvii
Konso, xvii
Korahe, 139, 143
Korean war, 159
Korem, 206, 207
Korro, 105
Koso, 59
Kumsa Noroda, 106
Kunama, xvii, 252
Kushanas, 7
Kwara, 46, 47, 59, 60, 61, 69

Lalibela, Emperor, 12, 15
Lalibela town, 145
Land tenure and reform, xix, 49–50, 120, 173, 186, 190–191; nationalization, 192
Lasta, 10, 12, 19, 32, 46, 49, 52, 53, 68, 89
Laval, Pierre, 140, 142, 143

League of Nations, 121, 122, 124, 126, 139, 140, 141, 156; sanctions against Italy, 143
Lebna Dengel, Emperor, 29, 30–33
Legarde, Léonce, Governor of Obok and Duke of Entoto, 94, 102
Leka, 81
Lekemti, 236
Lend-lease treaty, 153
Limu-Enerea, 40, 48, 56
London Conference (May 1991), 230–231
Lorenzo Taezaz, 151
Luba, 36
"Lucy," 1

Machinery, 155
"Mad Mullah," 114
Mahdi, 82
Mahdists. *See* Sudan and Sudanese
Mahrabete, 38
Mai Alba, 261
Maji and Goldiya, 134
Makeda, Queen of Saba, 16, 17, 18
Makonnen, Ras, 84, 91, 94, 102, 105, 108
Makonnen Habte Wolde, 134
Mandefera, 260
Mao-style Communism, 224
Mareb River, 74, 91, 96, 142
Maria Theresa dollar, 54, 54n, 131, 137, 156
Maru, Dej., of Begemdir, 56, 57
Maru, Dej., of Tigray, 56
Marxism-Leninism, xvii, 176, 186, 194, 196, 200, 203
Marxist-Leninist League of Tigray (MLLAT), 210, 228, 256
Mary, Church of (Entoto), 90
Marye, Ras, of Yeju, 57
Mass political organizations, 192, 193, 203–204
Matako, Fit., 79
Matara, 4
Mattewos, Abuna, 90, 112
Maychew, Battle of, 145
Mecca, 10, 11

Mecha, 46
Medhane Alem at Lalibela, Church of, 12, 13
MEISON. *See* All-Ethiopia Socialist Movement
Mekdela, 66, 70, 71, 72, 73, 80
Mekele, 143, 144, 207, 212, 229, 230, 234, 253
Melazo, 4
Meles Zenawi, xi, 217, 222, 227, 229, 232, 233, 235, 236, 237, 238, 239, 240, 241, 244, 247, 248, 251, 253, 257, 262; trip to London and Washington, 230–231
Melka Kontoure, 2
Mendez, Afonso Bishop, 40
Menen, Empress, 133
Menen, Itegue, 57, 57n, 58, 59, 60, 61
Mengesha Seyoum, Ras, 222, 223, 224, 252
Mengesha Yohannes, Ras, 89, 91, 95, 96, 108
Mengistu Haile Mariam, Lt. Col., president of the PDRE, xvii, 179, 185, 187, 189, 190, 194, 195, 196, 200, 201, 209, 212, 214, 216, 217, 221, 231, 240, 254, 257, 260, 262; election as president of PDRE, 211; and formation of COPWE/WPE, 203, 204, 207
Mengistu Neway, Brig. Gen., 169, 170, 172
Menilek I, Emperor, 17, 73
Menilek II, King of Shewa and Emperor, xviii, 65, 66, 67, 70, 72, 73, 74, 75, 77–80, 83, 84, 85, 86, 87, 88 fig. 17, 89, 91, 92, 93, 101, 106, 107, 117, 150; accession to imperial throne, 89–90; decline and death of, 108, 109, 110, 111, 112, 113; expansionism of, 94, 104, 105, 150; postwar foreign policy of, 102–103; relations with Italy, 83, 96–100; submission to Yohannes, 75, 79. *See also* Treaties and international agreements
Mentewab, Dowager Empress, 46, 47

Menz, 38, 67, 76
Merchants, Arab, 125
Merchants, Indian, 107, 120, 122, 125, 127
Merid Mengesha, Gen., 169, 170, 171, 174
Meroë, 8
Mesfin Seleshi, Ras, 167
Metema, 54, 57, 61, 86, 87, 89
Mikail, Abuna, 24, 25
Mikail, Ras (later King [Negus] of the North), of Welo, 73, 76, 87, 89, 113, 116, 117
Mikail Imru, 187, 189
Mikail Sehul, Ras, 46, 47, 51, 56
Military Coordination Commission, 263
Military expeditions, 55
Military review, Addis Abeba, 1862, 108
Military training and assistance, 137, 138, 157, 159, 161, 162. *See also* United States and Americans: military assistance
Mitchell, Lieut. General Sir Philip, 152
Mitmaq, Council of, 25
Mitsiwa, 13, 19, 27, 37, 40, 46, 54, 56, 59, 69, 70, 71, 73, 74, 79, 81, 82, 85, 92, 158, 197, 200; in Ethio-Eritrean campaigns of 1998 –2000, 239, 249, 255, 262; Italian occupation of, 83
Mixed Commission (of Ethiopia and Eritrea), 239, 247, 249
Modalities for the Implementation of the OAU Framework Agreement on the Settlement of the Dispute between Ethiopia and Eritrea, 258, 259. *See also* Ethio-Eritrean campaigns of 1998–2000
Money, 6, 7, 125, 131, 137; introduction of new currency and coinage in 1945, 156
Monophysitism, 8
Moroda of Nekemte, 106
Mugabe, Robert, 217
Muhammad, 10
Muhammad Abdullah, Seyyid, of Somaliland, 114

Muhammed Ali, Imam of Welo. *See* Mikail, Ras (later King [Negus] of the North)

Muhammed Ali, Viceroy of Egypt, 53, 59

Muhammed ibn al-Seyyid Abdullah of Sudan, 82

Mulugeta, Yigezu, Ras, 128–129, 144

Munzinger, Werner, Pasha and Governor-General of Eastern Sudan, 73, 74

Musk, 54, 94

Mussolini, Benito, 138, 139, 141, 143, 144, 147; war calculations, 140

Nakfa (currency), 250, 265 fig. 38, 266, 267

Nakfa (place), 200, 202, 203, 227, 262

Nadaw Abba Welo, Ras, 121

Nagadrases, 119

Naod, Emperor, 29

Napier, Sir Robert (later Lord Napier of Magdala), 70, 82

Nasibu Zamanuel, Dej., 134, 143

Nasser, Gamel Abdul, 159

National Bank of Egypt, 107, 131

National Charter (July 1991). *See under* Federal Democratic Republic of Ethiopia (FDRE)

National Coffee Board, 167

National Democratic Revolution, Program of, 194

Nationalism, Ethiopian, 96

Nationalities question, 194

Nationality. *See* Ethnicity

Nazret, 172

Neftennya-gabbar system, 105, 106, 120

Negaso Gidada, Dr., 230, 244

Neguse Welde Mikail, 68, 69

Nekemte, 106

Netherlands, 106

New Economic Policy (NEP), 236–237

Nicea, Psuedo-Canon of, 8n

Nile River, 8, 40, 82, 108; Blue, 10, 14, 127; White, 105

Nilo-Saharan languages, xvii

"Nine Saints," 8

Nomadism, 30

Nongovernmental organizations, 214

Obok, 84, 94

Occupied Enemy Territory Administration (OETA), 152, 153

Ogaden, xix, 84, 94, 114, 116, 126, 138, 143, 153, 154, 157, 173, 199, 247; Ethio-Somali peace agreement (1988), 212; Somali invasion (1977), 197, 198

Oilseeds, 162

Oligarchy, 120, 125, 155, 156, 173, 176

Omo River and valley, xvii, 164

Omotic languages, xvii

Orero, Gen. Baldassare, 92

Organization for African Unity Proposal for a Framework Agreement for a Peaceful Settlement of the Dispute between Eritrea and Ethiopia, 258, 259. *See also* Ethio-Eritrean campaigns of 1998–2000

Oromia, 231, 234

Oromo, xvii, xviii, 30, 34, 35, 37, 38, 39, 40, 43, 44, 45, 46, 47, 48, 51, 53, 58, 61, 65, 67, 79, 84, 106, 144, 145, 230, 232, 234, 235, 247, 248; *gada* system, 35–36, 106; post–WW II dissatisfaction of, 165, 178; relationship with PMAC, 186

Oromo Liberation Front (OLF), 215, 230, 232, 233, 248; vs. OPDO (1992), 231, 234–235

Oromo Peoples Democratic Organization (OPDO), 230, 247, 248; vs. OLF (1998), 231, 234–235

Orthodox Church. *See* Christians

Orthodox Church of Ethiopia, 230

Paez, Father Pedro, 39

Palestine, 23

Parastatal organizations, 205

Parliament, 134

Pastoralism and nomadism, 30

Patriotic Association for the Union of Eritrea and Ethiopia, 158

Patriotic movement. See *Arbenyotch* (patriots)

Peasantry, 56, 128, 154, 216–217.
  See also Bale
Peasants' associations (PAs), 192, 200,
  203–204
Peoples Democratic Republic of Ethiopia
  (PDRE), 194, 203, 211, 232, 233.
  See also Provisional Military Adminis-
  tration Council and its successors
Peoples Front for Democracy and Justice
  (PFDJ). *See* Eritrean Peoples Libera-
  tion Front
Peoples Liberation Front. *See* Eritrean
  Peoples Liberation Front
People's militia, 196, 198
Periplus of the Erythraean Sea, 5
Persia, 7, 10, 14
Petroleum, 155
Point Four Agreement, 160
Police, imperial, 132
Portal, Sir Gerald Herbert, 85
Portugal and Portuguese, 33, 34, 39, 42
Posts, Telegraphs, and Telephones,
  Ministry of, 107, 108, 119, 131
"Prester John," 14, 26, 27, 33
Prime minister, office of, 111
Printing press, 107, 122
Proclamation on Freedom of the Press, 21
  October 1992, 241
Producers' Cooperatives, 205. *See also*
  Agriculture
Program of Naitonal Democratic
  Revolution, 193–194
Protestant missionaries, 69
Proto-Cushitic languages, 3
Proto-Semitic languages, 3
Provisional Government of Eritrea (PGE),
  231. *See also under* Eritrea
Provisional Military Administration
  Council and its successors, 188–189,
  193, 195, 196, 203, 205–207;
  declaration of the PDRE, 211;
  Declaration of Socialism, 190;
  compared to Haile Sellassie regime,
  201, 204, 206; military losses on all
  fronts, 1990–1991, 216; Program of
  National Democratic Revolution,

193–194; Provisional Office of Mass
  Organizational Affairs, 193, 194, 200;
  resettlement and land reform programs,
  190–191, 193, 108–209, 212; Yekatit
  '66 Political School, 193, 200
Provisional Office of Mass Organizational
  Affairs. *See under* Provisional Military
  Administration Council and its
  successors
Provisional Regional Map of 1991, 234
Pulses, 122

Qallu (Oromo leaders), 35, 36

Racism, 73, 93, 96, 97, 100, 103, 123,
  140, 149
Radio Marina, 158
Radio Mogadishu, 178
Rahad River, 61
Rahita, 55
Railway: Addis Abeba–Djibouti, 107,
  126, 138, 146, 147, 153, 156; Somlia-
  Eritrea, 124
Ras, 44
Rassam, Hormuzd, 70
Raya Oromo, 53
"Red March," 195
Red Sea, 35, 37, 40, 49, 54, 82
Red Star Campaign, 202–203
"Red Terror," 195, 201. *See also* Mengistu
  Haile Mariam, Lt. Col., president of
  the PDRE
Relief and Rehabilitation Commission
  (RRC), 205, 206, 207, 208
Religion. *See* Christians; Islam and Mus-
  lims; Roman Catholics; Traditional
  religion
Revolutionary Ethiopia Women's
  Association, 203
Revolutionary Ethiopia Youth Association,
  203
Revolution of 1974–1975. *See* Coup of
  1974; Provisional Military Adminis-
  tration Council and its successors
Rhinoceros horn, 4
Rinderpest, 86, 93, 94

Roads, 136, 137, 160, 161, 166; Italian-built, 150, 155
Rodd, Lord Rennel, 103
Roha, 12
Roman Catholics, 39, 40, 68, 69
Rome, Eastern Empire of, 7, 9, 10
Roosevelt, Franklin Delano, 156
Rubattino Company, 75
Rural life, 50–51, 125, 165
Rwanda. *See* United States: United States–Rwanda Plan for Peace

Sabaeans (South Arabians), 3, 4, 5
Sabbatarians. *See* Ewostathians
Sabradin, 21
Sahati, 85, 86
Sahil, 6, 202
Sahle Dengel, Emperor, 57
Sahle Sellassie, King of Shewa, 53, 55, 56, 57, 58, 65, 66, 67, 79
Saho, xvii
Saint Chrischona Institute (Basel), 69, 71
Salama, Abuna, 58, 59, 63, 64, 71, 72
Salariat, 119
Salimbeni, Count Augusto, 92, 93
Salomon III, Emperor, 52
Salt and salt bars, 7, 49, 54, 155
Salt trade, 252
San'a, 10
San Marzano, General Alessandro Asinari di, 85, 86
Sarsa Dengel, Emperor, 37
Sasaw, 10
Sassanid Dynasty of Persia, 10
Savoia, Armadeo di, Duke of Aosta, 150
Sebagadis, Dej., of Tigray, 57, 71
Segele, Battle of, 117
Seifu Sahle Sellassie, Dej., 67, 68
Seka monarchy, 48
Semitic languages and speakers, xvii, 3, 38
Senafe: Battle of (1895), 96; in Ethio-Eritrean campaigns of 1998–2000, 260
Sennar, 39, 40, 61
Seraye, 22, 74
Seyoum Mengesha, Ras, 143, 144

Shams, 5
Sharecropping, 124, 176, 191
Shashamane, 236
Shengo, 210
Sheraro, 222, 226, 252
Shewa, xvi, xvii, 15–16, 19, 20, 22, 32, 37, 38, 39, 44, 45, 47, 53, 54, 57, 66, 67, 68, 74, 75, 76, 77, 84, 85, 87, 147, 150, 164, 180, 206, 216; Haile Sellassie's opinion of, 118; trade and expansionism of, 54, 55, 56, 65, 75, 77, 78, 79, 81, 94. *See also* Menilek II, King of Shewa and Emperor
Shida monument, 266 fig. 40
Shifta, 59
Shillings, East African, 156
Shimbra Kure, Battle of, 32
Shire, 226, 252; Battle of, 145
Siad Barre, Somalian president, 197, 199, 212
Sidama, xvii, 150
Sidamo, 32, 127, 147, 164, 178, 198, 206
Simen, 44, 53, 57
Sinclair Oil Company, 157
Sisay Habte, Major, 195
Skins, 54, 122
Slaves, 13, 19, 22, 40, 48, 54, 55, 56, 81, 86, 94, 120, 121, 130–131, 134
Snake deity, 5
Soaiba, Bay of, 11
"Socialist Federation" of the Horn of Africa and Yemen, 197
Société Ethiopienne de Commerce et d'Industrie, 118
Society for the Unification of Ethiopia and Eritrea, 158
Solidus, Roman, 7
Solomon, King, xvi, 16, 17, 18
Solomonic dynasty and mythology ("restored"), xviii, 17, 18, 33, 38, 45, 48, 53, 55, 65, 104
Somalia and Somalis, xvii, 26, 30, 34, 94, 163, 173, 178; Greater Somalia, 154, 157, 173, 178; 1977 war against Ethiopia, 196–199; 1963 war against

Ethiopia, 173–174, 189; Radio Mogadishu and anti-Amhara propaganda, 178; Soviet military assistance to, 174, 176

Somaliland, Italian (Somalia), 108, 114, 124, 126, 150; infiltration into Ethiopia from, 138; use of Somali troops in Ethiopia, 149

Somali Youth League, 157

Sost lidot. See Christians: and Monophysite theology

Southern Ethiopian Peoples Democratic Front (SEPDF), 247

South Yemen, 178, 197, 199

Special Court, 131, 132

State farms, 204, 205

Stela erected by Ezanas, on Atbara and Nile, 8

Stresa, Conference of, 141

Structural Adjustment Program (SAP), 236

Student movement. *See* Addis Ababa University

Suakin, 5, 40

Succession, 28, 29

Sudan and Sudanese, 5, 8, 10, 19, 59, 73, 82, 86, 87, 101, 102, 134, 178, 247

Sudanic peoples, xvii

Suez Canal, 151

Sugar, 161

Susneyos, Emperor, 39, 40, 43

Sweden, 138, 161

Swedish military training mission, 138

Switzerland, 123

Syphilis, 113

Syria, 8, 28, 175, 178

Tadjoura, 74, 82, 84

Tafari Makonnen, Ras. *See* Haile Sellassie, Emperor

Tafari Makonnen School, 122

Taferi Benti, Gen., 191 fig. 28, 195

Taitou Betul, Empress, 73, 80–81, 92, 93, 98, 111, 112, 113

Takusa, Battle of, 62, 63

Taltal, 54

Tamrat Layne, 232, 244

Tana, Lake, 19, 41, 59, 60; dam, 124, 127

Tanning, 125

Technical assistance, 69, 154

Teff *(ragrostis tef)*, 3

Tekeze River, 6, 44, 46, 52, 57, 143

Tekle Giorgis I, Emperor, 52

Tekle Giorgis II, Emperor, 72, 73

Tekle Haimanot, King (Negus) of Gojam, 73–74, 76, 69, 86, 87, 108; coronation as king, 80

Tekle Haimanot I, Emperor, 45

Tekle Haimanot II, Emperor, 51–52

Tekle Wolde Hawariat, Afanegus, 134, 155

Temben: first battle of, 144; second battle of, 145

Temporary security zone, 263

Teranafit, 224

Tesemma Nadaw, Ras, 105, 111, 112, 113

Tesemma Welde Mikail, 69

Tesenay, 209

Tesfaye Gebre Kidan, Gen. and acting president of the PDRE, 231

Tesfaye Habbiso, 232

Tewabetch, Woiz., 60

Tewahdo. See Christians: and Monophysite theology

Tewodros I, Emperor, 64

Tewodros II, Emperor (Kassa Hailu), 48, 57n, 59, 60, 61, 62, 63, 64, 66, 67, 71, 72, 73; coronation, 64; foreign policy of, 70; national policies and internal violence, 68, 69, 70

Tewoflos, Emperor, 45

Textiles, 155, 156

Tigray, Regional Education Board of, 252

Tigray and Tigrayans, xvi, xvii, 16, 21, 33, 37, 38, 44, 46, 47, 51, 52, 53, 54, 57, 62, 63, 68, 69–70, 72, 73, 74, 76, 86, 91, 94, 95, 96, 108, 128, 142, 143, 144, 145, 150, 154, 180, 206, 209, 210, 211–212, 213, 216; Greater Tigray, 239, 252, 256

Tigray National Organization (TNO), 221–222

Tigrayan Peoples Liberation Front
(TPLF), xi, 195, 209, 210, 213, 214,
216, 221, 222, 223–224, 225,
226–229, 232, 247, 252; differences
with the EPLF, 226–228, 229;
Fighters Congress (1976), 223; First
Manifesto (1976), 223; Gederef-
Tigray road, 228; mass organizations,
224, 230; military strategy, 223, 224;
political approach of, 223, 224–226;
political crisis of 1989–1990, 230;
victory in Tigray (1989), 230
Tigrinya, 3
Tools, 155
Tortoise shell, 4
Trade, 13, 19, 21, 40, 48, 49, 53, 54, 55,
56, 73, 74, 75, 125; arms trade, 84,
94, 123, 124; trade routes, 5, 19, 54,
55, 78, 79. *See also* Axum; Economy,
command; Economy, national;
Economy, world; Shewa
Traditional religion, xvii
Transitional Government of Ethiopia
(TGE), 221, 233, 234–235
Treaties and international agreements:
Aglo-Egyptian-Ethiopian Treaty
(1884), 82, 83, 85; Anglo-Ethiopian
Agreement (1942), 153; Anglo-
Ethiopian Agreement (1944), 154;
Anglo-Ethiopian Treaty (1897), 103;
Anglo-Franco-Italian treaties of Bon
Voisinage (1938), 150; Anglo-Franco-
Italo-Ethiopian Arms Agreement
(1930), 131; Anglo-French Exchange
of Notes about Harer (1888), 95;
Anglo-French-Italian Tripartite Treaty
(1906), 108; Anglo-Italian Exchange
of Notes (1925), 124; Anglo-Italian
Protocol (1894), 95; Anglo-Shewan
Treaty (1841), 66; Congress of Berlin
(1885), 90; Ethio-American Lend-
Lease Agreement (1943), 153; Ethio-
Italian Treaty (1889), 89, 90, 92, 93,
94, 95; Ethio-Italian Treaty of Peace
(1896), 99–100; Ethio-Somali
Agreement (1988), 212; Franco-

Ethiopian Commercial Agreement
(1908), 107; Franco-Ethiopian
Convention (1897), 102; Franco-
Ethiopian Secret Treaty (1897), 102;
Franco-Shewan Military Agreement
(1843), 66; Italo-Ethiopian Frontier
Agreement (1897), 139; Italo-
Ethiopian Frontier Treaty (1908), 139;
Italo-Ethiopian Treaty of Friendship
and Arbitration (1928), 126; Italo-
Shewan Treaty (1883), 78; Mussolini-
Laval Pact (1935), 140; Supplemen-
tary Agreement to the Treaty of
Wichale, 1 October 1889, 91; U.S.-
Ethiopia Technical Assistance Agree-
ment (1952), 160; U.S.-Ethiopia
Treaty (1953), 159. *See also* Ethio-
Eritrean campaigns of 1998–2000:
peace proposals and negotiations
Tributary states, 28
Trucks, 155
Tsadkan Gebretensae, Gen., 247, 257
Tsorona, 251, 260, 261
Tunisia, 138, 140
Turkana, Lake (formerly Lake Rudolf),
104
Turkey, 33, 34, 37, 38, 49, 69, 70
TWA, 159

Uganda, 247
Umberto I, King, 92
Unctionists. *See* Christians: and
Monophysite theology
Unionist Party, 158
Union movement, 232
Union of Soviet Socialist Republics
(USSR), 174, 176, 196, 197, 201,
206, 212
Unitary state, xi
United Nations, 158, 159, 161; UN
Mission in Ethiopia and Eritrea
(UNMEE), 263
United States and Americans, 126, 127,
156, 157, 159, 161, 171, 174, 175,
194, 196, 206, 215, 230, 233, 234;
economic assistance, 159–160,

161–163, 235–236; military assistance, 159, 162, 163, 174, 176, 247–248; policies during WW II, 153–154; United States–Rwanda Plan for Peace (1998), 258
University College of Addis Abeba, 161, 170–171
Urban life, 164–165

Victoria, Queen, 70, 92
Villages, fortified *(ketema)*, 105, 125
Villagization. *See* Provisional Military Administration Council and its successors: resettlement and land reform programs

Wadla Delanta (west-central Welo), 11
Wag, 10, 46, 52
Walamo, 96, 119, 168
War, Ministry of, 134
Warder, 138, 139, 157
War reparations, 156
Warsaw Pact, 206
Weaponry, modern, 70, 72, 73, 74, 75, 78, 79, 80, 83, 84, 87, 95, 108, 128, 131, 133, 137, 144, 196, 198, 209, 213. *See also* Arms embargo, post–WW I
Wegera, 44, 57, 60
Welega, xvii, 37, 80, 106, 119, 147
Welo, xvi, xvii, 1, 11, 37, 38, 44, 46, 47, 54, 55, 56, 62, 66, 67, 68, 69, 70, 73, 76, 80, 83, 86, 87, 89, 113, 116, 117, 128, 180, 205, 206, 213, 214, 216
Welwel, 85n, 138, 139
Were Ilu, 80
West Somali Liberation Front, 197
Wichale, 89
Wilhelm II, Emperor, 92
Wingate, Major Gen. Orde Charles, 151
Wolde Gabriel, Dej., of Tigray, 52
Wolde Giorgis, Ras, 104, 113
Wolde Giorgis Wolde Yohannes, minister of Pen, 158
Wolde Lul, Ras, 46

Wolde Sellassie of Tigray, Ras, 52, 53, 56, 57, 71
Wole Betul, Ras, of Yeju, 73, 74, 80
Women, 1, 11n, 16, 17, 18, 29, 46, 57, 57n, 58, 59, 60, 66, 73, 80, 81, 92, 113, 116, 133, 203
Wond Bewossen, Dej., of Begemdir, 51
Wool blankets, 49
Workers' Party of Ethiopia (WPE), 205, 206, 207, 210, 215, 232
Working People's Control Commission, 203
Workneh Gebeyehu, Lt. Col., 167, 169, 170, 171
World Bank, 236
World War I, 114
Wossen Seged, Ras, of Shewa, 53
Woyane movement, 223
Woyane uprisings (Welo and Tigray), 128, 154, 223
Wube, Dej., of Simen and Tigray, 57, 58, 59, 60, 61, 63, 64, 68

Yakob, Abuna, 22
Yalta Conference, 156
Yeha, 4
Yeju, 49, 52, 57, 58, 62, 66, 73, 74, 80, 89
Yekatit 12, 148
Yekatit '66 Political School. *See under* Provisional Military Administration Council and its successors
Yekuno Amlak, Emperor, 16, 17, 20, 46
Yemane Kidane, Gen., 247
Yemen, 40
Yifat, 20, 21, 26, 29
Yimam, Ras, of Yeju, 57
Yishak, 17
Yitbarek, Emperor, 16
Yohannes I, Emperor, 44
Yohannes II, Emperor, 57n, 58, 60
Yohannes IV, Emperor, 71, 72, 73, 74, 75, 76, 77, 78, 79, 80, 81, 84, 85, 86, 108
Yosef Neguse, Geraz., 89, 93
Yostos, Emperor, 45

Young Ethiopians (Abyssinians) and
    educated elites, 120, 128, 130, 134,
    160, 166–167, 170–171, 172–173

Za Dengel, Emperor, 39
Zagwe dynasty, xviii, 12, 13, 14, 15–16,
    19, 42; political economy, 15
Zalembessa, 251, 260, 261, 261 fig. 39,
    262

Zamacha, 192
Zamana Masafent ("Age of the princes"),
    47, 56, 57n, 60, 61, 62, 68
Zara Yakob, Emperor, 24–29
Zawditu, Empress, 80, 116, 117, 118,
    127–128, 129
Zeila, 19, 31, 54, 75
Zimbabwe, 217, 231
Zula, Gulf of, 5, 82

Cartographer: Bill Nelson
Compositor: Star Type
Text: 10/13 Galliard